AF522307

Crime Beat: Selected Journalism

Crime Beat: Selected Journalism

Vivek Tyagi

RANDOM PUBLICATIONS
NEW DELHI (INDIA)

Crime Beat: Selected Journalism

ISBN 978-93-5111-631-8

Published in 2017 in India by

RANDOM PUBLICATIONS

4376-A/4B, Gali Murari Lal, Ansari Road
New Delhi-110 002
Phone : +9111-43580356, 011-23289044, 011-43142548
e-mail: sales@randompublications.com,
info@randompublications.com, randomexports@gmail.com

Reprinted 2024

Type Setting by : Friends Media, Delhi-110089
Digitally Printed at: Replika Press Pvt. Ltd.

Preface

Every news organization covers crime. It's a staple of daily reporting. But not every news organization covers crime as a beat. Too often, crime stories are just accounts of incidents as they occur, with little context or depth. To cover crime well, reporters need to look for patterns and trends as well as for the impact of crime on individuals and communities. That means spending time on the crime beat, hanging out at police stations, firehouses, and with emergency medical technicians, getting to know their problems and procedures.

Reporters who cover crime also need to pay attention to the potential impact of the coverage itself. Research has found that news reports tend to feature more minorities as perpetrators of crime and fewer as victims of crime than the actual data would support.

Although most TV journalists are general assignment reporters who cover a variety of stories including crime, newspapers have traditionally assigned one or more reporters to the "crime beat" or to "cops and court reporting." In many cases, especially in smaller markets, it is rookie reporters who are assigned to cover crime. In part, young people get these assignments because they often require working nighttime hours, visiting neighborhoods with high crime rates, and venturing out in inclement weather. It also means dealing with victims who may be distraught and in physical pain.

The book presents a very systematic presentation of the subject matter in simple and lucid language.

I would like to thank my team for standing beside me throughout my career and writing this book. My special thanks go to "Random Publications" who have published the book.

– Vivek Tyagi

Contents

1

Bias in the Mass Media

INTRODUCTION

Political bias has been a feature of the mass media since its birth with the invention of the printing press. The expense of early printing equipment restricted media production to a limited number of people. Historians have found that publishers often served the interests of powerful social groups. John Milton's pamphlet *Areopagitica, a Speech for the Liberty of Unlicensed Printing*, published in 1644, was one of the first publications advocating freedom of the press. In the nineteenth century, journalists began to recognize the concept of unbiased reporting as an integral part of journalistic ethics. This coincided with the rise of journalism as a powerful social force. Even today, though, the most conscientiously objective journalists cannot avoid accusations of bias.

Like newspapers, the broadcast media (radio and television) have been used as a mechanism for propaganda from their earliest days, a tendency made more pronounced by the initial ownership of broadcast spectrum by national governments. Although a process of media deregulation has placed the majority of the western broadcast media in private hands, there still exists a strong government presence, or even monopoly, in the broadcast media of many countries across the globe. At the same time, the concentration of media in private hands, and frequently amongst a comparatively small number of individuals, has also lead to accusations of media bias. There are many examples of accusations of bias being used as a political tool, sometimes resulting in government censorship.

In the United States, in 1798, Congress passed the Alien and Sedition Acts, which prohibited newspapers from publishing "false, scandalous, or malicious writing" against the government, including any public opposition to any law or presidential act. This act was in effect until 1801.

During the American Civil War, President Abraham Lincoln accused newspapers in the border states of bias in favour of the Southern cause, and ordered many newspapers closed. Chancellor Adolf Hitler of Germany, in the years leading up to World War II, accused newspapers of Marxist bias, an accusation echoed by pro-German media in England and the United States. Politicians who favored the United States entering World War II on the German side asserted that the international media were controlled by Jews, and that reports of German mistreatment of Jews were biased and without foundation. Hollywood was said to be a hotbed of Jewish bias, and films such as Charlie Chaplin's The Great Dictator were offered as proof.

In the 1980s, the government of South Africa accused newspapers of liberal bias and instituted government censorship. In 1989, the newspaper *New Nation* was closed by the government for three months for publishing anti-apartheid propaganda. Other newspapers were not closed, but were extensively censored. Some published the censored sections blacked out, to demonstrate the extent of government censorship. In the USA during the labour union movement and the civil rights movement, newspapers supporting liberal social reform were accused by conservative newspapers of communist bias. Film and television media were accused of bias in favour of mixing of the races, and many television Programmes with racially mixed casts, such as *I Spy* and *Star Trek*, were not aired on Southern stations.

During the war between the United States and North Vietnam, Vice President Spiro Agnew accused newspapers of anti-American bias, and in a famous speech delivered in San Diego in 1970, called anti-war protesters "The nattering nabobs of negativism."

Not all accusations of bias are political. Science writer Martin Gardner has accused the entertainment media of anti-science bias. He claims that television Programmes such as *The X-Files* promote superstition. In contrast, the Competitive Enterprise Institute accuses the media of being biased in favour of science and against business interests, and of credulously reporting science that purports to show that greenhouse gasses cause global warming.

ROLE OF LANGUAGE

Mass media, despite its ability to project worldwide, is limited in its cross-ethnic compatibility by one simple attribute - language. Ethnicity, being largely developed by a divergence in geography, language, culture, genes and similarly, point of view, has the potential to be countered by a common source of information. Therefore, language, in the absence of translation, comprises a barrier to a worldwide community of debate and opinion, although it is also true that media within any given society may be split along class, political or regional lines. Furthermore, if the language is translated, the translator has room to shift a bias by choosing weighed words for translation.

Language may also be seen as a political factor in mass media, particularly in instances where a society is characterized by a large number of languages spoken by its populace. The choice of language of mass media may represent a bias towards the group most likely to speak that language, and can limit the public participation by those who do not speak the language. On the other hand, there have also been attempts to use a common-language mass media to reach out to a large, geographically dispersed population, such as in the use of Arabic language by news channel Al Jazeera.

Many media theorists concerned with language and media bias point towards the media of the United States, a large country where English is spoken by the vast majority of the population.

Some theorists argue that the common language is not homogenizing; and that there still remain strong differences expressed within the mass media. This viewpoint asserts that moderate views are bolstered by drawing influences from the extremes of the political spectrum. In the United States, the national news therefore contributes to a sense of cohesion within the society, proceeding from a similarly informed population. According to this model, most views within society are freely expressed, and the mass media are accountable to the people and tends to reflect the spectrum of opinion.

Language may also be a more subtle form of bias. Use of a word with positive or negative connotations rather than a more neutral synonym can form a biased picture in the audience's mind. It makes a difference whether the media calls a group "terrorist" or "freedom fighters" or "insurgents". For example, a 2005 memo to the staff of the CBC states:

Rather than calling assailants "terrorists," we can refer to them as bombers, hijackers, gunmen (if we're sure no women were in the group), militants, extremists, attackers or some other appropriate noun.

In a widely criticized episode, initial online BBC reports of the 7 July 2005 London bombings identified the perpetrators as terrorists, in contradiction to the BBC's internal policy. But by the next day, Tom Gross and many others noted that the online articles had been edited, replacing "terrorists" by "bombers".

In another case, March 28, 2007, the broadcaster paid almost $400,000 in legal fees in a London court to keep an internal memo dealing with alleged anti-Israeli bias from becoming public. BBC was accused of pro-Palestinian bias over a documentary about Israel developing a nuclear weapon during the second Palestinian intifada in 2000.

NATIONAL AND ETHNIC VIEWPOINT

Many news organizations reflect or are perceived to reflect in some way the viewpoint of the geographic, ethnic, and national population that they primarily serve. Media within countries is sometimes seen as being sycophantic or unquestioning about the country's government. Western media are often criticized in the rest of the world (including eastern Europe, Asia, Africa, and the Middle East) as being pro-Western with regard to a variety of political, cultural and economic issues.

Al Jazeera has been frequently criticized in the West about its coverage of Arab world issues. The Israeli-Palestinian conflict and wider Arab-Israeli issues are a particularly controversial area, and nearly all coverage of any kind generates accusation of bias from one or both sides. This topic is covered in a separate article.

ANGLOPHONE BIAS IN THE WORLD MEDIA

It has been observed that the world's principal suppliers of news, the news agencies, and the main buyers of news are Anglophone corporations and this gives an Anglophone bias to the selection and depiction of events. Anglophone definitions of what constitutes news are paramount; the news provided originates in Anglophone capitals and responds first to their own rich domestic markets. Despite the plethora of news services, most news printed and broadcast throughout the world each day comes from only a few major agencies, the three largest of which are the Associated Press, Reuters and Agence France-Presse.

Although these agencies are 'global' in the sense of their activities, they each retain significant associations with particular nations, namely France (AFP), the United States (AP) and the United Kingdom (Reuters). Chambers and Tinckell suggest that the so-called global media are agents of Anglophone values which privilege norms of 'competitive individualism, laissez faire capitalism, parliamentary democracy and consumerism.' They see the presentation of the English language as international as a further feature of Anglophone dominance.

VIS-A-VIS RELIGIOUS ISSUES

Media bias towards religion is most obvious in countries where the media are controlled by the state, which is in turn dominated by a particular religion. In these instances, bias against other faiths can be explicit and virulent. But even in countries with freedom of religion and a free press, the dominant religion exerts some amount of influence on the media. In nations where Christianity is the majority faith, reporters tend to focus on the activities of the Christian community, to the exclusion of other faiths. But the opposite may also occur, with media self-consciously avoiding reporting on any religious matters at all in order to avoid the appearance of favoring one faith over another, or presenting religious faith and phenomenon in a negative light.

This type of bias is often seen with reporting on new religious movements. It is often the case that the only view the public gets of a new religious movement, controversial group or purported cult is a negative and sensationalized report by the media. For example, most new or minority religious movements only receive media coverage when something sensational occurs, *e.g.* the mass suicide of a cult or illegal activities of a leader in the religious movement. According to the Encyclopaedia of Social Work (19th edition), the news media play an influential role in the general public's perception of cults.

As reported in several studies, the media have depicted cults as problematic, controversial, and threatening from the beginning, tending to favour sensationalistic stories over balanced public debates. It furthers the analysis that media reports on cults rely heavily on police officials and cult "experts" who portray cult activity as dangerous and destructive, and when divergent views are presented, they are often overshadowed by horrific stories of ritualistic torture, sexual abuse, mind control, etc. Furthermore, unfounded allegations, when proved untrue, receive little or no media attention.

OTHER INFLUENCES

The apparent bias of media is not always specifically political in nature. The news media tend to appeal to a specific audience, which means that stories that affect a large number of people on a global scale often receive less coverage in some markets than local stories, such as a public school shooting, a celebrity wedding, a plane crash, or similarly glamorous or shocking stories. For example, the deaths of millions of people in an ethnic conflict in Africa might be afforded scant mention in American media, while the shooting of five people in a high school is analyzed in depth. The reason for this type of bias is a function of what the public wants to watch and/or what producers and publishers believe the public wants to watch.

Bias has also been claimed in instances referred to as conflict of interest, whereby the owners of media outlets have vested interests in other commercial enterprises or political parties.

In such cases in the United States, the media outlet is required to disclose the conflict of interest. However, the decisions of the editorial department of a newspaper and the corporate parent frequently are not connected, as the editorial staff retains freedom to decide what is covered as well as what isn't. Biases, real or implied, frequently arise when it comes to deciding what stories will be covered and who will be called for those stories.

Accusations that a source is biased, if accepted, may cause media consumers to distrust certain kinds of statements, and place added confidence on others. For example, if readers believe that a particular newspaper is conservatively biased, they may feel that a pro-liberal article in that paper *must* be true. Conversely, they may assume that a pro-conservative article in that paper is suspect. Because of the possibility of influencing the public in this way, accusations about which media outlets are biased, and how, have become a very common occurrence. Media ethics is the subdivision of applied ethics dealing with the specific ethical principles and standards of media, including broadcast media, film, theatre, the arts, print media and the internet. The field covers many varied and highly controversial topics, ranging from war journalism to Benetton advertising.

TREATMENT OF MEDIA BIAS

Media bias is studied at schools of journalism, university departments (including Media studies, Cultural studies and Peace studies) and by many independent watchdog groups from various parts of the political spectrum. In the United States, many of these studies focus on issues of a conservative/ liberal balance in the media. Other focuses include international differences in reporting, as well as bias in reporting of particular issues such as economic class or environmental interests. A widely-cited public opinion study documents a correlation between news source and certain misconceptions about the Iraq war. Conducted by the Programme on International Policy Attitudes in October 2003, the poll asked Americans whether they believed statements about the Iraq war that were known to be false.

Respondents were also asked which was their primary news source: Fox News, CBS, NBC, ABC, CNN, "Print sources," or NPR. By cross referencing the responses according to primary news source, the study showed that higher numbers of Fox News watchers held certain misconceptions about the Iraq war. The director of Programme on International Policy (PIPA), Stephen Kull said, "While we cannot assert that these misconceptions created the support for going to war with Iraq, it does appear likely that support for the war would be substantially lower if fewer members of the public had these misperceptions."

The Glasgow Media Group carried out the Bad News Studies, a series of detailed analyses of television broadcasts (and later newspaper coverage) in the United Kingdom. Published between 1976 and 1985, the Bad News Studies used content analysis, interviews and covert participant observation to conclude that news was biased against trade unions, blaming them for breaking wage negotiating guidelines and causing high inflation. Martin Harrison's *TV News: Whose Bias?* (1985) criticized the methodology of the Glasgow Media Group, arguing that the GMG identified bias selectively, via their own preconceptions about what phrases qualify as biased descriptions. For example, the GMG sees the word "idle" to describe striking workers as pejorative, despite the word being used by strikers themselves.

Herman and Chomsky (1988) proposed a propaganda model hypothesizing systematic biases of U.S. media from structural economic causes. They hypothesize media ownership by corporations, funding from advertising, the use of official sources, efforts to discredit independent media ("flak"), and "anti-communist" ideology as the filters that bias news in favour of U.S. corporate interests. Their propaganda model first and foremost disuses self censorship through the corporate system; that reporters and especially editors share and/ or acquire values with corporate elites in order to further their careers. Those that don't are usually weeded out or marginalized. Such examples have been dramatized in fact based movie dramas as "Good Night, and Good Luck" and "The Insider" or demonstrated in the documentary "The Corporation". George Orwell originally wrote a preface for his book "Animal Farm", which focuses on British self censorship.

"The sinister fact about literary censorship in England is that it is largely voluntary.... [Things are] kept right out of the British press, not because the Government intervened but because of a general tacit agreement that 'it wouldn't do' to mention that particular fact." As if to prove the point, the preface itself was censored and is not published with most copies of the book.

The propaganda model posits that advertising dollars are essential for funding most media sources and clearly have an effect on the content of the media. For example, according to Fair, 'When Al Gore proposed launching a progressive TV network, a Fox News executive told Advertising Age (10/13/03): "The problem with being associated as liberal is that they wouldn't be going in a direction that advertisers are really interested in.... If you go out and say that you are a liberal network, you are cutting your potential audience, and certainly your potential advertising pool, right off the bat."

Furthermore "an internal memo from ABC Radio Networks to its affiliates reveals scores of powerful sponsors have a standing order that their commercials never be placed on syndicated Air America programming that airs on ABC affiliates.... The list, totaling 90 advertisers, includes some of largest and most well-known corporations advertising in the U.S.: Wal-Mart, GE, Exxon Mobil, Microsoft, Bank of America, Fed-Ex, Visa, Allstate, McDonald's, Sony and Johnson and Johnson. The U.S. Postal Service and the U.S. Navy are also listed as advertisers who don't want their commercials to air on Air America."

The academic study cited most frequently by critics of a "liberal media bias" in American journalism is *The Media Elite,* a 1986 book co-authored by political scientists Robert Lichter, Stanley Rothman, and Linda Lichter. They surveyed journalists at national media outlets such as the New York Times, Washington Post, and the broadcast networks. The survey found that most of these journalists were Democratic voters whose attitudes were well to the left of the general public on a variety of topics, including such hot-button social issues such as abortion, affirmative action, and gay rights. Then they compared journalists' attitudes to their coverage of controversial issues such as the safety of nuclear power, school busing to promote racial integration, and the energy crisis of the 1970s.

The book's most thorough case study involved nuclear energy. The survey of journalists showed that most were highly skeptical about nuclear safety. However, the authors conducted a separate survey of scientists in energy related fields, who were much more sanguine about nuclear safety issues. They then conducted a content analysis of nuclear energy coverage in the media outlets they had surveyed. They found that the opinions of sources who were cited as scientific experts reflected the antinuclear sentiments of journalists, rather than the more pro-nuclear perspectives held by most energy scientists. The authors concluded that journalists' coverage of controversial issues reflected their own attitudes, and the predominance of political liberals in newsrooms therefore pushed news coverage in a liberal direction. They presented this tilt as a mostly unconscious process of like-minded individuals projecting their shared assumptions onto their interpretations of reality.

At the time the study was embraced mainly by conservative columnists and politicians, who adopted the findings as scientific proof of liberal media bias. Many of the positions in the preceding study are supported by a 2002 study by Jim A. Kuypers: Press Bias and Politics: How the Media Frame Controversial Issues. In this study of 116 mainstream US papers (including The New York Times, the Washington Post, Los Angeles Times, and the San Francisco Chronicle), Kuypers found that the mainstream print press in America operate within a narrow range of liberal beliefs. Those who expressed points of view further to the left were generally ignored, whereas those who expressed moderate or conservative points of view were often actively denigrated or labeled as holding a minority point of view.

In short, if a political leader, regardless of party, spoke within the press-supported range of acceptable discourse, he or she would receive positive press coverage. If a politician, again regardless of party, were to speak outside of this range, he or she would receive negative press or be ignored. Kuypers also found that the liberal points of view expressed in editorial and opinion pages were found in hard news coverage of the same issues. Although focusing primarily on the issues of race and homosexuality, Kuypers found that the press injected opinion into its news coverage of other issues such as welfare reform, environmental protection, and gun control; in all cases favoring a liberal point of view.

Studies reporting perceptions of liberal bias in the media are not limited to studies of print media. A joint study by the Joan Shorenstein Centre on Press, Politics and Public Policy at Harvard University and the Project for Excellence in Journalism found that people see liberal media bias in television news media such as CNN.. Although both CNN and Fox were perceived in the study as being left of centre, CNN was perceived as being more liberal than Fox. Moreover, the study's findings concerning CNN's perceived liberal bias are echoed in other studies. There is also a growing economics literature on mass media bias, both on the theoretical and the empirical side. On the theoretical side the focus is on understanding to what extent the political positioning of mass media outlets is mainly driven by demand or supply factors. According to Dan Sutter of the University of Oklahoma, a systematic liberal bias in the U.S. media could depend on the fact that owners and/or journalists typically lean to the left.

Along the same lines, David Baron of Stanford GSB presents a game-theoretic model of mass media behaviour in which, given that the pool of journalists systematically leans towards the left or the right, mass media outlets maximise their profits by providing content that is biased in the same direction. They can do so, because it is cheaper to hire journalists that write stories which are consistent with their political position. A concurrent theory would be that supply and demand would cause media to attain a neutral balance because consumers would of course gravitate towards the media they agreed with. This argument fails in considering the imbalance in self-reported political allegiances by journalists themselves, that distort any market analogy as regards offer: (...) *Indeed, in 1982, 85 per cent of Columbia Graduate School of Journalism students identified themselves as liberal, versus 11 per cent conservative*", quoted in Sutter, 2001.

This same argument would have news outlets in equal numbers increasing profits of a more balanced media far more than the slight increase in costs to hire unbiased journalists, notwithstanding the extreme rarity of self-reported conservative journalists. As mentioned above, Tim Groseclose of UCLA and Jeff Milyo of the University of Missouri at Columbia use think tank quotes, in order to estimate the relative position of mass media outlets in the political spectrum. The idea is to trace out which think tanks are quoted by various mass media outlets within news stories, and to match these think tanks with the political position of members of the U.S. Congress who quote them in a non-negative way. Using this procedure, Groseclose and Milyo obtain the stark result that all sampled news providers -except Fox News' Special Report and the Washington Times- are located to the left of the average Congress member, *i.e.* there are signs of a liberal bias in the US news media.

However, the news media also show a remarkable degree of centrism, just because all outlets but one are located –from an ideological point of view-between the average Democrat and average Republican in Congress. The methods Groseclose and Milyo used to calculate this bias have been criticized by Mark Liberman, a professor of Computer Science at the University of Pennsylvania. Liberman concludes by saying he thinks "that many if not most of the complaints directed against GandM are motivated in part by ideological disagreement — just as much of the praise for their work is motivated by ideological agreement. It would be nice if there were a less politically fraught body of data on which such modeling exercises could be explored."

Sendhil Mullainathan and Andrei Shleifer of Harvard University construct a behavioural model, which is built around the assumption that readers and viewers hold beliefs that they would like to see confirmed by news providers. When news customers share common beliefs, profit-maximizing media outlets find it optimal to select and/or frame stories in order to pander to those beliefs. On the other hand, when beliefs are heterogeneous, news providers differentiate their offer and segment the market, by providing news stories that are slanted towards the two extreme positions in the spectrum of beliefs.

Matthew Gentzkow and Jesse Shapiro of Chicago GSB present another demand-driven theory of mass media bias. If readers and viewers have a priori views on the current state of affairs and are uncertain about the quality of the information about it being provided by media outlets, then the latter have an incentive to slant stories towards their customers' prior beliefs, in order to build and keep a reputation for high-quality journalism. The reason for this is that rational agents would tend to believe that pieces of information that go against their prior beliefs in fact originate from low-quality news providers.

The economics empirical literature on mass media bias mainly focuses on the United States. Steve Ansolabehere, Rebecca Lessem and Jim Snyder of the Massachusetts Institute of Technology analyse the political orientation of endorsements by U.S. newspapers. They find an upward trend in the average propensity to endorse a candidate, and in particular an incumbent one. There are also some changes in the average ideological slant of endorsements: while in the 40s and in the 50s there was a clear advantage to Republican candidates, this advantage continuously eroded in subsequent decades, to the extent that in the 90s the authors find a slight Democratic lead in the average endorsement choice.

John Lott and Kevin Hassett of the American Enterprise Institute study the coverage of economic news by looking at a panel of 389 U.S. newspapers from 1991 to 2004, and from 1985 to 2004 for a subsample comprising the top 10 newspapers and the Associated Press. For each release of official data about a set of economic indicators, the authors analyse how newspapers decide to report on them, as reflected by the tone of the related headlines. The idea is to check whether newspapers display some kind of partisan bias, by giving more positive or negative coverage to the same economic figure, as a function of the political affiliation of the incumbent President. Controlling for the economic data being released, the authors find that there are between 9.6 and 14.7 per cent fewer positive stories when the incumbent President is a Republican.

Riccardo Puglisi of the Massachusetts Institute of Technology looks at the editorial choices of the *New York Times* from 1946 to 1997. He finds that the *Times* displays Democratic partisanship, with some watchdog aspects. This is the case, because during presidential campaigns the Times systematically gives more coverage to Democratic topics of civil rights, health care, labour and social welfare, but only when the incumbent president is a Republican. These topics are classified as Democratic ones, because Gallup polls show that on average U.S. citizens think that Democratic candidates would be better at handling problems related to them. According to Puglisi, in the post-1960 period the Times displays a more symmetric type of watchdog behaviour, just because during presidential campaigns it also gives more coverage to the typically

Republican issue of Defence when the incumbent President is a Democrat, and less so when the incumbent is a Republican.

Alan Gerber and Dean Karlan of Yale University use an experimental approach to examine not whether the media are biased, but whether the media influence political decisions and attitudes. They conduct a randomized control trial just prior to the November 2005 gubernatorial election in Virginia and randomly assign individuals in Northern Virginia to (a) a treatment group that receives a free subscription to the Washington Post, (b) a treatment group that receives a free subscription to the Washington Times, or (c) a control group. They find that those who are assigned to the Washington Post treatment group are eight percentage points more likely to vote for the Democrat in the elections. The report also found that "exposure to either newspaper was weakly linked to a movement away from the Bush administration and Republicans."

Another unaffiliated group, Media Study Group, established seven categories of poor journalistic practice: for example, the journalist stating personal opinion in a report, asserting incorrect facts, applying unequal space or treatment to two sides of a controversial issue; then analyzed The Age Newspaper (Melbourne Australia) for the frequency of infraction of this code of practice. The resultant instances were then analyzed statistically with respect to the frequency they supported one or other side of the two-sided controversial issue under consideration. The goal of this group was to establish a quantitative methodology for the study of bias.

A self-described progressive media watchdog group, Fairness and Accuracy in Reporting, in consultation with the Survey and Evaluation Research Laboratory at Virginia Commonwealth University, sponsored a rigorous academic study in which journalists were asked a range of questions about how they did their work and about how they viewed the quality of media coverage in the broad area of politics and economic policy. "They were asked for their opinions and views about a range of recent policy issues and debates. Finally, they were asked for demographic and identifying information, including their political orientation". They then compared to the say or similar questions posed with "the public" based on Gallup, and Pew Trust polls. Their study concluded that a majority of journalists, although relatively liberal on social policies, were significantly to the right of the public on economic, labour, health care and foreign policy issues.

This study continues: "we learn much more about the political orientation of news content by looking at sourcing patterns rather than journalists' personal views. As this survey shows, it is government officials and business representatives to whom journalists "nearly always" turn when covering economic policy. Labour representatives and consumer advocates were at the bottom of the list. This is consistent with earlier research on sources. For example, analysts from the centrist Brookings Institution and conservative think tanks such as the Heritage Foundation and the American Enterprise Institute are those most quoted in mainstream news accounts; liberal think tanks are often invisible. When it comes to sources, 'liberal bias' is nowhere to be found."

EXPERIMENTER BIAS

A major problem in studies is experimenter bias. Research into studies of media bias in the United States shows that Liberal experimenters tend to get results that say the media has a conservative bias, while conservatives experimenters tend to get results that say the media has a liberal bias, and those who do not identify themselves as either liberal or conservative get results indicating little bias, or mixed bias. This same problem with experimenter bias extends to the studies of experimenter bias, of course. Whether bias is toward the left or the right depends on where you stand.

The study "A Measure of Media Bias" (pdf) by political scientist Timothy J. Groseclose of UCLA and economist Jeffrey D. Milyo of the University of Missouri-Columbia, purports to rank news organisations in terms of identifying with liberal or conservative values relative to each other. They used the Americans for Democratic Action (ADA) scores as a quantitative proxy for political leanings of the referential organizations.

Thus their definition of "liberal" includes the RAND Corporation, a nonprofit research organization with strong ties to the Defence Department. According to Media Matters for America (a non-profit progressive research and information centre), "the study employed a measure of "bias" so problematic that its findings are next to useless".

What is "liberal" in the United States may not be "liberal" by world standards. FAIR suggests that a benchmark for each country be set by scientific polling of a cross-section of the citizens. Another source of bias is the fact that some studies are reported by the media, and other stories are not. The case study "A Measure of Media Bias" discussed above was widely reported in the United States. George Orwell pointed out that in the UK during the last century businesses did not undermine their own interests by reporting leftist (anti business or pro-labour) information. In the United States Ben Bagdikian documents a long history of advertisers pulling out support when media content becomes too controversial.

TOOLS FOR MEASURING AND EVALUATING MEDIA BIAS

Richard Alan Nelson's (2003) study cited above on *Tracking Propaganda to the Source: Tools for Analyzing Media Bias* reports there are at least 12 methods used to analyse the existence of and quantify bias:

- Surveys of the political/cultural attitudes of journalists, particularly members of the media elite, and of journalism students.
- Studies of journalists' previous professional connections.

- Collections of quotations in which prominent journalists reveal their beliefs about politics and/or the proper role of their profession.
- Computer word-use and topic analysis searches to determine content and labeling.
- Studies of policies recommended in news stories.
- Comparisons of the agenda of the news and entertainment media with agendas of political candidates or other activists.
- Positive/negative coverage analysis.
- Reviews of the personal demographics of media decision makers.
- Comparisons of advertising sources/content which influence information/entertainment content.
- Analyses of the extent of government propaganda and public relations (PR) industry impact on media.
- Studies of the use of experts and spokespersons etc. by media vs. those not selected to determine the interest groups and ideologies represented vs. those excluded.
- Research into payments of journalists by corporations and trade associations to speak before their groups and the impact that may have on coverage.

EFFORTS TO CORRECT BIAS

One technique used to avoid bias is the "point/counterpoint" or "round table," an adversarial format in which representatives of opposing views comment on an issue. This approach theoretically allows diverse views to appear in the media. However, the person organizing the report still has the responsibility to choose people who really represent the breadth of opinion, to ask them non-prejudicial questions, and to edit or arbitrate their comments fairly. When done carelessly, a point/counterpoint can be as unfair as a simple biased report, by suggesting that the "losing" side lost on its merits.

The Skeptics Society has accused reporters of misusing the point/counterpoint format by giving more time to superstitions than to their scientific rebuttals. Using this format can also lead to accusations that the reporter has created a misleading appearance that viewpoints have equal validity (sometimes called "false balance"). This may happen when a taboo exists around one of the viewpoints, or when one of the representatives habitually makes claims that are easily shown to be inaccurate. One such allegation of misleading balance came from Mark Halperin, political director of ABC News. He stated in an internal e-mail message that reporters should not "artificially hold [George W. Bush and John Kerry] 'equally' accountable" to the public interest, and that complaints from Bush supporters were an attempt to "get away with... renewed efforts to win the election by destroying Senator Kerry."

When the Drudge Report published this message, many Bush supporters viewed it as "smoking gun" evidence that Halperin was using ABC to propagandize against Bush to Kerry's benefit, by interfering with reporters' attempts to avoid bias. An academic content analysis of election news later found that coverage at ABC, CBS, and NBC was more favorable towards Kerry than Bush, while coverage at Fox News Channel was more favorable towards Bush. Scott Norvell, the London bureau chief for Fox News, stated in a May 20, 2005 interview with the Wall Street Journal that "Even we at Fox News manage to get some lefties on the air occasionally, and often let them finish their sentences before we club them to death and feed the scraps to Karl Rove and Bill O'Reilly. And those who hate us can take solace in the fact that they aren't subsidizing Bill's bombast; we payers of the BBC license fee don't enjoy that peace of mind.

Fox News is, after all, a private channel and our presenters are quite open about where they stand on particular stories. That's our appeal. People watch us because they know what they are getting. The Beeb's (British Broadcasting Corporation) (BBC) institutionalized leftism would be easier to tolerate if the corporation was a little more honest about it".

With the release of the 2008 book *What Happened: Inside the Bush White House and Washington's Culture of Deception* by George W. Bush's press secretary Scott McClellan, there are some who contend that this is evidence of Mark Halperin being correct instead of biased. In his book, McClellan admits to lying to the media, and describes the contempt he felt for reporters who so easily believed his lies, and were cowed by the fear that if they exposed the lies, they would be accused of "liberal bias".

Another technique used to avoid bias is disclosure of affiliations that may be considered a possible conflict of interest. This is especially apparent when a news organization is reporting a story with some relevancy to the news organization itself or to its ownership individuals or conglomerate. Often this disclosure is mandated by the laws or regulations pertaining to stocks and securities. Commentators on news stories involving stocks are often required to disclose any ownership interest in those corporations or in its competitors.

In rare cases, a news organization may dismiss or reassign staff members who appear biased. This approach was used in the Killian documents affair and after Peter Arnett's interview with the Iraqi press. This approach is presumed to have been employed in the case of Dan Rather over a heavily biased story that he ran on 60 Minutes in the month prior to the 2004 election that attempted to impugn the military record of George W. Bush by relying on obviously fake documents that were provided by a Democrat Party operative. Finally, some countries have laws enforcing balance in state-owned media. Since 1991, the CBC and Radio Canada, its Francophone counterpart, are governed by the Broadcasting Act. This act states, amongst other things:

The programming provided by the Canadian broadcasting system should (i) be varied and comprehensive, providing a balance of information, enlightenment and entertainment for men, women and children of all ages, interests and tastes, (...) (iv) provide a reasonable opportunity for the public to be exposed to the expression of differing views on matters of public concern.

NEWS BIAS IN NEWS SOURCES

Some scholars and journalists argue American journalism in the 1990s suffers from a credibility crisis. Public perceptions of bias in the news media were detected as early as the 1960s. However, trend data suggest the American public views the media as increasingly less trustworthy, paralleling - possibly surpassing - a downward slide in trust for other American institutions.

This study examines perceptions about bias in the news media, specifically in the use of news sources by public affairs journalists. It proposes a link between the naivete of news consumers with respect to source bias and their belief that media are biased in their news coverage.

Bias and the news media:

Bias, although viewed as an important dimension of source credibility, is understudied. Credibility research about news media more often explores the importance of expertise as an attribute of news sources or a newspaper, or comparatively between newspaper and electronic news sources.

Carl Hovland and Walter Weiss conceptualized expertise and trustworthiness as the two dominant dimensions of source credibility at the inception of social science Enquiry into this topic.

Even trustworthiness, however, is conceptually problematic with respect to judgements about the news media. One might expect trust in the news media to be a function to some extent of the degree to which the media are perceived to be objective or biased. Therefore, this study is concerned with news consumers' perceptions of bias on the part of news sources. Some government officials and political pundits have criticized what they perceive to be a systematic ideological bias in the news media.

Although empirical evidence suggests that the liberal bias charge against the media is largely unfounded, some scholars argue that at certain times the American press has been more liberal or conservative, reflecting the climate of the country at the time. Psychological research shows partisan individuals from both sides of a controversial issue are likely to perceive the same media coverage as biased in opposite directions. Albert Gunther and Dominic Lasorsa found that greater importance individuals placed on an issue led to their increasing trust of newspaper coverage on that issue.

It would be, of course, self-serving on the part of journalists to claim that news consumer partisanship is the sole reason for accusations of media bias. As Gaye Tuchman argues, journalists provide a constructed reality that legitimizes the status quo and reflects the social reality of the newsroom. Journalists' perceptions and presentation of social reality may differ markedly from their audiences.

W. Lance Bennett maintains news media present biased information by focusing on trivial aspects of important news events, like personality flaws and behavioral gaffes; primarily cover events, leaving no professional convention for addressing many of the most serious problems confronting contemporary societies, like hunger, racism, resource waste and depletion; fragment the news, which distorts larger issues; and rely on too many of the same types of sources - authoritative officials who offer views that normalize the news for members of an average public.

Most research on news and public affairs information bias centers on the use of selected, elite sources, those who are easy to identify and access, often governmental officials.

Possible relation of news source bias perceptions and media bias perceptions. Accusations of systematic bias are frustrating and painful for journalists. Reporters are trained to operate under a professional code of values and ethics, where fairness and balance reign supreme.

All the while, audiences are showing increasing signs of distrust. Some of that distrust may be due to extreme partisan positions on the part of some consumers. This, however, is hardly likely to explain a more widespread questioning of media objectivity. The structural limitations of journalism, and the patterns of sources typically used, may constrain and bias news coverage. These problems and limitations in contemporary journalism may dispose news consumers to be critical of the news media. It may be that the way journalists approach balance and fairness is misunderstood, even rejected, by news consumers.

The problem of journalistic objectivity, of course, is a particularly difficult one. While journalists may seek to exclude their own feelings or opinions from a story, they are dependent upon sources - who usually have such opinions - in developing and presenting the story. Journalists, in most reporting contexts, finesse this problem through the convention of story balance. This practice may often mean purposefully seeking out biased sources to present one side's view and the other side's view.

Clearly, there is more to the use of sources from two sides of an issue in the name of fairness and balance that leads to perceptions of bias or distrust in the news. However, as Stephen Lacy, Frederick Fico and Todd Simon point out, fairness or balance in any given news story is typically a matter of affording equal coverage of opposing views. In their study of news stories in 21 newspapers, they found many lacked balance.

In 28 per cent of instances the two clear sides of a controversial issue were not contacted, and no explanation was offered by the story's writer. In an additional 6 per cent, no contact was made, but an explanation suggested efforts for such contact failed. Nonetheless, the extent to which members of the public perceive the news media as unbiased must depend in part on perceptions of story balance, as well as its actual occurrence.

This study examines an assumption of journalists, that using quotations from two sides of an issue, or balancing sources and material, presents a fair, balanced perspective to the news consumer. Bias may be defined as a perceived attribute of a news source whereby the individual news source, or the group the news source represents, has a clear, vested interest in a cause or action relative to maintaining or changing the status quo.

The person's credentials are such that one might predict how that individual would respond ideologically on political, economic and social issues. Thus, if background information describes an individual's positions and accomplishments but that information does not suggest a position on social, economic, political and other concerns, the source is interpreted as low in bias. A highly biased source generally would be presented in a journalistic account as operating to alter the status quo in some fashion, like eliminating taxes or making abortions illegal. A biased journalistic perspective, then, would mean only one side, not two or more sides, of an issue is presented.

Although not any one single source in public affairs journalism may present a biased perspective, from either comments made or background affiliation information presented, this study focuses on sources considered high and low in biased perspectives, based on their affiliations, an allegiance to some group or cause, or tendency towards promoting social reform.

The Lacy et al. results suggest one obvious problem, a discrepancy between the journalistic value of presenting two sides of an issue and the actual practice of doing so. However, in this study we propose that there may also be a more fundamental problem, or opportunity, based on studies about bias. Journalists might benefit from becoming more knowledgeable about their audiences. Indeed, their reliance on limited types of sources may constrain them in gaining insight into the lives of more average members of the populations they serve. The success of the convention of story balance assumes that the news consumer shares the reporter's assumptions concerning the bias, or lack thereof, of the various sources cited. This assumption has received little empirical examination.

One recent study suggested that, at least among college students, there was very little ability to recognize and acknowledge bias among message sources. It may well be that many members of the general public are relatively naive with respect to judging the extent of bias of news sources. On the other hand, journalists have extensive opportunity in working with news sources to experience first-hand the extent of their bias or self-interest. We might expect, then, that there would be a difference in perceptions of news source bias between professionals in the news industry and members of the general public.

In particular, we might expect to find that professionals in the journalism industry will more readily attribute bias to sources with a strong probable self-interest related to the news story. The nature of the differences with respect to sources with relatively less self-interest is more problematic.

On one hand, members of the public may be simply less attuned to bias judgements, and more inclined in the case of both high and low bias sources to make neutral judgements. On the other hand, members of the public may tend to assume less bias than the more experienced and perhaps more cynical journalism professionals even among relatively less apparently self-interested sources.

What might be the consequences of such a mismatch between journalist and public perceptions of bias? The problem is most easily apparent in the case of news sources who demonstrate higher levels of bias. Story balance is achieved by offering the views of competing biased sources in counterpoint. If the bias of these sources is not well-distinguished by some news consumers, they are unlikely to grasp the nuances of story balance. Such news consumers, then, should be more likely to perceive bias in the news media.

Therefore:

*H*1: The less bias that members of the general public perceive in high biased journalism sources, relative to journalism professionals' own judgements, the greater their perceptions of general media bias.

This, of course, represents a counterintuitive prediction. In the absence of the process described above, one would expect that members of the public who tend to perceive bias in media institutions would also be quick to attribute bias to individual news sources as well. After all, such sources are also normally affiliated with social institutions, and ones with clear political and social agendas of their own.

However, the more audience members attribute bias to the journalists or media institutions, the less likely individual sources would be blamed. Audience members might perceive sources as individuals caught up in the news events or crises and not think of the sources' predetermined vested interests manifested in their media statements. It is not known how much individual news consumers actually weigh what sources say in balance to make an assessment of the bigger picture.

The issues around perceptions of sources who are lower in their level of bias are more complex. On one hand, members of the public may be, as discussed earlier, more likely to make neutral judgements about sources.

On the other, they may tend to consistently perceive less bias among low bias sources as well as among high bias sources. Either case, though, might under different circumstances reduce the ability to recognize and correctly process the story balance convention. Sometimes, a low-bias source is used to provide presumably objective comment on an issue. If news consumers perceive the source as biased, then the intended effect of increased objectivity is lost. If less-biased sources are used to provide opposing viewpoints, the inability to perceive potential bias inherent in embracing a given viewpoint will interfere with acceptance of the story balance convention.

Therefore:

H2: Differences between journalism industry profe-ssionals and the general public in perceptions of bias among apparently less-biased journalism sources will be associated with greater perceptions of media bias.

Method A telephone random sample of 245 individuals over 18 who live in a mid-sized Western community represented the population under study. Trained students interviewed the respondents using random-generated numbers, with a response rate of about 70 per cent. Males were oversampled in an attempt to balance the number of male and female respondents.

Those in the sample responded to statements about the news media's use of sources. They indicated their level of agreement, using a Likert-type 5-point response scale that ranged from strongly agree to strongly disagree to statements such as: "I can trust the information I get from news stories," "Most news stories present issues accurately," "Most news stories are presented in a balanced and fair manner," "News stories usually quote at least two sources - one from each side of an issue."

To investigate specific differences in perceptions about the use of biased sources, eight descriptions were generated about sources. Similar to experimental conditions that manipulate bias in the source credibility literature, four types of sources were described in individual paragraphs.

Political, scientific, religious and business-related sources were presented as either low or high in bias, depending on information provided about their allegiances, affiliations and background experiences. Expert judges in communication studies provided validation that each source was either high or low in bias. Names that were used were male, to avoid a sex bias confound.

An example of a high bias source description: A researcher in environmental ethics at the University of California at Berkeley, who also heads the California chapter of Earth First. He has been arrested seven times for chaining himself to trees to prevent logging in old growth forests in the Pacific Northwest. He recently received a $70,000 grant from the National Endowment for the Arts to build an art museum display commemorating the northern spotted owl.

An example of a low bias source description:

A man who was a tenured professor in international political science at Michigan State University and who is now a private consultant to U.S. and foreign government trade organizations. His areas of expertise include world population growth and environmental economics.

The sample responded to a question that asked how biased they considered each of the eight possible sources to be, using a 7-point scale that ranged from unbiased to biased. This study also required a benchmark of professional journalists' assessments of these high and low biased sources, from which public perceptions of source bias could be compared.

Thus, 28 representatives from the daily newspaper serving the community from which the public sample was drawn responded to similar questions about news and bias. Means of the journalists' responses were used to create distance, or discrepancy, scores for each member of the public sampled regarding where they were in relation to the journalists.

In order to create an index for each respondent that represented a discrepancy between public perception of bias and journalist perceptions of bias, difference scores were calculated for the perception of each source description in the sample. For the high biased source description, each respondent's raw score measuring the perceived bias of a source description was subtracted from the mean of the journalists' assessment of the same source description.

This was done for the eight source descriptions. For the low biased source description, the mean of the journalists' assessment of a source description was subtracted from each respondent's raw score measuring perceived bias of the same source description. Again, this was done for all eight source descriptions. These discrepancy scores were added to form indices of high source bias discrepancy and low source bias discrepancy. These measures were found reasonably reliable.

Results

The mean education level of the sample was somc college, the mean age 54. Forty-five per cent were male and 55 per cent female, reflecting the conventional female bias of a telephone sample. The primary news source of the general public sample was listed as television for international news (73 per cent); television for national news (74 per cent); television for state news (34 per cent), followed closely by their local newspaper (29 per cent); and their local paper for local news (87 per cent). The two measures of perceptions about news reporting that were clearly different between the sample and the newspaper employees were:

- Fairness and balance and
- Presenting quotes that represent two sides of an issue.

Testing Hypothesis 1 involved running a statistical test to determine if less bias source perception led to greater perception of general media bias, in this case presenting quotes from two sides of issue in public affairs stories. This was the case, supporting Hypothesis 1.

Hypothesis 2 was also supported. The more discrepant the perceptions of low source bias between members of the sample and the journalistic norm, the less likely the public perceived the news media to present fair, balanced information and to present quotes from two sides of issues.

Thus, the greater the difference between journalists and their audience members, the greater the perceptions of media bias. The results provide preliminary and provocative evidence that consumers' inability to perceive news media conventions may contribute to consumer distrust in media.

The study found:

- A difference between the public and the news media's perceptions of bias in sources and of general perceptions about using quotes and presenting different sides of issues and
- The difference in perceptions of bias in sources between professional journalists at the small daily newspaper and members of its own public is related to the public's perceptions that the media are generally biased.

The more different the public's perceptions are from journalists about source bias, the less likely members of that public are to believe journalists present quotes from two sides of issues or present fair, balanced news coverage.

The tendency of respondents from the general public to fail to discriminate news source bias in the same way journalism professionals did, influencing their perceptions about the quality of the news media presentations, has broader implications for the working journalist. If a sizable percentage of news consumers are not making the same assumptions regarding the bias of self-interested news sources as is the journalist, the news story may not be interpreted as it was intended. The reverse hypothesis offers an alternate explanation, that people who are distrustful of media may pay more attention to source attributes.

Another interpretation is that of a displacement effect, whereby lower audience bias perceptions about sources shift bias perceptions about the story or the writer upward, making news organizations look responsible for unfair or unbalanced presentations. It could be news audience members are unsympathetic to journalists in their use of sources, viewing source abuse as a problem and therefore perceiving the journalists as manipulative of sources. Audience attribution of a problem of bias, then, might lie with the journalists.

What must the reporter or the editor do to clarify the biases of the news sources, and the implications of these biases for the story? Perhaps journalists should try to better educate the public about multiple sides of issues presented in stories. Perhaps journalists need to interpret types of source presentations, in order for news consumers to better comprehend the use of opposing views.

Although efforts in public journalism are controversial, one latent benefit of increasing dialogue with members of one's publics is to close the gaps of misunderstandings about practices, norms, and the rationale, as well as constraints, for certain types of news reporting practices. It is possible this dialogue, in and of itself, might lead to greater trust in journalism.

Changing journalistic norms about reporting the news in as fair, balanced way as possible might be met with the most controversy.

This might mean journalists becoming more interpretive, particularly with stories about issues with multiple sides. It would seem more realistic and pragmatic to have journalists learn more about audiences and try more educational means. It is important that future research clarify the extent of the differences found in this study regarding news story interpretation, rather than merely assuming such problems exist because of limited discrimination of news source bias. These results, preliminary though they may be, suggest a problem. Unsurprisingly, the overall patterns of these results suggest that journalism employees perceive journalism more favorably than their audiences.

The results of this study are clearly preliminary and are obtained only from a single location. However, the sample uses the newspaper from which the benchmark of newspaper employees' perceptions was derived.

This link between a medium and its intended audience lends a certain robustness to these findings, given media audience research tends to investigate audiences in isolation, apart from examinations of sources, communicators and messages those audience members receive.

Greater reliability of measures and more realistic clips (these two likely go hand-in-hand) would augment these findings, including more generalizability.

If audience perceptions of news source bias are in fact often inaccurate from the journalist's perspective, the success of the story balance convention may be less certain and news consumer interpretation of stories in some cases more distorted than journalists assume. The mainstream media cover issues with often striking similarity. Whether it is domestic issues, foreign policy, or political scandal, the media follow each other's lead as they "converge" on the same topics and interpretations, often limiting the range of views on important policy debates. Indeed, considering that thousands of journalists cover such "media events" as economic summits, political conventions, and most recently, the Persian Gulf War, remarkably few divergent points of view emerge.

This phenomenon is partly rooted in pack journalism, the routine based on the psychological need of reporters and their editors, in the highly ambiguous world of news, to confirm their work with others. But in addition, a more "systemic" convergence is encouraged by the common socialization patterns of newsworkers, large conglomerate ownership of news organizations, information subsidies through public relations efforts, and the dominance of a few key wire and syndicated news services.

By relying on a common and often narrow network of sources — newsmakers, experts, and commentators, in other words — the news media contribute to this systemic convergence on the conventional wisdom, the largely unquestioned consensus views held by journalists, power-holders, and many audience members.

The perspective that guides our analysis in this study of these news sources is based on elite theory, which directs attention towards the structure of power in society. This approach focuses on commonalities, cohesion, and coordination among those individuals at the top rungs of society, and rejects the traditional pluralist notion of power distributed across a number of competing and balancing blocs. C. Wright Mills, for example, in his influential work *The Power Elite"*, traced the convergent interests of business, economic, and military elites, as forming an apex atop the social structure pyramid.

More recently, network analysis has found a broad-based group, or "social circle," of elites, supporting a cohesive and unified conception of elite power. Among the few scholars who have applied this approach to the media, Dreier, who examined the interlocks between media boards of directors and others, found the strongest interconnections between the elite media companies and other powerful institutions.

This same theoretical perspective can be usefully applied to the study of news sources, because it focuses attention on the interconnections among those sources. We already know that elites, both governmental and corporate, receive privileged access to news channels, but here we examine the extent to which the news sources on which the national media rely form an interlocking structure across Programmes and issues.

Locating a large, cohesive, interconnected group of sources, which addresses a number of issues, would support a conception of sources comparable to the "higher circles" found by elite as economic summits, political conventions, and most recently, the Persian Gulf War, remarkably few divergent points of view emerge.

This phenomenon is partly rooted in pack journalism, the routine based on the psychological need of reporters and their editors, in the highly ambiguous world of news, to confirm their work with others. But in addition, a more "systemic" convergence is encouraged by the common socialization patterns of newsworkers, large conglomerate ownership of news organizations, information subsidies through public relations efforts, and the dominance of a few key wire and syndicated news services.

By relying on a common and often narrow network of sources — newsmakers, experts, and commentators, in other words — the news media contribute to this systemic convergence on the conventional wisdom, the largely unquestioned consensus views held by journalists, power-holders, and many audience members.

The perspective that guides our analysis in this study of these news sources is based on elite theory, which directs attention towards the structure of power in society. This approach focuses on commonalities, cohesion, and coordination among those individuals at the top rungs of society, and rejects the traditional pluralist notion of power distributed across a number of competing and balancing blocs. C. Wright Mills, for example, in his influential work *The Power Elite*", traced the convergent interests of business, economic, and military elites, as forming an apex atop the social structure pyramid.

More recently, network analysis has found a broad-based group, or "social circle," of elites, supporting a cohesive and unified conception of elite power. Among the few scholars who have applied this approach to the media, Dreier, who examined the interlocks between media boards of directors and others, found the strongest interconnections between the elite media companies and other powerful institutions.

This same theoretical perspective can be usefully applied to the study of news sources, because it focuses attention on the interconnections among those sources. We already know that elites, both governmental and corporate, receive privileged access to news channels, but here we examine the extent to which the news sources on which the national media rely form an interlocking structure across Programmes and issues.

Locating a large, cohesive, interconnected group of sources, which addresses a number of issues, would support a conception of sources comparable to the "higher circles" found by elite sources likely to appear on the other news shows also value a chance to appear on the Sunday Programmes. We consider all of these news Programmes to be members of the mainstream press, with greater similarities than differences, and so expect to find substantial connections across these shows via their source selections.

This emphasis on news sources as the basic building blocks of the structure departs from many content studies, which tend to organize news coverage by topics or issues: "war," "the economy," or "the campaign." A source focus is consistent with a number of media sociology studies. Gans, Sigal, and others since them have emphasized the important role sources play in actively shaping the news.

When we look at who says what in the news, it helps get us beyond imprecise statements about what "the media" say about an issue: the media express views by allowing newsmakers to express theirs. Thus, although the media are often said to be "powerful," in large part that power derives from media's ability to amplify the views of certain powerful sources, such as the president, members of Congress, and other elites. Thus, no analysis of news media content is complete without a close look at the sources of that content.

Increasingly, many of the opinion leaders who dictate the conventional wisdom that concerns us here are found on television. According to David Shaw, the media critic for the *Los Angeles Times*", "it is increasingly television that drives the journalistic consensus today, especially on Washington-based public affairs stories". He adds that "predictability is a major factor in the conventional wisdom dispensed by the TV talk shows", and this predictability is served up within a narrow range of opinion and superficial analysis.

Shaw further notes that although the some 20 public affairs talk and interview shows on television barely register on the ratings, they are in fact influential beyond their audience size because they reach important opinion leaders and other journalists: "Television increasingly acts as a megaphone, broadcasting the conventional wisdom back to its vast audience — which includes other print journalists".

Because television must distill news into a dramatic format, with a beginning, middle, and end, Hallin argues that television provides more explicit ideological guidance than newspapers and strives for a more coherent ideological vision. This suggests that television should display more readily than print media a discernible structure of source selections.

LINKAGES IN THE SOURCE STRUCTURE

We assume that the joint appearance of two or more sources in a television news story or on a public affairs show indicates a "relationship" between those sources. They are considered to "go together" for the purposes of presenting the media treatment of an event or story. These sources are assumed to be more involved with each other than with oth ers who do not appear, even if that relationship is largely symbolic as it relates to their political positions or the interests they represent.

In other words, the linking of two or more sources in this manner does not assume anything about the intentions or actions of the sources themselves, who obviously do not usually control the appearance of others with them, nor does it assume that they even communicate with each other. We do assume that these links tell us something meaningful about the actual structure of sources who appear to discuss important national issues, upon whom news content is based.

In addition, and just as importantly, these sources by their joint appearance are considered by writers, reporters, or talk show producers to represent the essential players or range of views on a topic. By their selection of sources, television news gatekeepers implicitly define the limits of discourse on an issue.

This selection of sources confines the debate and carries with it implicit assumptions about who is important. For example, when National Security Adviser Brent Scowcroft, and former advisers Henry Kissinger and Zbigniew Brzezinski were chosen by the producers of "This Week with David Brinkley" to be the best people to talk about the Persian Gulf crisis, it revealed much about the range of opinions considered important.

On "Nightline", for example, Republican Rep. Robert Dornan and Democratic Sen. Christopher Dodd appeared to discuss a Nicaraguan peace plan with Assistant Secretary of State Elliot Abrams. Behind the co-appearance of these three lay many behind the scenes decisions and institutional arrangements, but their presence ultimately reveals the voices and interests that the present system of newsgathering considers to go together. These officials were not the only ones involved in the Nicaraguan issue, but by selecting this configuration of views, "Nightline" framed the debate.

Both strong Contra supporters, Dornan and Abrams strongly opposed the Nicaraguan Sandinista government; Dodd was presumably picked to "balance" the other two as a critic of administration policy. His contribution, however, was limited to commenting on a procedural controversy, whether House Speaker Jim Wright had the right to meet with visiting Nicaraguan president Daniel Ortega against State Department advice.

Ultimately, he differed only tactically from Dornan and Abrams, arguing that if the peace process worked — if the Sandinistas shaped up — "there'll be no reason to support Contra aid," that is, to punish them militarily. In the example given above, we have three sources and three links, reflecting both disagreement and agreement, yet taken together they show the group called upon to represent debate on the Nicaraguan issue.

This linkage approach resembles the co-citation technique used to identify intellectual areas within academic disciplines, where linkages are based on the joint citation of studies by others. For example, if two journal articles are cited together within a later article they are considered to go together, even if one is an effort to "disprove" the other.

This linking of research (whether defined as articles, books, authors, or journals) adds a new, structural dimension to the conventional ranking of research by sheer frequency of citation, just as we go beyond listing frequent sources to showing their arrangement.

It is important to note that conceptualizing links as we do allows the source structure to encompass several dimensions, connecting sources across different points in time, news "reports," and issues.

To illustrate, we can expand the example above with three other Programmes. In addition to the "Nightline" appearance, Dodd and Abrams appeared a few days earlier on "MacNeil/Lehrer" to discuss peace in Nicaragua, joined by Republican Sen. John McCain.

Thus, the link between Dodd and Abrams remains, with both now being linked to an additional source, McCain. Abrams also appeared on "Nightline" (October 7) paired with Alejandro Bendana, the Secretary General of the Nicaraguan Foreign Ministry (discussed in greater detail below), and on "MacNeil/Lehrer" (November 30) with Democratic Rep. Walter Fauntroy to discuss democracy in Haiti, thus linking Abrams across two issues.

THE PUBLIC AFFAIRS SHOWS

Our look at television goes beyond the half-hour network newscasts to include the broader range of news Programmes on television that add important emphasis and interpretation to breaking stories. These public affairs shows place the news into context by drawing on more extensive conversations with newsmakers, experts, and commentators, and because these Programmes are usually presented live, their spontaneity makes the choice of guests critical.

The proliferation of news on television in recent years, including the public affairs Programmes, adds less than ought to be expected to the diversity of opinions. The Sunday public affairs shows in particular — "Brinkley", "Face the Nation", et al. — concentrate on Washington officialdom. As Tuchman observes, producing a successful talk show requires a certain predictability in what guests will say. This leads to typifications of guests into definable categories to make possible a routinization of guest selection. Familiar commentators serve the same purpose for television public affairs shows — their predictability safely fits the "format," and their views can be balanced with others who are also well known.

As producers come to rely on a limited number of these elites for news, viewers also develop psychological relationships with these often-seen sources. Thus, sources gain credibility by appearing often, and that credibility helps ensure their continued selection in a self-justifying cycle. Television relies on the same news sources as do the print media, and, in cases like "MacNeil/ Lehrer", depends regularly on print reporters themselves as guests. Despite their importance, however, much less scholarly attention has been directed at these Programmes than at the traditional evening newscasts.

In recent years, "Nightline" and "MacNeil/Lehrer" have come under particular scrutiny. The media watchdog group Fairness and Accuracy in Reporting has conducted systematic content analyses showing that both Programmes focus on elites, with heavy reliance on administration sources.

"MacNeil/Lehrer", although twice as long and broadcast on non-commercial PBS, is also heavily dependent on the power elites, usually white, male Capitol Hill pundits. The most frequent "Nightline" guests, appearing more than ten times in a three-year period between 1985 and 1988, were, in order, Henry Kissinger, Alexander Haig, Elliot Abrams, Jerry Falwell, Lawrence Eagleburger, Jesse Jackson, Arthur Miller, and William Hyland, thereby demonstrating the program's strong tilt towards government and former government elites. Our analysis will require that we look at specific people such as these-including those like Kissinger who appear frequently, and on more than one show.

SOURCES IN THE NEWS

Like the print media, television news in general relies heavily on institutional sources, that is, officials speaking through routine channels. In particular, the networks have been oriented towards Washington news, with regular attention given the president and Capitol Hill. In addition to officials, we consider two other important categories: experts, and journalists themselves.

THE EXPERTS

Media analysts in recent years have begun to give greater attention to expert sources. These academics, think-tankers, and retooled political insiders have become an important element in many stories. In addition, these expert commentators in network newscasts appear to have a strong impact on public opinion, as shown by Page, Shapiro, and Dempsey, who suggest that their potency may stem from their expression of elite consensus. Journalists find it easier and more predictable to consult a narrow range of experts than to call on new ones each time.

Albert R. Hunt, Washington bureau chief for the *Wall Street Journal*", says he grew so annoyed at seeing the same experts quoted in his paper all the time that he banned the use of several of them for a couple of months last year. "The ban ended when I did a column and had to quote a couple of them," he says, sheepishly.

Cooper and Soley confirm this tendency in their study of "experts" on network newscasts, noting that correspondents showed a clear pattern of reliance on a homogeneous handful of the same experts to put events in context in an apparently neutral and objective fashion. They were mostly men, East Coasters, and Republicans, ex-government officials from Republican administrations and "scholars" from conservative Washington think tanks. Among the top ten most-quoted experts or analysts in 1987 and 1988 on ABC, CBS, and NBC were William Schneider and Norman Ornstein (both of the conservative American Enterprise Institute, AEI), and Stephen Hess (of the centrist Brookings Institution). These experts are valued for their succinct and predictable responses, which further reinforce the conventional wisdom.

In addition, Steele argues, university experts are particularly attractive to television news producers, who usually have already decided what they want said before calling these sources to "reinforce their own understanding of a story" and to create "the illusion of objective reporting".

Although few of these academics provoke or challenge, hearing them creates the impression that an objective analysis has been given. Their value depends on their presumed impartiality and lack of bias, which helps producers and reporters round out stories. Political scientist Ornstein, typical of many experts, promotes himself into the news, hawking his largely descriptive commentary to the mass press in publications like *TV Guide*". His centrist viewpoint both ensures his audience appeal and certifies his suitability.

JOURNALISTS AS SOURCES

Journalists themselves — broadly including authors, columnists, and commentators — have also become important sources. The use of print media journalists, commentators, and columnists anchors the television world to the print media, encouraging group consensus. On network newscasts, these journalists stay behind the scenes, but on the interview shows they are as likely as anyone to appear on camera. The "Brinkley" programme, for example, has several rotating journalists, who appear with regulars Sam Donaldson and George Will.

These have included Cokie Roberts (NPR), Hodding Carter (former Carter State Department spokesperson and now PBS commentator), Tom Wicker (*New York Times"* columnist), Morton Kondracke (*New Republic"*), Ellen Goodman (syndicated columnist), Mary Anne Dolan (syndicated columnist), and the late Robert Maynard (*Oakland Tribune"* editor).

Similarly, "Nightline" and "MacNeil/Lehrer" also make extensive use of journalists as sources. From a producer's standpoint, journalists are a boon.

They are usually articulate, up on the issues, accessible, predictable, and desire the exposure. In fact, journalist sources effectively subsidize the cost of a show by relieving the news program's own reporters from the task of digging up information.

Because the journalists themselves have already made the investment in compiling their "stories" they can "repackage" that information on television for a modest incremental cost in their own time. Thus, the relationship between journalists and the public affairs shows is symbiotic.

A network perspective alerts us to the collection of working press figures, pundits, and commentators who span the public affairs talk shows. "The Capital Gang" on Cable News Network (CNN), for example, provides a forum for Washington insiders to discuss political issues. These guests include columnist Robert Novak, *Wall Street Journal"* Washington bureau chief Al Hunt, the *Washington Post'"*s Mark Shields, and Pat Buchanan (presidential aspirant and former director of communications for Reagan), who also has appeared regularly on "The McLaughlin Group" on PBS, among others, and writes a column. Hunt has appeared on "Meet the Press", "The McLaughlin Group", and PBS's "Washington Week in Review".

Others can also be seen across several shows, expressing essentially the same view on each. Shields has been featured weekly as a commentator on "MacNeil/Lehrer" with David Gergen, former *U.S. News and World Report"* editor and Reagan staff member (most recently a Clinton staff member). Hunt is a regular on a number of shows, as is Hedrick Smith of *The New York Times"*.

These "interlocking directors" effectively knit these shows into a seamless forum of mainstream journalism and provide a centripetal force towards consensus. view. In both cases, key metaphors help illustrate their differences. The agenda metaphor — underlying the agenda-setting approach to media effects-has been especially strong in the way it has directed the study of news content towards a "topical" emphasis.

The very term "agenda" implies a list of prioritized and discrete topics or issues, and "agenda-setting," the transmission of those priorities to the public.

At the risk of oversimplifying, the method for analysis that often follows is to establish a fixed number of news "issues" and measure the relative amount of coverage devoted to each. Like any metaphor, however, this one highlights one view of reality while hiding another. We can readily see that if the sources, articulated interests, and perspectives were the same for each issue on the *nominal* agenda, then the diversity implied by the agenda metaphor would be effectively much less.

In keeping with the elite model, consider the metaphor of a "framework." This signifies a more interlaced, interconnected view of news content, with the structure of sources being one important component. We can imagine the key load-bearing poles of this framework anchored in the institutional foundations of Capitol Hill and Wall Street.

On its outer surface lie the words and images about events in the news at any given time, but the interconnecting structure draws attention to how the whole set-up, the "system" itself, is geared towards certain stories and points of view. This model leads us in this study to consider a number of news Programmes together, as different components of this news framework — an approach that emphasizes commonalities across Programmes rather than differences.

Of course, some news media occupy a more pivotal location than others: the power of *The New York Times"* and the "MacNeil/Lehrer Newshour", for example, lies not in their circulation or ratings but in their ability to colour the way issues are presented in other media. Even specialized publications and the alternative press can be seen as part of the framework, in the sense that they must contend with the way events have been framed elsewhere.

Thus, the elite model we adopt as a theoretical perspective requires an approach to news content indicated by this "framework" conception, an important part of which is the source structure. We now turn to measuring this structure, specifically within the framework constituted by television news.

DIFFERENCES BETWEEN MEDIA ETHICS AND OTHER FIELDS OF APPLIED ETHICS

The issues of freedom of speech and aesthetic values (taste) are primarily at home in media ethics. However a number of further issues distinguish media ethics as a field in its own right. A theoretical issue peculiar to media ethics is the identity of *observer* and *observed*. The press is one of the primary guardians in a democratic society of many of the freedoms, rights and duties discussed by other fields of applied ethics. In media ethics the ethical obligations of the guardians themselves comes more strongly into the foreground. Who guards the guardians? This question also arises in the field of legal ethics.

A further self-referentiality or circular characteristic in media ethics is the questioning of its own values. Meta-issues can become identical with the subject matter of media ethics. This is most strongly seen when artistic elements are considered. Benetton advertisements and Turner prize candidates are both examples of ethically questionable media uses which question their own questioner. Another characteristic of media ethics is the disparate nature of its goals. Ethical dilemmas emerge when goals conflict. The goals of media usage diverge sharply. Expressed in a consequentialist manner, media usage may be subject to pressures to maximize: economic profits, entertainment value, information provision, the upholding of democratic freedoms, the development of art and culture, fame and vanity.

Yellow journalism is a type of journalism that downplays legitimate news in favour of eye-catching headlines that sell more newspapers. It may feature exaggerations of news events, scandal-mongering, sensationalism, or unprofessional practices by news media organizations or journalists. Campbell (2001) defines Yellow Press newspapers as having daily multi-column front-page headlines covering a variety of topics, such as sports and scandal, using bold layouts (with large illustrations and perhaps colour), heavy reliance on unnamed sources, and unabashed self-promotion. The term was extensively used to describe certain major New York City newspapers about 1900 as they battled for circulation. By extension the term is used today as a pejorative to decry any journalism that treats news in an unprofessional or unethical fashion, such as systematic political bias. Yellow Journalism can also be the practice of over-dramatizing events.

Frank Luther Mott (1941) defines Yellow Journalism in terms of five characteristics:

- Scare headlines in huge print, often of minor news
- Lavish use of pictures, or imaginary drawings
- Use of faked interviews, misleading headlines, pseudo-science, and a parade of false learning from so-called experts
- Emphasis on full-colour Sunday supplements, usually with comic strips (which is now normal in the U.S.)
- Dramatic sympathy with the "underdog" against the system.

Present day (successful) exponents of the yellow journalistic style would include the British red top tabloids, notably The Sun and its German equivalent Bild, and in Australia the Daily Telegraph. The term originated during the Gilded Age with the circulation battles between Joseph Pulitzer's New York World and William Randolph Hearst's New York Journal. The battle peaked from 1895 to about 1898, and historical usage often refers specifically to this period. Both papers were accused by critics of sensationalizing the news in order to drive up circulation, although the newspapers did serious reporting as well. The New York Press coined the term *yellow kid journalism* in early 1897 after a then-popular comic strip to describe the down market papers of Pulitzer and Hearst, which both published versions of it during a circulation war. This was soon shortened to *yellow journalism* with the New York Press insisting, "We called them Yellow because they are Yellow."

Joseph Pulitzer purchased the World in 1883 after making the *St. Louis Post-Dispatch* the dominant daily in that city. The publisher had gotten his start editing a German-language publication in St. Louis, and saw a great untapped market in the nation's immigrant classes. Pulitzer strove to make *The World* an entertaining read, and filled his paper with pictures, games and contests that drew in readers, particularly those who used English as a second language. Crime stories filled many of the pages, with headlines like "Was He a Suicide?" and "Screaming for Mercy." In addition, Pulitzer only charged readers two cents per issue but gave readers eight and sometimes 12 pages of information (the only other two cent paper in the city never exceeded four pages).

While there were many sensational stories in the *World*, they were by no means the only pieces, or even the dominant ones. Pulitzer believed that newspapers were public institutions with a duty to improve society, and he put the *World* in the service of social reform. During a heat wave in 1883, *World* reporters went into the Manhattan's tenements, writing stories about the appalling living conditions of immigrants and the toll the heat took on the children. Stories headlined "How Babies Are Baked", "Burning Babies Fall From The Roof" and "Lines of Little Hearses" spurred reform and drove up the *World's* circulation.

Just two years after Pulitzer took it over, the *World* became the highest circulation newspaper in New York, aided in part by its strong ties to the Democratic Party. Older publishers, envious of Pulitzer's success, began criticizing the *World*, harping on its crime stories and stunts while ignoring its more serious reporting — trends which influenced the popular perception of yellow journalism, both then and now. Charles Dana, editor of the New York Sun, attacked *The World* and said Pulitzer was "deficient in judgement and in staying power." Pulitzer's approach made an impression on William Randolph Hearst, a mining heir who acquired the *San Francisco Examiner* from his father in 1887. Hearst read the *World* while studying at Harvard University and resolved to make the Examiner as bright as Pulitzer's paper..

Under his leadership, the *Examiner* devoted 24 per cent of its space to crime, presenting the stories as morality plays, and sprinkled adultery and "nudity" (by 19th century standards) on the front page. A month after taking over the paper, the *Examiner* ran this headline about a hotel fire:

Hungry, Frantic Flames. They Leap Madly Upon the Splendid Pleasure Palace by the Bay of Monterey, Encircling Del Monte in Their Ravenous Embrace From Pinnacle to Foundation. Leaping Higher, Higher, Higher, With Desperate Desire. Running Madly Riotous Through Cornice, Archway and Facade. Rushing in Upon the Trembling Guests with Savage Fury. Appalled and Panic-Striken the Breathless Fugitives Gaze Upon the Scene of Terror.

The Magnificent Hotel and Its Rich Adornments Now a Smoldering heap of Ashes. The "Examiner" Sends a Special Train to Monterey to Gather Full Details of the Terrible Disaster. Arrival of the Unfortunate Victims on the Morning's Train — A History of Hotel del Monte — The Plans for Rebuilding the Celebrated Hostelry — Particulars and Supposed Origin of the Fire.

Hearst could go overboard in his crime coverage; one of his early pieces, regarding a "band of murderers," attacked the police for forcing *Examiner* reporters to do their work for them. But while indulging in these stunts, the *Examiner* also increased its space for international news, and sent reporters out to uncover municipal corruption and inefficiency. In one celebrated story, *Examiner* reporter Winifred Black was admitted into a San Francisco hospital and discovered that indigent women were treated with "gross cruelty." The entire hospital staff was fired the morning the piece appeared.

NEW YORK

With the *Examiner*'s success established by the early 1890s, Hearst began shopping for a New York newspaper. Hearst purchased the New York Journal in 1895, a penny paper which Pulitzer's brother Albert had sold to a Cincinnati publisher the year before. Metropolitan newspapers started going after department store advertising in the 1890s, and discovered the larger the circulation base, the better. This drove Hearst; following Pulitzer's earlier strategy, he kept the *Journal's* price at one cent (compared to *The World's* two cent price) while providing as much information as rival newspapers.

The approach worked, and as the *Journal's* circulation jumped to 150,000, Pulitzer cut his price to a penny, hoping to drive his young competitor (who was subsidized by his family's fortune) into bankruptcy. In a counterattack, Hearst raided the staff of the *World* in 1896. While most sources say that Hearst simply offered more money, Pulitzer — who had grown increasingly abusive to his employees — had become an extremely difficult man to work for, and many *World* employees were willing to jump for the sake of getting away from him. Although the competition between the *World* and the *Journal* was fierce, the papers were temperamentally alike. Both were Democratic, both were sympathetic to labour and immigrants (a sharp contrast to publishers like the *New York Tribune's* Whitelaw Reid, who blamed their poverty on moral defects), and both invested enormous resources in their Sunday publications, which functioned like weekly magazines, going beyond the normal scope of daily journalism.

Their Sunday entertainment features included the first colour comic strip pages, and some theorize that the term yellow journalism originated there, while as noted above the New York Press left the term it invented undefined. *Hogan's Alley,* a comic strip revolving around a bald child in a yellow nightshirt (nicknamed The Yellow Kid), became exceptionally popular when cartoonist

Richard Outcault began drawing it in the *World* in early 1896. When Hearst predictably hired Outcault away, Pulitzer asked artist George Luks to continue the strip with his characters, giving the city two Yellow Kids.

The use of "yellow journalism" as a synonym for over-the-top sensationalism in the U.S. apparently started with more serious newspapers commenting on the excesses of "the Yellow Kid papers."

In 1890, Samuel Warren and Louis Brandeis published "The Right to Privacy," considered the most influential law review article of all time, as a critical response to sensational forms of journalism, which they saw as an unprecedented threat to individual privacy. The article is widely considered to have led to the recognition of new common law privacy rights of action.

SPANISH-AMERICAN WAR

Pulitzer and Hearst are often credited (or blamed) for drawing the nation into the Spanish-American War with sensationalist stories or outright lying. However, the vast majority of Americans did not live in New York City, and the decision makers who did live there probably relied more on staid newspapers like the *Times, The Sun* or the *Post.* The most famous example of the exaggeration is the apocryphal story that artist Frederic Remington telegrammed Hearst to tell him all was quiet in Cuba and "There will be no war." Hearst responded "Please remain. You furnish the pictures and I'll furnish the war." The story (a version of which appears in the Hearst-inspired Orson Welles film *Citizen Kane*) first appeared in the memoirs of reporter James Creelman in 1901, and there is no other source for it.

But Hearst became a war hawk after a rebellion broke out in Cuba in 1895. Stories of Cuban virtue and Spanish brutality soon dominated his front page. While the accounts were of dubious accuracy, the newspaper readers of the 19th century did not expect, or necessarily want, his stories to be pure nonfiction. Historian Michael Robertson has said that "Newspaper reporters and readers of the 1890s were much less concerned with distinguishing among fact-based reporting, opinion and literature."

Pulitzer, though lacking Hearst's resources, kept the story on his front page. The yellow press covered the revolution extensively and often inaccurately, but conditions on Cuba were horrific enough. The island was in a terrible economic depression, and Spanish general Valeriano Weyler, sent to crush the rebellion, herded Cuban peasants into concentration camps and caused hundreds of thousands of deaths. Having clamored for a fight for two years, Hearst took credit for the conflict when it came: A week after the United States declared war on Spain, he ran "How do you like the *Journal's* war?" on his front page.

In fact, President William McKinley never read the *Journal*, and newspapers like the *Tribune* and the *New York Evening Post*. Moreover, journalism historians have noted that yellow journalism was largely confined to New York City, and that newspapers in the rest of the country did not follow their lead. The *Journal* and the *World* were not among the top ten sources of news in regional papers, and the stories simply did not make a splash outside New York City. War came because public opinion was sickened by the bloodshed, and because leaders like McKinley realized that Spain had lost control of Cuba. These factors weighed more on the president's mind than the melodramas in the *New York Journal.*

Hearst sailed directly to Cuba, when the invasion began, as a war correspondent, providing sobre and accurate accounts of the fighting. Creelman later praised the work of the reporters for exposing the horrors of Spanish misrule, arguing, "no true history of the war... can be written without an acknowledgment that whatever of justice and freedom and progress was accomplished by the Spanish-American war was due to the enterprise and tenacity of *yellow journalists,* many of whom lie in unremembered graves."

AFTER THE WAR

Hearst was a leading Democrat who promoted William Jennings Bryan for president in 1896 and 1900. He later ran for mayor and governor and even sought the presidential nomination, but lost much of his personal prestige when outrage exploded in 1901 after columnist Ambrose Bierce and published separate columns months apart that suggested the assassination of McKinley. When McKinley was shot on September 6, 1901, critics accused Hearst's Yellow Journalism of driving Leon Czolgosz to the deed. Hearst did not know of Bierce's column and claimed to have pulled Brisbane's after it ran in a first edition, but the incident would haunt him for the rest of his life and all but destroyed his presidential ambitions.

Pulitzer, haunted by his "yellow sins," returned the *World* to its crusading roots as the new century dawned. By the time of his death in 1911, the *World* was a widely-respected publication, and would remain a leading progressive paper until its demise in 1931. Other newspapers, especially the new tabloids in the big cities, adopted the flashy techniques of Yellow Journalism, most notably the New York *Daily News*, founded in 1919.

STANDARDS AND REPUTATION

Among the leading news organizations that voluntarily adopt and attempt to uphold the common standards of journalism ethics described herein, adherence and general quality varies considerably. The professionalism, reliability and public accountability of a news organization are three of its most valuable assets. An organization earns and maintains a strong reputation, in part, through a consistent implementation of ethical standards, which influence its position with the public and within the industry.

GENRES AND ETHICS

Advocacy journalists — a term of some debate even within the field of journalism — by definition tend to reject "objectivity", while at the same time maintaining many other common standards and ethics. Creative nonfiction and Literary journalism use the power of language and literary devices more akin to fiction to bring insight and depth into often book-length treatment of the subjects about which they write. Such devices as dialogue, metaphor, digression and other such techniques offer the reader insights not usually found in standard news reportage. However, authors in this branch of journalism still maintain ethical criteria such as factual and historical accuracy as found in standard news reporting. Yet, with brilliant prose, they venture outside the boundaries of standard news reporting in offering richly detailed accounts. One widely regarded author in the genre is Joyce Carol Oates, as with her book on boxer Mike Tyson.

New Journalism and Gonzo journalism also reject some of the fundamental ethical traditions and will set aside the technical standards of journalistic prose in order to express themselves and reach a particular audience or market segment. Tabloid journalists are often accused of sacrificing accuracy and the personal privacy of their subjects in order to boost sales. Supermarket tabloids are often focused on entertainment rather than news. A few have "news" stories that are so outrageous that they are widely read for entertainment purposes, not for information. Some tabloids do purport to maintain common journalistic standards, but may fall far short in practice. Others make no such claims. Some publications deliberately engage in satire, but give the publication the design elements of a newspaper, for example, The Onion, and it is not unheard of for other publications to offer the occasional, humorous articles appearing on April Fool's Day.

RELATIONSHIP WITH FREEDOM OF THE PRESS

In countries without freedom of the press, the majority of people who report the news may not follow the above-described standards of journalism. Non-free media are often prohibited from criticizing the national government, and in many cases are required to distribute propaganda as if it were news. Various other forms of censorship may restrict reporting on issues the government deems sensitive.

VARIATIONS, VIOLATIONS, AND CONTROVERSIES

There are a number of finer points of journalistic procedure that foster disagreements in principle and variation in practice among "mainstream" journalists in the free press. Laws concerning libel and slander vary from country to country, and local journalistic standards may be tailored to fit. For example, the United Kingdom has a broader definition of libel than does the United States.

Accuracy is important as a core value and to maintain credibility, but especially in broadcast media, audience share often gravitates towards outlets that are reporting new information first. Different organizations may balance speed and accuracy in different ways.

The New York Times, for instance, tends to print longer, more detailed, less speculative, and more thoroughly verified pieces a day or two later than many other newspapers. 24-hour television news networks tend to place much more emphasis on getting the "scoop." Here, viewers may switch channels at a moment's notice; with fierce competition for ratings and a large amount of airtime to fill, fresh material is very valuable. Because of the fast turn-around, reporters for these networks may be under considerable time pressure, which reduces their ability to verify information. Laws with regard to personal privacy, official secrets, and media disclosure of names and facts from criminal cases and civil lawsuits differ widely, and journalistic standards may vary accordingly. Different organizations may have different answers to questions about when it is journalistically acceptable to skirt, circumvent, or even break these regulations.

Another example of differences surrounding harm reduction is the reporting of preliminary election results. In the United States, some news organizations feel that it is harmful to the democratic process to report exit poll results or preliminary returns while voting is still open. Such reports may influence people who vote later in the day, or who are in western time zones, in their decisions about how and whether or not to vote. There is also some concern that such preliminary results are often inaccurate and may be misleading to the public. Other outlets feel that this information is a vital part of the transparency of the election process, and see no harm (if not considerable benefit) in reporting it.

TASTE, DECENCY AND ACCEPTABILITY

Audiences have different reactions to depictions of violence, nudity, coarse language, or to people in any other situation that is unacceptable to or stigmatized by the local culture or laws (such as the consumption of alcohol, homosexuality, illegal drug use, scatological images, etc.). Even with similar audiences, different organizations and even individual reporters have different standards and practices. These decisions often revolve around what facts are necessary for the audience to know. When certain distasteful or shocking material is considered important to the story, there are a variety of common methods for mitigating negative audience reaction. Advance warning of explicit or disturbing material may allow listeners or readers to avoid content they would rather not be exposed to. Offensive words may be partially obscured or bleeped. Potentially offensive images may be blurred or narrowly cropped. Descriptions may be substituted for pictures; graphic detail might be omitted. Disturbing content might be moved from a cover to an inside page, or from daytime to late evening, when children are less likely to be watching. There is often considerable controversy over these techniques, especially concern that obscuring or not reporting certain facts or details is self-censorship that compromises objectivity and fidelity to the truth, and which does not serve the public interest.

For example, images and graphic descriptions of war are often violent, bloody, shocking and profoundly tragic. This makes certain content disturbing to some audience members, but it is precisely these aspects of war that some consider to be the most important to convey. Some argue that "sanitizing" the depiction of war influences public opinion about the merits of continuing to fight, and about the policies or circumstances that precipitated the conflict. The amount of explicit violence and mutilation depicted in war coverage varies considerable from time to time, from organization to organization, and from country to country. Reporters have also been accused of indecency in the process of collecting news, namely that they are overly intrusive in the name of journalistic insensitivity. War correspondent Edward Behr recounts the story of a reporter during the Congo Crisis who walked into a crowd of Belgian evacuees and shouted, "Anyone here been raped and speaks English?"

CAMPAIGNING IN THE MEDIA

Many print publications take advantage of their wide readership and print persuasive pieces in the form of unsigned editorials that represent the official position of the organization. Despite the ostensible separation between editorial writing and news gathering, this practice may cause some people to doubt the political objectivity of the publication's news reporting. (Though usually unsigned editorials are accompanied by a diversity of signed opinions from other perspectives.) Other publications and many broadcast media only publish opinion pieces that are attributed to a particular individual (who may be an in-house analyst) or to an outside entity. One particularly controversial question is whether media organizations should endorse political candidates for office. Political endorsements create more opportunities to construe favoritism in reporting, and can create a perceived conflict of interest.

INVESTIGATIVE METHODS

Investigative journalism is largely an information-gathering exercise, looking for facts that are not easy to obtain by simple requests and searches, or are actively being concealed, suppressed or distorted. Where investigative work involves undercover journalism or use of whistleblowers, and even more if it resorts to covert methods more typical of private detectives or even spying, it brings a large extra burden on ethical standards. Anonymous sources are double-edged - they often provide especially newsworthy information, such as classified or confidential information about current events, information about a previously unreported scandal, or the perspective of a particular group that may fear retribution for expressing certain opinions in the press.

The downside is that the condition of anonymity may make it difficult or impossible for the reporter to verify the source's statements. Sometimes sources hide their identities from the public because their statements would otherwise quickly be discredited. Thus, statements attributed to anonymous sources may carry more weight with the public than they might if they were attributed. The Washington press has been criticized in recent years for excessive use of anonymous sources, in particular to report information that is later revealed to be unreliable. The use of anonymous sources increased markedly in the period before the 2003 invasion of Iraq.

SCIENCE ISSUES

The mainstream press is often criticized for poor accuracy in reporting science news. Many reporters are not scientists, and are thus not familiar with the material they are summarizing. Technical information is also difficult to contextualize for lay audiences, and short-form reporting makes providing background, context, and clarification even harder. Food scares are an example of the need for responsible science journalism, as are stories connected with the safety of medical procedures.

EXAMPLES OF ETHICAL DILEMMAS

One of the primary functions of journalism ethics is to aid journalists in dealing with many ethical dilemmas they may encounter. From highly sensitive issues of national security to everyday questions such as accepting a dinner from a source, putting a bumper sticker on one's car, publishing a personal opinion blog, a journalist must make decisions taking into account things such as the public's right to know, potential threats, reprisals and intimidations of all kinds, personal integrity, conflicts between editors, reporters and publishers or management, and many other such conundra. The following are illustrations of some of those.

- The Pentagon Papers dealt with extremely difficult ethical dilemmas faced by journalists. Despite government intervention, The Washington Post, joined by The New York Times, felt the public interest was more compelling and both published reports. (The cases went to the Supreme Court where they were merged and are known as New York Times Co. v. United States, 403 U.S. 713.
- The Washington Post also once published a story about a listening device that the United States had installed over an undersea Soviet cable during the height of the cold war. The device allowed the United States to learn where Soviet submarines were positioned. In that case, Post Executive Editor Ben Bradlee chose not to run the story on national security grounds. However, the Soviets subsequently discovered the device and, according to Bradlee, "It was no longer a

matter of national security. It was a matter of national embarrassment." However, the U.S. government still wanted The Washington Post not to run the story on the basis of national security, yet, according to Bradlee, "We ran the story. And you know what, the sun rose the next day."

- The Ethics Advice Line, a joint venture, public service project of Chicago Headline Club Chapter of the Society of Professional Journalists and Loyola University Chicago Centre for Ethics and Social Justice, provides some examples of typical ethical dilemmas reported to their ethical dilemma hotline and are typical of the kinds of questions faced by many professional journalists.

A partial listing of questions received by The Ethics Advice Line:

- Is it ethical to make an appointment to interview an arsonist sought by police, without informing police in advance of the interview?
- Is lack of proper attribution plagiarism?
- Should a reporter write a story about a local priest who confessed to a sex crime if it will cost the newspaper readers and advertisers who are sympathetic to the priest?
- Is it ethical for a reporter to write a news piece on the same topic on which he or she has written an opinion piece in the same paper?
- Under what circumstances do you identify a person who was arrested as a relative of a public figure, such as a local sports star?
- Freelance journalists and photographers accept cash to write about, or take photos of, events with the promise of attempting to get their work on the AP or other news outlets, from which they also will be paid. Is that ethical?
- Can a journalist reveal a source of information after guaranteeing confidentiality if the source proves to be unreliable?

2

Crime Reporting and the Media

INTRODUCTION

The gay newspaper account of his murder indicated, "Patrick was too trusting of people and that he had been warned not to take strangers home". Perhaps this statement from the gay press was issued as a warning to the gay community about the criminal practice of gay baiting. That is, posing as gay in order to rob, assault, or in this case murder a gay man. The documentary film License to Kill, by documentarian Arthur Dong, presents interviews with seven convicted murderers of gay men. Dong interviews five of the convicted killers who sought out their victims by "baiting them" in the geography of the gay community such as parks, bars, and other known meeting places.

Patrick brought the wrong person home that night. He was found in his bed stabbed to death. The mainstream (straight) newspaper The Louisville Courier never called attention to his murder as a gay related hate crime. Mainstream USA news media, often deletes the details of peoples' sexual orientations, the chief motive in hate crimes. When the media does include gays and lesbians as part of the news frame, the image (photograph) shown often does not make the point. This was the case in the CNN October 1991 coverage of National Coming Out Day. The media reported the rise in anti-gay violence and chose for its example an attack on one gay man at Columbia University in New York City. From the TV image, the man did not look the least bit damaged from the attack (even though he said his ribs were broken), and that was the only example selected to present the problem.

Gay related hate crimes had not yet become a part of public discourse until the murder of 21-year-old University of Wyoming student Matthew Shepard in 1998. In his father's words, at the sentencing phase of the trial, he described his son as "a hero whose death had focused world-wide attention on hate", reported the popular television show American Justice.

Gay, lesbian, and transgendered people are at-risk for hate crime victimization. While hate crime legislation goes beyond the scope of my present analysis, some critics point out that media attention to bias motivated violence, along with examples of such crimes to achieve "empirical credibility", is helping at the state and federal levels to move towards legislation to protect gay and lesbian people from such crimes. A bias-motivated crime is different from a hit-and-run accident; a store clerk killing of a material witness; a domestic homicide; a greedy drug deal gone sour.

Not all crimes are motivated by hate. People who object to hate crime legislation often repeat the familiar mantra "murder is murder" and maintain these laws "create special victims and special rights". Bias (hate) crime is at the centre the loathing of certain groups or identities as is the decision to act on such loathing. More likely, there are objections from citizens who feel that any law that promotes the legitimacy of gay and lesbian people is a bad law. Consequently, mass media such as film, television, print, and broadcast news, play an important social role in reporting hate crimes and the threat they pose to gay and lesbian and other at-risk communities. As hate crime expert Valerie Jenness makes clear "[T]he media plays a large role in the construction of hate crimes and hate crime victims".

My main thesis is that whether fictional or nonfictional narratives are employed, media texts that represent what Henry Giroux calls symbolic forms of violence may help educate the public with regard to the hate crimes of which gay, lesbian, and transgendered people are at a particularly high risk for being victimized. First, I consider why we are seeing more media attention paid to the gay and lesbian community, which has historically been on the fringes of the media landscape, because of having to establish its own cultural artifacts-often invisible to those outside the subculture. To some extent, the mainstreaming of gays and lesbians as a co-cultural group in the semiotic network of magazines, newspapers, television, film, and the news is the result of an ethic of media activism most visible from the post-Stonewall gay and lesbian movement. This opening up to gay and lesbian representation in popular culture is the result of the influence of other texts produced from and for the movement.

A second part of my analysis is concerned with improving the important social role print and broadcast journalism can play in covering victims of violent crime in the mass media. Reflecting on research in the Victims and the Media Unit at the University of Central Oklahoma, we were led to believe that sensitively written stories about victims and trauma may help society remember (not forget) victims, and further may educate communities about the ramifications of such needless acts of hate and violence. Cote and Simpson, who wrote the first book on victims of violence make clear that "better reporting about trauma can help readers and viewers gain empathy for the suffering of victims and enrich our awareness of the powerful role trauma plays in our lives". Such research will help to differentiate codes of violence in the media, some of which can be broadly designated as "symbolic" and will aid a collective understanding of the victims' experiences; while other representational forms coded as "ritualistic", offer little insight into the trauma that real human beings suffer.

THE DEFINITION OF CRIME

The commission of a crime marks one as a deviant. It places the criminal outside of the consensus and identifies him as an enemy of the state. However, because the criminal is outside the consensus, he also may be described as an enemy of the people. Thus, crime as a category helps determine the borders of the consensus and the consensus helps provide legitimacy to the state's definition of crime. In this way, crime "provides hegemonic services for the state." The extent of these hegemonic services, however, is limited because the definition of crime is politically contested. Crime is not just what the state wants it to be, but what it comes to be signified as.

While there is general agreement that criminal acts are wrong, not everyone agrees on what acts should be criminal. Traditional or mainstream views of crime tend to focus almost exclusively on acts of individuals that threaten violence to persons or property.

This mainstream or state definition of crime is criticized by those who note that, under this view, harmful conduct of the wealthy and powerful is either not conceived of as crime or, if so, rarely prosecuted or punished.

These critics would propose an alternative definition of crime, one which would define a broad range of human rights violations - *e.g.*, racism, sexism, economic exploitation - as crime. Even within these two general camps there is wide disagreement over which specific acts ought to be criminalized.

This is true because in the most fundamental respect the definition of crime is politically determined. Its definition derives from the political give and take generated as various interests compete for control of the state apparatus. The formal definition of crime, then, will vary as different interests gain power or as groups in power redefine their needs in response to changing social conditions.

Viewing crime as politically contingent only partially explains why the state definition of crime is so prevalent. It prevails because the functional definition of crime (*i.e.*, the definition used to determine the imposition of punishment, whether from mainstream or alternative formulations) is built from deeper, more fundamental concepts of criminality. The fundamental definition of crime is not found in criminology courses or in criminal law texts. When people talk about crime, they draw on social images from "the available field of practical ideologies." These images provide the structure for any discourse about crime.

When the journalist, or the judge, or the members of the ordinary public have to respond to, or explain, troubling events, like "mugging", they tend to draw, often in a piecemeal and unreflexive manner, on the social images, the "ideas of society", the sources of moral anxiety, the scattered meanings which frame their everyday experience in order to construct, out of them, social accounts which carry credibility.

These fundamental images build up slowly over time, accruing from society's total experience with crime and its ideological reaction to it. These images are the result of politically contingent, functional definitions of crime percolating in the public consciousness until they reach the level of "truism." When definitions of crime enter into the social reservoir of ideas, they retain their political and ideological character.

Thus, the limited range of explanatory paradigms within which we structure our thinking about crime is greatly influenced by those who inject ideas about crime into the public consciousness, or those whom Hall refers to as the "definers" of crime.

Hall distinguishes between primary and secondary definers of crime. "Primary definers" are authority figures in powerful and high status positions. They are considered to have greater expertise and to have "access to more accurate or more specialized information on particular topics than the majority of the population." As a consequence, it is primary definers who are able to provide the primary definition or the most widely accepted "take" on crime.

"Secondary definers" are those who reproduce as secondary sources the definitions established by primary definers. In industrialized countries, these are primarily the media. Hall points out that the media are forced into heavy dependence on the statements of primary definers by their desire to produce an "impartial" and "objective" product under constant deadline pressure, since primary definers provide a readily accessible source of authoritative opinions.

The realities of news production, then, work to create" a systematically structured over-accessing to the media of those in powerful and privileged institutional positions." This means that the opinions and viewpoints of primary definers are much more likely to be widely disseminated than those of others. They will be credited as authoritative by the media, and ultimately accepted by the majority of the public.

Over time, as these opinions work themselves into the social reservoir of ideas, they will exert a greater and greater influence over all signification about crime that takes place within that culture. I do not mean to suggest that alternative perspectives on crime cannot be expressed.

Indeed, there are alternatives to the mainstream view of crime both at the functional and the fundamental level. But these alternative views generally lack credibility." Counter-definers," or those who produce alternative definitions of crime, are severely handicapped in their ability to influence the production of meaning. It is difficult for most counter-definers to gain access to the media and thereby participate in the defining process. Those that can, by reason of the fact that they have won some degree of legitimacy from the system (such as law professors or criminal defence attorneys)," must respond in terms pre-established by the primary definers and the privileged definitions, and have a better chance of securing a hearing and influencing the process precisely if they cast their case within the limits of that consensus." Counter-definers who fail to respond in the familiar framework established by the primary definers run the risk of having their opinions de-authenticated and dismissed as" radical" or" extreme."

Thus, it comes as no surprise that a close inspection of the way that crime is reported reveals a heavy reliance on the statements of police, prosecutors, government officials, and other spokespersons of the established institutions of criminal justice.

To the extent that lay opinion is represented at all in this field, it is represented by the advocates of victims. Rarely are the opinions of those perceived as criminals solicited, unless they are the views of reformed lawbreakers, employed now as consultants to crime control organizations.

The alternative perspective is offered, if offered at all, by a small coterie of criminal defence attorneys and civil libertarians, whose opinions are made to seem more and more nonsensical, even though they are always careful never to challenge the fundamental assumptions of the criminal justice system.

In this section, I have shown how the meaning of crime is produced through a semiotic process of signification. Crime determines the consensus, but the consensus also determines crime. At the raw functional level, the meaning of crime is determined through a process of articulation as competing interests vie to establish their own self-interested definitions of crime. Thus, the working definition of crime is politically contingent and therefore relational.

The meaning of crime is also relational in the sense that the working, or functional, definition of crime is constructed from deeper, foundational notions that have been cloaked in the veneer of common sense. These common sense notions are themselves the result of a semiotic process at work. They are but distilled and refined versions of politically contingent, functional definitions of crime that have been worked and reworked through an extended process of signification. These fundamental views of crime comprise a cultural inventory of basic assumptions that structure all discourse on crime.

In the next Part, I examine the way that crime is signified in popular culture in order to reveal the basic assumptions about crime and criminals that are at work.

Making Meaning: The Depiction of Crime In Popular Culture

Investigating the way that crime is signified in popular culture can show how the image of crime is worked into the popular consciousness. Exploring popular culture, then, can expose the codes that govern the way that significations about crime take their meaning, since it is from this deep level that all subsequent discourse about crime is structured. The popular culture serves as a window into the shaping of the consensus. It is the means through which the consensus expresses itself, as well as the means via which key definers can shape the consensus. The term" popular culture" can cover a lot of ground. For my purposes, I am concerned mainly with television as a representative of popular culture. I choose television because television is the primary means through which we learn about and make sense of our world. Whether offered as" fact" or" fiction," representations of crime invade all aspects of television programming.

For convenience, I divide my comments into:

- Observations about dramatized accounts of crime
- Non-fiction reporting of incidents of crime.

Crime on Prime Time Television

Crime is a staple of prime time television. A 1985 survey revealed that more than forty per cent of prime time hours during the 1985-86 television season were devoted to shows featuring police officers, detectives, private investigators or other law enforcement agents.

There is substantially more crime on the nation's television screens than on the nation's streets. The principal investigator in a two decade-long survey of prime time television claims ten times more crime is depicted on television shows than occurs in real life.

The average viewer watches six violent crimes during each hour of prime time viewing and two-thirds of all major dramatic characters are involved in some violence, typically brought about by the commission of or the consequences of a criminal act. As a result, television viewers are immersed, hour after hour, in a world where crime takes on exaggerated importance.

Not only is the amount of crime on television dramas exaggerated, but also the types of crime depicted are exaggerated. Television crime is bloodier and more violent than crime is in reality. As flawed as known indicators of crime are, it is clear that the vast majority of serious crime is directed at property. Yet, the type of crime most frequently depicted on television dramas is murder. On television, the bulk of crime depicted is crime against the person, and the victims of crime are disproportionately white and female. The perpetrators of crimes are also portrayed unrealistically. Surprisingly, criminal characters on prime time shows are frequently played by white middle-class males. While real criminals are dispropor-tionately poor, television criminals are often rich and greedy. Such a stereotype makes little sense, as white collar or victimless crimes are seldom the focus of television dramas.

Criminals are generally presented unsympathetically. Rarely are they depicted as victims of circumstance or motivated by concerns or needs, other than greed, with which the average viewer can empathize.

In the world of television crime, there are only two acceptable motivations for criminal behaviour: greed and insanity. When crime cannot be explained by these two factors, it is presented as just senseless - the consequence of an uncontrollable evil will. In short, instead of real people with histories, personalties, and relationships that frame and explain their conduct, criminals are represented as one-dimensional demons to be feared and destroyed. Viewing crime presented in a manner that suggests that it cannot be explained discourages us from looking for its causes.

The structure of television drama does not allow for the accurate representation of criminal defence attorneys, nor does it permit an adequate explanation of their function and/or necessity. Since most crime dramas end with an arrest, "[a]rraignments, pretrial hearings, jury selection, bonding, plea bargaining, trials, sentencing, and other postarrest processes are rarely shown." Furthermore, since we typical see the perpetrators as they commit their crimes, television criminals are, of course, almost always guilty. Consequently, criminal defence attorneys are either superfluous or corrupt. According to legal ethics scholar Steven Stark, "`criminal defence lawyers are usually depicted on crime shows as figures of derision and betrayers of the public trust.'"

Contrasting sharply with the image of the criminal and the criminal defence attorney is the image of the television "crime-fighter." Law enforcement agents are central heroic figures in prime time crime dramas. Whether police officers, detectives, private investigators, federal agents (FBI, DEA, Treasury) or even medical examiners or attorneys, the common characteristic shared by crime-fighters is their archetypical role as instruments of crime detection and enforcers of the established order.

Police officers are represented in particularly glamorous, but unrealistic ways. Their role as fighters of crime is exaggerated and other mundane, but more common aspects of the police officer's role are diminished. The life of a television crime-fighter is exciting. He rarely makes mistakes, and seldom makes a false arrest.

Crime dramas rarely focus on complaints of police brutality. When they do, the complainant is belittled and the brutality characterized as necessary. Studies have repeatedly disclosed that the constitutional rights of those suspected of crime are routinely violated on television crime shows. Not only are witnesses assaulted, but homes and offices are routinely broken into without warrants, highly suggestive identifications are solicited, and confessions are flagrantly coerced.

Notwithstanding the blatant illegality of fictional police conduct, the television representation of crime-fighters is generally positive and presumably perceived as such by much of the audience. Several studies indicate that police officers are held in high regard by members of the general public. The illegal conduct of television cops is accepted, even encouraged, in large part because in the context of such shows, illegal conduct is framed as pragmatic and necessary. In the words of one researcher: In most crime shows the audience sees the crime committed, so they know who committed the crime, a position the television police do not enjoy. So when the police violate the Fourth Amendment and conduct an illegal search, it seems acceptable because guilt has already been established as far as the audience is concerned.

Police violence and illegal conduct are presented on television as an effective, quick, and simplistic solution to society's crime problem. Constitutional guarantees are presented as obstacles to effective law enforcement, causing more harm to citizens if taken too seriously. Police officers are frequently portrayed in a highly romanticized manner as macho individualists, who are not afraid to do whatever it takes to get the job done.

Since on television, the real threat to a prosperous life comes from criminals and not from a faceless government, the viewing public is encouraged to place their trust in the hands of violent, but effective, law. The ideological impact of the way crime is signified on television dramas was pointed out by George Gerbner over twenty years ago, in a study prepared for the Surgeon General's Scientific Advisory Committee on Television and Social Behaviour.

Gerbner's research disclosed that the vast majority of dramatic themes represented on television "revolved around threats to and the preservation of the moral, social and global order." Violence, including crime, is used in these contexts because it is an inexpensive and emotionally charged way to communicate messages about appropriate and inappropriate social behaviour and the consequences of each. "The typical plot," notes Gerbner, "ends by reaching a reassuring and usually foregone conclusion about who is the better man." Violence operates symbolically to show us how it may be used to advance our causes and to avoid being hurt. Violence demonstrates who is heroic or empowered and what values should triumph over others. In this way, "symbolic violence is one of society's chief instruments for achieving the aims of real violence without having to commit any."

Gerbner found that "the lion's share Of representation went to types that dominate the social order...." Not surprisingly, "less... representation was allocated to those lower in the domestic and global power hierarchy....". This uneven representation of character types, combined with their placement in television's matrix of violence and crime, encourages the reproduction of dominance and rigid social order. Gerbner concluded:

The pattern of allocation of violence appears to project the fears, biases, privileges, and wishful thinking of dominant institutions onto a cosmic canvas.... The fundamental function and social role of ritualized dramatic violence is, then, the maintenance of power. The collective lessons taught by drama tend to cultivate a sense of hierarchical values and forces. Their conflicts expose the danger of crossing the lines, and induce fear of subverting them.

More Crime at Eleven: Television News and the Signification of Crime

Because television news ostensibly deals with the portrayal of reality, one might think that the representation of crime in the news would differ significantly from that offered in the fantasy world of entertainment television. But the distinction between television news and television entertainment is not sharp. The "reality" of television news broadcasts is highly selective. In fact, television news "is much closer to definitions of narrative construction than unmediated experiences or conceptions of real life." In this way, its reality mirrors the reality of television drama.

Both real and dramatic television are significations produced by an external and active will. Both reproduce the conventional cultural pressures of the existing social order. Consequently, both "compliment and reinforce each other as they repeat the same propositions about life and society."

Television's selective eye makes it all the more persuasive. Television has the power to concentrate its attention on one or two themes and strengthen its message through repetition. Crime reporting is a major feature of television news Programmes. This constant focus on crime, its frequency and its danger, reinforces the perspective on crime generated by television crime dramas.

The news media does not create its discourse about crime from whole cloth. It recycles concepts and terms already in the cultural lexicon. Thus, while a newscast may be furnishing information cast as facts, it is also constructing a tale that either "fits" or contradicts broader and deeper concepts of crime that operate as "myths."

Most news accounts of crime (whether reports of specific incidents of crime or more general accounts of crime statistics and trends) come from official government sources. News reporters and editors work closely with the police. Television stations routinely report bulletins, lookouts and warnings about criminal activities. While such activities lend an aura of respectability to television newscasts, they also reinforce the credibility and authoritativeness of the official sources upon which they rely.

Media reliance on official sources, in the end, permits police officials to shape the nature of news coverage of crime.) It gives government authorities input into the decision of which stories will be covered and which will not. Ultimately, the offenders and victims selected as newsworthy will tend to be those fitting established preconceptions.

Television news reinforces the perception that we are living in a "mean and dangerous world." A prominent place in each evening newscast is reserved for reporting some serious and violent crime - a shooting, robbery, carjacking, abduction, or rape - or the efforts of some law enforcement agency to control crime - a drug bust, increased street patrols, or a similarly newsworthy event. Those who are arrested, accused or convicted of crime are represented as malevolent and incorrigible outcasts.

Unlike the wealthy criminals depicted on prime time shows, criminals shown on the news are, more often than not, poor members of racial or ethnic minority groups arrested for crimes of violence. Newsreporting can thus interact with and feed on racial stereotypes, promoting a further deterioration in already strained race relations.

The exploitation of stereotypes is even more exaggerated on so-called" reality" programming such as Fox Network's" COPS" or NBC's" Rescue 911." These shows present a highly emotional and sensational product that is even more objectionable because the shows exploit a format that has become associated with objective reporting. Shows such as these blur the distinction between entertainment and news even further.

Television news influences society's concepts of order and normality in a manner which often goes unnoticed. Through its coverage and presentation of crime, television news signifies that violent crime is increasingly the norm and that greater imposition of state control and police intervention are necessary to maintain some semblance of order.

The end result is that television news coverage encourages the impression that we are living in a society that is under siege by the forces of crime and that it is only through the efforts of our local police forces that civilization as we know it endures. Through television news, crime works to reintegrate society, to reinforce notions of who is inside the" thin blue line" and who should be cast outside it. Media coverage, then, provides a vehicle for communicating" the necessity for strong social control." In this way, the news media have assumed the functions of ideological reproduction previously performed by public punishment. Where once public hangings were necessary to develop a sense of community and obeisance to authority, now nightly broadcasts of crime serve much the same role.

The Attitudinal Effects of Television Crime

Attempts to measure the effects of television viewing on attitudinal change have always been controversial. Given the pervasiveness of the medium of television and the difficulty of controlling for other influences that might interact with watching scenes or shows, opinion research based on exposure to television has always been qualified. Nonetheless, an impressive number of studies suggest that not only are the effects of television viewing measurable, but that television plays a tremendous role in the socialization process and in the formation of attitudes and opinions.

Several studies have concluded that exposure to television fosters the belief that we are living in an increasingly dangerous and violent world. Heavy television viewers tend to believe there is a greater incidence of crime than light viewers do. Heavy viewers are also more likely to fear victimization as a result of crime than are light viewers. Consequently, heavy viewing of television contributes to the development of a sense of distrust towards others, a factor which may make it difficult for a criminal defendant to convince jurors of the sincerity of a defence.

Another disturbing consequence of television's portrayal of crime is its tendency to undermine the rights of criminal defendants. Heavy television viewers are more likely to think that a person who has been arrested of a crime is guilty of something. Several studies have demonstrated that, on the whole, viewing television crime shows discourages support for civil liberties. Carlson concluded that" while crime show viewing does not explain a large proportion of the variance in attitudes towards civil liberties... its contribution is significant and greater than many other factors which presumably are important in the socialization of democratic values such as social status, achievement in school, and family structure."

Findings such as these support Gerbner's conclusion that" television profoundly affects the social and political climate and the institutional setting in which courts work." While most empirical studies have focused on crime drama viewing, the viewing of news Programmes," reality" shows, and televised trials can only exacerbate the effect.

Because the media tends to report only the most dramatic and spectacular crimes, news (and pseudo-news) coverage of criminal trials can only" warppublic understanding of the judicial process." Furthermore, the depiction of crime on television encourages the widespread belief that Blacks and other people of colour are the source of crime. Adeno Addis makes this point about the effects of the" media's daily narrative about crime":

The media paints a picture of the black criminal threatening the innocence of white America. Indeed," crime" has virtually become a metaphor to describe young black men. Not only does the mainstream media present news stories about African Americans that" are more often negative, focusing on crime or other negative attributes than are stories about whites," but also quite often the media, especially television, uses the picture of young black men to illustrate a point about the pervasiveness of crime and drug abuse in the society.

Television's linkage of crime with race may lessen any public concern over racial abuses in the criminal justice system and make it more difficult for people of colour to receive a fair trial.

Consequently, all television's offerings having to do with crime, whether designed for purposes of entertainment or information, are both creatures and creators of the consensus. Operating through the consensus, television contributes to the "exploitation of popular prejudices and the cultivation of public support for the suppression of threats and challenges to the social order." Television works, then, to extend hegemony and to create a populace that is more respectful of authority and power. Thus, heavy television viewers, while subject to varying ideological influences, tend to take unmistakably conservative positions on issues. insofar as crime is concerned, television viewing "can... be expected to contribute to receptivity to repressive measures and to apparently simple, tough, hard-line posturings and `solutions.'"

Television draws its images from a cultural reservoir stocked by and large with images of dangerous criminals, shady defence attorneys, and virtuous prosecutors and police. What television takes from the cultural reservoir, it also replenishes through the process of signification.

Thus, as television is influenced by the consensus, television also influences it. Television teaches that a particular type of social order is appropriate and normal, a social order that is conservative, dominant, racially-biased, and rigid. Television represents a social order that excludes and vilifies not only criminals, but also those who are merely charged with crime. Television teaches us that these people are already guilty. They have only yet to be provided with the formality of a trial. In the next section I discuss how the images of crime and justice represented on television, structured as they are in conservative notions of law and order, are replicated and reinforced in the criminal trial.

The Trial as Text

The trial is a highly ritualized formal narrative that is the culmination of the adversarial process. Like the image of the criminal, the trial too is socially constructed. Our ideas of what rights are fundamental, what procedures are fair, indeed the very notion of fairness itself, all spring from the same cultural reservoir as do the images that are represented on television. The consensus influences and is influenced by the trial just as it influences and is influenced by television. In a word, the trial is a "text."

The ostensible purpose of the trial is to determine the guilt or innocence of the accused. This determination is reached by a jury made up of lay persons drawn from the community and is based on highly abstracted and formulaic presentations of evidence made by the state and the accused. From these highly abstracted presentations it is the job of the jury to ascertain the facts. Indeed, there are no facts before evidence is presented to the jury; it is the job of the jury to find them.

The trial, and as a result the jury's verdict, function "as if legal proof, which is largely a matter of formal procedure, and knowledge, which is largely a matter of the substance of the facts, are the same thing." Consequently, the verdict is treated as realistic: not as just one version of the truth, but as "the whole truth." But legal proof is not knowledge and verdicts can never embrace the whole truth. The realism of the verdict is, at best, "belief" masquerading as "truth." "As realism, the trial does not embody real social relationships but cultural mythologies about those relationships." The verdict of the trial is as constructed as the trial itself. The consensus on crime reaches its ultimate expression in the device of the trial. The trial is where society both assesses and responds to behaviour it marks as deviant. The cultural mythologies that work to produce the verdict are forged in an environment that can best be described as a "metaphorical morality play." As a morality play, the trial has its own stage or setting, players, and conventions as to how the script is to unfold.

As in any morality play, the actors in the criminal trial play symbolic roles. The adversarial posture of the parties symbolizes the clash of good and evil. But in the allegory that is the trial, good is supposed to triumph over evil. The adversary nature of the criminal trial must be re-examined in this light. If good is to win over evil, good must be more powerful then evil. For the trial to play out its symbolic mission, the prosecution and defence cannot be two evenly matched adversaries. The prosecution must have the upper hand. The criminal trial can only be adversarial in the sense that the prosecution and defence oppose each other as the symbolic representatives of good and evil.

Here we have a departure from the typical notion of what the adversarial process is all about. The common view depicts the adversarial process as a contest waged between two opponents who have a roughly equal chance of convincing the fact finder that their version of events is true. While the trial does proceed in this way on its surface, at a deeper level, the notion of "trial as morality play" works at cross purposes to the "trial as fair contest" ideal.

In the remaining sections of this Part, I review those attributes of the trial that make it resemble a morality play. My analysis of the setting, participants, and staging of the trial reveal the working of the same ideology that pervades popular culture and that is made manifest in television's representation of crime.

The Setting

Trials typically take place in buildings with imposing architectural designs. It is not uncommon for courthouses to evoke associations with glorious empires of the past. The courthouse is represented as a place where justice in the philosophical sense is done. To underscore this projection, quotations from great moralists, esteemed jurists, or classical works of morality or law are frequently inscribed on courthouse walls.

The courtroom, where the trial actually takes place, is a familiar venue to most as a result of its frequent appearance on screen and description in print. A courtroom is formal space. Stately and ceremonial, the design of a courtroom is intended to provide a dignified setting for the trial. Adding to the courtroom's sense of decorum are emblems and symbols of state authority and power. Through items such as these, the courtroom and all that occurs in it are stamped with the mark of officialdom, evoking all the prestige and supremacy of the state.

The typical courtroom shares much in common with a playhouse, further accentuating the trial's relationship to theater. The well of the courtroom serves as the stage. On this stage are the props around which the drama will revolve: tables and chairs for the prosecution and defence and, often, a podium.

In many courtrooms, the table closest to the jury is reserved for the prosecution. The judge sits on a podium overlooking the well of the court, as if to direct the drama that is to unfold on the stage below.

The immediate audience for the story is the jury, which is seated in a bleacher-like jury box to the side of the well of the court. More removed is an area of auditorium-style seating for the general public. These seats are normally separated from the rest of the courtroom by a barrier or "bar," which emphasizes to those that sit behind it that they are spectators, not participants.

The setting of the trial not only suggests the presence of theater, but it also sets up a commanding "environmental resonance," or atmosphere, of authority and power. Within this space the state is on home turf. All others are made to feel uncomfortable and out of place. The defendant is not the beneficiary of the courtroom's formality and sterility. Instead, the defendant stands out as an object to be regarded and examined. The very structure and design of the courtroom works to legitimate the prosecution and delegitimate the defence.

THE PLAYERS

There are many participants in a trial. However, the defining characters in any criminal trial are the judge, the prosecutor, and the defence attorney or public defender. They are the ones who will ultimately determine how the story is told.

- *The Judge*: The judge is the representative of the state's judicial power. The judge serves as the ultimate legal authority, decisionmaker, and referee over the adversarial contest that takes place during the trial. During the course of the trial, the judge is responsible for governing the conduct of the trial. In this sense she is like the director of a play. At the conclusion of the trial, the judge instructs the jury as to the law they should apply during their deliberations.
- The judge is treated with utmost dignity and respect. Her demeanor is authoritarian and aristocratic. Like any other autocrat, the judge commands an entourage of aides and assistants. Indeed, the judge personifies hierarchical power. The judge's authority comes from a number of ancient and well-entrenched sources: the prestige and prominence of the clan leader (from whom the role of the judge evolved); the special authority traditionally afforded to the landed gentry and/or aristocracy in European cultures; the might and supremacy of the state; and the stature and distinction of the judge's age and social status. The judge carries all of this elite-based power and privilege into the courtroom to aid her in her functions. Of the trial's three key participants, the judge is by far the most prestigious.
- The judge can use her power and prestige to influence the course of the adversarial process. Akin to a sports umpire, the judge is in a position to ensure a fair contest or throw the game in favour of one

party or another. As creatures of the consensus, judges are more likely than not to favour the prosecution. Although the trial is itself weighted in favour of the prosecution, the judge polices this imbalance and works to insure that the outcome of the, trial comports with commonsense notions of justice - *i.e.*, that the symbolic function of the morality play is realized.

- *The Prosecutor*: The prosecutor represents the state as a legal entity before the court and is the proponent of the state's case against the defendant. Prior to trial, the prosecutor decides what charges to bring and what penalties to seek. The prosecutor's power in this regard is enormous; although the decision to charge is subject to review in most states by grand jury or preliminary hearing, the meaningfulness of this review is limited since" a prosecutor seldom has any difficulty in making a prima facie case against a defendant." When trial commences, the prosecutor is responsible for presenting the government's case-in-chief. That is, the prosecutor tells a story that he urges the jury to accept as the preferred version of the facts.
- After judges, prosecutors are the most important state government officials in the criminal justice system. Prosecutors have prestige not only because they are attorneys but also because they are representatives of the state. Prosecutors trade on the authority of the state. They are cautioned in trial manuals not to refer to themselves as" the prosecution" but rather as" the state," " the government," or, in the most extreme version of this practice," the, people." Thus, to the eyes and ears of the jury, it is" the state" that rests," the government" that alleges, or" the people" that object. The prosecutor, then, is not just some employee of the government; the prosecutor is the alter ego of the state - the government personified. To the extent that the state engenders authority, power, and respect, so too then does the prosecutor.
- Prosecutors consciously position themselves in the mainstream. On the whole, prosecutors are cleancut and wholesome, representing the image of efficiency and professionalism. The image and appearance of the prosecutor is not happenstance. It is partially a function of seeking to reflect majoritarianism and to avoid identification with any" special interest group." But the prosecutor's grooming, dress, and demeanor are also intended to demonstrate an identification with generally conservative (or" moderate") political ideology. The image that the prosecutor projects embraces and endorses the mainstream, and thereby, embraces and endorses hierarchy and power.
- As the judge can use the authority and prestige of her office to influence the conduct and outcome of a trial, so too can the prosecutor.

By determining whom to charge with crime, prosecutors engage in the labelling function that crime in its social role permits. More importantly, prosecutors draw on the moral superiority that is theirs as representatives of the consensus. Their role as definers of crime allows them to speak to the jury as one in a shared community. This permits a prosecutor to position himself and the jury as" us" and the defendant and his attorney as" them."

- *The Public Defender*: The public defender is most often a state or county employee retained or appointed for the purpose of providing free legal assistance to criminally charged indigents. Public defenders act as ombudsmen for their clients as they confront a hostile criminal justice system. Public defenders must employ a variety of skills to advance their clients' interests, including negotiation, bureaucratic maneuvering, and legal challenge. Although it is the most visible, representing his clients at trial is only one aspect of the public defender's job. It is, however, the most important in terms of the allegorical nature of the criminal justice process.

At trial, the public defender directly opposes the prosecutor. The public defender works to counter the government's case by offering the jury an alternative story, one that may conflict with the government's version of events, or one that may agree with the state's account but raises an affirmative defence. But, no matter which approach the public defender takes, the public defender is hampered by the restrictive discourse regarding crime that is produced by the consensus.

While public defenders have the prestige of being members of the bar - they are respected to that degree by court officials, witnesses, and laypeople - that prestige is tempered by two factors: they represent "criminals," and they are the opponents of the state. All defence attorneys oppose the state and thus oppose, in the minds of the public, all that the state stands for - security, order, justice, and consensus. Retained attorneys may compensate for this negative identification by the positive force of their own public image or that of their comparatively well-to-do clients. The public defender cannot. Further-more, the public defender's clients are the epitome of the class of individuals that the public is convinced is the cause of crime. Public defender clients are uniformly poor, mostly Black, and routinely perceived as social outcasts.

Unlike the case with prosecutors, it is not unusual to find flamboyant and eccentric personalities among the ranks of public defenders. Many take pride, in maintaining an appearance that is out of the ordinary and a little risky. Rather than embrace the status quo, the public defender purports to stand somewhere outside of the mainstream. The public defender projects the image of the anti-establishmentarian rebel more so than that of the efficient and professional public servant.

STAGING THE TRIAL

The trial begins, appropriately enough, with opening statements from the prosecution and the defence. In these, the parties outline their respective cases to the jury by summarizing what they expect the evidence to be. Through their opening statements, the attorneys inform the jury of their theory of the case and explain how they expect to prove it. Although it is important that the jury receive a "roadmap" of what to expect when the evidentiary portion of the trial commences, it is equally, if not more, important for the attorneys to use this opportunity to establish rapport with the jurors.

"First impressions," so the saying goes, "are lasting impressions." As a result, it is significant that the prosecution gives its opening statement first. The prosecution gets the first opportunity to make a lasting impression in the minds of the jurors. The prosecution's theory of the case and "take" on the evidence will be the yardstick against which all others' will be measured. After all, the government can make a compelling case. The prosecutor represents the state - the state that we all expect to protect us from crime. And it is the state that accuses the defendant, the state that tells us all of its resources have identified this defendant as the perpetrator, and the state that tells us, in its disciplined and professional way, how it will prove the defendant's guilt. From the very beginning of the trial, the government is able to bring into play all of the myths and symbolism that the jurors have already learned about crime. The defendant, especially, appears dangerous and antisocial. Thus, the government's accusations seem reasonable, even common-sensical.

The prosecution starts with much more legitimacy and credibility than does the defence. To the jury, every word the prosecution utters is suspended in a web of meaning that has been spun and re-spun every day of their lives. Every teacher's mention of "Officer Friendly," every parent's caution not to trust strangers, every book, every television show, every newspaper report of crime, collectively work to suggest a guilty defendant and an earnest prosecutor committed to justice.

The prosecution draws on its credibility to strengthen and mobilize the consensus. The jury can be addressed as a community of law-abiding citizens who share, along with the prosecution, a common interest in eradicating crime. This legitimates the prosecution's narrative and invests it with a persuasive power that the defence cannot muster. As a consequence, "guilt" and "innocence" are determined more by the definitional work of the consensus than by the arguments of either the prosecution or the defence.

The public defender has a tremendous hurdle to overcome, even before he or she utters a word about the defence's case to the jury. The public defender must work to overcome the jurors' natural biases and suspicions against his client, which have just been reinforced by the prosecutor's opening remarks. Somehow, the public defender must counter the prosecution's advantage and establish a rapport with the jurors. The first task of the public defender is to quickly raise some doubt in the minds of the jurors about the tightness of the government's case. Then, the public defender must go further and attack the jury's tendency to stereotype his or her client as a "criminal." The public defender must personalize the defendant, establish him or her as a human being, separate him from the demonic image that the jurors carry ready-made in their heads. This can be done, and it often is, but it is a decidedly uphill battle. Despite the supposed level playing field, it is the government that claims the jurors' allegiance and has every opportunity to keep it.

After the opening statements, the trial proceeds to the presentation of evidence stage. As with opening statements, the prosecutor goes first. The prosecutor is not content to just let his or her witnesses tell their stories. Like any trial attorney, the prosecutor meticulously prepares the witnesses he or she intends to call. What is recounted at trial is not "reality," but rather a rigidly structured narrative, the telling of which is accomplished through question and answer.

By the time a witness testifies at trial, every question and every answer has been crafted and practiced to bring the utmost advantage to the prosecution. The skillful prosecutor uses this opportunity to rework each witness's testimony so it "fits" the expectations created by the consensus. For the prosecution this is a relatively easy task. The fit is natural because jurors have already been educated to place each element of the trial, whether symbolic or real, into its proper place.

Not only is the content - of a witness's testimony scrutinized, but much energy is expended on its presentation as well. Witnesses are primed to look good and to be believable. It is important that witnesses appear sensible and sympathetic. Attorneys intuitively know that aesthetic factors such as these greatly influence a juror's decisions at trial. Prosecution witnesses are generally respectable police officers, doctors, ballistic and forensic experts, and average citizens. A defence attorney attempting to cross examine witnesses such as these may find it difficult to undermine their credibility with the jury. This is especially true when the attorney is an anti-establishmentarian public defender, who lacks the authority of the prosecutor and represents a suspected criminal.

Notwithstanding the fact that the state has brought the charges and bears the burden of persuasion, permitting the prosecution to present its case first, like permitting the prosecution to deliver its opening statement first, allows the government to establish its story as the story. Within the context of the adversarial trial, the prosecution determines which account becomes the preferred version of events, a version which, once accepted as the status quo, can shape the remainder of the jury's deliberations and limit the way in which the defence can respond. If the jurors were to have any doubts about the importance of the evidence to be relied on by the state, the fact that it is presented by the prosecutor organizes it in a way that makes it more believable.

The prosecution's story is invariably conservative. In its telling, the prosecutor focuses on the "facts," which are presented as "objective" and "immutable." By so doing, the prosecutor shifts the contest from the courtroom to the consensus where the prosecution is more apt to win out. This strategy can be observed in the prosecution's constant appeal to the "common-sense" of the jurors. By asking the jurors to trust their common-sense, the prosecutor is telling them to rely on that which they already have accepted as true via the operation of the consensus.

At the close of the prosecution's case the defence has two choices: the defence may present evidence of its own, or the defence may present no evidence and argue that the government failed to meet its burden of proof beyond a reasonable doubt. Typically, the defence will present evidence at the close of the prosecution's case. The defence can cast doubt on the government's case-in-chief by seeking to undermine the credibility of the government's witnesses or by attacking the prosecution's logic. On the other hand, the defence may bypass a direct assault on the validity of the government's version of events and, instead, attempt to establish an affirmative defence. Whatever course the defence chooses, it is of equal importance that the defence construct its case in a manner that will humanize, as well as generate sympathy for, the defendant. Given the way the defendant is constructed in popular culture, this is not an easy task.

Like the prosecution's case, the defence's case is also a highly stylized and structured narrative. Witnesses for the defence are also carefully selected, and their testimonies are painstakingly rehearsed. But this preparation does not endow defence witnesses with the kind of credibility that prosecution witnesses have by virtue of association. Instead of working with the consensus, the defence must work against it. While public defenders would like to present attractive and sympathetic witnesses, this rarely occurs. Public defenders are constrained by the class position of their clients.

Furthermore, police officials will not ordinarily be available to testify in favour of a criminal defendant, or they will be reluctant to do so. Rarely will witnesses with equivalent high status, such as professionals and members of the clergy, be among a criminal defendant's social contacts.

It is more likely that the defendant's witnesses will be like the defendant - poor people, working class people, racial minorities, or members of the defendant's family. If the defendant is involved in criminal activity (which is often the case in criminal trials), or has been so in the past, then the defendant's witnesses will more often than not be tainted with a criminal past. This makes it all the easier for the prosecutor to impeach their testimonies.

The most unattractive witness in the defendant's case may be the defendant himself. Of course, the defendant need not testify, but that is a course that is itself fraught with danger. Jurors frequently wish to hear the defendant testify, if only to hear the defendant's denial of the charges from his own mouth. But whether the defendant testifies or not, the jury will silently evaluate his demeanor and appearance.

The defendant, the jurors will often be reminded, looks the way they would expect a criminal to look. It is the congruence of the defendant's image with the socially constructed image of the criminal that ultimately convicts. If the defendant is a "criminal," then, so the reasoning goes, he cannot be trusted, his defence is merely a scheme to evade justice, and he is certainly capable of all that which the prosecution accuses him.

Thus, as the defence presents its evidence, it must attend to the double duty of both contradicting the established, official story of the prosecution and lessening the negative socially constructed conceptions that jurors may already have of the defendant or of defendants in general. At the close of the defendant's case the prosecution has an opportunity for rebuttal. Thus, the prosecution has the opportunity for the last word at the presentation of evidence stage, as it does when opening statements are delivered to the jury. While the opportunity for surrebuttal is available to the defence, as a practical matter it is rarely invoked.

The prosecution also gets the last word at the argument stage of the trial. At argument, the parties may give their opinions of the evidence and attempt to persuade the jury as to how it should vote. The usual procedure at closing is for the prosecution to go first, followed by the defence, leaving the prosecution an opportunity for rebuttal.

Closing arguments are critical to the outcome of the trial. Often, at the conclusion of a trial, jurors are left with a mass of conflicting testimony and confusing instructions from the judge. Closing arguments can help the jury place this evidence in perspective and can supply common sense interpretations of arcane legal rules.

A good closing argument should tell a jury why it should vote a particular way and how it can do so. While a closing argument is not likely to persuade a jury to convict or acquit in the face of overwhelming evidence to the contrary, a closing argument may provide the margin of victory in a close case.

In a close case the prosecution has a distinct advantage. If confronted with two equally plausible stories, the jury will naturally gravitate towards the prosecution's version of events. The prosecution has the upper hand because its version is the one stamped with the authority of the state, and the jury has simply heard the prosecution's story earlier and with greater frequency than it has heard the point of view of the defence.

The closing argument is opinion, and the prosecutor's opinion is apt to have greater weight with the jury than the defence's opinion. To a jury, the prosecutor's argument is likely to appear more attractive. It implies that the system works, that the right suspect is in custody, and that the government is taking steps to reduce the threat that crime poses to the community at large. The defence, on the other hand, must rely on the discomforting contention that the system cannot be trusted to do anything about crime, and that, in this case, the government has arrested and prosecuted the wrong person.

Following closing arguments, the court instructs the jury on its deliberations about the case. The instructions tend to be worded in a technical and archaic prose that is hard for the uninitiated to comprehend or understand. Because jurors do not understand the very instructions that are supposed to guide them in carrying out their responsibilities, it is difficult for a defendant to receive the theoretical benefits of a trial by jury. Instead, jurors are more likely to fall back on common sense notions of crime - common sense notions that unavoidably favour the state.

Even when jurors do understand them, instructions are often slanted in favour of the prosecution. Sometimes this bias results from the legal rule or element that is addressed by the instruction which may itself favour the prosecution. On other occasions, however, bias occurs as a matter of emphasis - either in the words chosen to express the legal principle or how those words are delivered by the judge. As representatives of state authority, judges are more likely to sympathize with the prosecution, and their instructions to the jury are apt to reflect their pro-prosecution orientation. Rarely are judges pro-defence.

The requirement that the state prove its case beyond a reasonable doubt is often viewed as a heavy burden for the state to meet and a rigorous line of defence for the accused. In reality, it is neither.

First of all, it is notoriously difficult to arrive at a precise definition of what proof beyond a reasonable doubt is. Absent any meaningful direction from the court, jurors are at liberty to apply their own idiosyncratic views of the matter, which are likely to be at variance with the defendant's expectations. Moreover, no matter how the standard of proof might be interpreted, a number of evidentiary presumptions help the prosecution meet its burden of proof. Finally, and most importantly, jurors are generally reluctant to acquit defendants whom they believe to be guilty, although the state's evidence may be insufficient to erase all reasonable doubts. Thus, from the beginning to the end of the trial, the advantages lie decidedly in favour of the prosecution. The jurors come to the courthouse already biased in favour of the government. The prosecution gets the first opportunity to confront the jurors with its "official" view of reality. Throughout the trial, the defence must labour to contradict this established version of events, a version cloaked with the credibility of the state.

The prosecution has better resources at its disposal - more thorough investigation, more attractive witnesses, greater respect and deference from the judge. The trial even takes place in a venue that reinforces the state's prestige at the expense of the defendant. In the face of such concrete inequities, physical as well as psychological, the advantages supposedly conferred on the defendant by a mostly theoretical presumption of innocence and a seemingly high, but ephemeral, burden of proof are quickly overwhelmed.

The Trial in Context

The adversarial criminal trial, when examined in isolation, presents a majestic facade. Justice is served, it appears, because the state's accusation of crime is not taken for granted.

The government is first required to prove its case beyond a reasonable doubt before a jury of the defendant's peers. The defendant is given an opportunity to contest the government's charges and is provided with an attorney, if he cannot afford his own, to help make his case. In addition, the defendant is provided with a panoply of rights that regulate the trial process in a fair manner and protect the defendant from government overreaching.

But it is misleading to analyse the trial as a free-standing institution. A more revealing way to approach the trial is as it actually functions in its social context. That is, the trial must be viewed as the result of a semiotic process - a text - a medium through which the reader can signify, drawing on a long chain of significations that reach deep into the recesses of culture.

As text, the trial is the property of no one. All are free to signify through it. But all significations, all attempts to make meaning manifest, are constrained by he significations that have been produced before. Thus, the genealogy of significations - of things, ideas, and institutions - can be traced.

The criminal trial cannot stand apart from the images of crime that are at work in the popular culture. The very same process of signification that produces these images also produces the notions of justice, conceptions of rights, and patterns of rituals that make up the criminal trial.

That is, the trial is linked to a specific system of signification that is governed by particular themes and codes. These themes and codes structure all discourse, including the adversarial criminal trial, in ways that make some interpretations of meaning appear more appropriate and others less so. A general ideology or "consensus" arises from this interplay of structured meaning. Since the process of signification is dominated by powerful elites who can give their articulations wider circulation, a consensus is produced that vilifies the defendant while it glorifies social order.

The adversarial criminal trial is a social construction and, like any other social construction, it is made out of bits and pieces produced through the consensus. The consensus on crime structures the trial in ways that favour the prosecution. No matter what formal rights the defendant may have, in practice, procedures are adopted, rights interpreted, judgements made, and meaning determined in ways that disadvantage the defendant in the criminal trial.

Consequently, both judge and jury perceive the defendant negatively; jury instructions and court procedures are biased in the prosecution's favour; the legitimacy of the prosecution's case is reinforced by the authority of the state; and the prosecution's case is strengthened through repetition and strategic positioning at the beginning and end of the presentation of both argument and evidence. Through the working of the consensus, these disadvantages, and others, are made to seem "fair."

Consequently, the trial as "text" follows a tried and true formula. Upon reading the text, one can see that the criminal trial is not constructed in such a way as to match its formal signification as an institution of even-handed justice. The "rights" of the criminal defendant are not fully enforced, and as a result, the adversarial system is not all that adversarial. More importantly, no matter how secure a defendant's rights may be, the entire criminal justice system is permeated by an ideology that frustrates their realization. Within the structure that culture provides and the consensus shapes, the moral of the story told in the criminal courtroom - and the meaning of the allegory of the trial - is that the defendant is guilty and deserves to be punished.

The foregoing is not meant to suggest that the defendant is never capable of winning at trial. Instead, it is offered as a realistic assessment of the obstacles that stand in the way of acquittal and that create imbalance in the adversarial process. The possibility exists, of course, that an especially competent defence attorney may be able to overcome these obstacles, or that an inept prosecutor may fritter away the advantages that flow from representing the state. That defendants are disadvantaged by the adversarial trial process would be of little significance if their attorneys were in a position to reasonably compensate for the imbalance. In the next section, I ask whether public defenders are prepared to handle the extra burdens that the ideology of crime places on them in the adversarial process.

PUBLIC DEFENDERS: CREATURES OF THE CONSENSUS

The myth of criminal justice suggests that the state acts as a civilizing influence on the expression of public outrage about crime. It is assumed that the state, through its ordered system of criminal justice, prevents vigilante behaviour and mass tyranny. Justice is supposedly above culture and popular sentiments.

Although culture may influence the criminal justice system, the state compensates for this by providing counsel and a protective regime of rights. Thus, whether the myth of criminal justice is truly a myth depends to a large extent on the effectiveness of counsel. Good legal representation may be able to help ameliorate the influence of negative cultural attitudes towards the defendant. In this section, I concentrate my analysis on the type of representation that the state provides to criminally charged indigents: public defenders. I focus on public defenders for a variety of reasons. First, they serve a vast majority of the nation's population. Second, in most cases they are professionals, devoting full-time service to indigent defence. Finally, as governmental agencies, public defender offices may be readily compared to prosecutor's offices.

Public defender agencies are a relatively recent addition to the criminal justice system. A public defender system may be defined as an organization "in which salaried lawyers devote all or a substantial part of their time to the specialized practice of representing indigent defendants." The first publicly supported, indigent defence programme was established by the city of Los Angeles in 1914. Public defenders did not become commonplace, however, until several decades later, in the 1940's and 1950's.

There is a great deal of diversity in the way that public defender offices are organized and structured. Most are organized at the local level and depend on local finances. In 1982, only 13 states operated public defender systems organized exclusively at the state level. Several states provide some support to local budgets, but the vast majority of public defender offices in the country are either part of county government or are organized by local trial courts.

Public defender systems should be distinguished from the two other major means of providing for the defence of indigents: assigned counsel systems and contract systems. Assigned counsel systems utilize private counsel, who are appointed as needed from a list of available attorneys. Assigned counsel Programmes are the most widely used form of indigent defence services. Contract systems rely on one or more private attorneys to provide indigent defence services, but these attorneys are not appointed on a case-by-case basis by the court. Instead, they provide representation pursuant to contractual arrangements with the appropriate state or local governmental entity.

Many public defenders are hard-working professionals who are committed to their work and concerned about their clients. This is not to say, however, that the typical public defender agency is sufficiently equipped to carry out its formal role as worthy adversary of the prosecution. Indeed, most public defender offices are vastly outgunned by the prosecution, in terms of both the tangible and intangible resources at their disposal.

Material Disparities

In comparison with other governmental expenditures, very little is spent on criminal justice Programmes, whether for prosecution, defence, police protection or the courts. No matter how inadequate support for criminal justice Programmes may be generally, funding for indigent defence is abysmally low. There is a great disparity between the level of support provided for indigent defence and that provided for the prosecution of crimes. In 1990, only slightly more than two per cent of all criminal justice expenditures nationwide was spent on indigent defence. By comparison, prosecution agencies received more than three times this amount. Virtually every public defender office in the country is vastly underfunded. Numerous studies have concluded that the level of support for indigent defence is entirely too low.

This low level of financial support translates into lower salaries, higher caseloads, and less secretarial and other basic support for public defenders than their prosecutorial counterparts receive. Because of low funding, public defenders may not be able to adequately prepare their cases for trial due to nonexistent or overburdened investigative services, inadequate libraries or insufficient office space. Dean Norman Lefstein spoke to the importance of the funding issue in a 1982 study he conducted for the American Bar Association. As Dean Lefstein succinctly put it:

Criminal defence services for the poor must be adequately funded in order for comprehensive and effective repre-sentation to be provided. Experience teaches that when funding is insufficient, some defendants are not represented at all, despite having a constitutional right to counsel. If representation is by public defenders, their numbers must be adequate to avoid excessive caseloads, and they must be paid salaries that are competitive with those earned by prosecutors and by lawyers in private practice.

Unfortunately, few jurisdictions have heeded Dean Lefstein's admonition. Salaries remain low, caseloads remain high, and, consequently, many clients of public defenders continue to receive less than adequate representation.

Generally, there is a considerable gap between the typical public defender's salary and that of the average prosecutor. For example, in Gainesville, Florida, the entry level salary for public defenders is $23,000. Entry level prosecutors earn $25,000. Prosecutorial duties in the District of Columbia are the responsibility of the U.S. Attorney for the District of Columbia. The starting salaries for beginning Assistant U.S. Attorneys is $47,670.

By comparison, attorneys at the Washington D.C. Public Defender Service with comparable experience earn only $39,048. Why these differences? Is the rationale that prosecuting is that much harder than defending, or that there is a need to attract better talent to prosecution offices, or that the market for prosecutors demands that they be paid more?

These assumptions can be justified only if one thinks that defence work is somehow less important than prosecutorial work. There is little reason why public defender salaries should be so much lower than prosecutors'.

The responsibilities of the individual line prosecutor are not substantially different from those of trial attorneys employed by public defender offices. For every investigative, research, or litigation task performed by prosecutors there is a substantially parallel task that must be performed by public defenders. The practical effect of the salary disparity between these positions is that it becomes more difficult for defender Programmes to attract talent.

Thus, indigent defence is left to those who cannot find other employment or to those ideologically committed individuals who can afford to forego the economic considerations of maintaining a middle-class lifestyle or supporting a family. It is not uncommon for many students who are interested in criminal litigation to choose to begin their careers at the state or district attorney's office rather than the public defender's office because the salaries offered by the public defender are too low.

Another problem with low salaries is that they make it difficult for the public defender to retain employees for the period of time necessary to develop expertise.

Consequently: where the salary is low the staff attorney is likely to be a young lawyer who will leave for a better job within two or three years, for example to join the staff of the prosecuting attorney. Like any other lawyer, the defender will usually do a better job of representation as he gains experience. But if the experienced lawyer is replaced by a beginner within a fairly short time, the quality of representation afforded the indigent is bound to be different from one year to the next.

After reviewing the low salaries present in the mid 1960's at the time of his report, Silverstein concluded that a large proportion of the reported salaries were not" career" salaries," even if one allows for differences in the cost of living and in a lawyer's income in communities of different sizes...."

If an insufficient number of attorneys is hired, then those present in the office will naturally have to labour under heavy caseloads. An excessive caseload is a frequently cited problem for public defenders; nonetheless, it remains pandemic in the defence of indigents. Low funding also restricts the number of cases that receive pretrial investigation and the degree of investigation provided to those cases that are lucky enough to receive any investigation at all.

Misdemeanor cases suffer especially, but felony cases are also vulnerable, particularly if other, more complex or more serious cases are being tried at or around the same time. Inadequate investigation is a common occurrence for criminal trials. It is at this level that defenders and their clients are most at a disadvantage in comparison with the prosecution. The prosecution is usually able to avail itself of the comparatively well-funded and extensive investigative resources of the police.

Poor funding can also be made manifest in other, less dramatic ways. Often, public defenders are unable to obtain decent secretarial support. This means that, instead of concentrating on providing legal assistance to their clients, many public defenders must spend their time typing motions or handling other clerical duties. As a general rule, this of course means that the unsupported public defender will ultimately file fewer motions and less vigorously represent his or her client. In many offices, it is not uncommon for public defenders to have to furnish their own office supplies. Frequently, public defenders are forced to work in cramped, run-down quarters that make it difficult to interview clients in privacy or store files or other needed materials.

Systemic Disparities

To the extent public defenders lack independent and adequate funding, they remain subject to the whims of the funding sources they do have: typically county governments and courts of general jurisdiction. One of the most frequently raised critiques of public defender Programmes, from their proponents and detractors alike, is their lack of autonomy.

This lack of autonomy can manifest itself in two ways. First, lack of funding independence can have a chilling effect on the public defender agency's interest in providing vigorous representation.

Public defenders may be reluctant to undertake unpopular forms of representation that might jeopardize funding sources. After studying the operation of public defender offices in three jurisdictions, sociologists James Eisenstein and Herbert Jacob concluded:

Public defenders become adept at modifying office policy in anticipation of possible consequences and reactions of their governing boards.... They cannot forget that actions which disrupt the felony disposition process may generate opposition from the governing board and appropriating agencies. A public defender office that demands jury trials in all of its cases is likely to experience swift budget cuts and attacks on its personnel.

Second, outside funding sources may acquire direct or indirect control over a public defender's practices or policies by virtue of their control over finances. For example, if the court oversees the public defender's expert witness funds, then the court can exert influence over litigation strategy and policies by simply agreeing or not agreeing to allow expert witnesses to be used in certain cases. In a case that addressed whether public defenders acted" under colour of law" for purposes of permitting suit under 42 U.S.C. [sections] 1983, Justice Blackmun noted:

The county's control over the size of and funding for the public defender's office, as well as over the number of potential clients, effectively dictates the size of an individual attorney's caseload and influences substantially the amount of time the attorney is able to devote to each case. The public defender's discretion in handling individual cases - and therefore his ability to provide effective assistance to his clients - is circumscribed....

The lack of autonomy observed in the operation of most public defender offices implies a lack of adversariness or a failure on the part of the public defender agency to vigorously advance the interests of its clients. The more extreme version of this theory would condemn the public defender as a" police state" tactic simply because it is not believed possible for the state to both prosecute and purport to defend the accused at the same time.

A more widely held belief is that the institution of the public defender is a poor method for insuring the vigorous representation of the rights of indigents because the public defender's office cannot help but settle into a form of institutional entropy with the prosecuting agency that is its regular opponent. Because of the close cooperation between prosecutor's offices and public defender agencies, the reasoning goes, public defenders are conditioned to not make an issue of the morality of the police, the criminal justice process, or the courts. In exchange, the defendant's guilt is treated in a matter-of-fact fashion. What results is a criminal justice system that does not operate along ideological lines - such as due process ideals or retributionism - but instead functions as "a system of `bureaucratic justice' - a system in which discretionary actions are governed by fairly rigid adherence to informal means and procedures designed to pigeonhole defendants into a few rough groupings with as few exceptions as possible."

Many observers have noted this tendency, but whether the alleged nonadversariness of public defenders actually harms their clients is a point of view that has been challenged. Most of the researchers who have studied the problem have failed to find any relationship between the fact that a defendant was represented by a public defender and the ultimate outcome of the case. But this could very well result from the fact that excellence in the provision of defence services is hard to quantify and that case outcomes may not provide the best measure of the quality of representation.

These findings may also be skewed by the fact that public defenders, by virtue of the numbers of cases they handle, may "lock in" all other practitioners. As Peter Nardulli described it, public defenders and other courtroom regulars (or "insiders") act "as creators and protectors of the status quo. In this view... insiders play a crucial role in the formulation and evaluation of norms which govern particular types of cases. Once established they affect cases involving both insiders and outsiders on a routine and systematic basis." The sad fact may be that - except for that rare criminal attorney who brings outside clout - the type of representation provided by the public defender, although deficient, may be typical.

Finally, although much insight may be gained from quantitative analyses of criminal justice processes, one should not expect too much from statistical depictions of reality. The limits of quantitative enquiry have been widely debated in the social sciences. Particularly in the case of criminal court research, one should be wary of focusing on case outcomes. Researchers, such as McIntyre, who conclude that social science research has discredited the claim that public defender clients receive less effective representation greatly overstate their case. The burdens that the typical public defender must labour under do have an effect, although one that may not be easily quantified. They would do well to remember that: discussions with criminal court veterans who have watched these changes unfold over the years reveal the salience of environmental factors for courthouse communities. Students of criminal courts who ignore them because they fail to have a "statistically significant effect" upon case outcomes do so at great peril and at great cost.

When we look at the criminal trial process in its larger context, the fact that there are glaring disparities between the public defender and the prosecution is inescapable. There are disparities in funding, salaries, resources, training, and physical facilities. These disparities cause or contribute to the way that public defender clients are disadvantaged vis-a-vis other criminal defendants and the state. While statistical evidence suggests that the claim that public defenders lack adversariness and autonomy is false, at best these data simply show that public defender clients do not fare any worse than do criminal defendants generally. Comparisons of case outcomes alone, then, cannot measure the ways that criminal defendants as a class are handicapped in their ability to contest the state's accusation of guilt.

The Symbolic Importance of Material and Systemic Disparities

To expose the way that defendants in general - and public defender clients in particular - are poorly equipped to compete for the hearts and minds of jurors in the adversarial arena of the criminal trial, it is helpful to consider how the material and systemic disparities discussed above work symbolically. What cultural values are implicit in the ways that criminal defendants are treated and what meaning can be extracted from the way that the role of the public defender is constructed?

Money takes on a central importance in this culture. It is not simply a matter of "getting what you pay for" (which presumes a sellers market), but it is also a matter of "paying what one thinks things are worth." When public defenders are offered salaries that are thirty per cent less than those offered to state's attorneys, obviously this signifies a belief that the services of public defenders are worth less than those provided by prosecutors. According to a commission charged by President Johnson to investigate the administration of justice in the nation's courts, low wages unavoidably impose a stigma of inferiority on the defence of the accused. If the status of the defence bar is to be upgraded and if able lawyers are to be attracted to criminal practice, it is undesirable to perpetuate a system in which representation for the poor seems to be obtained at a discount.

The lessened importance that the public attaches to providing defence services to indigents can be measured by the fact that over three times as much is spent to support prosecution agencies than is spent on all forms of indigent defence. If the prosecution and the defence were truly seen as evenly matched counterparts of one another, then the nation would not be spending a fraction of what it spends to prosecute crimes on the defence of crimes.

Nothing underscores this point more than the disparity in facilities and physical plant that is often a feature of public defender offices. The objective needs of the prosecution and the defence are pretty similar in respect to facilities. They both need offices with sufficient space for filing and support services to allow the attorneys to ply their trade with a sufficient amount of dignity. There is no particular reason why prosecutors would need larger or more modern offices or facilities that are more pleasing to the eye. Yet, in virtually every jurisdiction, there are readily observable differences in the quality of the work spaces afforded the prosecution and those afforded the defence. The commentary to the A.B.A. Standards for Criminal Justice points out why this discrepancy is harmful:

It is essential to the efficient operation of the defender programme that facilities be provided in which clients can be interviewed in privacy. Without offices and facilities befitting the nature of a lawyer's professional calling, the accused may very well lack confidence in the defender and, ultimately in the system of justice itself. Appropriate facilities are also necessary to attract and retain career personnel.

Where appropriate facilities are not provided, is this not an indication that society does not view public defenders as entitled to display "the dignity of the legal profession"? The fact that public defender offices are almost uniformly less desirable than prosecution buildings and workspaces may be taken as clear evidence of the public defender's lower prestige and authority.

The differences in salaries and work facilities that exist between defenders and prosecutors cannot be explained by differences in either the market conditions or the required functions of each job. Instead, these disparities are clearly representative of the opinion that the majority of society holds about the type of work that is done by public defenders and prosecutors. Whether public defenders can be conclusively shown to be less effective than other attorneys or not, "it is clear that those that represent the poor are not generally held in high esteem, either within the legal profession or outside of it." It is a commonplace observation that "a lack of respect and influence is a common characteristic of public defenders.

Within the courthouse, public defenders are at the end of the pecking order." The truth of this observation may be emphasized by the following comments made by a public defender in Chicago:

We are the gophers sic, we run for things. Whenever there's something the judge needs done, if there is not a clerk available, the judge gives it to the public defender and has him do it. They would never think of having a state's attorney do it. But public defenders have to do this silly stuff. The problem runs deeper than is demonstrated by the treatment public defenders may receive at the hands of autocratic judges. Public defenders are not perceived as "real" lawyers by the public, their peers, or by their clients. The professional life of public defenders is characterized by their attempts to cope with the deep stigma attached to the work that they do. Yet, the stigma is hard to escape. Even in Washington, D.C., which is serviced by what is arguably the country's best public defender organization, defendants often pass up representation by the public defender in favour of less-experienced and much more costly private defence lawyers.

Trained professionals, who ought to know better, offer no greater support for public defender organizations. As the A.B.A. Special Committee on Criminal Justice in a Free Society concluded in its 1988 report, "the criminal justice system is shunned by the mainstream bar, and it will never be able to attract funds and public support if it cannot even garner the respect and support of the bar."

Considerations such as these have led many to conclude that "the pivotal concern" that led to the establishment of the public defender was not justice, but "judicial economy," or "efficiency, particularly as it affected the smooth flow of guilty pleas." Also, as Lisa McIntyre has pointed out, public defenders increase judicial legitimacy by encouraging public confidence in the administration of justice. Yet, neither of these rationales for the establishment of defender Programmes necessarily calls for a viable, wellfunctioning and adversarial enterprise.

All that is needed to account for judicial economy and legitimacy is a public defender who appears competent, no matter how rough an appearance it may be. If the motivation for the creation of a public defender organization is anything less than supplying equal justice under law for its own sake, then a "paper tiger" public defender may be just as good as the real thing.

It is certainly true that if public defenders were more successful and "won consistently and often, their successes would undermine the legitimacy of the courts and ultimately jeopardize support for them." Indeed, the entire criminal justice system is premised on the expectation that defendants will be proven guilty and locked away. There is no room for the proposition that an adequately functioning criminal justice system might result in the release, without sanction, of a majority of those who have been charged with crime.

Of course, such a state of affairs might suggest that something is terribly wrong with the criminal justice system, something overlooked in the midst of the commonly heard anti-crime rhetoric. Such a situation might demonstrate that the state is intervening in the lives of too many of its citizens via unjustifiable arrests and prosecutions. However, this possibility is never seriously considered. It is easier, both politically and economically, to simply validate what the police and courts are doing by gutting the ability of the public defender to defend his or her client. In a society that excludes "criminals" from the consensus, and that, in fact, uses crime to shape the consensus, the inadequacies of public defenders appear normal.

DEFENDER GENERAL

Remedies and Ihe Importance of Reform

I have attempted to demonstrate that the mere identification of formal rights for criminal defendants does little to ensure a fair trial. Instead, as I have explained, the difficulty is external to the legal system and lies, rather, in the way that the community at large seeks to define crime and the type of justice to which criminal defendants are entitled. Because the disparity in the criminal justice system is culturally based, one could argue that it presents an unsolvable problem. The difficulty is that any attempts at reform are likely to be subverted by the very cultural processes that led to the imbalance in the adversary system in the first place. But this is a point of view that can lead to paralysis. Notwithstanding my broad critique of the criminal justice system, I feel compelled to offer something in the way of a concrete and pragmatic solution.

A factor favoring reform is that the process of signification is, in a sense, democratic; that is, the state or dominant social groups cannot monopolize the production of meaning. There is always room for alternative interpretations and resistant readings and recodings of texts. It is possible that, through disciplined and rigorous cultural work and the raising of consciousness, the allegorical meaning of the criminal trial could be changed, or at least contested.

Admittedly, the ostracism of the criminal (and the subsequent failure to take the rights of criminal defendants seriously) is a deep and pervasive problem that is not subject to easy, instrumental solutions.

Howevcr, the government can still be expected to do what it can to improve the adversarial process and, at the very least, prevented from taking actions that aggravate the situation. If the state were to take the role that the public defender plays in the adversarial process seriously, then perhaps the public would too.

The first step, then, to improve the adversarial criminal trial process is to infuse the criminal defendant's right to counsel with new meaning. Having argued that the problem lies outside of the formal legal structure and its collection of rights, it would seem to make little sense to retreat into the rhetoric of rights in order to resolve it.

Yet, that is what I propose to do here. While the designation of something as a "right" does not necessarily ensure justice, greater importance can be attached to how a "right" is interpreted, both by courts and by the broader culture. The creation of rights and their subsequent treatment by the state can play a significant role in the shaping of the consensus, and this in turn can play a role in constructing the meaning that is attached to rights.

BEYOND ASYMMETRY

As I see it, the core of the problem with the adversarial system is the current imbalance in the degree of attention the government pays to the act of prosecution as opposed to its obligation to provide for the defence of citizens whom it accuses of crime. While it cannot be argued that prosecuting crime is one of the central concerns of government, there is no legitimate reason for the current excessive focus on prosecution at the expense of individual rights (other than illegitimate reasons of social control). If there is to be balance in the adversarial process, there must be balance in the role that the state plays within that system.

The state's commitment to prosecution is institutionalized in the office of the attorney general. At both the federal and state level, the attorney general is a high government official responsible for supervising the state apparatus for the prosecution of crimes, in addition to rendering formal legal opinions and advising government agencies.

The attorney general also has an important political role and may have significant input in the formation of national or state policy.

The federal Attorney General, often referred to as "the nation's chief law enforcement officer," has the greatest symbolic importance. The Attorney General for the United States heads the Department of Justice and is the fourth ranking member of the President's Cabinet. The U.S. Attorney General provides legal advice to the President and the various executive and military departments of the U.S. government. Moreover, the Attorney General "has overall responsibility... for representing the United States in all state and federal courts." The duties of the Attorney General include the "supervision of United States Attorneys and other government counsel" in, inter alia, the investigation and prosecution of crimes against the United States.

In addition to these criminal litigation functions, the U.S. Attorney General is also charged with investigative authority, chiefly through the Federal Bureau of Investigation and the Drug Enforcement Administration. While the commitment to the act of prosecution is institutionalized, the commitment to defence is haphazard. There is no defence counterpart to the Attorney General. Perhaps there should be. In addition to prosecuting crimes, the government also has an overriding duty to provide for the general public welfare.

In theory, this duty would require the government to expend as much effort on preventing erroneous convictions as it does on obtaining justified ones. Certainly, the governmental undercommitment to the defence function has deep symbolic import. What the public sees stamped with the authority of the state is the act of prosecution - this is what has allegorical power, and this is what skews the defendant's ability to obtain a fair trial in an adversarial context.

Conceptualizing a Federal Defender General

In order to balance the government's symbolic relationship to the criminal justice system, I would propose the creation of a "Defender General" at the federal level. Like the Attorney General, the federal Defender General would also be a high government official, although not necessarily a member of the President's Cabinet.

However, there are many differences in the way that cases are prosecuted and the way they are defended that would call for the Defender General's Office to be structured somewhat differently from that of the Attorney General.

First, there is no uniform system for the provision of defence services comparable to the network of U.S. Attorneys and local state prosecutors.

Secondly, although assuring that criminal defendant's receive the effective assistance of counsel is a governmental concern, the actual representation of criminal defendants is not primarily accomplished through the state's employees. Third, and most important, while all prosecutors theoretically represent the state, each defence counsel represents the unique interests of his or her own client.

Perhaps the Surgeon General would provide a better model for a Defender General than would the Attorney General as that office is presently conceived. The delivery of medical services is, quite possibly, even more fragmented and diversified than is the delivery of defence services. Although the Surgeon General does provide some direct medical care through the Public Health Service and its Commissioned Corps of doctors, most Americans receive their medical treatment from private physicians.

And, while government plays a substantial role in paying for the health care of many people, doctors, like defence lawyers, consider their primary duty to be to their patients, not the government.

Prior to the reorganization of the Executive Branch in 1966 the Surgeon General was responsible for the administration of the Public Health Service and the promulgation of "regulations necessary to the administration of the Service." In addition, the Surgeon General was required by statute to "encourage, cooperate with, and render assistance to other appropriate public authorities, scientific institutions, and scientists in the conduct of... research... and studies relating to the causes, diagnosis, treatment, control, and prevention of physical and mental diseases."

In carrying out this responsibility, the Surgeon General was given broad authority, including the ability to issue publications, provide research facilities, maintain research fellowships, and "make grants in aid to universities, hospitals, laboratories, and other public or private institutions." Even though the Surgeon General no longer exercises the same authority, he is still recognized as the symbolic leader of the medical profession and, when it comes to health matters, continues to exert great influence.

A Defender General patterned after the Surgeon General (as the office was originally envisioned in the Public Health Act) could serve as the symbolic leader of the criminal defence bar and enable criminal defence lawyers to claim more prestige vis-a-vis the prosecution. The Defender General could also serve as a source for necessary training and as a catalyst for improving the delivery of defence services.

By committing its resources to the establishment of a viable and vital Defender General Office, the government would be signaling the importance and significance of the right to counsel.

By improving the ability of criminal defendants to compete for the hearts and minds of jurors, the government would increase the chances that those accused of crime would receive a fair trial.

Thus, the federal Defender General I propose would have the following responsibilities:

- Give leadership and direction to the nation's criminal defence Programmes and practitioners.
- Contribute to the advancement of criminal defence techniques through research and clinical Programmes.
- Disseminate that knowledge to legal professionals and the general public.
- Assure the adequate training and personnel development of criminal defence practitioners.
- Improve the organization and delivery of defence services in the communities. In order to carry out these responsibilities, the Defender General would be empowered to make grants in aid to public defender organizations, law schools, universities and other public or private institutions; offer fellowships to promising or renowned defence attorneys; offer scholarships to deserving students in exchange for a commitment to practice criminal defence for an appropriate time; retain experts, scholars and consultants; issue publications; and provide technical advice and assistance to appropriate public and other nonprofit organizations and institutions.

Obviously, many details remain to be worked out before a federal Defender General could ever become a reality - such as whether the Defender General should be a part of the Justice Department, the Department of Health and Human Services, or an independent agency in the judicial branch.

But what is important about the concept of the Defender General is the idea of committing the state to the provision of defence services in a way that parallels the government's commitment to the act of prosecution. By committing the government to the defence of accused persons in such a concrete and substantial way, the Defender General would make an important symbolic statement.

It would teach respect for individual rights and infuse the presumption of innocence with real meaning. A Defender General would help make the right to a fair trial and the right to adequate counsel more than just empty promises. As a result, this country would go a long way towards making the myth of criminal justice a reality. The functioning of the adversarial criminal trial cannot be determined solely by reference to the ideals that are set forth in the Constitution, the mandates found in statutes, or the guarantees that are promised in court opinions. The adversarial trial takes its real meaning from the culture from which it springs, after it has been worked and reworked by the play of semiotic processes.

The adversary system has been socially constructed so that its requirements may be easily met by the provision of an overburdened and undertrained public defender, who has a scant chance of providing his or her client with a fair trial. If the trial is to be made more than a simple way station on the road to a sure conviction, then public defenders must be given the ability to contest the government's case from a position of equality. To facilitate the task of re-envisioning and reconstructing the allegory of the criminal trial, the state must afford the defence the same dignity and resources that it affords the prosecution.

CRIME REPORTING

Crime reporting is not separate from the objective, interpretation and investigative form of reporting. Here it is separately dealt with because it is a separate and important beat in all big and medium level daily newspapers. There is a tremendous public interest in crime stories and no newspaper can afford to ignore them without damage to its circulation and credibility. Attempts made by some newspapers to keep crime out of their columns, proved to be counterproductive and were soon abandoned. Crime is a part of life and it is a newspaper's duty to inform the readers of what crimes are going on in their city, state or country. However, crime reporting should not aim at satisfying morbid curiosity or sensation mongering. Although crime reporting is usually assigned to one of the junior reporters in a newspaper, it is a highly responsible and specialized job.

The reporter should not only have the ability to shift the grain from the chaff, and the truth from lies, he should also have good contacts in the police and other departments of the administration as well as a working knowledge of the penal codes and law on libel and other relevant matters. Besides, he must observe a code of honour. He should be as objective as is humanly possible and avoid resorting to sensationalism or cheap gimmicks to catch the attention of the readers. He should not suppress news of public interest. Nor should he seek to settle personal scores with police officers or lawyers or judges. And he must be careful that in the course of this work, he does not unnecessarily invade a citizen's privacy. There has been much criticism of the press reporting of crime and not all of it is baseless. Some reporters have been found quality of unethical standards, thus causing much pain and sorrow to their victims or their families and friends. In the case of the brutal murder of two Bombay nuns, some newspapers published totally baseless allegations conveyed to them by irresponsible police officials that the nuns were in the habit of receiving male visitors. The reports offended all decent citizens, particularly the members of the Christian Community.

A leading newspaper once published a fictitious report about a couple having been waylaid by a gang on the national highway. The report said that the husband was beaten up and the women were molested. The story was subsequently-found to be incorrect, the product of the imagination of a reporter anxious to get his by-line in-the paper. Reports glorifying the activities of criminals or making heroes of them should be discouraged as much as a resort to sensationalism. The crime reporter must never violate standards of decency and good taste.

Crime as News : There are several types of crime news-murders, fires, accidents, robberies, burglaries, fraud, blackmail, kidnapping, rape, etc.

Fires : The reporter must get his facts correct about the essential elements of a fire story the number of persons killed or injured, the extent of damage to property, the loss of valuables, etc. He must also find out if the fire brigade responded in time or was guilty of delaying the fire-fighting operations through sheer lethargy or incompetence or a lack of water supply. He should question eyewitnesses about any acts of bravery or cowardice. All these are essential ingredients of a fire story. The lead in a fire story would normally suggest itself. If, for instance, lives have been lost, it needs highlighting in the lead. Where possible, list the names of the dead and the injured.

- *Example*: A major fire caused extensive damage to New Delhi's Vigyan Bhavan, the premier venue for international and national conferences, on Monday night. A chowkidar on duty received minor burns. According to preliminary investigations, the fire broke out in 'the kitchen and soon spread to other rooms on the ground floor. The chowkidar raised an alarm which alerted the head clerk on duty who informed the fire brigade and the police. Ten fire tenders soon arrived on the scene. However, their fire-fighting operations were hampered by lack of water in the hydrants. By the time water tankers rushed to the site, the fire had engulfed a large area and damaged files, furniture, curtains and ceilings.

The police suspect an electric short-circuit as the cause of the fire.

Homicides : In cases of a major murder, the reporter should rush to the scene as soon as possible after receiving a tip and gather all the relevant facts. In nine cases out of ten, crime reporters in, say, Delhi, depend on police information about the murders and there is a 'time lapse before they can begin their investigations. This often hampers their search for the truth. The reporter must, in any case, exercise great care in how he handles the story. Otherwise he runs the risk of causing offence. From reporting dowry deaths or alleged dowry deaths, for instance, the reporter should refrain from levelling uncorroborated statements by one party or the other. He must therefore get his facts correct-by talking to the investigating police officer, the girl's in-laws and her parents, and, if possible, the neighbours.

- *Example*: A 25 year old housewife, Sushmita Malik, died in Pant Hospital on Monday morning from burns received in a kitchen fire. The housewife's parents allege that she was murdered by her in-laws who had been dissatisfied with the dowry she brought at the time of her wedding a year ago. However, the husband, Keshav Malik, a garmant merchant in Chandni Chowk, and his father who were in the house at the time of the accident maintain, that Sushmita's sari caught fire when she was lighting a stove in the kitchen. Since the kitchen door was closed, they did not hear her cries for help. The police are questioning the women's relatives as well as neighbours and are reluctant to offer an opinion until the investigations are complete. At the insistence of Sushmita's parents, however, they have registered a case against her in-laws.

Accidents : Most accidents are reported on the basis of police bulletins or information supplied 'by police spokesmen. However, wherever possible the crime reporter must rush to the scene of a major accident to give authenticity to his story.

- *Example*: Three members of a family-husband, wife and daughter—were killed on the spot when a speeding truck rammed into their car on the road to the Indira Gandhi International Airport on Sunday morning. A fourth member of the family had a providential escape. According to the police, the truck driver lost control of the vehicle and swerved sharply to the right and hit the car coming from the opposite direction. Those killed are Ramkishore Singh, a businessman from Agra, his wife, Sumitra Devi, and their daughter, Sapna. The second daughter, Tanuja, had a miraculous escape and suffered only minor bruises on her arms and legs. She was treated at the Safdarjung Hospital and allowed to go home. The truck has been seized by the police but the truck driver, Milkha Singh is absconding.

TRANSGENDERED HATE CRIMES IN THE MEDIA

The final part of my analysis examines symbolic narratives of hate crimes in the media. Primarily, this semiotic analysis focuses on the February MTV production of the Matthew Shepard Story Anatomy of a Hate Crime (2001) and gives examples of news texts and other media representations that discuss hate crimes and victims.

Anatomy of a Hate Crime (2001) was broadcast in February 2001 to tell the Matthew Shepard story to an obviously younger audience. The film was produced for MTVs Fight For Your Rights: Take a Stand Against Discrimination Campaign. Immediately following the films' exhibition there were interlocutors from gay and lesbian organizations, even a personal friend of Matthew Shepard from the university, and a member of the National Legal Defence Fund. After this discussion, seventeen hours of continuous examples of hate crimes involving race/ethnicity, sexual orientation, transgendered, and hate crimes of gender were broadcast.

Giroux (1996) distinguishes a second code of violent films (beyond ritualistic), which he refers to as "symbolic violence". "Symbolic violence attempts to connect the visceral and the reflective. It couples the mobilization of emotion and the haunting images of the unwelcome with an attempt to give meaning and import to our moral twitchings.... It shakes everything up, reforming the fictive environment around itself.

Anatomy of a Hate Crime (2001) uses the code of symbolic violence to teach viewing audiences about this horrific hate crime that should never be forgotten or repeated. This docudrama using the code of social realism is effective at showing some of the realities that often face gay and lesbian victims of hate crimes. For instance, the profile of Matthew Shepard's assailants Russell Henderson and Aaron McKinney fits the empirical data on perpetrators: they are often young males, often acting together with other younger males, all of whom are strangers to the victim(s).Biographical accounts of the crime itself by Rob Debree, the sergeant who was the first official on the scene, testified to the maliciousness, what he called absolutely pre-meditated acts of violence by these young perpetrators. The film implies "gay baiting" showing Russell Henderson and Aaron McKinney coming on to Matthew Shepard.

Verbal and nonverbal codes in the film reveal this gay baiting tactic and offering Matt what turns out to be his last ride. This scene leading to the beating is the most symbolic moment in the film recreating for the audience the gay baiting tactics of the assailants.

- *McKinney*: Hey man what's up?
- Matt: Not much. You guy's winning over there? (In reference to their pool game)
- *McKinney*: Hell no. Some fresh gear man. (Looking at Matt's clothes and crotch)
- *Matt*: Yeah. Thanks.
- *McKinney*: You doing something after this?
- *Matt*: (hesitating). No, I'm just going home to study.
- *McKinney*: Shoot we're looking for some action?
- *Henderson*: Yea, we were hoping there was something going on after this?
- *Henderson*: My name's Russ (shakes hand). This is Aaron. (They shake hands)
- *Matt to bartender*: Hey bud will you call me a cab?
- *McKinney*: We'll give you a ride home near campus. It's on our way.
- *Matt*: Alright. Matt sort of staggers out and forgets to pay his bill.

According to Sergeant Rob Debree, Russell Henderson's confession "went into great detail about how they pretended to be gay to lure [Matt] out, changed their voices [to] an effeminate voice, and probably did some touching. There's absolutely no doubt in my mind that Matthew did anything at all to start this. McKinney's claim in his confession and the trial that Matt had grabbed his genitals was, Debree asserts, a 'flat lie'".

Anatomy of a Hate Crime clearly shows the homophobic mentality responsible for allowing the killing of such an innocent victim as Matthew Shepard. The film does teach viewing audiences some of the forms of re-victimization that gay and lesbian people involved in hate crimes often face.

For instance, it shows the court and officials constructing the crime in such a manner that Matt deserved what he got because he came on to Aaron McKinney. In the trial and the film, the "homosexual panic defence" was invoked. Berrill and Herek state that the tactic is often used most "successfully when victims are dead and unable to respond to the defendant's allegations". The defence attorney, Jason Tangeman argued that Aaron McKinney who delivered what would become "fatal" blows to Shepard from the 357 magnum pistol was threatened by him because of sexually traumatic events in his past life, coupled with alcohol and drug abuse.

"Tangeman told the jury that as a teenager McKinney had 'engaged in homosexual acts with a cousin, and at twenty had been distraught after he accidentally entered a gay and lesbian church in Florida'. He argued that Matt must have been looking for a sexual encounter that night and 'five minutes of emotional rage and chaos' ensued after Matt allegedly grabbed McKinney's crotch and licked his ear". Due to the public nature of the case, the attorney told the local newspaper, the Star Tribune that the defence team had not ever stated specifically a gay panic defence. One newspaper in Laramie, The Boomerang published what looked like a textbook case of the gay panic defence used by Tangeman on the first day of the trial.

The defence attorneys, Custis and Tangeman, brought in witnesses to testify that Matt had come on to them to prove their argument that he was sexually predatory and thus, as one of the defendant's girlfriends pointed out in her confession, "needed to be taught a lesson about coming on to others". These kinds of "revictimization" strategies are commonly used in gay and lesbian hate crime defences. Often the police and other authorities, prosecutors, judges, and juries blame the gay person in a manner similar to that in reports from victims of rape. A hate crime victim who lives may not report his or her assault to the police and the press because of possible "secondary victimization", due to heterosexism. In the film, Anatomy of a Hate Crime, McKinney says, "The stupid, whiney, little bitch. He's not going to tell anybody. Who'd believe him!" Beth Loffreda's reading of the event, from interviewing many people associated with the trial, believes "that Matt was an innocent victim-of which there is no doubt-doesn't mean that we need to see him as innocent of sex, of desire; but in the minds of many I spoke to that year, to think the latter seemed to taint the former". Symbolic media such as this anatomy of a gay hate crime in the media serves to educate the public about existential dilemmas that victims often face.

Likewise, people in the media have a social responsibility to report with accuracy material about hate crime victims. Much of the research on victims and the media has focused on understanding how to report on rape trauma and, yes, parallels can be made to hate crime victims. "People tell of the hurt and anger they experience from seeing news reports containing their names and their personal information framed in ways that makes the victim into a villain". It is generally well documented that rates of anti-gay hate crimes historically have been underreported for many years, because of the stigma surrounding homosexuality and the fear of revealing one's sexual preference to the police and other authorities. Analogously, rape survivor and author, Migael Scherer points out in regard to the news coverage of her own attack: "The unpredictable public scrutiny, the implication of blame, the focus on the suspect that shifts attention away from victims-all adds to our private anguish". The manhunt for Andrew Cuananan, for instance, seemed to say a lot about him but not about hate crimes by the ways the media were reporting his killings and disappearing acts. Consequently, he became somewhat of a celebrity gay killer.

Cote and Simpson not only recommend support for victims, but they have also found that there is some catharsis for victims telling their stories of rape in magazines, newspapers, and other public forums. Consistent with this research, these narratives are symbolic forms of violence which the public needs to understand to prevent them from happening again. This initial study calls for revisions to as well as more study of how the media reports hate crimes, citing the important social responsibility the media must exercise in reference to victims' rights and their support.

It cannot be underestimated how much hate crimes define vicious acts. Rob Debree, the investigating deputy in the Shepard case, thinks that it was not as the media reported that McKinney asked if Matt could read his license plate, and since he could read the numbers, McKinney resumed the pistol whipping. "I think essentially what happened Matt probably made a statement, 'Don't do this to me, I've got your license plate.' I think he's [Matt] doing anything he can to get out of this situation. Right there-right there is premeditation. Everybody is so used to TV that they think you plan this thing for a week or so and then go and do it. But right there if you have any doubt about first degree-that was it".

Russell Henderson held Matthew Shepard while McKinney did the uncontrollable beating, this was determined by the blood splatter on his coat. To Rob, these were vicious people. He couldn't abide the excuses, the laying of blame on drugs and childhood. He states, "[T]here were quite a few things that affected me emotionally-the viciousness of the crime, how small he was. [But] I think the thing that affected me the most was actually seeing the fear in the gay community". Loffreda's analysis suggests that McKinney and Henderson showed "homophobic violence as it more usually expresses itself: half hatched, half-confused, complex and impure, deeply cruel, and utterly stupid". And in the Matthew Shepard case, not without punishment.

The Shepard family was called in for plea bargaining on the second degree murder verdict of Aaron McKinney, for which he could still get the death penalty in the sentencing phase of the trial. He was given life sentences without the possibility of parole. Biographical accounts of the trial indicated that part of the plea bargaining was that McKinney would never be allowed to speak to the media about the killing of her son. Russell Henderson was also given life sentences without the possibility of parole. Judy Shepard commented, that she did not want to see McKinney on Geraldo Rivera or any other programme getting public notoriety. The Shepard family emphatically did not want these killers to become media celebrities. After all, Matthew Shepard did not live to tell his side of the story.

Another film that shows the terrible tragedy of a hate crime is the documentary about a transgendered life and death The Brandon Teena Story and the Hollywood produced Boys Don't Cry, portraying hate crimes as the violent acts of hatred they are. For instance, Teena's real mother says in the documentary that "she had so many knots on her head from the beating, rape, and then ultimately being shot and stabbed repeatedly to death in the tragic conclusion of the film". In a similar last brutal act, Matthew Shepard was shown getting the butt of the gun thrust heavily upon his head in Anatomy of a Hate Crime. It seems necessary to show as much victim "pain" as possible for the empathie responses these films require. Any Mother's Son about a hate crime involving a murdered young serviceman who was gay, a crime covered up by the military was shown on the Lifetime Channel. The independent (gay) film Relax It's Just Sex turns queers against gay bashers while it tackles with some humour quite serious issues facing gay and lesbian people. License to Kill by Arthur Dong is another documentary about gay killers and their methodical seeking out of victims.

Documentary television responded to both the Matthew Shepard Story and the Billy Jack Gaither story. Although Gaither's killing and burning by homophobes in Alabama in 1997 did not receive near the media attention from the straight press as did the Shepard's. Hour long educational news Programmes, such as 20/20, Dateline, and AaE, have done segments on both hate crime victims to educate the public about how these vicious acts affect this once invisible gay community now in and Out of the media.

In brief, my preliminary study links up the problems of how victims of violence are covered by the media. Distinctions made between ritualistic and symbolic forms of violence characterize different media forms, such as print and broadcast media and the media landscape of popular culture. Following Erni, further calls for queer-focused analyses can provide a sustained examination of how gays and lesbians are represented in mass culture. My study also attempts to bridge these related areas of investigation so that we might better represent gays and lesbians in the media. All of us partake of, and must live in, this culture; hopefully, not to the exclusion of the Other. Mainstream news media must pay more attention to the social concerns of gay and lesbian people. Journalists and other media personnel must be aware of diverse groups and how they represent them in the media. Accurate and responsible journalism and the increasingly important symbolic domain that popular culture can fulfill is evident in the exemplary MTV production Anatomy of a Hate Crime. Together, (1) gay and lesbian media studies and (2) victims and the media studies can provide a new framework for a socially responsible mass media semiotics.

Global competition, the globalizetion of corporate operations, and the complexity of social, cultural, and political systems across countries have created a greater need for international public relations theories and frameworks. Although the professional development of international public relations has begun to address these needs, scholarship in the field has yet to mature. Several international studies have identified the personal influence model as an additional dimension of Grunig's four models. Yet, it is still unclear why certain public relations practices are more common in international settings. International public relations researchers need to determine the status of the public relations profession in their respective countries, as well as explore the linkages between public relations and the environmental variables relevant to their regions, including culture, media environment, political system, level of activism, and level of economic development. Thus, certain questions need to be addressed.

Why is public relations perceived only as media relations in a given country? Why does the personal influence model have more explanatory power in specific international settings? To answer these questions, this study focuses on prevailing practices in media relations, the most dominant public relations practice in South Korea, and analyses its underlying factors from a cultural and societal framework. Such knowledge will further expand our understanding of the unique media relations components of public relations, based on the country in which they are practiced.

Practitioners increased their interest in international public relations beginning in the 1990s. Despite this growing interest, there is little empirical research on the nature of public relations practices in different regions of the world. Indeed, Culbertson has pointed out the imbalance between the need for such research and its availability. When considering public relations on an international scale, one must consider the importance of culture. Culture is embedded in every aspect of a nation, from interpersonal communication to its political system. Culture also influences the methods of public relations in a given country. Of particular importance in South Korea is the culture of Confucianism.

Confucianism is a religious and philosophical system developed from writings attributed to the Chinese philosopher Confucius. In South Korea, Confucianism has permeated state ideology and educational efforts for more than 500 years. Confucian ideas, values, morals, and norms have been internalized as a standard for judgement and behaviour in South Korea. In a Confucian society, spiritual harmony among different classes and subgroups is emphasized, and individual interests are sacrificed for the greater good.

The subjugation of personal self-realization to authority has served as a guide for maintaining harmony within South Korean society since the Lee dynasty in the fourteenth century. This Confucian notion of harmony is deeply related to collectivism. Further, an emphasis on propriety in human relationships has dominated interpersonal relationships for centuries. Propriety has a role in groups, organizations, and the collectivistic society as a whole. Confucianism focuses mainly upon relationships among individuals and emphasizes harmony and unity, which are considered key values in interpersonal relationships.

In South Korea, media relations tactics are derived mainly from the Confucian concept of harmony. Individual or social accommodation is emphasized over individual or social confrontation, even at the expense of ignoring ethical dilemmas. Challenging traditions or deviating from these norms is considered improper communication. Huang found that Confucianism also is closely related to public relations practice in Taiwan. Hwang assumed "the Western starting point of the atomic individual is alien to Chinese considerations of man's social behaviour, which see man as a relational being, socially situated and defined within an interactive context." Applying Hwang's conceptualization, Huang noted that the rationale of the personal influence model could be explained by the guanxi, a mixed-tie relationship outside of an individual's immediate family.

Individualism-collectivism has been recognized as a useful dimension to theorize cultural differences between the West and the East. Collectivist culture stresses group goals in which individuals are more likely to be attached to their employers. South Korea is a society with high power distance, high collectivism, little tolerance of uncertainty, high masculinity, and high Confucian dynamism.

Huang argued that collectivism has had a negative relationship with excellence in public relations. Contrary to Huang's findings in Taiwan, however, Rhee found that collectivism and Confucianism are positively correlated with public relations excellence in South Korea. She interpreted the collectivistic notion as signifying that the ultimate purpose of communication is the creation of harmony among people. Although there may be common agreement between the teachings of Confucianism and public relations objectives in terms of ultimate values, the processing components to that end may be in conflict. As Huang notes, excellent public relations stresses fairness, openness, and equality, whereas Confucianism values harmony and obligation to the group leader.

With reasoning similar to that of Huang, Park and Kim addressed the negative impact of Confucianism in South Korea. They argued that collectivism often thwarts an open system, fairness, and equality by stressing the selfish interests of family, social group, and organization. Further, collectivism does not fit with the public relations theories as developed in the United States.

VICTIMS AND THE MEDIA

Recent research from victims and the media studies questions some of the ritualistic practices of crime reporting, concluding that they are bereft of social benefit to victims. In some ways, broadcast and print news room practices of "faceless" victim coverage are similar to the types of disembodied violence common on primetime television drama shows. According to a National Television Study conducted in 1994-1995, "few depictions of unrealistic television violence suggest how trauma has injured the person or how long a reasonable degree of recovery requires. The context researchers warn, is important because it tells us what to expect in violent interactions".

Cote and Simpson are critical of ubiquitous media violence, claiming the amount and frequency of violence that we are exposed to on television and in newspapers is an institutional problem with "crime news leading and taking up more than half of local television newscasts and violent stories making up a quarter or more of the locally generated stories in newspapers". They also note the types of shows on television that emphasize violence in a ritualistic fashion, with "few Programmes offering any warnings about violence or any useful information about its consequences". Research by George Gerbner in his Cultural Indicators Project makes clear that violence on television appears to be calculated to induce fear in what he calls the "Mean World Syndrome". Statistics show that crime rates are down in major urban areas, but violence, nevertheless, still dominates the first several minutes of news shows. "Many stations have the practice, if not policy, that 'if it bleeds, it leads'". Henry Giroux refers qualitatively to those types of formulaic violence shown in popular film genres such as action-adventure, Hollywood drama, and splatter and gore films as ritualistic. He reads this code of ritualistic violence as "pure spectacle in form and superficial in content. Audiences connect with such depictions viscerally; yet, it is not edifying in the best pedagogical sense, offering few insights into the complex range of human behaviour and struggles". In contrast, we will examine the MTV production Anatomy of a Hate Crime dealing with the Matthew Shepard story because it seems to be using the code of "symbolic violence" in order to show audiences the horror of what it means to be a victim of a hate crime. Further, cultural criticism of how the media relayed the Matthew Shepard case to the public will be examined from biographical details of the case assembled by Beth Loffreda, an English professor at the University of Wyoming at Laramie, in her recent book about this tragedy entitled Losing Matthew Shepard. These two views are detailed in order to understand victim narratives and codes. The structural semiotic investigation of how victim stories are misrepresented by "irresponsible" news gathering practices is evident when we examine the Matthew Shepard case.

VICTIM REPRESENTATION

Where the victim is placed in these multiple stories of crime and violence on television and news broadcasts? Institutional problems abound in media representations of stories of violence and victims. Cote and Simpson are particularly critical of victim coverage by television and print journalism because of their tendency to emphasize the crime or the event, rather than the punishments and outcomes. They claim journalists are guilty of trotting out easy explanations or simplistic ironies to quickly summarize violent acts. This was the case in the Laramie, Wyoming trial of the hate crime that led to the death of Matthew Shepard. The media went on a "feeding frenzy" descending upon the small town and painting pictures of it as lawless and backward. Of course, hate crimes can happen anywhere; yet, the media suggested this was a dangerous community in which to be gay. Bob Beck, news director of Wyoming Public Radio, and Jim Osborn, a student and leader of the campus gay organization Lesbian, Gay, Bisexual and Transgendered Association (LGBTA) at the University of Wyoming, both testified to the inaccurate statements made by the media that served to re-victimize an already traumatized and grieving community. Beck talks about the first television news report he saw.

It was this woman reporter outside the Fireside doing what we call a bridge, a stand-up: "Hate: it's a common word in Wyoming". Beck couldn't believe it, but that mirrored precisely the assumptions of most of the media representatives he encountered that week. Journalists who interviewed him began with comments like, "Well this kind of thing probably happens a lot up there", or "You have the cowboy mentality in Wyoming, so this was bound to happen". Reporters criticized Laramie, he says, for not having a head trauma unit, not having gay bars, not pushing back homecoming. Jim Osborn, said the tone of the journalistic questioning was hostile. Jim says the press he spoke to wanted to hear this was a hateful, redneck town, that Wyoming was in the inane rhyming of some commentators, "the hate state". But Jim insisted on what he considered accurate: "Nobody expects murder here-nobody. This is not a place where you kill your neighbour, and we see each other as neighbours. This is a good place".

Lull and Hinerman describe this frenzied, overly dramatized type of journalistic reporting as a "pyschodrama scandal", when something extraordinary happens to an ordinary person, making for big news. Examples would be the Lorenna Bobbit and Susan Smith psychodrama scandals in the media. Both became "media stars" when Bobbit cut off her husband's penis in a moment of rage, and Smith drowned her children and blamed it on a black man. These scandals instantly became grist for the television, print and infotainment (Court TV, reality television) mills. Lull and Hinerman suggest that reporting (some) media scandals may be necessary or educative because they show transgressions that are of social import to the wider community. Too often, it seems that some of these stories are dramatized for their tabloid market value, rather than for their potential to inspire critical reflection of social problems deserving widespread media discussion. The real tragedy of narrativizing stories of victims of horrific violence and those connected with those events is that journalists and others can injure traumatized people by not being aware of what psychiatrist Sandra Bloom sees as an often denied reality, that "trauma is a central organizing principle in the formation, development, and maintenance of human society". Cote and Simpson make clear in their efforts to educate media professionals "that the public interest in knowing about the event can generally be served along with due regard for the needs of people who have been harmed".

Journalists may add insult to injury in their race to explain a horrific event involving victims, neighbours, friends of victims, people at risk, as in the Matthew Shepard case the whole community of Laramie, Wyoming. Rumors and hearsay are not a sound fact gathering practice and tended to fuel the media fire in the Shepard murder case. Mr. Beck referred to the scenario as "pack journalism". Beck recalls, "I remember going to the courthouse, and somebody would say, 'Hey I understand he got burned-which wasn't true by the way-'where did he get burned?' Oh, on his face, and they're all taking notes, and they were sources for each other. One person would announce that he heard such and such from a deputy, and they would go with it; no one [else] went and interviewed the deputy". These structural problems foster inaccurate reporting. Such practices are insensitive to traumatized people, and they tend to feed our society's fascination with violence, while offering little solace to the experience of victims. What does it mean to be a victim and, specifically, a victim of a hate crime?

In commonsense terms, we routinely label persons who have been unjustly harmed or damaged by forces beyond their control as victims. The emotional toll of suffering victimization and trauma is just beginning to be taken into account by news staffs. According to Cote and Simpson, the most important idea is that the "traumatized person has become a different person emotionally. If news practices take that into account, reporting their stories can help victims". The victims and the media maxim of giving the "victim equal space" has pedagogical potential when film, news, and other media examine the social problem of hate crimes and other victimization through human cruelty.

In the case of hate crime, we can point in particular to racial minorities injured by racially motivated violence, as well as to gays and lesbians harmed by violence motivated by hate and women harmed simply because they are female. The Hate Crimes Sentence Enhancing Act passed by the U.S. Congress in 1994, defines a hate crime as criminal conduct wherein "the defendant intentionally selected any victim or property as the object of the offence because of the actual or perceived race, colour, religion, national origin, ethnicity, gender disability, or sexual orientation of any person". According to the National Institute of Justice Hate Crime statistics from 1997-1999, there were 3,000 identifiable hate crimes in the United States. Race and sexual orientation had the highest frequency of occurrence. It was not until the Shepard hate crime in October of 1998 that the media gave much attention to hate crimes involving gay and lesbian people. Therefore, it is important for media practitioners to be aware of the important symbolic role they fulfill in educating the public about victims. Victim representation is important to the domain of popular culture, where narratives of hate can be addressed in a symbolic manner, showing the suffering of real human beings so that these vicious acts will never be forgotten, nor repeated

Giroux codes different types of films based upon their pedagogical and consciousness raising potential, versus more ritualistic representation which is gratuitous at best saying nothing about the complexities of the human condition. Much of the ritualistic routine of news delivery by print and broadcast journalism does not compel viewers or readers to empathize with victims. Even more problematical is that the perpetrator(s) of violent acts may receive more coverage than the victim. This seemed to be the case with Newsweek magazine's coverage of Columbine Colorado high school killers Dylan Kleibold and Eric Harris. The killers were foregrounded by large framing shots, while the murdered children were put in tiny box shots.

Journalists are finally beginning to recognize the importance of incorporating an ethic of sensitivity to victims in their work. Symbolic forms of news writing focus on the healing process; for instance, by publishing different installments about how a family deals with the loss of their daughter after a murder. These kinds of follow-up stories can humanize and may actually aid the healing process of victims. In writing news stories about victims, getting details wrong such as names, ages, job descriptions, and other information that is a part of a persons' identity can be harmful to victims and their grieving families.

3

The Ethical Aspect of Sting Operation

INTRODUCTION

This is not to deny that hidden cameras and related techniques have been used at times with great courage and foresight for very clear public interests. Such efforts deserve our applause. But these rare causes should not prevent us from being critical of the more frequent 'sting operations' of a highly dubious nature. In some cases, even the identity of those who carried out the sting operation is not known, even though the contents of the videotapes make headlines all over media. In other cases, entirely unsubstantiated, incidental allegations made about people, not at all involved in the sting operation, are also splashed around indiscriminately.

The debate on various aspects of sting operations may be quite intense today, but actually it is only a small part of the much wider, increasingly urgent debate on the relevance, credibility and ethics of media. In the modern, globalised world, the reach of media is so wide (and getting wider) that its importance in mirroring as well as shaping our daily lives and views is not questioned many more.

To give a recent example, the USA Presidential election last year was clearly a very important event for the entire world as millions of people in many countries, not just the USA, could draw a link between how this electoral choice could impact their own lives in important ways. It was equally clear that the debate carried out in the media, particularly on TV, played a very important role in shaping the views of a very large number of voters. It was even stated at one time that a single documentary on the 9/11 terrorist attack could play a decisive role, although this was probably exaggerated.

On the whole, while the importance of the role of media cannot be denied, questions of great urgency need to be raised about how ethical this role is. With the media reaching out to an increasing number of people and claiming more of their time, can we rest assured that people are now better informed about important events and issues? In the recent American Presidential election, the 9/11 terrorist attack and Iraq were obviously two very important issues.

In this context two key points of the debate were — Did any significant WMDs, more specifically nuclear weapons, exist in Iraq prior to the invasion of Iraq by the USA and its allies? Did any evidence exist to establish a close link (or for that matter, any link) between the Al Queda and the Saddam Hussain regime?

All available evidence indicated negative answers to both these questions. But at the same time, several surveys and polls indicated that a significant number of American citizens believed the answers to be positive.

How could such a situation emerge that widely known facts regarding crucial election issues could not reach American voters when the election campaign was so extensively covered by the media? Why did American voters remain misinformed about some of the most crucial issues when they had access to several TV channels, radio news, newspapers, journalists and Internet? One reason may be that several leading politicians made false statements on these crucial issues and these were prominently splashed in media, often without any adverse editorial comment. One strategy is to confuse the ordinary people with some prominently displayed statements by well-known persons so that they remain confused.

Thus even in a country like the USA where freedom of the press is so persistently emphasised at least at the surface level, it is possible for the media to present facts in such a distorted way that a large number of people, perhaps even a majority, remain misinformed on some of the most crucial issues, even at election-time. It is complex but also fascinating to try to understand how despite the apparent freedom to publish a very diverse range of facts and opinions, vested interests eventually succeed in ensuring that it is their viewpoint that eventually reaches the majority of people.

Today, the world faces several threats of such a serious nature that we should start worrying about a crisis of survival. These threats include climate change, the accumulation of WMDs and the highly accelerated rate of loss of many species of life.

But the media has by and large failed to accord adequate importance to such issues or to present these in a proper perspective. More specifically, only technological solutions are presented for problems, which require basic changes in the way we think, live and organise our world.

At the same time, the media has created its own world of glamour, sex and sensation, which has played an important role in distracting attention from the real issues of our times. This aspect of the media has played an important role in the rise of crimes (including sexual crimes) and commodification of women.

The media has also contributed to the trivialisation of human sensitivities, which makes violence and injustice more acceptable. Media has promoted consumerism and glamour to the exclusion of the most essential concerns of our difficult times. The occasional sting operations try to create a mistaken public impression of a crusading role of media, but there is no doubt that very basic changes are needed before the real potential of the media in effectively tackling the most important issues of our time can be realised.

EFFECTIVENESS OF STING OPERATION

They are familiar sights on our TV screens these days: The grainy, curiously distorted images, the awkward camera angles, the unclear audio and the anchors promising startling revelations just ahead.

They're sting operations; the exposés conducted by journalists in much the same manner as investigative agencies conduct undercover operations. And what's more, they're flourishing: Indeed, age could be called the year of the sting operation.

MAJOR STING OPERATIONS IN INDIA

Aaj Tak

Tihar Jail Bani Ghoos Mahal: Officials at Tihar Jail taking bribes.

Ghoos Mahal: 82 employees of the Delhi sales tax office taking bribes.

Operation Duryodhan: 11 MPs caught taking bribes to raise questions in Parliament.

Star News

Ayaash IG: Jharkhand IG suspended for sexually exploiting a tribal woman.

Doctor selling infants from a hospital.

Operation Chakravyuh: MP's caught misusing MPLAD funds.

Wife caught on camera beating her husband.

NDTV India

Delhi policeman taking a bribe to hand over the body of a man to his family.

Railway policemen extorting money from passengers.

India TV

Bihar MLAs having sex with call girls.

Holy men sexually exploiting women devotees.

Operation Casting Couch: Actor Shakti Kapoor propositions journalist posing as actress.

Operation Casting Couch: Actor Aman Verma takes journalist posing as an actress to his bedroom.

Sahara Samay

Corruption in Delhi PWD.

Kokh Mein Qatl

Sting operations by media are largely aimed at uncovering scandals and corruption. Major scandals including Tehelka, the Judeo bribery, the existence of the casting couch or the case of MP's taking money to ask Parliament questions are some of the examples of the media exposes. It was either money or sex that sensationalized these stories. But there are rare cases in the history of TRP-driven modern media when a sting is launched against social malpractices. Social stings is a term unheard of in the Indian media also because the sting operations in itself is a recent phenomenon. Hence, there is no documentation of sting operations dealing with issues of social concern in India.

One such operation titled *Kokh Mein Katl* (murder in the womb) has highlighted the severity of the discrimination against the girl child and the risk involved in conducting such operations. The operation was launched by a team of journalists in Rajasthan. It was a campaign based on the personal commitment of the team. With this operation the genre of sting operation has entered a new era.

Suppression and discrimination of women was the starting point of this operation run jointly by Sripal Shaktawat, the Bureau Chief, Rajasthan, Sahara News and Dr. Meena Sharma, a freelance journalist. Sripal Shaktawat has been crusading against the social malpractices and atrocities especially crime against women for over a decade while Meena has been a young freelance reporter committed to the social upliftment of the society. Both of them have given new meaning to the sting operations led by media. Meena left her assignments with the local media and her college lectureship to devote herself to the operation.

They planned to launch a sting operation in February- March,2005 to expose the breed of doctors conducting illegal abortions after sex determination in the state. They travelled a distance of 13,000 km across the districts of Rajasthan and MP, Gujarat, and UP.

This sting "Kokh Mein Katl" was telecast on Sahara channel from 4th April,2006. The team had footage of about 100 doctors. Out of them 80 were telecast. Some of the footages were held back because of the poor quality. Together, the team travelled a distance of 1300 km across the districts of Rajasthan, MP, Gujrat, and Haryana. There were pressures from the political and social circles but the team continued to resist all pressures to expose the killer Doctors. The local media and journalist associations and social groups came in open support of the sting team.

The operation was conducted in the following phases:

The First Phase

- Planning and strategy of operation.
- Search for a pregnant lady to act as a decoy.

- After 4 month of search a lady got ready to help as a decoy in the operation.
- Her husband was taken into confidence.

She was a graduate with 6 months pregnancy and she did not demand any money in exchange. The operation began in Jaipur, Bundi and Kota districts.Meena impersonated as an attendant of the lady willing to terminate pregnancy after identifying a girl child in sex determination. She took along a camera in her bag.She was a beginner in camera handling, therefore the quality of shots was poor.

She had been working as an anchor on regional channels and was recognized by the doctors who could not be trapped because of her disclosed identity.

Realising the problem she left the anchoring and engaged herself with the operation. They encountered the inhuman doctors ready to abort a 6-7 month pregnancy for money. This realization forced the duo to re think and re- plan the entire exercise in a big way.

The Second Phase

Watching the reality closely the team could visualize the gravity of the problem in a wider perspective and smelled that there could be a wider network across the state. With this knowledge they widened the scope of operation. The team did not want to restrict itself to mere 5-6 exposes. Rather than touching the tip of the iceberg they wanted to reach the root and catch the perpetrators red handed on camera. Search for a pregnant decoy continued.

A decoy met them but after accompanying them to one clinic refused to help. In order to prevent the leak (of both the idea and the sting) they could not reveal and seek help openly. The search continued and so the obsession with the issue. Meena was desperate and she asked her pregnant sister and sister-in- law and her aunt to act as a decoy. All her close acquaintance disappointed her and refused to help her in the crusade. The family members dissuaded her from continuing with the operation.

Another decoy offered to help though she didn't reveal it to her family. Her husband agreed to the idea and they stayed with the team for 25 days. With her a major target was covered. During this period the targets gave hint about the wider network extended to Agra, Gwalior, Palampur and Ahmadabad.

The team explored and planned to go beyond the boundaries of the state of Rajasthan.

The decoy left. Another decoy extended help. The team covered 7 districts with her.

First ever arrest under PNDT Act in Palwal foeticide case. The team had planned to go to Haryana and Punjab but had to postpone plans after the judgement to play safe. Now the task ahead was more challenging than before.

The strategy was changed and the further coverage was done with week long break after week long shoot.

By this stage the team had collected enough evidences and caught the instigators of the offence in camera. The team had become more confident and cautious about handling the embarrassing moments.

They did not hesitate to carry the camera into the chamber and even to the Operation theatre.The operation slowed down because of the Palwal judgement. Besides, all through the operation it was a major challenge to search and persuade a pregnant lady to join the operation as a decoy. Without their assistance this operation would not have reached to its destination. It was risky to take along 6-7 months pregnant woman and travel long distances. Interestingly all the five decoys had one child.

The team would take care of the decoy's health, her child and husband who would all travel along the team. The camera was seen by the doctors in Jaipur, Chittorgarh and Palampur.

The team had to run away to avoid any tussle and consequent disclosure of the operation and motive. There arose situations when the team allowed the decoy to be taken to the Operation Table and Meena accompanied her as attendant in the OT.

Narrating the incident during the live telecast and personal interaction Meena says that ".... I still shiver to recall the incident......the decoy was taken to the OT...the medicines were were unwrapped ....the injections were ready......Sripalji couldn't enter the OT.....I barged and stopped the doctors ......and rushed back with the decoy ....and cried our heart out in the van ..... any untowards happening would have caused a life long burden on our conscience...."

It was risky but this way only the team could record the conversation of the team of doctors and take the visuals of the illegal MTP.

The Final Showdown

The climax of the episode came as a shock to the team. On 4th April, 2006 a culprit, a Jaipur doctor at Deep Nursing Home manhandled Shripal and Meena, whose contribution through their bold participation at the risk of their and decoy's life helped make this initiative one of the leading sting operations in the country, one that has added a new dimension to media activism. Dr Rekha Gupta of Deep Nursing Home hampered the further schedule of the Sting. Despite many hurdles from various quarters the team engaged in the sting operation successfully and managed to capture on camera around 140 doctors, among them 100 odd doctors seemed in great hurry to abort the girl child from the mother's womb.

The undercover operation was recorded in last one year covering 36 cities. The team members travelled a distance of 1300 kms in four states. The faces exposed so far are just the tip of an iceberg; many more are yet to be exposed. ...But financially and politically well connected medical practitioners were panicky and worked overtime for face saving.

The case has been registered against 33 doctors in all the states the sting was conducted. The most speedy action was taken in Gujarat with the intervention of the state health minister. The sting was conducted at four clinics of Palampur. Just after the live telecast of the sting the government ordered immediate seizure of the clinics. The government also ran a campaign to check the F- form containing details of the patient undergone termination of pregnancy and cancelled registration of Ultra Sound Machines of about 58 clinics.

The issue has emerged as a major social blot on the progressive societies and a debate has begun at various forum. At some places the police have been proactive in registering the cases against the accomplices of the crime. There has been an awakening about the extent and gravity of the problem.

The government was initially reluctant to take action against the culprits. The journalists and the opposition party (Congress) boycotted the assembly (Rajasthan) proceedings until the issue was taken up for debate in the house. Because of the pressure of the journalists, political and social organizations, the issue was debated in the Rajasthan Assembly and the Home Minister had to make a statement that the government will not spare the culprits.

The issue was also raised in the Rajya Sabha by Brinda Karat, Sushma Swaraj and other female MPs. The Health Minister Ramodas assured to launch a sting operation on behalf of the government. The central and the state governments and Rashtriya Mahila Morcha of BJP also appealed the religious leaders to sensitize the mass about this malpractice. The caste leaders and associations like Bhil Samaj, NGOs like Aangana Patel and Akhila-CEFAR expressed their concern with the issue and declared that the community will boycott the persons engaged in female foeticide. The political and social organizations staged demonstrations all across the country demanding urgent attention to the issue and arrests of the guilty. The local media especially the print media carried the follow up stories and editorials- campaigning the arrest and legal action against the culprits, sensitizing the masses and building opinion against the practice.

The visiblity of the issue in media and the sensitive treatment by the media persons is welcome change. Since the issue came to the limelight there has not been a single week the newspapers did not publish a story on female foeticide and the trend continues. The gruesome stories on throwing the foetus in the well now receive front page space. Recent cases (in the month of July-August) of a man carrying female foetus in polybag for dumping (Bharatpur) or three foetus lying near a lake in the lake city (Udaipur), 25 foetus in a well (Patiala) or a five month female foetus and body of a new born girl child near government hospital (Jaipur) have been highlighted in right earnest by media and cases have been registered in all the cases.

It was unfortunate that some unidentified criminals stormed the house of Shripal and threatened his wife and children with dire consequences one night. It was April 19, 2006, and the perpetrators warned against the further telecast of the sting operation. The doctors offered money and threatened the team constantly. The police and politicians lay direct or indirect pressures on the team members and their family not to pursue the case further. The state government the state Home Minister Gulab Chand Kataria not only ordered police cops to find out the decoy who helped in the sting operation but said, " Hum kise ke saath anyaay nahi karenge.

Nyaay ke liye zaroori hai ki un mahilaon ke jaanch ho ki w-oh garbhwati hai bhi ki nahi." (we shall not do injustice to anybody. For justice it needs to be investigated whether the decoy who helped in the whole operation was pregnant or not?). One of the reasons for the government reluctance to take harsh action against the guilty doctors was the doctor brother Ashutosh Bansal of a Superintendent of Police who was one of the accomplices caught on camera at Deep Nursing Home engaged in sex determination tests.

The district and the state authorities have *suo motu* powers to take action against violators of PC/PNDT and MTP Acts, but the CMHOs and the Directorate of Family Welfare hesitated to take any action. The harassment of the team still continues with the police-culprit nexus. The cases have been registered at various Police Thanas of the districts and the journalist duo have also been prosecuted for being thc witnesses of the doctors' involvement in sex determination and willingness to abort the female foetus.. They are being summoned at all the districts wherever the cases have been registered for evidences.

Instead, the police should have collected the evidences on the basis of the visuals (CDs) provided by the journalists rather than harassing and prosecuting the journalists. The dilemma the journalists face in such cases is whether to restrict themselves to alarming and mobilizing the society and let the law take its course or fight the whole battle as an activist at the expense of their professional commitments.

SHAKTI KAPOOR STUNG BY STING OPERATION

Shakti Kapoor is one of the topmost villains of Bollywood. But one sting operation claims to have revealed that he is a 'bad guy' in real life too. He has been filmed purportedly making verbal and physical advances against a young woman and casting aspersions on several film personalities in a sting operation conducted by a private TV channel.

Kapoor did not deny making the advances but maintained he was set up. He claimed he had not made any specific statements about his fellow stars but only spoke in generalities.The sting was conducted by producer Suhaib Ilyasi for his "India's Most Wanted" programme that has now shifted to the India TV channel.

The channel aired the 40-minute clip. In it, Kapoor is seen to be making sexually explicit verbal and physical suggestions to an India TV reporter posing as an aspiring film star.

The reporter is told of various "services" that would have to be provided if she were to make it big.

Kapoor then turns his wrath on Ilyasi and the cameraman when he discovers he is being filmed.

"Kapoor had the choicest of verbal abuses reserved for us when he realised what happened. He threatened us with dire consequences and even said he would stab the girl," Ilyasi said.

"It was a trap," Kapoor later told a press conference. "This girl had been in touch with me for close to five months, calling me up in the middle of the night and asking for roles. She even sweet-talked me into meeting her. Any man would fall for this," he claimed.

What sort of topics do sting operations deal with? Perhaps the most obvious target for these stings has been government corruption. However, stings increasingly deal with other topics as well. For example, India TV aired a series of exposés centering around sleaze including what came to be known as the 'casting couch' story: Bollywood personalities propositioning an undercover journalist posing as an aspiring actress.

CNBC Awaz regularly conducts sting operations on issues concerning consumer rights and private sector malpractices. Stings have also become commonplace on crime shows, though these have no wider impact.

Nevertheless, the most publicized topic for stings remains government corruption. The Tehelka exposé was on corruption in arms deals, Operation Duryodhan on MPs taking bribes to raise questions in Parliament, Operation Chakravyuh exposed misuse of the MPLAD fund, while Aaj Tak's "Ghoos Mahal" was on corruption in Tihar Jail and a sales tax office. The CNN-IBN exposé showed us a UP minister willing to transport narcotics. Kairali TV also recently carried out a sting exposing a state minister. All these sting operations dealt with misuse of power by the authorities- crooked politicians, government officials and policemen.

So what happened after these exposés? At least with Operation Duryodhan, the reaction was swift. All the 11 MPs caught on camera were dismissed from their respective parties. Then, less than two weeks after the scandal broke out, the 11 men were suspended from parliament in an unprecedented and somewhat controversial move. The immediate fallout of Operation Chakravyuh was less dramatic, but still noteworthy: The Lok Sabha speaker ordered an enquiry and told the accused MPs not to attend parliament until their names were cleared. The UP Minister exposed by CNN-IBN resigned from his position, as did the Kerala minister caught in the Kairali TV sting.

These are all remarkable examples of the power of the media. Sting operations have unflinchingly exposed the rot in the system and brought corruption into focus. Though a lot of what they reveal is depressing, none of it is especially surprising. Stings have only confirmed what were once mere suspicions or allegations. They have also put pressure on politicians and bureaucrats to take action against their colleagues caught with their hands in the till.

News channels usually insist that their sting operations are done in public interest. They point out that stings are expensive, unpredictable affairs. Large sums of money go into paying bribes; budgets cannot be fixed in advance and can increase dramatically. And after all that, there is no guarantee of success.

However, sting operations do bring some benefits for news channels. The most obvious is that they have a major, albeit temporary impact on TRPs- they are a great way for a station to get noticed. Perhaps the most important aspect of this is the footage itself- those characteristic visuals showing corrupt netas or government officials making shady deals, and wads of currency changing hands. These visuals not only give substance to the claims of the news channel, they bring in troves of curious viewers. A lot more people end up watching that particular channel simply because the footage is unavailable to competitors.

Whatever the motivations behind sting operations maybe, their immediate effects are often impressive. However, some questions remain over the long-term benefits. One reason for this is that news channels usually fail to follow up on their stings adequately. This may be because of a sense that the story is 'over'.

How much did things really change after the 2001 Tehelka exposé? In 2003, a sting exposed Dilip Singh Judeo, a minister while he was apparently taking a bribe. Now, some five years after Tehelka, a series of stings have shown us that corruption is rife as ever in government. Politicians, it seems can still be bribed easily, not just to ask questions in parliament or misuse taxpayers money but to, in the case of the UP minister exposed by CNN-IBN, actually transport narcotics in his own car. What happened in all those intervening years? No matter how many stings are carried out, it still seems like business as usual among the corrupt.

The story is clearly not 'over' once footage from a sting operation is aired. The Aaj Tak sting on a sales tax office may have led to the suspension of some 30 employees but it certainly does not mean an end to graft there. Unfortunately, the way stories of political corruption are treated on TV leaves little scope for follow-ups. Instead, the focus tends to be on specific individuals whom the channel has exposed rather than the systemic problems that allow for corruption in the first place. This may be because of a feeling that audiences are more interested in stories about those individual personalities rather than in analysis of systemic issues.

For example, Aaj Tak's coverage of Operation Duryodhan was dominated by myriad details of the expose- who the MPs were, how much money each of them took and whether political parties would suspend the errant parliamentarians-not the issue of widespread political corruption. After catching on camera a UP minister agreeing to take drugs in his own car, CNN-IBN focused on whether he would be made to resign rather than the larger implications of it's own exposé. Yet with the novelty of sting operations fading and returns diminishing viewers are now more and more likely to question why little seems to be changing.

Indeed news channels seem to be shortchanging themselves by not following up on their own audacious journalism. Armed with little more than tiny cameras and great deal of gumption, a relatively small but committed group of Indian journalists has taken the challenge of exposing corruption head on. And they have been remarkably successful so far. What's needed now is a more sustained commitment from the media to ensuring that the gains they have made are consolidated and the powers that be are held accountable.

PREVENTION OF CHILD PORNOGRAPHY AND SOME MAJOR STING OPERATIONS

The Supreme Court upheld laws prohibiting child pornography in 1982, law enforcement agencies embarked on an impressive effort to stamp out the trade in this illicit material. With the rise of the Internet, however, child pornography proliferated beyond what anyone could have imagined. In the later half of the 90s, federal law enforcement agencies began directing their efforts online. This era also witnessed the rise of greater cooperation between federal, state, and local law enforcement agencies and between nations. The following stings represent some of the largest conducted around the world in recent years. Not featured here, but no less important, is the work being done in local communities all across the globe.

Operation Hamlet

Date: On August 9, 2002, U.S. Customs Service Commissioner Robert Bonner announced the results of an investigation dubbed Operation Hamlet.

Subject: The investigation centered on a group of approximately 20 individuals who were molesting their own children and trading the images and videos with others in the group.

Background: Operation Hamlet began in November 2001 when a group called Save the Children was alerted to a picture of a young girl being abused by an unidentified man. A company logo was visible in the picture and Save the Children alerted the National Police in Denmark, where the company was located. Within 24 hours the man was identified and apprehended along with his wife. A search of their home and computer equipment revealed information about others in the group, including a Clovis, California father of four who appeared to be the ringleader.

Results: Twelve Americans and ten Europeans were arrested in connection with the group. One member was found with more than 1 million images and 450 CDs containing hardcore pornography and child abuse. Thirty-seven children in the United States and eight children in Europe were rescued and taken into protective custody.

Operation Candyman

Date: On March 18, 2002, FBI Executive Assistant Director Bruce Gebhardt and Attorney General John Ashcroft announced the first phase of Operation Candyman.

Subject: The investigation centered on a Yahoo! Egroup that invited people to trade pictures of child pornography. The FBI estimates that there were more than 7,000 subscribers to the group, with around 2,400 living abroad. Those subscribing to the Candyman group were targeted in this investigation, but other Egroups were under scrutiny at the time Candyman was announced.

Background: Operation Candyman began in January 2001 when an undercover FBI agent joined the site. He had instant access to about 100 images and video clips, most of which showed prepubescent children engaged in sexual acts with themselves and adults. Within a month, the agent received 500 e-mail messages, some of which included child pornography. By the time Candyman was made public, all 56 FBI field offices were involved with the investigation.

Results: More than 100 Americans have been arrested. The group administrator, Mark Bates, was sentenced to 30 years in prison. Those arrested included day care workers, clergy members, law enforcement personnel, a U.S. Army Sergeant, and others in positions of trust or authority. German authorities are investigating 1,400 people in connection with Candyman and British police have identified more than 2,000 people suspected of acquiring illegal material from the sites in question.

Operation Avalanche

Date: On August 8, 2001, Attorney General John Ashcroft and Chief Postal Inspector Kenneth Weaver announced Operation Avalanche. By this time, the two-year undercover operation had already made more than 100 arrests on charges related to child pornography, and had secured the convictions of the masterminds of the business, Thomas and Janice Reedy.

Subject: The investigation centered on Landslide Productions, Inc., a Fort Worth Internet business engaged in advertising and conspiring to distribute child pornography. Landslide offered subscriptions to more than 250 web sites, many of which were devoted to child pornography. Landslide collected 300,000 subscribers, earning as much as $1.4 million dollars a month. It is known as the largest commercial child pornography enterprise ever encountered.

Background: Operation Avalanche began in 1999 when a Minnesota postal inspector passed a tip along to another inspector in Fort Worth who then contacted the Dallas police. Working with thirty federally funded Internet Crimes Against Children (ICAC) Task Forces, the Department of Justice, and the U.S. Postal Inspection Service, the Dallas Police department infiltrated Landslide and arrested its owners.

Results: Thomas and Janice Reedy of Landslide Productions were sentenced to 1,335 and fourteen years in prison respectively. More than 250 Americans have been arrested to date, but the subscriber list contained names of more than 35,000 Americans. People from 60 countries have subscribed to Landslides sites. Police in Switzerland are investigating around 1,300 people in Operation Genesis, the German police have launched Operation Pecunia to investigate more than 1,400 suspects, British authorities have launched Operation Ore to investigate more than 7,200 names, and Ireland conducted more than 100 raids as part of Operation Amethyst. Canada is also investigating suspects in Operation Snowball.

Operation Blue Orchid

Date: On March 26, 2001, the U.S. Customs Service announced results of an on-going international child pornography investigation called Operation Blue Orchid. *Subject:* The investigation centered on the Blue Orchid Web site, run by Russian pedophiles for the purpose of posting and selling pictures and videos of young boys being sexually abused.

Background: Operation Blue Orchid began in May 2000 when the Moscow Police Department contacted the U.S Customs Attaché for help identifying the owners of the Blue Orchid site. The Attaché requested the Customs Service CyberSmuggling Center in the United States to make an undercover purchase of pornographic materials. The information gleaned from the purchase led Moscow police to two men responsible for producing and distributing a number of tapes depicting sodomy and rape of young boys.

Results: Moscow police seized 400 videos, equipment, and billing records. The resulting information led to more than 50 leads around the world. Investigations have been completed in Sweden, Denmark, and the Netherlands and are ongoing in several other European nations. The U.S. Customs Service has announced four arrests and the execution of fifteen other search warrants across the country.

Operation Snowball

Date: Details of Canada's on-going Operation Snowball first appeared in the press on January 16, 2003. *Subject:* The investigation centers on the more than 2,300 Canadians who allegedly subscribed to child pornography through Landslide Productions, a Fort Worth, Texas-based company.

Background: Operation Snowball can trace its roots to the start of the United States' investigation, Operation Avalanche, in April 1999. When American law enforcement officers analyzed Landslide's business records, they discovered hundreds of thousands of subscriber from all over the world. Canadian investigators went to Dallas in June 2000 to retrieve the names of 2,329 Canadians. Six months later, police held a private briefing to determine a national strategy to investigate the crimes.

Results: By the time of the first press reports, Canadian police had made up to 100 arrests. This represents less than five percent of the names contained on a list of Canadian subscribers. Canadian police say the country is woefully unprepared to handle such large-scale investigations.

Operation Ore

Date: Details of Britain's Operation Ore first began to appear in September 2002 when two police officers who had worked on a high-profile child abduction case were arrested for child pornography offences.

Subject: The investigation centers on the more than 7,200 Britons who allegedly subscribed to child pornography through Landslide Productions, a Fort Worth, Texas-based company.

Background: Operation Ore can trace its roots to the start of the United States' investigation, Operation Avalanche, in April 1999. When American law enforcement officers analyzed Landslide's business records, they discovered hundreds of thousands of subscriber from all over the world. After the Reedys were convicted, U.S. investigators released the names of international subscribers to Interpol. Britain received its list of suspects in September 20013 and began dividing them between 43 regional forces. Police targeted those in positions of authority or proximity to children first.

Results: To date, British police have arrested 1,500 people, including more than 50 police officers, judges, two Members of Parliament, doctors, and legendary rock star Pete Townshend of The Who. News reports also indicate that the FBI is ready to turn over another 8,000 leads as a result of a separate child pornography investigation. Police have determined that nearly one in five of those arrested was also sexually abusing children.

Operation Twins

Date: On July 02, 2002, police in seven countries arrested 50 people suspected of crimes involving child abuse and child pornography.

Subject: The investigation centered on a high-tech pedophile group that called itself the "Shadowz Brotherhood." This group of around 100 individuals employed sophisticated encryption software to avoid detection and maintained a "star" rating system that indicated what level of access certain members had. *Background:* Operation Twins began in early 2001, when Swedish intelligence discovered the club. Netherlands- based Europol coordinated the yearlong investigation. At one point before the early July raids, British investigators flew to Georgia to rescue a young girl who was being raped by her father.

Results: Police forces in several countries have arrested 50 people in connection with the "Shadowz Brotherhood." Investigations into other suspected members of the group are ongoing. Police have also ordered 62 Internet Service Providers to remove material related to the group from more than 240 web sites.

Operation Artus

Date: On March 20, 2002, the U.S. Customs Service announced that eight American and as many as 30 international warrants were served in an international child pornography sting dubbed Operation Artus. *Subject:* The investigation centered on a private Internet group that exchanged and downloaded child pornography on the Internet. The group contained suspects in ten countries around the globe, in addition to the United States.

Background: Operation Artus began in November 2001 when German National police searched the house of a man accused of distributing child pornography. The man cooperated with investigators to identify other members of the group. In all, international law enforcement identified 46 suspects, of which eight were from the United States.

Results: Police forces in eleven countries investigated 46 individuals suspected of trading and producing child pornography. By the time the investigation was announced, twelve suspects had already been arrested5 and twelve computers were seized, along with 600 CDs, 200 videos, and a book on how to seduce children. Three of the suspects have been identified as previously unknown members of the Wonderland child pornography ring that was broken up in 1998.

Operation Candy Box

Date: Operation Candy Box, which started with some intelligence passed on to American authorities, was initiated in the U.S. in May 2001 by DEA and FBI agents in New York City. It eventually became an operation which encompassed 16 cities in the U.S. and three in Canada. March 31, 2004- More than 130 people were arrested today in a two-nation crackdown on a huge drug trafficking ring that manufactured large quantities of Ecstasy and marijuana in Canada and then shipped them to cities around the United States.

Subject: One outcome of this three-year investigation, called Operation Candy Box, was the discovery that Ecstasy trafficking, which had largely been controlled by Russian and Israeli gangs, had now spread to groups with ties to Southeast Asia. The two principal targets of this investigation were Ze Wai Wong, a Chinese national, and Mai Phuong Le, a Vietnamese national.

Background: A second outcome of the operation was the disruption of a sizable money laundering business and the discovery of significant weaknesses in the U.S. financial system that make money laundering possible. The Drug Enforcement Administration, under its Administrator, Karen Tandy, has made financial investigations a priority of the agency.

Results: The large number of arrests was only part of the story of Operation Candy Box. The investigation also resulted in the seizure of large quantities of drugs and organizational assets, including manufacturing labs.

Operation Predator

Date: On July 9th, 2004 The Department of Homeland Security's new Bureau of Immigration and Customs Enforcement (ICE) delivered a pointed message Wednesday to any foreign national who might come to the U.S. planning to sexually exploit American children for pleasure or for profit.

Subject: Operation Predator is a new initiative developed by the Department of Homeland Security's Bureau of Immigration and Customs Enforcement (ICE) to protect children world-wide. As the President has made clear anyone who harms a child will be a priority target of law enforcement in this Administration.

This comprehensive DHS program will identify child predators and remove them from the United States (if subject to deportation). Operation Predator will also work to identify children depicted in child pornography to help rescue them, and to assist in prosecuting the people responsible for making and distributing the pornographic material.

Background: This Homeland Security initiative is being driven by ICE's Cyber Smuggling Center in conjunction with every facet of the ICE organization.

In addition, ICE will partner with other important law enforcement entities such as DHS's own Bureau of Customs and Border Protection, the U.S. Secret Service, the U.S. Postal Inspection Service, the FBI, and other state and local law enforcement agencies. This initiative is also being conducted in partnership with the National Center for Missing and Exploited Children (NCMEC).

Results: Since March 1, ICE has made 88 additional arrests, garnered 56 indictments, obtained 77 convictions, executed 134 seizures of contraband and launched 192 new investigations into suspected sexual predators of children.

Operation Falcon

Date: January 15, 2004 An Indictment has been unsealed, charging a Belarus-based child pornography enterprise and a Florida credit card billing service in a global Internet pornography and money laundering scheme involving thousands of paid memberships to some 50 pornography web sites, U.S.

Attorney Christopher J. Christie, Assistant Attorney General Christopher A. Wray of the DOJ Criminal Division, Michael J. Garcia, Assistant Secretary of U.S. Immigration and Customs Enforcement, Internal Revenue Service Special Agent in Charge Patricia J. Haynes, and U.S. Postal Inspector in Charge Martin D. Phanco announced.

Subject: Regpay Co. Ltd. is a credit card processing company providing billing services to child pornography web sites and also operated its own web sites, which accounted for nearly a quarter of the $3 million in credit card membership fees it generated in the six months ending in August 2003, according to the Indictment and separate criminal complaints unsealed yesterday. Late yesterday, the chief executive officer of Connections USA, of Ft. Lauderdale, Fla., another credit card processing company doing business as "IServe", pleaded guilty in federal court in Newark to a conspiracy to launder money for Regpay and its principals.

Background: Under the recently enacted Protect Act, the violations of Title 18, United States Code, Section 2251 carry a mandatory minimum penalty of 15 years in prison and a maximum penalty of 30 years, and a fine of $500,000 or the gross profits to the defendant or gross loss to any victims of this offence, whichever is greatest. The violations of Title 18, United States Code, Section 2252 carry a mandatory minimum penalty of 5 years in prison and a maximum penalty of 20 years, and a fine of $500,000 or the gross profits to the defendant or gross loss to any victims of this offence, whichever is greatest. The violations of Title 18, United States Code, Section 1956 carry a maximum penalty of 20 years in prison, and a fine of $500,000 or twice the value of the monetary instrument or funds involved in the transportation, transmission or transfer, or of the gross profits to the defendant or gross loss to any victims of this offence, whichever is greatest.

Results: Also today, 15 people were arrested or surrendered in New Jersey as part of the wider investigation targeting individual subscribers of child pornography internet sites connected to the Belarus enterprise. They and another nine suspects already charged were found during court-approved search warrants to have possessed child pornography on their home computers. Initial court appearances will be occurring at 2 p.m. before U.S. Magistrate Judge Madeline Cox Arleo in Newark. Arrests in New Jersey have included a family physician, at least three previously convicted sex offenders, a campus minister, part-time teacher and church youth coordinator, and an 85-year-old retired engineer. Additionally, at least 20 other individuals have been arrested nationwide during the investigation of Belarus-based Regpay Co. LTD, which sold memberships to dozens of child pornography web sites, including at least four of its own.Christie credited Special Agents of the IRS Criminal Investigation section, among others, with aiding in the success of this operation. Christie also thanked Mastercard and VISA for their cooperation in the investigation.

Operation Cyber Sweep

Date: Since Operation Cyber Sweep began on Oct. 1, investigators have uncovered more than 125,000 victims who have incurred losses of more than $100 million. November 20, 2003 - Federal law enforcement agencies today announced the arrests or convictions of 125 people and the return of 70 indictments in a coordinated nationwide enforcement operation designed to crack down on the leading types of online fraud. The ongoing operation, known as Operation Cyber Sweep, was spearheaded by the U.S. Department of Justice in coordination with numerous federal, state, local and foreign law enforcement agencies.

Subject: The case includes: The investigation targeted a variety of online economic crimes that involved schemes including fraud, software piracy and the fencing of stolen goods. One man who admitted to obtaining stolen credit card numbers from various individuals and used the information to purchase more than $80,000 in computer equipment and electronic devices from Kent, Conn.-based Outpost.com.

A 21-year-old man who pleaded guilty to two felony charges of securities fraud and was sentenced to 14 months in prison. Another man who was indicted on charges of hacking into computers across the country to launch spam e-mail attacks criticizing the Philadelphia Phillies baseball team. He was also charged with identity theft for illegally using the e-mail address of reporters at Philadelphia newspapers and a woman who pleaded guilty to conspiracy to possessing unauthorized access devices. The defendant engaged in by sending fake e-mail messages to America Online customers, advising them to update their credit card and personal information on file with AOL to maintain their accounts.

Background: In the first nine months of 2003, the Internet Fraud Complaint Center, a joint project of the FBI and the National White Collar Crime Center, referred 58,392 Internet-related fraud complaints to law enforcement officials. That compared to 48,000 Internet-related fraud complaints referred to law enforcement in all of 2002. As part of the effort, ClearCommerce Corp. has provided information to the FBI about fraudsters that have preyed on some its members' customers as well as the various ways they're perpetrating online fraud, according to Katherine Hutchison, a spokeswoman for ClearCommerce. ClearCommerce is a founding member of the Merchant Risk Council, a group of merchants fighting online fraud.

Results: More than 125 investigations, in which more than 125,000 victims lost more than $100 million. More than 350 targeted subjects, resulting in more than 125 arrests or convictions thus far; and More than 70 indictments to date, and the execution of more than 90 search/seizure warrants. Our last operation of this type, Operation E-Con, ran from January 1 to May 16, 2003. That operation involved more than 90 investigations, the execution of more than 70 search and seizure warrants, and the charging or conviction of more than 130 individuals. Combined, these online investigations have saved consumers and businesses hundreds of millions of dollars.

Operation E-Con

Date: Today, May 19, 2003- the United States Department of Justice announced the successful results of nationwide Cyber Crime investigation called Operation E-Con. The investigation was coordinated at the federal level between the Department of Justice, the FBI, the U.S. Postal Inspection Service, the U.S. Secret Service, and the Federal Trade Commission. A number of state and local law enforcement agencies, along with the National White Collar Crime Center (NW3C), also contributed greatly towards the success of the operation.

Subject: The lawless, Wild-Wild-Web days of the early Internet are coming to a jail door slamming end as the FBI reports the arrests of more than 130 individuals and the seizure of more than $17 million in cases involving internet fraud and abuse. The arrests and seizures resulted from Operation E-Con, an effort coordinated by 43 United States Attorneys Offices nationwide, the Federal Bureau of Investigation (FBI), the Federal Trade Commission (FTC), the Postal Inspection Service, Secret Service, and the Bureau of Immigration and Customs Enforcement alongside a number of other state and local law enforcement agencies both in the United States and a number of countries around the globe. Among the alleged online crimes committed by those arrested were multimillion-dollar swindles, online auction scams, identity theft, business-opportunity frauds, and piracy of software and other copyrighted material.

Background: In a press conference announcing the results of Operation E-Con, Assistant Attorney General Michael Chertoff warned high-tech scammers and schemers to "think again" before trying to hijack the Internet. "The Department of Justice will track them down and prosecute them the same way weve gone after traditional hucksters," Chertoff told reporters. According to FTC statistics, incidents of Internet fraud pose an ever-increasing threat to consumers. Three years ago, 31 per cent of all fraud complaints filed with the FTC involved Internet-based scams. By 2002, that number had grown to 47 per cent. By the end of 2003, the FTC expects Internet-related complaints will account for well over 50 per cent of all fraud complaints filed.

Results: So far, Operation E-Con has initiated more than 90 investigations of complaints filed by 89,000 victims who reported total losses estimated at more than $176 million. In addition, the execution of more than 70 search and seizure warrants has led to the formal charging conviction of more than 130 individuals. During a single week alone, 55 Operation E-Con searches resulted in the arrests of 50 people, the filing of 48 individual indictments and 12 guilty pleas. The Internet Fraud Complaint Center (IFCC) - a joint project of the FBI and the National White-Collar Crime Center - reported in 2002 that it referred more than 48,000 Internet-related fraud complaints to law enforcement.

Operation Pipe Dreams

Date: February 24, 2003 Washington,DC— Attorney General John Ashcroft and Acting DEA Administrator John B. Brown, III today announced the indictment of 50 individuals on charges of trafficking in illegal drug paraphernalia. The charges are the culmination of two nationwide investigations code-named Operation Pipe Dreams and Operation Headhunter and include indictments against national distributors of drug paraphernalia and businesses nationwide. DEA offices in Boise, Idaho; Des Moines, Iowa; Pittsburgh, Pennsylvania; and Dallas and Tyler, Texas were involved in these investigations.

Subject: With the advent of the Internet, the illegal drug paraphernalia industry has exploded," Ashcroft said. "The drug paraphernalia business is now accessible in anyone's home with a computer and Internet access. And in homes across America we know that children and young adults are the fastest growing Internet users. Quite simply, the illegal drug paraphernalia industry has invaded the homes of families across the country without their knowledge.

This illegal billion-dollar industry will no longer be ignored by law enforcement. Today, the Organized Crime Drug Enforcement Task Force, under the leadership of Deputy Attorney General Larry Thompson and Associate Deputy Attorney General Karen Tandy has taken decisive steps to dismantle the illegal drug paraphernalia industry by attacking their physical, financial and Internet infrastructures."

Background: The investigation leading to the indictments in this case was led by the Drug Enforcement Administration and the Organized Crime Drug Enforcement Task Force, along with the U.S. Marshals Service, U.S. Customs Service, U.S. Postal Inspection Service, Immigration and Naturalization Service, Pennsylvania State Police, City of Pittsburgh Police, Allegheny County (Pa.) Sheriff, Stowe Township Police, Chippewa (Pa.) Police Department and the Duquesne (Pa.) Police Department. Named in the indictments announced today are 17 individuals who operated 10 national distribution companies of drug paraphernalia. Ten individuals who sold drug paraphernalia in retail shops in the Western District of Pennsylvania also face charges of conspiracy, offering for sale, and selling drug paraphernalia.

Results: Recently the federal government has implemented "Operation Pipe Dreams" and "Operation Headhunter," which have resulted in the indictment of 55 online paraphernalia distributors.

Operation Web Sweep

Date: May 8, 2002 - New Jersey Attorney General David Samson and Christopher J. Christie, United States Attorney for New Jersey, announced that as of 6:00 A.M. DST today, hundreds of law enforcement officers throughout New Jersey, the United States and across the globe began a coordinated and unprecedented effort to identify nearly 200 individuals alleged to be engaged in the possession, receipt and distribution of child pornography.

Subject: Samson said that the ongoing investigation, dubbed "Operation Web Sweep," was initiated and coordinated by the New Jersey Division of Criminal Justice Computer Analysis and Technology Unit (CATU) - a team of specially-trained state investigators who go on-line to track, investigate, arrest and prosecute individuals who use technology and computer systems to commit criminal acts in New Jersey. Additional law enforcement resources and expertise was provided by the U. S. Attorney's Office for New Jersey, the Federal Bureau of Investigation, the National Center For Missing and Exploited Children and over 65 international, federal, state, county and local law enforcement agencies.

Background: To date, the investigation has identified nearly 200 potential suspects in 16 nations (including the U.S.), 29 states and 24 New Jersey communities. The investigative actions initiated today include the execution of court authorized search and seizure warrants at the residences and/or business locations of those individuals who subscribed to the site and who provided child pornography images. The warrants authorize the seizure of computers, computer systems, Programmes, hardware and software which might contain evidence relating to the possession and/or distribution of child pornography.

Results: With the cooperation of the server operator, investigators said they determined the site contained images of "clearly prepubescent" boys along with advertising describing the site's content and images. It charged a membership fee of $19.99. In February, authorities disabled the site and removed all child pornography, then created a replacement at the same domain address. The Web site, which contained no illegal content, was styled to resemble the original. Previous subscribers were informed the site was rebuilding its collection of images. Through an assigned user name and password, subscribers could upload or transmit pictures to the site.

4

Investigative Journalism

INTRODUCTION

Investigative journalism is a branch of journalism that usually concentrates on a very specific topic and typically requires a lot of work to yield results. It is an in-depth article or series of articles based on research and investigation, usually over a long period of time. The subject often involves legal or controversial issues, such as the mafia, the tobacco industry, now a days political controversies are forming a major part of investigation.

During the 1972 campaign for the White House, when Richard M. Nixon was seeking a second term in office, five persons, acting on orders, broke into the Democratic national offices in the Watergate complex in Washington and planted electronic eavesdropping devices.

Their purpose remains unclear till date. Bob Woodward and Carl Bernstein, reporters with the Washington Post, became curious when a short news item appeared regarding a burglary at the Watergate office of the Democratic Party and began to make Enquiries. Through their investigations, it was discovered that it was not a simple act of burglary but a case of political corruption and manipulation involving the highest office in the land.

Investigative journalism is a distinctive aspect of the work undertaken by the media. Essentially an information-gathering exercise, it looks for facts that are not easy to obtain by simple requests and searches, or those that are actively being concealed, suppressed or distorted. Where such investigative work involves the use of covert methods, it raises issues that tend to further blur the line between law and ethics.

An informed citizenry – the bedrock of a democracy, holding the government accountable through voting and participation – requires investigative journalism. In many cases, the subjects of the reporting wish the matters under scrutiny to remain undisclosed. A healthy democracy cannot sustain itself on asymmetric dissemination of information. The political elite are ever sensitive to news; and news about economic or political wrongdoing can trigger judicial or quasi-judicial scrutiny.

Various methods are employed for their fact-finding – the study of often neglected sources like archives, phone records, address books, tax records and license records; anonymous sources; and going undercover. It is often suggested that anonymous sources are double-edged - on the one hand they may provide especially newsworthy information, such as classified or confidential information about current events, information about a previously unreported scandal, or the perspective of a particular group that may fear retribution for expressing certain opinions in the press; but the downside is that the condition of anonymity may make it difficult or impossible for the reporter to verify the source's statements. By going undercover, the reporter tries to infiltrate a community by posing as somebody friendly to that community.

The Bhagalpur Blindings provide a lesson in the crucial contribution that journalistic research can make in creating public awareness of human rights, more so in a society in which entrenched abuse is likely to be overlooked. Over three years, from 1979 to 1982, policemen blinded 33 criminals in Bhagalpur Jail using acid. Codenamed Operation Gangajal, a report carried by The Indian Express, the incident became a national scandal and 14 policemen were suspended. Of the 14 policemen, 13 were acquitted and reinstated in service. When The Indian Express brought the issue into national focus, the Supreme Court accepted it as a writ petition. In Bhagalpur, many people campaigned for the suspension of the policemen, arguing that such punishment deterred crime more effectively than protracted legal cases. It took a sustained campaign on the rights of prisoners along with the impact of the pictures of the blinded men to touch the public conscience.

A journalist once said, "News is something someone somewhere doesn't want to be published – all the rest is advertisement". That may be considered a far-fetched definition in today's media world which considers advertisements the lifeblood of journalism and a starlet delivering a baby more attractive news than a wave of suicides among exploited farmers.

However, any newsperson worth his/her salt knows that uncovering a hidden story is far more challenging and satisfying than covering a prime minister's foreign tour or hunting for Page 3 gossip in a celebrity party. Regrettably, this breed of committed reporters is fast vanishing, thanks to the bulldozing forces of the market that are converting the media profession in India into an enterprise like any other industry producing consumer goods.

Modern investigative journalism is a discipline, rigorous and demanding. Modern journalism, despite its many aberrations, is considered the most effective monitor and upholder of democratic values. And the powerful instrument to fulfill this obligation is investigative reporting. Democracy involves accountability of elected representatives and civil servants. There are many mechanisms for checks and balances, but these can be abused, circumvented, ignored or made ineffective. Investigative reporting steps into this vacuum to scrutinise and expose the wrong-doings of those in authority which hurt public interest and make them accountable to the people.

We rejoice at the robustness of our democracy. We celebrate the vibrancy of the sparkling free press of India. But we know that the constitutional instruments to make the establishment accountable are weakening or failing. The parallel democratic institutions, which are supposed to nourish these instruments, are not fully evolved.

Leave alone the ordinary citizen, neither our political leaders nor the academicians and intellectuals have fully cultivated a democratic mindset and culture which should involve transparency, professional commitment and accountability. To that extent, our democracy is fragile and — to use an unpleasant word — underdeveloped.

The importance of the "organic" relationship, as described by Walter Lippman, between a healthy democracy and the free press need not be elaborated here. One cannot sustain without the other. Indian media is so intoxicated with its so-called freedom (freest press in the world, one might say) that it fails to understand that it is also equally underdeveloped and fragile, that freedom carries certain grave responsibilities and that as upholder of democratic values and freedom (not just another profit-making industry) it has some specific obligations and duties towards the society. It is so obsessed with itself that it does not realise that it is throwing to winds its credibility, respectability and power by not attending to its basic obligations.

What goes under the name of investigative journalism (with some honourable exceptions) in India, can hardly be taught in a journalism school as classic investigative journalism. The so-called investigative reporting in India in the Bofors case, Fodder scam, Jain Diary Case, Petrol Pumps largesse scandal and even Satyendra Dubey's murder case have been either rankly partisan political exercises or half-hearted attempts to show off the fearlessness of those media units.

Has anyone followed Satyendra Dubey's case to the end? Who are the murderers? Are they arrested? Who leaked Satyendra's confidential letter from the PMO? Is that person booked? And the mafia contractors of the Golden Quadrilateral? Has any paper or channel pursued them?

One remembers the sensation caused by Arun Shourie's series of 'investigative' stories on the then chief minister AR Antulay of Maharashtra in early 1980's. Shourie, then, was acknowledged as the pioneer of modern investigative journalism in India. One also remembers the first sentence of his first story.

Paraphrased in memory, it ran something like this "...look at these political rats; how they run when cornered..." Now, any news editor worth his/her salt would spike that story. It broke all the tenets of not only investigative journalism, but also of ordinary reporting. Shourie's stories were written in a style that was blatantly partisan and spiteful. Moreover, he had not uncovered anything that had not been published earlier, that too, with much more detail, in local newspapers. Antulay's sins of omission and commission, his acceptance of cheques for his public trust in front of TV cameras, was public knowledge in the entire state of Maharashtra. But Shourie, instead of writing scathing comment pieces on the edit page, wrote 'investigative' news stories on the front pages of his newspaper!

POLITICAL EXPEDIENCE

Bofors, St.Kitts, none of the stories were followed thoroughly and with the rigour that investigative journalism demands. The pursuit was half-hearted; the stories tapered off occasionally, but were revived vigorously whenever a political occasion demanded.

No doubt, there have been laudable attempts at exposing some major scandals at local or state levels. But, often, the exposure is made in one sensational burst and then the press loses interest. The story tapers off or is not followed at all. Clearly, the Indian media has not nourished the discipline of classic investigative reporting. The political, economic and social scenario of India is so complex and rotten and the media's credibility, despite its enormous power, is so low that even conscientious bureaucrats do not dare to blow the whistle. One whistle-blower who dared was murdered. And the press has nearly forgotten him.

Basic Requirements of Investigate Journalism

For investigative reporting to flourish, what is required is: an independent and pluralistic media which is fearless, committed to democracy, universal human values, journalists with commitment who can identify problems and have the grit, perseverance, patience and skills to do research and owners and editors professionally non-partisan and without vested interests.

We have a fantastically free press, so free that it does not have a professional self-regulatory mechanism to monitor fundamental ethics of the press. Not even the journalists' associations, which are more interested in begging for more perks from the government and corporate bodies than in the health of their own profession. Many journalists may have the aptitude and skills for investigative journalism. But their owners and editors do not have the will, even if they have the resources, to encourage them. The owners and the editors too have multiple vested interests — in political parties, individual leaders, corporate bodies and so one.

Indian bureaucracy, notorious for its red-tapism, does not easily part with even ordinary information, never mind the information acts on the book, and, as mentioned earlier, those who really want expose the malefascence do not trust the press.

The Ethics of the 'Sting' in Investigating Journalism

Most discussions about ethics in investigative journalism have focused on the methodology. What methods are valid to reveal wrongdoing? Is deception legitimate when the aim is to tell the truth? Is any method justifiable no matter the working conditions and the difficulties in getting information? Can television reporters use hidden cameras to get a story? Can journalists use false identities to gain access to information?

Operation Westend brought some particularly acute questions to the fore. Many argued that a vast gulf existed between 'snaring' or 'tempting' people into accepting 'gifts' or 'bribes'; and the exposure of corruption regarding specific deals. Is it ethical to hold someone responsible for a crime that would not have been committed if the undercover journalist had not encouraged the act? Also, how ethical was it to use prostitutes in order to expose corruption in defence deals? Tarun Tejpal, Tehelka editor, had justified the methods by saying that 'extraordinary circumstances justified the use of extraordinary methods'.

Clearly, there can be no consensus on the ethics of sting operations when the methods and objectives of each operation vary so vastly. In fact, the legal implications of reporters' actions are, by far, more clear-cut than the ethical issues involved. Ethics, dealing with distinguishing right and wrong, uses philosophical principles to justify a particular course of action. Any action can be judged ethical, depending on what framework is used to justify it, and what values are prioritized. Fortunately for this particular dilemma, the media's cherished values are not a matter of much debate. What journalists and editors need to determine is who will benefit as a result of the reporting. If journalism is committed to democratic accountability, then the question that needs to be asked is whether the public benefits as a result of specific investigative reports. Does the press fulfill its social responsibility in revealing wrongdoing? Whose interests are being affected? Whose rights are being invaded? Is the issue at stake a matter of legitimate public interest?

One can debate endlessly about the ethics of these issues, and not be any closer to resolution, except where motive is clear. Most people would consider the sting operation on Dilip Singh Judeo as unethical because it was motivated – not by concerns of informing the citizens, but for political one-upmanship. The 'reverse sting' on Ajit Jogi and his son falls in the same category.

At best, a case by case analysis may be undertaken to distinguish ethically right journalistic method from wrong. However, if one were to move beyond ethics and enter the realm of law, the determination of what is legally right method is easier. Such an enquiry is also apt in the context of the much-anticipated Broadcasting Bill. Undoubtedly, the starting point for any such discussion has to be the freedom of the press.

In such circumstances, what does a restless committed journalist do? He takes a hidden camera with him and broadcasts countrywide bulletins of responsible people accepting bribes. If documents, receipts, accounts, papers or files are not forthcoming as proof, here's how the journalist furnishes the proof. Live on screen. Tarun Tejpal and Tehelka's sting operation and subsequent imitations by others have raised a hornet's nest questioning the ethical propriety of this kind of journalism. A positive outcome indeed.

Media Credibility

The press is losing credibility because of its blatant partisanship and rank commercialism. So take the camera and expose. Never mind, it is one-time exposure of a part. But the proof is there, clearly visible on the screen to make an impact on the minds of the people. This will at least shake the people and those who are concerned out of their slumber.

No, this is not investigative journalism. But it is the sting. An occasional sting operation made with professional commitment may serve the cause for the time being. But that is no alternative to investigative journalism. To build its credibility and ensure its freedom under democracy, the media in India will have to turn to serious investigative reporting.

The Tehelka style of investigative journalism has brought about a change in the way we look at news, amidst new notions of editorial freedom. Stirring stuff like the kind shown in 'stings' has a fair amount of shock value.

There is no denying the fact that a sting operation is by far the most effective way of exposing the truth. With a society and a system of governance that defies transparency, the doubting public demands credible proof. Being 'caught in an act' on camera leaves little scope for evasive answers by those who shamelessly manipulate the system for vested interests.

Public figures are often reminded that they have nothing to hide from the public, which has a right to know everything. The stinging truth however, is the easy conscience with which corruption is tolerated and allowed to plague the political system.

Operation West End

Newsgathering acquired a new meaning with Tehelka's 'Operation West End', which left the common man with deep revulsion for the political system and contempt for those in the defence establishment who are willing to trade national interest for vested interests.

It is not just governance but also other systems of everyday life, which if left unchecked spell disaster for the common man. Also the argument that it is virtually impossible to discover the real state of affairs through normal ways of investigation deserves a fair hearing.

The most explosive sting by Tehelka in recent times is the one, exposing the twists behind the Best Bakery case.Zaheera Sheikh, who has become a symbol of thc Gujarat carnage has been continuously changing her testimony in the case. The Tehelka tapes allege that Zaheera was paid Rs 18 lakh by a BJP MLA. The startling revelation has led the judiciary to now examine the possibility of a dubious deal. But whether the 'sting' is a legitimate weapon of the new media is an issue worth debating upon. Investigative journalism is synonymous with controversies. While it does reflect upon a vigilant media, it also allows the survival of a sensationalist press, which confuses cheap thrills with journalism.

To assume that a mere expose' can keep the audience hooked is the media's fatal error. Public opinion will eventually expose dumbed down journalism to sharp criticism.

Such exposures can thus stand the test of time only on account of credibility and veritable proof of the alleged facts. There are also occupational hazards to be battled when engaged in a sting operation. In the case of Tehelka, the associates were made to pay a heavy price, virtually grounding the organization operationally and financially.

But the fact remains that there is only so much that the press can endeavour to do. It cannot punish the guilty nor can it command accountability from those occupying positions of power.

Launched in 2000, Tehelka began as an on line news-views portal, unaligned of any of India's established media groups. Since then, it has become the sub continent's fastest growing independent weekly newspaper. Published by Tarun Tejpal, Tehelka's 2001 sting Operation West End captured several members of the then ruling party BJP - Bangaru Laxman accepting bribes to approve defence contracts. George Fernandes resigned after the tapes were made public. In the aftermath of these exposes,

Tehelka drew the ire of the government and was at the receiving end of a destructive un-constitutional assault eventually forcing its closure. After a widespread public appeal to loyal readers, Tehelka re-launched in 2004 as a weekly newspaper, committed to free, fair and fearless journalism. Tehelka's reputation for ground- breaking investigations, tenacious public interest journalism, exposes of corruption, fiery reportage and fine writing, has earned it a strong national following and widespread international acclaim. Tehelka's in depth investigative stories on witness bribery in the Best Bakery Fire case, corruption over airline pilots' qualifications and child sex scandals in resort areas are among the many that have contributed to changing the fundamental nature of Indian media.

EVIDENCE FOR DETERRENCE EFFECTS

Returning to our central theme, in general terms it is a traditional expectation of sentencing practices that they should deter individuals from committing crimes. Outside the realm of penology and legal philosophy, this is also an expectation of the citizenry-at-large. Much has been written about whether the public believe that the courts are too lenient or too punitive, and it is widely thought that the news media play a pivotal role in shaping perceptions of this, for example by giving more publicity to sentences that are thought too lenient than those that seem unduly harsh.

These influences notwithstanding, more soberly conducted opinion surveys do not show the public to be as punitive or as vengeful as is often alleged; on the contrary, they are often firmly in favour of rehabilitation. It is nevertheless commonly assumed that there is a widespread, fundamental belief that crime and punishment belong together; that the latter brings home to the individual what he or she has done and thereby engenders appropriate change. If that exepectation is indeed widespread, how well-founded is it? There are seven types of evidence that are potentially relevant to the question of whether deterrence measures in criminal justice have an impact on recidivism. In what follows as suggested, examine each of them in turn.

They are:

- The effects of sentencing, as judged from criminal statistics;
- Relationships between imprisonment and crime rates;
- Effects of enhanced punishments;
- Meta-analytic reviews of outcome studies;
- Controlled trials of deterrence measures;
- Self-report surveys;
- Research on the death penalty.

THE IMPACT OF SENTENCING

A first source of doubt regarding the impact of punishment arises from official statistics of offender re-convictions. In the United Kingdom, the effectiveness of sentencing has traditionally been assessed by employing large-scale criminological data on the sequelae of different court 'disposals'. During the 1990s, this exercise achieved a higher level of sophistication by applying the tools of statistical prediction. It is now fairly well established in criminology that rates of criminal recidivism among groups of offenders can be predicted with a reasonable degree of accuracy on the basis of a combination of certain key variables.

They include gender, age at first offence, current age, number of previous convictions, number of previous incarcerations and type of current offence. This process of prediction is limited to aggregate data and cannot be extrapolated for use at the individual level. In the United Kingdom, the Home Office, through its Research Development and Statistics Directorate, developed an instrument of this kind, the Offender Group Reconviction Scale. The original version of this scale was employed for the prediction of discretionary conditional release and also to enable comparisons to be made between different types of court sentences. A second, refined version has since been developed, which allows prediction over a wider age range and for specific offence types, though only in very broad categorical terms. The advent of this measure thus allowed comparisons to be made between custodial and community penalties, respectively. One longstanding problem is that simple comparisons between raw rates of re-conviction following different types of court disposals are not valid or meaningful, due to prior differences in risk levels between groups. For example, if people sent to prison are regularly found to be poorer risks for re-conviction, it is hardly surprising if larger numbers of them are later re-convicted than those subject to other disposals.

Thus 'any attempt to compare the effectiveness of sentences through the simple comparison of reconviction rates is likely to produce very misleading results'. These difficulties were resolved by Lloyd and his associates, who reported on a carefully controlled comparison of the four main types of sentence used by the criminal courts for more serious offences. In England and Wales, when this study was done, these were imprisonment, community service orders, probation orders and probation with additional requirements. The *actual* rates of re-conviction over two years following release from prison or discharge from community penalties were compared with the *predicted* rates: those which would be expected on the basis of offenders' previous criminal histories.

Lloyd and his colleagues found some interesting differences between the groups given different types of sentence. But the real import of their data lies in the side-by-side comparison of predicted with actual rates within each sentence type. In no case was this difference larger than 3 per cent. 'When account was taken of background variables and pseudoreconvictions, most of the differences between the disposal groups disappeared'. In other words, the rate at which individuals re-offended was very close to the rate at which they were probably going to re-offend, regardless of the type of sentence imposed upon them. The sentence of the court had no clear differential impact on the outcome. It could be argued that it is a virtual irrelevance. Walker and Padfield expressed similar dismay at the result: 'the differences between expected and actual percentages are disappointingly small'. When similar analyses are done across successive years, fairly consistent patterns emerge.

This powerfully bears out the trend originally found by Lloyd and his colleagues. Summarizing these trends, Kershaw concluded that 'After taking into account all relevant factors, there is no discernible difference between the effect of immediate custody and community penalties on reconviction rates'. We might reasonably have expected that some suppressant effect of the more punitive sanction, imprisonment, would emerge from these figures, especially given almost unanimous acceptance of a necessary and desirable link between 'crime and punishment'. On the contrary, the findings imply that the sentencing system has a virtually negligible impact on criminal behaviour, certainly as far as the perspective of utilitarian justice is concerned.

IMPRISONMENT AND CRIME RATES

At any one time, only a fraction of those committing crimes in society is apprehended and punished. Yet the public visibility of this process is held to act as a general deterrent for the remainder of the population, including those likely to offend. If general deterrence operates to an extent that justifies its central position in society, there should be some association between the activity of the criminal justice system and the total amount of crime. The broadest, though possibly weakest, kind of evidence pertaining to this comes from studies of the relationship between the numbers of persons incarcerated in a society and its general rate of recorded crime.

For example, where opportunities have been available to monitor recorded levels of crime across periods when rates of incarceration were steadily changing, no clear relationship materializes, even allowing for possible time-lags. This emerges particularly in studies of, and projections based upon, the increased use of incarceration in parts of the United States. Reviewing the evidence bearing on this point up to 1997, Nagin described the conceptual and other difficulties posed in researching this question, but could find no study that can be taken seriously as demonstrating a deterrence effect of imprisonment on general rates of crime. Furthermore, recent research has failed to establish any relationship, in a direction that would be predicted by deterrence theory, between lengths of prison sentences and rates of recidivism. Gendreau *et al.* have systematically reviewed this area in a report for the Solicitor General of Canada.

The research group reviewed 23 studies yielding 222 comparisons of groups of offenders who spent longer versus shorter periods in prison. The groups were similar on a series of five risk factors. Contrary to what would be predicted by deterrence theory, offenders who served longer sentences had slight increases in recidivism of between 2 and 3 per cent; there was a small positive correlation between sentence length and subsequent rates of re-conviction. Incidentally, even Robert Martinson, in his widely cited and highly influential paper which gave 'very little reason to hope that we have in fact found a sure way of reducing recidivism through rehabilitation', also concluded that there was no evidence of an association between recidivism and sentence length. The foregoing review integrated information from many sources and was conducted on a mammoth scale. But smaller-scale research, for example on the comparative impact of fines and short jail sentences on rates of drinking and driving, have not unequivocally shown that the deterrence effect of the latter is necessarily any more powerful than that of the former.

Another frequently heard claim regarding deterrence is that it is more likely to work with 'white-collar' crimes, committed by mainly middle- or upper-class offenders. Weisburd and Chayet followed the criminal careers of 742 offenders convicted of such crimes. The sample, which was divided into those who received and those who did not receive prison sentences, was followed up for a total of more than ten years. There was no observable effect that could be attributed to specific deterrence.

ENHANCED PUNISHMENTS

During the 1970s, the proclaimed failure of education, training or psychotherapy to have their intended impact on criminal recidivism has been associated with a shift towards a more punitive stance in a number of legislatures. Particularly in the United States, from that decade onwards there was a progressive move towards harsher punishments and 'turning up the heat' on offenders. At an institutional level, such sentences included the use of boot camps and shock incarceration. In the community, intensive supervision, electronic surveillance, random drug testing, curfews and various permutations of each were tried and tested. Primary studies and evaluations of 'enhanced' and intermediate punishment therefore flourished during the 1980s and 1990s as the use of these types of sanction became more widespread. This created opportunities for controlled trials, in which more severe punishments were compared with standard punishments or 'business as usual' within the criminal justice system.

Participants in the stricter forms of treatment were sometimes allocated randomly, on other occasions selected on a voluntary basis. Analysis of outcomes in such studies is made difficult by the fact that although the harshness of punishment was intensified, in many cases additional elements of education, counselling and other types of rehabilitative activity were also introduced. Petersilia and Turner reported an evaluation of intensive supervision in probation and parole conducted in 14 American states. A sample of nearly 2,000 individuals across numerous sites was allocated randomly to experimental and control groups.

Follow-up evaluation found no impact of the more intensive and restrictive supervision, which in some agencies included close surveillance, electronic monitoring, random drug testing and other innovations, on recidivism. The only positive result along these lines to emerge was an association between clients' participation in drugs and alcohol counselling and subsequent reductions in re-offending rates of the order of 10–20 per cent. However, the possibility that this was due to a selection effect could not be eliminated. Nevertheless, Petersilia was led to conclude that 'The empirical evidence regarding intermediate sanctions is decisive: Without a rehabilitation component, reductions in recidivism are elusive'. Examining this and other evaluations of intermediate punishment, Gendreau *et al.* concluded that none of the hoped-for goals of reduced prison numbers, reduced costs or reduced recidivism were delivered by these programmes. A more recent evaluation of the effectiveness of electronic monitoring in Canada, taking account of participants' risk levels, also drew negative conclusions.

Bonta and his colleagues judged that the effectiveness of electronic monitoring 'as a true alternative to incarceration and reducing recidivism has yet to be demonstrated... If one is interested in reducing recidivism, then offender treatment, rather than sanctions, is the most promising approach'. For institutionally based sanctions, a similar large-scale evaluation was undertaken of the impact of shock incarceration or 'boot camps' for the US National Institute of Justice. Here, boot camp inmates were compared with other prisoners, prison parolees or probationers at a number of sites in eight states. Again, however, the results were not supportive of deterrence theory. The impact on recidivism was concluded to be 'at best, negligible... based on the totality of the evidence, boot camp programmes did not reduce offender recidivism'. This overall finding is very close to that obtained from evaluation of detention centres designed to deliver a 'short, sharp shock' in the United Kingdom in the early 1980s.

Evaluation of this initiative concluded that 'the introduction of the pilot project regimes had no discernible effect on the rate at which trainees were reconvicted. A number of ways in which effects on reconviction might have been masked were considered and discounted'. In a further test of deterrence effects, MacKenzie *et al.* have recently reported a review of 29 evaluative studies of correctional boot camps. The authors found that there was 'an almost equal odds of recidivating between the boot camps and comparison groups'. On the basis of their review, they therefore concluded that, 'in our overall metaanalysis of recidivism, we found no differences between the boot camp and comparison samples... the results of this systematic review and metaanalysis will be disappointing for many people... boot camps by themselves have little to offer as far as moving offenders away from criminal activities' is concerned. In both institutional and community settings, then, while the innovations being researched here were ones designed to impose stiffer penalties on offenders, no useful effect of this escalation in toughness was found. Where positive outcomes were observed, they were usually associated with an investment of time and effort in rehabilitative activities.

META-ANALYTIC REVIEWS

The findings from large-scale reviews of 'offender treatment' were surveyed. Some of the meta-analytic reviews described there included studies of criminal sanctions. We noted that the estimated 'grand mean' across all reviews, of the order of an approximately 10 per cent reduction in recidivism levels, was probably diminished to some extent by the incorporation of studies that reported predominantly zero or negative effects. The average effect size was, in other words, dragged down by these particular results. Reviews that have examined criminal sanctions separately within a wide range of approaches to intervention have typically found deterrence-based programmes to have zero or negative effect sizes.

One meta-analysis specifically designed to dissect the relevant literature on community-based intermediate punishments yielded negative conclusions regarding the impact of the initially much-lauded enhanced punishments. In their reviews of 135 outcome studies of surveillance, 'smart sentencing' and other measures of this type, Gendreau *et al.* found a mean effect size just below zero.

DETERRENCE ON TRIAL

The studies just discussed involved evaluation of changes in sentencing practices in criminal justice services where many other factors that were operating could not be easily or satisfactorily controlled. A possibly more robust approach is to examine deterrence effects when these have been directly manipulated, though published reviews of this field are hard to find. Sherman has reviewed studies in which the effect of deterrence practices has been evaluated using randomized designs. The use of randomization in this context clearly raises ethical issues. The focus here is upon those circumstances where it has been feasible to evaluate the use of criminal sanctioning because offenders were randomly allocated to experimental and control conditions.

Of 21 studies included in Sherman's review, 14 found no differences in recidivism between experimental and control samples. In five studies, increased severity of penalties resulted in increased recidivism. Only two studies showed any impact of punitive sanctions. In one, this effect was observed only in some sub-samples and not across the experimental group as a whole. The remaining report, by Sherman *et al.*, focused on the effect of arrest and brief incarceration on perpetrators of domestic violence in Minneapolis. However, subsequent extension and replications of this study at other sites obtained mixed results, so much so that the question of whether arrest should be mandatory for spousal abuse has been re-opened by other authors. For example, in another study responding to 1,200 cases of domestic violence in Milwaukee, criminal justice intervention in some cases precipitated further harm. Short-term arrest had an initial deterrence effect, but had a criminogenic effect in the following 12 months; full arrest with many more hours detention made no difference either way. On that basis, alongside other factors, it has been argued that the nature of legal decisions made should be tailored to the circumstances and demands of each individual case.

The most comprehensive attempt to catalogue the potential impact of punitive sanctions as specific deterrents was undertaken by Weisburd *et al.*, who compiled a 'Registry' of randomized experiments. The Registry provides details of a series of 68 studies published between 1951 and 1984 involving random allocation to different levels of criminal justice sanction. The definition of the word 'sanction' was very broad, and encompassed both heightened levels of strictness in terms of prison, probation or parole, as well as other experiments in which rehabilitative activities were included in traditional sanctioning procedures. Of the 68 studies available, 44 reported no differences between experimental and control samples. Only two showed apparently better outcomes for interventions that could be construed as more punitive. In neither case did the authors report statistical significance and the conclusions they drew were based solely on apparent trends in the data.

In the remaining 22 experiments, rates of recidivism, parole violation or other similar outcomes favoured experimental over control groups. However, in all the latter studies, the increased 'sanction' consisted of provision of individual counselling, participation in group treatments such as social skills training, or other forms of intervention that entailed sanctioning only in the respect that participation was non-voluntary. Though defined as sanctions for the purpose of the Registry, and involving some coercion in terms of limits on an offender's freedom, these interventions contained few if any elements that would ordinarily be considered directly punitive. In another context, that of work with substance-abusing offenders, coercion into treatment has been shown to have effects equivalent to voluntary participation, and the provision of services within such a framework may not be intrinsically punishing.

Another type of research though in a similar vein has more direct bearing on the question of general than of specific deterrence. Sherman reviewed a series of 18 studies of the impact of police 'crackdowns' on rates of crime. Crackdowns were defined as combinations of three tactical elements: increased police presence, greater use of sanctions and threats of increased sanction certainty, conveyed through the media. That is, the police announced to the public that they would be working more intensively on certain types of crime, that people were more likely to be arrested and would be more severely dealt with by the courts. In six of the studies, crackdowns were short-term and most of these experiments focused on illegal parking, drink-driving and other 'distinctly middle-class' vehicle-related offences. In five studies in this group, residual effects of deterrence were observed; in other words, the effect continued after police 'back-off' or lifting of the crackdown. The remaining experiments were longer-term, and focused on offences such as drug sales and trafficking. However, only two of the 12 studies in this category obtained residual effects. In another two studies, there was disturbing evidence that other kinds of crimes had increased.

SELF-REPORT SURVEYS

This category of evidence could be regarded as relatively weaker than some of the others discussed here, since it involves reliance on the verbal reports of people already convicted of crimes, some of whom may be dishonest, and indeed have convictions for offences involving dishonesty. However, there is no reason to believe that participants have anything to gain or lose just as to how they respond to questioners in research of this kind. Some investigators have focused on the reactions of individuals arrested and then punished for crimes, inviting them to comment on the extent to which their experience of the process might be likely to deter them from future offending. Other researchers have focused more closely on patterns in individuals' thinking in the period immediately before committing offences.

Some of this work has been based on interviews with offenders during which they have been asked to describe their offending behaviour in some detail. The types of offences committed by those taking part in these research studies varied considerably in seriousness, from shop theft and vehicle-taking to drug-trafficking and armed robbery. As suggested, return to these studies a little later in the stage. In a series of surveys, Klemke and his colleagues collected self-report information on shoplifting by teenagers. Young people were interviewed at two points several months apart. Researchers found little evidence of deterrence in preventing repeated acts of shoplifting by this age group. While only a small proportion of those arrested was apprehended a second time, a far higher proportion admitted to further acts of theft. Thus the experience of arrest appeared to have had little impact on their behaviour. Conversely, although we cannot rule out the possibility that another proportion was deterred, other factors such as increasing age and maturation could also have explained their desistance.

The impact of arrest has also been investigated in some of the longitudinal studies. In the Denver Youth Survey, Huizinga *et al.* collected data on the relationship between ongoing involvement in offending and experience of being arrested by the police. First, they found that the majority of offenders whatever their level of seriousness were not arrested at all. Second, for those who were, their delinquent behaviour did 'not appear to be well described by their arrests'. That is, the more serious offenders were rarely apprehended for their gravest offences: they were more likely to be detained for a fairly minor offence. Third, the majority of cases showed either no change in behaviour or an actual worsening of behaviour following arrest; and 'in only 8 per cent of the cases was the serious offending rate of the arrested juvenile less than the matched control... being arrested is not a very strong deterrent against future delinquent behaviour'.

THE DEATH PENALTY

Research on the most extreme of sanctions, capital punishment or 'judicial execution', self-evidently has no bearing on the question of specific deterrence, but may provide evidence on the effectiveness of this extreme measure as a general deterrent. The presumption that it is a deterrent is certainly invoked as a rationale for imposing it. Among the 71 countries that still retained its use up to the year 2001, 'the most common political justification is the belief that it has a unique general deterrent capacity to save further innocent lives or reduce significantly other capital offences'. Of course, the issue of the death penalty is a highly emotive one and attitudes towards it are primarily influenced by a range of ethical and political beliefs, rather than by evidence bearing on its outcomes. But as this evidence has nevertheless been collected and is relevant to the present discussion, it is included in this survey. Such research as is available has failed to find that the availability of the death penalty as a sentencing option has any clear suppressant effect on rates of the most serious crimes, such as homicide, including the murder of police or prison officers. Some researchers claimed to have found deterrence effects in the United States for the period 1935–1969, to the extent of calculating a ratio of executions to numbers of lives saved. But other researchers who have analysed the same data or attempted to replicate the analyses with other data sets have ultimately dismissed such claims.

In a global survey conducted on behalf of the United Nations, Hood compared different countries allotted to discrete categories just as to their pattern of usage of capital punishment over a 40-year period. Some countries or states were *retentionist*–they had retained the use of the sentence throughout that period. Others were *abolitionist*–they either had not used it throughout the same period, or had at some point halted its use. Others, most notably all states of the USA, had a period when execution was not used, but following which its use was reinstated. Analysis of the data for rates of serious crimes such as homicide under these different jurisdictions yielded no evidence that capital punishment was associated with reductions in their frequency. The assumed effects of capital punishment in suppressing rates of homicide or violent crime have proved similarly elusive even when side-by-side comparisons are made between roughly equivalent localities differing only in their usage of it.

They also fail to appear in other circumstances predicted by general deterrence theory, for example where effects might be amplified through the publicity given to executions. Even in the state of Texas, 'by far the most active death penalty state' analysis of crime statistics for the period 1984–1997 has found no relationship between the execution rate and the murder rate. One other kind of evidence might seem only tangentially relevant to the points at issue here but is nevertheless worth considering. Does the potential threat of sudden death at the hands of a fellow citizen dissuade individuals from committing crimes? McDowall *et al.* tested the widely held view that possession of lethal weapons acts as a general deterrent to crime. Such an argument is often forwarded in defence of widespread gun ownership in the United States. McDowall *et al.* analysed five sets of crime data covering periods before and after significant changes in levels of gun ownership.

In two of these cases, following an apparent upsurge in serious crimes, police forces offered training to citizens in the use of firearms, and levels of ownership increased. In one instance in the town of Kennesaw, Georgia, a law was passed making it a legal requirement for every household to maintain a firearm. In two other cases, new laws were passed in local communities prohibiting the sale or ownership of handguns. Extended time-series analysis of rates of the target offences showed no impact of these changes. This was despite widely publicized claims that guns made a difference; based, as McDowall and his colleagues showed, on misleading analyses of data over short and unrepresentative periods of time.

INVESTIGATING SYNERGY EFFECTS

Synergy, a marketing term, refers to the benefits derived from selling two or more compatible products simultaneously (*e.g.*, a blockbuster movie, the book on which the movie is based, the movie soundtrack, and action figures derived from the story), as well as the harnessing of relations between two or more elements of a media production and distribution process, including the repurposing of content created for one medium for distribution by another. In the context of this study, synergy refers to the possibility of two contiguous media behaviours-on air and online news consumption-having a greater impact on perceptions of media credibility than exposure to either medium by itself. Although telewebbing emerged as a mass phenomenon in the late 1990s, the effects of cross-platform media use remain underexamined and little understood.

In addition to examining synergy effects in a real-time setting, this study adds to a small but growing body of research that has applied the experimental method to questions of television news credibility. The preponderance of studies on media credibility has been survey based, and most channel comparison studies have examined the credibility of television news in relation to newspapers. The survey approach to studying credibility allows researchers to track broad trends in public opinion about the media but the results of such surveys are limited in their ability to explain cause-and-effect relationships.

Survey research has established that use of a particular media channel correlates with high credibility ratings for that channel. But does media use lead to enhanced perceptions of credibility, or do people tend to use media they already consider credible? Survey studies, because they lack control and generally do not address the issue of temporal sequence, cannot effectively answer this question.

Surveys, moreover, are hampered in a data-gathering sense because they rely on reflections of past media use, an estimation process prone to distortion and social desirability biasing. Placing participants directly in different media settings (*e.g.*, telewebbing, television only, or Net news only) offers the opportunity to assess perceptions of credibility as they occur rather than relying on reflections of past media behaviour. The experimental situation also enables the researcher to control the sequence of presumed effects.

The documentation of synergy effects on perceptions of credibility could have important implications for the broadcast news industry, and network news organizations in particular, as audiences tend to pay more attention to and become more reliant on media they consider credible.

Perceptions of credibility have also been found to influence the processing of issue importance. When media are perceived as credible, acceptance of information veracity increases and agenda-setting effects-accepting issues given prominent media coverage as valid and important-are likely to occur. In an era of convergent media and twenty-four-hour news channels, when the future of the nightly newscast itself is being called into question, the networks are challenged with maximizing their believability, accuracy, fairness, and informational completeness across delivery platforms.

Media Credibility and Age Cohort. Studies of media credibility have consistently found an association between age and education with credibility assessments. In general, older, more educated audiences tend to be the most critical of media, while younger, less educated news consumers are more likely to be accepting of news coverage and to evaluate the media as credible. The youngest adults, 18-24 years old, are the most likely to rate news media highly believable. And it is network news, more than most other forms of media, that has been likely to elicit these demographic response patterns. Sophistication, life experience, and knowledge of the press-a type of news literacy-combine to make more seasoned audiences skeptical of the nightly news. Although displacement theory would suggest that a traditional medium such as television, besieged by new challengers and new communication technologies, would directly lose its audience to popular forms of new media, some studies conclude that the Internet supplements rather than replaces television viewing.

These findings are consistent with the idea that online sources provide what industry players like ABC-TV refer to as an "enhanced television" experience. Robinson and colleagues even found a positive relationship between computer use and television viewing.

Other researchers have argued, however, that television viewing is negatively affected by computer or Internet use. None of the aforementioned studies, however, explicitly considers telewebbing as a media behaviour that might influence the interpretation of these findings. In a time of rapid technological change and format experimentation, credibility remains central to understanding public perceptions of network news as well as encouraging acceptance of the Internet as a trusted source of news and information.

Documenting the potential contributions of online news operations to perceptions of network news credibility through experimental investigation may enhance industry and scholarly awareness of the nonmonetary value of the networks' online news operations beyond bottom-line issues of profitability and audience share. If such effects are found, this will suggest to the industry that investments in online news operations may be justified not on the basis of economic considerations alone but on the grounds of enhancing public perceptions of network news through multiple media channels.

Research Questions

To assess whether cross-platform media use of online and on-air news has a greater impact on audience perceptions of media credibility than exposure to either medium in isolation, this study of synergy effects is guided by the following research questions:

- *RQ*1: Do different audiences for news, specifically younger and older age groups, rate the credibility of on-air and online news differently?
- *RQ*2: What influence does media channel have on audience evaluations of media credibility?
- *RQ*3: Is there a combined, or synergy, effect between on-air and online news sources that enhances perceptions of credibility over use of either medium in isolation?
- *RQ*4: Is there an interaction between media channel and age group resulting in different synergy effects for younger and older news audiences?

Method

Operationally, this study took the form of a 4 (media channel) × 2 (age group) between subjects, factorial experiment. The first factor, media channel, had four levels: television news, Net news, both TV and Net news, and no exposure (control group). The second factor, age group, had two levels: undergraduate students and older adults.

Student subjects consisted of 84 undergraduates enrolled in communications courses at a large Midwestern university and ranged in age from 18 to 25 (M = 20). Adult subjects consisted of 83 members of a local community group and ranged in age from 26 to 80 (M = 49).

A total of 167 subjects participated in the study, populating each cell of the design with a minimum of 20 subjects. Student subjects received extra credit for their participation, while adults received a small monetary incentive. Slightly more than half of the study participants (52.1 per cent, n = 87) were female, while just under half (47.9 per cent, n = 80) were male.

Procedure. The study was conducted in the weeks immediately following the September 11 terrorist attacks. The news focus on terrorism remained prominent for the duration of the study, although the early emphasis on domestic security issues gradually gave way to a focus on the war in Afghanistan. Within each age group, subjects were randomly assigned to one of the four media channel conditions. To guard against primacy and recency effects, each condition had four randomized orders. At the beginning of the experiment, subjects completed a questionnaire asking about their media use, political attitudes and knowledge, and demographic information. Subjects assigned to the television condition were shown four, randomly ordered network news stories (from ABC, NBC, CBS, or MSNBC) about the World Trade Centre attacks and were asked to rate their responses.

The stories were recorded off-air from network news coverage beginning on the day of the attacks and for several days thereafter. Each story consisted of an anchor lead-in, followed by a news report about the attacks or Bush administration response to the crisis and a direct presidential sound bite in reaction to the unfolding events. Altogether, there were eight unique stories in the stimulus material, two from each network. The average length of each story was just over 2 minutes (M = 125.75 seconds). After viewing each story, subjects completed a series of evaluative measures and open-ended questions designed to elicit any specific impressions prompted by the stories.

Subjects assigned to the Net news condition were instructed to visit two unaltered network news sites (among ABC, CBS, NBC with Tom Brokaw, or MSNBC with Brian Williams) and perform either an interactive or reading task for approximately 5 minutes. The specific pages visited featured news stories, photos, graphics, and interactive features about the terrorist attacks, making the online content comparable with the broadcast news stories. The decision to not replicate the exact verbal content of the broadcast news stories and leave the Net news sites unaltered was made with the intention to maximize ecological validity and to deliberately test the effect of medium as opposed to modality. Consistent with previous channel studies, "news items were selected so that the same substantive information was included in each medium's version of the story, but the journalistic presentation varied as it actually does by medium."

After visiting each site, subjects completed a series of evaluative measures designed to elicit credibility assessments of the individual sites.

Subjects assigned to the cross-platform (synergy) condition, in randomly alternating order, first viewed four of the broadcast news stories and then visited two Net news sites. To guard against order effects, some subjects first viewed the broadcast news stories and then went online, while others went online first then viewed the stories. Again, after viewing each story and visiting each site, subjects completed a series of evaluative measures and open-ended questions.

At the end of each media condition, subjects completed a series of overall credibility measures separately for television and Net news. Media credibility, the focal concept of this study, was operationalized as the degree to which news consumers judge network newscasts and Web sites to be believable, fair, accurate, informative, and in-depth. Each item comprising the credibility construct was measured using a 7-point scale (1 = not at all; 7 = very). To determine the suitability of using the five items together in combined credibility indexes, a reliability analysis was performed for both TV news and Net news credibility. For both indexes the Cronbach's alpha coefficient was.89.

Subjects assigned to the control condition were not exposed to any media, but simply completed the experimental questionnaire and overall media credibility measures.

A between-subjects analysis of variance (ANOVA) was performed for the media channel and age group factors on the combined credibility indexes. For the age group factor, there were significant main effects for both the TV news index, eta-squared =.26, as well as the Net news index, eta-squared =.06. To reveal the contribution of individual items, a series of t-tests were run for each index separately. Across all items, the younger age group rated TV news credibility significantly higher than the older age group, reserving its highest ratings for informativeness and believability. Interestingly, both age groups rated TV news lowest on its depth. On the bottom row of the table the combined index scores show that younger audience members evaluated TV news to be significantly more credible overall than older audience members.

Students were much more inclined to rate online news as informative and in-depth than adult subjects. As with TV news, adults also considered Net news significantly less fair than students. Again on the bottom row of the table the combined index scores show that younger audience members evaluated Net news to be significantly more credible overall than older audience members.

Although students' credibility ratings are higher overall than adults, within age groups adults rate Net news to be significantly more credible than TV news. Within the younger age group, the reverse occurs: students rate TV news more credible overall than Net news. Another difference between the TV and Net news credibility ratings is revealed by the fewer degrees of freedom in the t-tests for the older age group when compared to the younger group (76 versus 83). Several of the older adult participants said they had no online experience and declined to even rate Net news credibility for this reason.

In response to the first research question, then, different audiences do seem to rate the credibility of on-air and online news differently. Younger audience members are much more inclined to assign both news channels higher credibility ratings than older audience members. But within groups, adults consider Net news to be more fair, informative, and in-depth, and therefore more credible overall, than TV news. Students, on the other hand, give TV news higher marks than Net news on every item except in-depth and regard television as the more credible news source. Care should be taken not to read too much into these results, since these age-group differences do not take into account the unique effect of channel exposure, which is analysed next.

The second research question asked what influence media channel had on audience evaluations of credibility. Analysis of variance produced a significant main effect for media channel on the TV news credibility index. Across all subjects, exposure to television news resulted in the highest TV news index scores of any media channel. These scores were significantly higher than the control group, which was exposed to no media, and the Net news-only group, as determined by Tukey post-hoc comparisons. Media exposure did not have a significant effect on ratings of Net news credibility, which varied comparatively little regardless of channel used.

The columns representing exposure to TV news suggest an effect of channel congruence on credibility evaluations, where perceptions of credibility are enhanced when the channel used is consistent with the news source being evaluated. Simply put, television news viewing results in the highest evaluations of TV news credibility of any condition. Going online has the same effect on evaluations of Net news credibility for students, at a level significantly higher than the control group ratings, but not for adults. In three out of four cases, then, channel congruence enhances credibility evaluations. In response to the second research question, direct media exposure mostly enhances credibility evaluations when the channel is consistent with the news source being evaluated, resulting in what might be called a congruence effect. When the channel is inconsistent, direct exposure still results in higher evaluations than no exposure for students but lower evaluations for adults.

The third research question asked whether there is a synergy effect between on air and online news sources that enhances perceptions of credibility over use of either medium in isolation. Subjects exposed to both broadcast and online news in the same experimental session (telewebbing) rated TV and Net news credibility higher overall than any other condition except for the TV congruency case (TV exposure producing the highest TV credibility evaluations). For both students and adults, telewebbing has a small positive impact on TV news credibility beyond Net news use and no exposure, but these individual comparisons were not significant in Tukey post-hoc comparisons.

The fourth research question asked whether there is an interaction between media channel and age group resulting in different synergy effects for younger and older news audiences. When exposed to either TV or Net news, however, students and adults reacted quite differently (as indicated by the divergent upward and downward lines in the centre of the graph). For adults, exposure had a negative effect and evaluations of Net news credibility fell from the control group level.

For students, exposure had a positive effect and evaluations rose. When adults were placed in the telewebbing condition (shown on the right side of the graph), with exposure to both TV and Net news, evaluations of Net news jumped to their highest levels. For students, telewebbing caused perceptions of Net news to dip slightly. The interaction for media channel and age group for evaluations of TV news credibility was not significant.

To summarize these findings, when adults were placed in the telewebbing condition, with exposure to both TV and Net news, evaluations of Net news credibility jumped to their highest levels. Evaluations of TV news credibility also benefited from telewebbing, compared to the control group and to Web use alone. For students, telewebbing caused perceptions of TV and Net news credibility to increase in relation to the control group, but dip slightly or show no difference compared to other forms of media exposure. In answer to RQ4, then, telewebbing potentially results in greater synergy effects of Net news credibility for adults than students, but these results only approached significance.

Discussion

This study of synergy effects, which adds to the experimental literature of media credibility, found significant main effects for media channel on evaluations of TV news credibility and for age group on evaluations of both TV and Net news credibility.

The ANOVA model also produced a near-significant interaction for the two factors on evaluations of Net news credibility, which may have achieved significance had the group sizes been larger. Consistent with survey studies of media credibility, younger audience members evaluated both TV and Net news to be significantly more credible overall than older audience members.

In particular, students regarded both forms of network news as more informative than adults, while adults considered both forms of news to be significantly less fair than students. Both age groups rated TV news lowest for its depth. Within age groups, adults rated Net news to be significantly more credible than TV news, while students rated TV news more credible. These results are somewhat surprising, given that the audience for broadcast news tends to be older, while the online audience tends to be younger. Each age group evaluated the less familiar medium more generously.

Media channel also influenced credibility evaluations. The ratings for television news suggested a channel congruence effect, where perceptions of credibility are enhanced when the channel used is consistent with the source being evaluated. This was the case for both students and adults. The finding of a congruence effect in an experimental setting differs from the common survey finding that media audiences regard the medium on which they are most reliant as the most credible because the evaluations here were generated in response to direct exposure to a particular medium and not based on reflections of past media use. Nevertheless, similar to the association of media reliance with high credibility evaluations revealed by surveys, audiences seem to regard media they have just used more favourably than media to which they are not exposed.

Going online had the same congruence effect on evaluations of Net news credibility for students, but not adults. When the channel used is inconsistent, adults tend to evaluate the source less favourably compared to the control group. Adults were noticeably less inclined to view TV news as credible after exposure to the Web. For students, any media exposure had a positive impact and evaluations rose relative to the control group.

As for cross-platform media use, the results provided some initial evidence for the existence of a synergy effect. The magnitude of these effects, though relatively small, was greater for adults than for students, perhaps reflecting students' propensity to multitask.

A recent study of the gratifications obtained from new media found that students spend on average a total of 10.5 hours per day with a range of different media technologies.The telewebbing condition was arguably more novel for adults, and thus had a greater impact on their credibility evaluations. Overall, subjects exposed to the telewebbing condition rated TV and Net news credibility higher than the control group or subjects exposed only to Net news. The only exception was that TV exposure by itself elicited the highest evaluations of TV credibility.

The fact that several of the mean credibility ratings for telewebbing pointed to synergy effects but were not significantly different at the $p < .05$ level suggests that a larger number of subjects in this between-subjects experiment would have produced more significant results. Between-subjects experiments with 20 or fewer subjects per group, as was the case with this study, are notoriously underpowered. To overcome this classic problem without having to involve hundreds of subjects in a costly and time-consuming data collection process, future experimental research should take advantage of within-subjects, repeated measures designs, which provide greater statistical power with fewer subjects since each subject responds multiple times and serves as his or her own control.

When studying network news, the demographics of the audience are an essential consideration. Young adults who are wired, and therefore on a trajectory for the higher socioeconomic status that characterizes network news viewers, represent the future of the on-air news audience. Whether members of this audience will ever completely migrate online for their news and information seems doubtful, at least at this stage of the Web's development. Students in this study reported almost two nights of network news viewing per week-even as members of a residential campus environment that provides "cost free," high-bandwidth online access. What seems almost certain, however, is a continued tendency by younger audiences to teleweb and, beyond that, multitask with a variety of information and communication technologies simultan-eously.

The results of this study suggest that media exposure has differential effects on student and adult perceptions of news credibility. Future research should keep this finding in mind and not attempt to generalize about the news audience from a convenience sample of undergraduates. The experimental nature of this study, while desirable for the control it offered over the news channels subjects were exposed to, was limited in its ability to simulate actual viewing conditions.

Subjects in the telewebbing condition, for instance, either saw a series of newscasts first and then went online, or spent some time online first and then watched a series of broadcasts. At home (or in the office), news consumers who teleweb may use both media at the same time.

Follow-up studies should attempt to recreate a real-time telewebbing or "enhanced television"experience in as naturalistic a way as possible. In addition, other genres of media content associated with telewebbing, such as live sports coverage or news specials, should be studied. Satisfying these two conditions may lead to more pronounced findings for synergy effects.

With the growth of telewebbing and multitasking as routine audience activities, it will become increasingly important to understand and measure perceptions of news credibility under conditions of simultaneous media use.

Considering the potential contribution of synergy effects resulting from cross-platform media use could help recast the debate about media credibility so that the realities, rather than the hyperbole, of online developments are adequately taken into account. The networks have adapted to the online environment and are making gainful use of both delivery platforms. Moreover, most audience members do not stop using a source as heavily relied on as television just because a new medium arrives on the scene; instead, their media repertoire may become wider and more varied.

The rise of telewebbing and two-screen households presents media research with the challenge of understanding the impact of this new consumer behaviour on evaluations of news content. With technological convergence, the independence of different delivery platforms is eroding.

Even so, the stylistic differences between on-air and online news may persist, withbroadcast news retaining its trademark chronological narrative and online (text-based) news embracing the inverted pyramid style of print reporting. Although both forms of news are similar in that they are delivered through electronic telecommunications terminals, they may be processed and evaluated with vastly different criteria, as is the case for assessments of newspaper and television news credibility.

From the perspective of the news audience, the ways in which television and the Web complement-and contravene-each other are only beginning to be understood. Research should investigate the different processing styles required for on-air and online news, with the aim of revealing the psychological mechanisms underlying credibility judgements.

Access to news making, that is, the chance to have our voices and experiences included in an influential public communication forum, is a critical political resource. Such access, especially the kind of serious voice routinely achieved by political elites, offers sources wide distribution for their ideas and the opportunity to significantly affect public debate.

Research suggests, for example, that news selections help set the public's issue agenda; that news constructions "prime"the audience in ways that affect evaluations of candidates and policies; and that journalists'framing choices can affect the audience's attribution of casuality and blame for social problems, and their tolerance for civil liberties. Consequently, the question of how news stories are created, and in particular whose voices are included in these constructions, has become a critical democratic question.

Access to the news is an especially important resource for social movement groups. For these groups, such as the women's or the environmental movement, communication is a central goal. They seek to change public attitudes and understandings on key social and cultural issues through the creation and communication of new information and new interpretive frameworks. To do so, however, they must reach mass audiences. Access to news media thus becomes an important mobilizing resource for such groups. In addition, as voices of political dissent and social change, social movements'ability to access news media provides a critical test of the media's ability to serve as a legitimate source of information in a democracy. But how open are news media to social movement communications? Can social change groups strategically access newsmaking processes? Can they achieve routine access to news? How have they done so and at what costs? This chapter investigates the media access strategies of the National Organization for Women (NOW), a central organization of the second wave of the U.S. women's movement. Using historical data gathered from NOW's archive and from a content analysis of New York Times coverage of NOW, it traces NOW's resource mobilization, strategy development, and media access during a fifteen year period, from its founding in 1966 to its institutionalization as a voice for women's issues by the 1980s.

NOW's ability to access news media in this period was the result of two key factors. First, NOW was able to mobilize the material resources-money, skills, technology, labour, organizational structure, and especially information-necessary to serve as a reliable and routine source for journalists. Second, the group was able to develop effective and reflexive media strategies by mobilizing its knowledge of the routines and discursive structures of news and using them in its own media communications. These two factors contributed significantly to NOW's public visibility over time and to the group's role in helping to create a public agenda for "women's issues"in the United States.

A single case study approach to these questions has its limitations, of course. NOW is not typical of all social movement organizations. It is a mass-based organization with a national office and local chapters, not a local grassroots organization. Its longevity-more than thirty years-is also unusual for an advocacy organization. However, NOW is also an important organization in its own right.

Though it has been seen as too "liberal"by some groups and too "radical"by others, there is widespread agreement in the women's movement that NOW played a central role as the public voice of feminism for many years. A recent history of the movement notes, "The fact is that if the National Organization for Women were to collapse and disappear, it would be taken as a signal of the end of this era of feminism."

Perhaps most critically for this analysis, though, NOW can be seen as something of a social movement "success story"in terms of media access. NOW has always been able to achieve at least some basic news access, and although early coverage was marginalizing, later news presented NOW as an important civil rights organization for women. In particular, around the Equal Rights Amendment (ERA) struggle of the late 1970s and early 1980s, NOW became a key source and definer of events for news media. Analyzing the resources and strategies that structured NOW's access, then, may help us understand the chances of other groups to access news media.

5

Election Campaigns

INTRODUCTION

Elections provide opportunities for formal participation in the political system, and the campaigns that lead up to Election Day are intended to generate interest and excitement that might translate into actual voting. And yet a steady decline in voter turnout since the 1960s has occurred despite increased access to news media, an expansion of literacy and civics instruction in schools, and the liberalization of procedures for voter registration.

News media and schools are implicated in efforts to stimulate voting given the presumption that these two institutions should provide knowledge and motivation for voting. Critics of conventional news coverage, for example, urge avoidance of overly negative campaign coverage, which is thought to induce cynicism and lethargy in the citizenry. Schools are likewise urged to implement curriculum reform that breaks down the barrier of adolescent indifference to political participation.

With respect to voting laws, the belief that registration procedures inhibit turnout has led to a series of reforms at the state and national levels. Beginning in the mid 1970s, several states implemented changes to liberalize voting laws, providing researchers with "laboratories" to assess the impact of various reforms.

Michigan, for example, established the first motor voter law in 1976; Tennessee mandated an early voting system in 1994 to allow voters to cast ballots during the two weeks prior to an election; and Oregon experimented with a vote-by-mail provision for the 1996 election. Comprehensive reform of the federal election law was enacted in 1993 with the National Voter Registration Act. In reviewing effects of eliminating requirements associated with time, place, and manner of voting, Calvert concluded that permissive rules marginally enhance turnout.

But in light of the dismal turnout for the 1996 presidential election, the success of these reforms was deemed less than overwhelming. Referring to the National Voter Registration Act, Knack observed that, "The most dramatic liberalization of voter registration procedures in American history coincided with not only the lowest level of turnout since 1924, but with the largest single four-year decline since 1920.

The theory that registration barriers are the chief cause of the gap between turnout rates for U.S. and other developed democracies suffered a devastating blow, as turnout in North Dakota - where voters aren't even required to register - was a mere 56 per cent of the voting population in 1996."

RETHINKING ASSUMPTIONS ABOUT POLITICAL ACTIVATION

Many mobilization efforts that rely on media, schools, or elections have failed to adequately address micro-social processes that generate motivation and competence for political involvement. This section critiques the activation strategies associated with each institution with respect to four themes: a presumption that low-SES groups are permanently disengaged; a restricted and unrealistic conceptualization of citizenship; a tradition of thinking about political involvement in terms of individual behaviour; and a top-down approach to activation. These interrelated tendencies in the way reforms are conceptualized and implemented help to account for the neglect of the family in efforts to stimulate citizenship.

NEGLECT OF LOW-SES GROUPS

Hyman and Sheatsley provided "some reasons why information campaigns fail" in what became a landmark article cited by scholars to justify pessimism about mass media interventions. Subsequent research has consistently shown the power of demographic variables to predict levels of political interest and behaviour, with education in particular strongly associated with nearly every indicator of civic involvement. Studies in mass communication suggest that campaigns designed to promote equality in citizenship are not only bound to fail, but are likely to exacerbate "knowledge gaps" between individuals of low and high socioeconomic status.

Survey research on political behaviour has tended to view SES as an individual disposition, despite the paradoxical and problematic implications of this theoretical construct. The assumption is that indicators of social status represent individual differences in terms of the ability to process information, of motivation to pay attention to political information, and of frequency of exposure to political discussion or news stories.

The level of a person's formal schooling might in fact be fixed, but the consequence of educational attainment for an individual varies across situations, in response to the flow of political stimulation within that person's social network. Media and schools have the potential to increase political interest in low-SES groups by stimulating political discussion during highly salient events such as election campaigns.

The shadow of Hyman and Sheatsley's pessimism, however, still appears to evoke images of "know nothings" among the planners of intervention campaigns. The failure to even attempt the engagement of low-SES groups is often evident in the goals of news media reforms. Efforts in civic journalism to create ideal speech situations - characterized by what might be considered elitist expectations for the rationality of discourse - will involve some sectors of a community but leave out citizens who are less skilled in public deliberation. Pauly observes that "Public journalism works within a thin and unconvincing account of the communities it hopes to serve.

Taking its cue from a variety of contemporary upper-middleclass reform groups and the language of sponsoring foundations such as Pew and Kettering, it uses terms such as `civic culture,' `civil society,' and `social capital' with a breezy selfconfidence."

Rosen argues that journalists should acknowledge that they represent a "political institution that has a legitimate stake in whether politics works for all or becomes the professional playground of a privileged few," but this rhetoric of inc fusion is rarely matched by practical suggestions for engaging low-SES groups. Rosen, for example, suggests methods for newspapers to convene with highly motivated voters so they can add to their knowledge of ballot issues. Charity describes the ideal reader, one who "would be eager to organize deliberative forums" if only she could get a little training. He provides practical tips and points to accessible resources useful for organizing a meeting among similarly motivated citizens.

We suspect that the lack of interest in Programmes that might politicize low-- SES groups stems from the longstanding assumption that dispositional barriers in the lower social strata create an enduring resistance to political stimulation. The preference for strategies aimed at the highly educated and already interested - or perhaps the "why bother?" approach to engaging the lower social strata - is reflected in the design of several recent innovations that derive from discursive models of deliberative democracy.

These Programmes provide blueprints for how to organize conversations among citizens during election campaigns; examples include deliberative opinion polling and the use of interactive media to create electronic town meetings. An emphasis on deliberative democracy in the design of interventions is not necessarily compatible with more inclusive approaches to participatory democracy.

The failure to engage low-SES groups has also been a persistent problem in the reform of voting laws. Constituencies in which there has been a relatively high proportion of non-voters are the ones least likely to take advantage of curtailed voting procedures. A more effective approach would involve the stimulation of motivation to vote by targeting primary groups as resources for political mobilization. Early field experiments demonstrated how interventions increase turnout among those least likely to participate by treating voting as social rather than individual behaviour. Eldersveld conducted an experiment in Ann Arbor, Michigan, concentrating his efforts on 500 election "apathetics" - people who did not vote in prior local elections.

His goal was to determine the comparative effectiveness of personalized contact and impersonalized canvassing via mail. The results showed that voting was higher for those personally contacted, particularly among those with only a high school education, those who lived in small households or lived alone, and those who had recently moved to Ann Arbor. In all three cases, these were people who tended to lack "social connectedness" and interpersonal political stimulation. The effect of person-to-person pressures, Eldersveld concluded, was to compensate for the absence of social interaction that would otherwise encourage voting.

In educational reform, a prominent theme is the desire to alleviate disparities in schooling opportunities and outcomes. While a substantial body of research has documented how differential opportunities in education generate job-market disparities, less scholarly attention has been paid to inequality in educational preparation for citizenship. We do know from empirical studies, however, that SES-based gaps in knowledge and other indicators of civic competence emerge during adolescence.

Low-SES children, for example, read the newspaper less frequently than their high-SES counterparts, and this gap widens during the formative years of adolescence. This differential pattern in developmental strides towards citizenship poses a challenge to civics instruction in the United States, which is intended to provide equal opportunity for participatory citizenship.

Findings from the Kids Voting studies provide reason for optimism about the efficacy of curriculum reform. As envisioned by Dewey, schools can function as laboratories for civic preparation, allowing young people to practice civic skills such as opinion expression in peer-group settings. Students represent a captive audience at school, which creates the possibility for widespread diffusion of political stimulation. As demonstrated by the scenario of "trickle-up influence," students can function as "opinion leaders" who extend classroom stimulation to low-SES parents.

Parent involvement, in fact, has become the focus of efforts to understand and alleviate the inequalities in educational outcomes in the United States. A plethora of policies and Programmes have been implemented across the country to enlist parents in children's formal education. But in the realm of civics instruction, low-SES parents are likely to remain disconnected from a child's schooling unless specific efforts are made to involve them.

Along with the tendency of low-SES parents to avoid discussion about politics, these parents might feel less welcome in the middle-class school culture. They are more likely to have inflexible work schedules, preventing involvement in school activities; and parents without prior success in school would tend to lack confidence in performing tasks such as helping with homework.

Desimone argues that despite the national attention focused on parent involvement, the social mechanisms needed to translate policies into effective practice are missing. The mediating effects of family interaction need to be identified, studied, and incorporated into practice. "It is imperative that we increase our understanding of how parent involvement best can be employed for all children, especially for those at risk of educational failure". We concur, but add that theorists of curriculum reform should extend their view of family influence beyond topdown effects of parents on children. Students have the capacity to activate the entire family as a setting for political involvement.

RESTRICTED VIEW OF CITIZENSHIP

In most daily interactions, the political self is confined to primary-group interaction. Political competence acquires social utility in intimate settings in which civic growth serves developmental and relational needs. By contrast, many traditional models of political participation seek to show how private interactions in the home, the church, and the workplace provide opportunities to develop and try out civic skills - such as public speaking and social networking - that are transferable for use in the formal political system.

That is, scholars are usually concerned with how private life recruits citizens to serve the needs of the political system. Our interest here is essentially the opposite - we are trying to understand how politics serves the family as a dynamic system, and how it serves the developmental needs of its individual members.

We view citizenship as a manifestation of human growth. It is a far broader concept than a sense of civic duty, or rational attempts to influence public policy. Citizenship in liberal democracy, however, is nearly always conceptualized in terms of self-governance. Communication campaigns should consequently prepare and motivate citizens for participation in the formal political system, according to this view.

For example, several civic journalism projects have set out to boost voter turnout by providing in-depth coverage of issues that help voters decide among candidates and ballot propositions. The liberalization of voting laws in many states, meanwhile, is intended to make registration and actual voting as easy as possible.

According to the model of political activation presented here, individuals are motivated to acquire civic knowledge, skills, and communication habits that make them competent for social interaction within their families and primary groups.6 Political behaviour outside the home is obviously important in any conception of participatory democracy, but increased political competence is most immediately useful within the context of an individual's primary groups, rather than being functional for participation in the political system, an activity that is for most people an abstraction or a remote possibility beyond the ritual of casting a ballot.

An intellectual tendency to extract individuals from their immediate if perhaps mundane - social environments, and to imagine them as participants in idealized participatory forums, is evident in the scholarship of both empirical research and normative conceptions of democracy. The reification of participation in constructs such as the "public sphere, " for example, while important in normative conceptions of democracy, describes participation at high levels of abstraction without explicating engagement in micro-social contexts.

If events such as an election campaign or a school intervention are to influence individual behaviour, such effects are contingent upon interactions of individuals within primary groups. The family is thus situated as an intervening agent that mediates the effect of exogenous influence on individual outcomes. Unfortunately, theorists' restricted view of citizenship as activity that occurs outside of the family has prevented the development of models that might effectively incorporate the dynamics of intra-family communication as a strategy for civic mobilization.

We urge an expanded view of citizenship in which political competence is manifest in political communication that serves relational and developmental needs of family members. Interrelated behaviours such as media use, knowledge, opinion formation, and discussion of politics are systemic to an individual during periods of heightened involvement, and systemic at the level of family interaction.

These mutually supportive activities constitute a single condition of the person and the family in that the behaviours are all part of the same structure of family communication. Citizenship consequently has an important intra-family function, apart from the more traditional understanding of involvement as participation in the formal political system. From a developmental perspective, we understand citizenship as an integration of political communication behaviours within the evolving structure of family interaction. Political involvement thereby allows for growth in family relationships as children and parents take advantage of opportunities to practice communication skills and develop competence.

This view of citizenship is consistent with recent critiques of liberal democracy that question traditional conceptions about the self and its relation to politics. Standard liberal democracy, as articulated by Madison and James Mill and incorporated into American pluralism, presumes that democracy is primarily of instrumental value for protecting interests that belong to individuals or groups prior to - and independent of- political life. Conceptions of liberal democracy, consequently, do not necessarily require theories of communicative competence or self-transformation through social interaction.

In contrast, theories of "expansive democracy" refer to conditions that enhance self-development and personal expression. Under this view, political preferences and identity are formed in social contexts in which individuals are required to make choices: "Individuals choose in order to become, and the nature of the opportunities given for the expression of choice affects the formation of the will". This broad conception of citizenship is reminiscent of Thurgood Marshall's assertion about the purpose of free speech: "The First Amendment serves not only the needs of the polity but also those of the human spirit - a spirit that demands self-expression".

INVOLVEMENT AS INDIVIDUAL BEHAVIOUR

Studies on civic behaviour usually conceptualize the individual as the unit of observation and analysis. While suitable for experimental and survey design, this approach limits the theoretical frameworks that can be used to develop intervention strategies. By focusing on political involvement as essentially individual behaviour, reform advocates fail to appreciate that the social networks surrounding people constitute resources for activation.

This tendency is evident in contemporary critiques of the press, which describe political involvement in terms of psychological engagement with news media content. Modern trends in political journalism are blamed for initiating what Pinkleton and Austin refer to as "a spiral of disaffection." Media-induced cynicism about politics and government is thought to result in a lack of motivation to obtain information, which leads to further cynicism, low levels of political efficacy, and ultimately, alienation.

Cappella and Jamieson, for example, criticize journalists' use of strategic frames, arguing that they activate cynicism that results in decreased political participation. Sabato and Patterson contend that unrelenting negative coverage of politicians, including the periodic "feeding frenzy" of attack journalism, encourages readers' cynicism and disgust.

Empirical studies on the relationship between news exposure and political involvement, however, indicate that purposeful use of media is associated with high levels of participation. McLeod and McDonald found that even as newspaper users were more likely to blame politicians, they also participated more in the political process. But the belief that media contribute to psychological disengagement is prevalent among academic critics, providing a misguided rationale for news media reform.

We do not believe that civic disaffection - or activation for that matter - can be explained by focusing exclusively on an individual's cognitive or affective response to media content. In the context of a mobilization effort, news media use is only an initial stage in a process of activation that requires the expression of political interest in primary-group interaction. But given a conviction that journalistic practices are responsible for the pathology of disengagement, it is only natural to assume that media-centered reforms will be sufficient to engage individuals.

Civic journalism, for example, advocates that the press become a partner with citizens and with local institutions to alleviate political disaffection while forging connections that might establish synergy to solve community problems.

This prescribed outcome, we note, does not explicate the process by which citizens become motivated for civic involvement in social environments. Advocates and critics of this reform movement have begun to address a missing link in the theory of civic journalism -the process by which press innovations activate citizenship at the micro-social level of grass-roots participation.

Civic journalism has thrived as an ongoing critique of traditional journalism, and as a debate among academic and media elites, but with respect to theory, the movement lacks a political sociology in which citizen behaviour might be explained in terms of media exposure and use.

TOP-DOWN ACTIVATION

By a top-down approach to political activation, we mean an attempt to impose or transmit civic orientations that promote regime stability and other needs of the political system. A democratic system functions by virtue of the consent of the governed, and in this regard, schools, media, and election campaigns act as societal agents to encourage voting, to affirm normative values, and to transmit knowledge of issues, candidates, and political traditions.

Research in political socialization has been criticized, however, for focusing on the functional requirements of the macro-political system instead of the developmental needs of the citizens themselves.

The liberalization of voting laws in the absence of efforts to generate motivation for voting reflects this top-down perspective. The intent of legal reform is not necessarily relevant to the lives of people who have personal priorities more pressing than political participation. Efforts to lower voting registration barriers share an assumption with many media-centered reforms, that the problem of anemic citizenship can be alleviated by increasing the "supply" of easily accessible experiences that stimulate political involvement.

The expectation is that by making voting easier - or by increasing the flow of political information via mass media - citizens will take advantage of the many opportunities for involvement. But these efforts are likely to fail without concurrent Programmes to stimulate "demand" for political stimulation within the context of social interaction. Supply-side strategies for activating political engagement invite an unflattering comparison with the nation's "war on drugs," a deployment of resources routinely criticized for focusing on the supply of drugs rather than addressing demand as the root cause of the problem.

Whether the behaviour is something to discourage such as drug use, or something to encourage such as voting, successful strategies hinge on the capacity to intervene in social settings that influence a person's motivation. Recent studies on voting behaviour show that turnout will increase despite restrictive election rules when political parties and advocacy groups make serious efforts to mobilize voters by reaching out to them in their homes and neighborhoods.

A top-down perspective is reflected in the failure of media interventions to recognize the potential for civic activation at the grassroots level. According to advocates of civic journalism, local media can function as the means through which citizens come to know parts of the community they do not regularly interact with. Because the community rarely comes together as a whole, a surrogate is needed to advance public life.

It is difficult to resist pointing out the irony of this seemingly democratic appeal to press reform - the elitist assumption is that people at the grassroots level - in their homes, schools, workplaces, and peer networks - are not capable of sustaining political engagement for themselves. Civic journalism proponents advocate that the media become more inclusive in drawing people into civic spaces, but missing from this perspective is the acknowledgment that citizens are already embedded in primary groups that periodically undergo episodes of heightened political involvement.

The notion of a functioning linkage between the press and the public originates from John Dewey's argument for the creation of conditions by which people could routinely participate in public life. Haas asks the pertinent question: "In what capacity; then, should journalists engage citizens in the democratic process? No one has so far addressed this issue in detail, although the literature of civic journalism suggests that journalists should engage citizens in their capacity as members of specific communities."

A common theme of press criticism is that news media should not only stimulate the political involvement of existing institutions, but should strive to create communities of civic engagement where they do not currently exists. One manifestation of this goal is the creation of "focus groups" in which strangers are brought together at the urging of local media to discuss issues of the day.

Glasser argues that interventions of this sort are too often conducted as patronizing gestures rather than serious attempts at civic activation: "Focus groups, town meetings, salons, and other attempts to convene the community amount to at best a contrived and artificial response to the need to cultivate citizenship. They create at most an ad hoc venue for discussion, a small and temporary site for a debate managed by and too often only for the press."

Schools in recent years, meanwhile, have been criticized for a top-down approach to civics instruction. In the traditional model of didactic learning, students are placed in the passive role of simply absorbing knowledge of the country's political heritage and governmental structure. Empirical research provides evidence that patterns of classroom interaction, rather than transmission of substantive information, predict outcomes conducive to citizenship.

Ehman demonstrated effects of an "open classroom environment," which occurs when students engage freely in making suggestions for structuring the classroom environment, and when they have opportunities to discuss all sides of controversial topics.

In this longitudinal study, Ehman concluded that perceived freedom to express opinions in class is a strong predictor of interest in politics.

These findings are consistent with Dewey's philosophical model of the democratic learning environment as elaborated in Democracy and Education. Dewey contended that schools educate for citizenship indirectly, by means of the environment they create. He believed that the most effective learning occurs when student activity is carried out in a social context characterized by free expression, peer interaction in cooperative activities, respect for diverse viewpoints, and equal participation in democratic decision making.

The participatory focus of the Kids Voting programme reflects this philosophy of civic education and provides a model for future efforts at curriculum reform. The goal of civics instruction as competence in political expression serves most immediately the social and developmental needs of the students themselves rather than the systemic requirements of the political regime.

A STRATEGY FOR POLITICAL ACTIVATION

Family-based interaction constitutes a valuable resource for mobilization efforts, but to appreciate this potential requires a reconceptualization of activation as a micro-social process. According to our functional model of family political communication, the family constitutes a social system that tends to maintain homeostatic balance in various domains of social interaction, including civic competence.

A civic intervention such as a school curriculum or a mass media campaign can heighten the political interest of the family member initially reached by the intervention, which might create tension if other family members perceive a need to increase their own civic competence. Developmental gains in citizenship occur when the family system adjusts to re-establish equilibrium in response to exogenous influences that create tension.

This framework contrasts with a tendency towards reductionist thinking in which campaign effects are evaluated in isolation to each other, and in the absence of social context. Interventions should strive to influence the structure of communication within primary groups rather than try to coax behavioural change from an individual independent of her social environment.

A family's response to an intervention takes the form of "endogenous feedback", whereby behavioral outcomes are interdependent in response to an exogenous influence. While any given member might be initially exposed to political stimulation, the family as a system responds by way of interactions that reflect mutual adjustment and reciprocal influence.

We have modeled this process as a sequence of five steps: stimulation of a family member who is most easily reached by an intervention; initiation of interpersonal communication; heightened expectations for political competence; a resulting increase in the capacity of family members to influence each other's political interest; and greater motivation for participation outside the home. With this process in mind, interventions should be based on two distinct but related strategies. The first challenge is to coordinate public institutions that normally operate in isolation to each other, so that they provide sufficient stimulation for families.

As a model of institutional integration, Kids Voting incorporates influences of schools, media, and elections, while simultaneously engaging the family as a social context in which the increased flow of political information is used in interpersonal communication. Students and parents become immersed in a social environment in which exposure to political communication is nearly unavoidable. Students essentially act as a conduit from the school to the family, allowing the programme to overcome social structural barriers that would otherwise prevent an information campaign from reaching low-- SES adults.

An integrative approach takes advantage of what each agent has to offer while avoiding the temptation to assume that any single reform will be sufficient to activate citizens. An integrative strategy also alleviates the tendency to miscast institutions in roles they are unable to perform. Much of the controversy surrounding civic journalism, for example, is stirred by disputes over what the press can realistically contribute. Critics contend that the press is not equipped to provide forums such as neighborhood focus groups, and neither is such a role appropriate given a need to preserve press autonomy. An integrative intervention bypasses this controversy by enlisting the press to focus on what it does best - providing stimulation at the macro-social level - in coordination with agents (such as schools and families) that are better suited for interactive citizenship.

Recognizing that no single institution creates conditions necessary for widespread civic participation, McLeod, Eveland, and Horowitz argue that for interventions to succeed, "There needs to be not only mobilization, but also cross-mobilizing of community institutions and organizations. The synergy of organizations that typically work separately can have a greater effect when these organizations work together." Ideally, an intervention would be comprehensive and integrative in scope to engage families, news media, schools, and elections to take advantage of symbiotic interactions among the various agents.

At a practical level, we are not calling for the invention of new Programmes for civic activation, but for strategies that incorporate the family. The Newspaper Association of America, for instance, sponsors Newspapers in Education to promote discussion of current affairs in classrooms. Educators should consider takehome assignments in which students ask parents about news topics.

The emerging popularity of media literacy also represents an opportunity to design curricula that would engage family members in co-use of traditional media and the Internet. For example, together a child and parent might dissect a political ad to identify its persuasive strategy, and thereby empower each other as sophisticated users of political content.

DebateWatch organizers could design Programmes in which each family as a social unit watches presidential debates, along with the conventional approach in which strangers or neighbours are brought together. Meanwhile, election officials and civic organizations could work with local school districts to establish "mock voting" Programmes so that children can vote alongside parents on Election Day. Programmes that encourage voting as a family activity might be more effective at boosting turnout than recent efforts to remove legal restrictions to registration. Indeed, prior research has shown that voting turnout tends to be a joint household activity, with adult family members either voting or staying home as a social unit.

The second challenge for intervention strategists is to identify the intrafamily motivations for acquiring political competence. Media-centered campaigns represent information control processes in that sponsors attempt to influence the information environment so that as many individuals as possible are exposed to a particular topic. But an intervention strategy should go beyond efforts to merely saturate a social environment so that everyone is exposed. Such an approach might result in a certain amount of passive learning as individuals gain knowledge despite minimal effort.

A more powerful strategy would be based on a careful analysis of how communication experiences are used in family interactions to serve relational needs or developmental goals. Information will be processed, knowledge gained, and opinions formed when these cognitive resources are functional in interactions that are meaningful to the individuals involved.

The scenario we describe as "trickle-up influence" took advantage of two developmental tendencies - the need for adolescents to assert independence via opinion expression, and the need for parents to maintain their leadership role in the family. The politicization of low-- SES parents becomes possible because of a particular stage within the family life cycle, in which teenagers are beginning to engage in "adult" conversations. Political communication might be functional for other stages in family development, such as when young adults enter the formative years of marriage and desire increased knowledge of a community while setting down roots.

And when their children eventually leave the home for college or work, retired couples might have more time for political discussion as they pursue other interests.While the genesis of political habits and orientations can be traced to family interactions and other socializing experiences, family life is routinely dismissed by reform advocates as private behaviour that individuals must transcend to pursue citizenship. Hays notes that "In the past, scholars have attributed low levels of political participation among voters under thirty to such distractions of youth as getting an education, finding a spouse, or having fun with friends." The description of acquiring education and entering marriage as "distractions" illustrates the failure of scholars to theorize about the relationship between family life and civic competence.

In response to institutions that periodically heighten the flow of political information, the family acts as a mediating agent that translates the raw material of political stimulation into motivation for civic participation. Far from being a barrier to involvement, the family constitutes a setting that amplifies intervention effects by translating individual involvement into interpersonal communication that politicizes the entire household. In the future, reforms incorporating the family as a social unit might demonstrate why interventions can succeed despite the dismal predictions of chronic disengagement.

6

Political and Crime News Coverage

ANALYTICAL PERSPECTIVES

Three analytical perspectives are useful tools for assessing these ethical implications because they point both to the potential ethical good and the ethical dangers of anecdote use.

A framework developed previously for studying coverage of news with an ethical dimension involves evaluating stories based on how thoroughly they portray the ethical issues relevant to a topic, the parties connected with those issues, the levels at which the ethical issues play out (individual, organizational/institutional, professional, and social), and the legal backdrop for those issues.

Although each story about ethics-laden topics cannot be expected to address all four of these elements comprehensively, coverage that addresses these areas well is considered to be ethical. The normative assumptions about journalism in this framework are in keeping with social responsibility and communitarian press theory, both of which emphasize the importance of not merely reporting events but also serving society.

The attention to levels of analysis reflects the importance of portraying individuals in news coverage. News coverage should include the ways that individuals and families are affected by decisions or events-such as a health maintenance organization's decision about whether to approve or deny coverage for a kind of cancer treatment. Anecdotes shine light on the difficulties that individuals face, and as such they are tools of ethical journalism.

The importance of the individual notwithstanding, journalists should go beyond that level to examine issues at the organizational/institutional, professional, and social levels. Attention to only one level of analysis, in an in-depth piece or a body of coverage, falls short of the moral obligation of journalists. In this light, anecdotes are morally a double-edged sword. While they can bring attention to the plight of individuals in riveting fashion, and even place that plight in institutional, professional, and social contexts, the attention remains on a representative, or perhaps unrepresentative, individual or family, as exemplification studies have shown.

Furthermore, previous work suggests that news coverage should include an array of sources, including neither exclusively professionals (such as doctors or businesspeople) nor nonprofessionals (patients or customers). Good anecdotes, although they focus on an individual, may point out how that individual interacts with other people, as well as with organizations and institutions. Attention to a range of relevant parties at a variety of levels, both in the anecdote and elsewhere in the story, can mitigate the potential ethical harm from anecdotes' narrow focus. But the exemplification literature suggests that the anecdote still would have power to shape readers' or viewers' perception of the broader issue.

Christians, Ferre, and Fackler's communitarian media ethic also provides ethical justification for using anecdotes to highlight the situations of individuals while it draws attention to the limitations of anecdotes. The idea of mutuality is central to this perspective, which has a variety of intellectual underpinnings including communitarian political theory and theology. Mutuality views humans as having their identity in relation to others and living both for others and themselves.

The relationship of persons and communities takes priority over either alone. This ethic is profoundly concerned with both society and the individual. The priority of justice creates a profound interest in the needs of the hurting or marginalized. "A press nurtured by communitarian ethics requires more of itself than fair treatment of events deemed worthy of coverage. Under the notion that justice itself-and not merely haphazard public enlightenment-is a telos of the press, the news-media system stands under obligation to tell the stories that justice requires." Part of telling "the stories that justice requires" involves telling the stories of individuals.

This is because justice addresses fair treatment of individuals. One of the most powerful ways, in fact, to draw attention to such individuals is through the telling of their stories, in words and images, in print and broadcast media.

Even as it provides an ethical underpinning for use of anecdotes, communitarian media ethics, with its deeply grounded concern for the good of society, calls into question the structure and choice of anecdotes. Again, this ethic does support the use of compelling individual cases to highlight broader social injustices.

However, sloppy use of anecdotes can undermine an effort to portray the broader issue, not simply because of the natural tendency of anecdotes to highlight individuals, but also because the particular choice of individuals can skew understanding towards one side of a controversial issue, resulting potentially in neglect of social justice.

The issue is not formulaic balance in news coverage; communitarian ethics calls for more than "fair treatment of events." Consonant with Durham's notion of "strong objectivity," Christians, Ferre, and Fackler call for highlighting the perspectives of the marginalized and, where needed, giving those perspectives attention that is out of balance with the play given to the stories of the powerful. However, since communitarian ethics also implies a concern for faithful portrayal of the whole community, it implies a need to portray the breadth of the community's concern.

Gilligan's feminist ethic of care supports the use of anecdotes because it, too, is concerned with persons in relationships. This perspective, developed out of psychological studies of women's distinctive conceptions of morality, underlines the importance of relationships and responsibilities.

Discussing one of her interviewees, Gilligan writes: "Her world is a world of relationships and psychological truths where an awareness of the connection between people gives rise to a recognition of responsibility for one another, a perception of the need for response."

Commenting on how another interviewee viewed activities of care, she writes: "The ideal of care is thus an activity of relationship, of seeing and responding to need, taking care of the world by sustaining the web of connection so that no one is left alone.

" This ethic of care in relationships, however, is not relevant only to women, Gilligan argues. "To admit the truth of the women's perspective to the conception of moral development is to recognize for both sexes the importance throughout life of the connection between self and other, the universality of the need for compassion and care."

Anecdotes are ethically significant in the context of this perspective because they can help to portray the web of personal relationships and responsibilities involved in ethical situations.

Anecdotes can dramatically represent the difficulties that an individual, including women facing illnesses such as breast cancer, face in relation to their families and others outside their families, such as physicians. In fact, use of anecdotes is in keeping with the attention to particulars that Gilligan found women bringing to their moral analysis. She discusses what happens when women go beyond hypothetical dilemmas:

However, the reconstruction of the dilemma in its contextual particularity allows the understanding of cause and consequence which engages the compassion and tolerance repeatedly noted to distinguish the moral judgements of women. Only when substance is given to the skeletal lives of hypothetical people is it possible to consider the social injustice that their moral problems may reflect and to imagine the individual suffering their occurrence may signify or their resolution engender.

This passage implies that anecdotes may awaken attention both to the suffering of individuals and the social context of their difficulties. It suggests that, despite the danger of distortion of the broader picture that the exemplification literature suggests, deep concern for the people behind issues that journalists report may arise only through telling the stories of individuals.

Even as it underpins the ethical value of anecdotes, the ethic of care also implies a need for careful attention to what anecdotes are chosen and what they portray. It implies a need for accurate understanding of responsibilities of individuals in the broader context of society, so that the web of relationships and people's responsibilities within them is rightly understood. All three perspectives suggest that anecdotes are best when they situate individuals they mention in the broader context of the issues being discussed.

These three perspectives all draw attention to the value of the individual and therefore imply that it is ethically justifiable to use anecdotes to draw attention to the needs and concerns of individuals. The communitarian ethic and the ethic of care complement the ethics coverage framework by emphasizing the individual in relationships.

Communitarianism puts priority on the hurting and marginalized. The ethic of care draws attention to the importance of the circumstances of the lives of individuals in prompting a depth of concern for them. Even as they draw attention to the individual, however, all three perspectives emphasize the need to think beyond the individual to the broader contexts of a problem, thereby implying that anecdotes should be carefully chosen for how they may limit or draw attention to these contexts.

NO WOMEN IN THE PUBLIC

It is interesting to note that even though 1920 marked the fruition of the women's movement's struggle to win the right to vote and the LippmannDewey exchange took place in the years immediately following this enormous reconfiguration of the political environment, neither man had much if anything to say about women and the public.

Looking at Lippmann, this empty space is not surprising. Lippmann supported the suffragette movement and could appreciate the movement's sophisticated mastery of the new art of publicity in making news? But his ability to see the world in compartmentalized terms and to see a clear line dividing the world between the scientific and the irrational, allowed him not to be overly troubled by the border between domestic and public life, between the public and the private sphere.

If the women's movement had the potential for signifying a new kind of politics or at least perhaps empowering the Progressive tradition, the aftermath of the presidential election of 1920 yielded, for Lippmann, a fairly ambiguous result. "Unless one is prepared to regard the election as the final twitch of the war mind (that is the way I regard it)," Lippmann wrote, "there would be cause for profound discouragement with universal suffrage."

Looking at Dewey, this lack of attention to gender in his consideration of the public is surprising. While up to and throughout the 1920s Dewey had written little about women, what he had written was consistent with the complex idea of democracy, science, and communication that has been examined here.

As early as 1894 Dewey wrote that "the prevalent theory of the essentially conservative nature of women's intelligence [is but] a fiction of the male intelligence, maintained in order to keep [her] inconvenient radicalism in check." In 1919 he wrote that while "women have as yet made little contribution to philosophy... when women set out to write it" their "viewpoint or tenor" will be very different from the male perspective because one's philosophical view is forged by one's "habitual purposes and cultivated wants," not "insight into the ultimate nature of things or information about the make-up of reality."

It seems clear that Dewey should have understood that in his analysis of the formation of the public, in the realization of democracy as a living, active relationship between the individual and society, the historical conditions of gender oppression would have to be addressed. And yet these matters were left unacknowledged.

Instead, Dewey like progressive social theorists to follow him, including Chistopher Lasch with his "haven in a heartless world" and Jurgen Habermas with his "life world," had a tendency to see in the domestic sphere an idealized counterpoint to the increasing scientization and industrialization of social life.

Dewey idealized the old-fashioned farm kitchen as a model for an organic and integrated life without recognizing that traditional domestic life was not just an organic counterpoint to the instrumental logic of industrial capitalism, but it was also a stronghold for the maintenance and reproduction of gender oppression.

As Jane S. Upin wrote in her study of the intersections between the work of Charlotte Perkins Gilman and Dewey, "despite his continual celebration of democratic values, Dewey did not see that the home can be a poor training ground for democracy."

At the same time, unlike Lippmann's work, which represented for all practical purposes a dead-end for thinking about gender politics in relation to the public and to democracy, Dewey's own work was in sympathy with many critical themes in feminist political theory and can even be used to critique his own neglect of women in his consideration of the public as well as contribute to contemporary theory.

Dewey's critique of scientism that "political facts are not outside human desire and judgement," that science understood as mere reason masks the ideology of scientism, that the work of publicity is not simply to disseminate information but to provide the conditions under which the validity of knowledge can be ascertained, not in its ability to control nature or people but in its capacity to realise the values of an inclusive public as judged by the same inclusive public, is very much in concert with the critiques of scientism by Sandra Harding, Carol Gilligan, and Dorothy Smith.

Dewey's understanding of democracy as community, as based on the fundamentally social character of human existence, of the misleading dichotomy between the private and the social, are observations that all resonate with the feminist political theory of Nancy Frazer, Johanna Meehan, and Barbara Marshall.

In fact, the correspondences between Dewey and feminism and the recent revival of Deweyian theory have, in part, contributed to a significant scholarly interest in re-examining the terrain linking feminism and pragmatism. What are the implications of the absence of women in this LippmannDewy debate that is now regarded as philosophically foundational by the public journalism movement? The news is not good.

Lippmann and Dewey's neglect of gender politics has made it easier for contemporary media scholars recovering this historic moment to also neglect gender, focusing on the metaphor of the work of the press as civic conversation, without facing up to the current material conditions which either continue to muffle women's voices in this conversation or continue to define women's issues as outside of or marginal to serious matters of the public and civic life.

For instance, as Nancy Frazer has written, poverty is viewed as a gender-neutral social problem even though structurally the United States has witnessed a progressive feminization of poverty over the last two decades. At the same time childcare is seen as a women's issue, as if the work of raising and educating children is not fundamental to the society as a whole.

Put somewhat differently, the neglect of gender politics by Lippmann and Dewey and the recovery and reconstruction of the neglect allow the public journalism movement to both ignore the politics of epistemology and the gendered character of those politics. In terms of the historical connections between the Lippmann-Dewey debate and current scholarly energy organized around the idea of the public sphere, the news is more hopeful.

The deeper impulses of Deweyian pragmatism and a pragmatic Critical Theory as developed by Habermas and others have carried forward the sophisticated concern for the interrelationship of epistemology, power and communication while leaving open the space for self-critique from the feminist tradition. Again, however, neither the epistemological politics of Dewey nor the feminist challenge to a patriarchal conception of the public sphere seem to have made much headway in the public journalism movement.

Lippmann, Dewey, and the Post-Factual Age Lippmann understood that simple bias was not all that would trouble the modern press. The problem went beyond bias, to the very questioning of the existence of facts. In short he saw the post-factual world and feared it. The absence of facts and the primacy of subjective perceptions meant for Lippmann, a world paralyzed by relativity. The post-factual world symbolized another step, after the decline of religion and erosion of the stabilizing forces of tradition, towards a world of dangerous uncertainty. At first Lippmann put his hope in science as the solution to the crisis of the fact. This was the solution he advocated in Public Opinion. The idea of separating facts from values had been around for some time in the practice of journalism, but in the 1920s, in the face of a growing recognition of the problem of subjectivity this idea became forcefully organized around the concept of objectivity and became a central principle in the professionalization of journalism.

It is ironic that even though Lippmann is often cited in journalism history as one of the central voices contributing to the establishment of the principle of objectivity in journalism, he himself did not believe the press could be objective, in part due to its organizational structure and in part due its commercial orientation.

Soon after, in The Phantom Public, Lippmann abandoned even his faith in science. Still he understood the importance of some form of moral authority in society.

By 1929, in A Preface to Morals, after dismissing religion and science, Lippmann wrote that his generation "having ceased to believe without ceasing to be credulous, hangs, as it were, between heaven and earth and is at rest nowhere." Lippmann ended up advocating a form of secular humanism which seemed oddly inconsistent with any of his arguments of the previous decade.

However, serving up hope seemed to be a better recipe for publishing success than serving up despair. A Preface to Morals became an instant success and his first book chosen for the Book-ofthe-Month Club. The Phantom Public, as noted earlier, disappeared after its first printing.

However, it was the Lippmann of Public Opinion who would prove prophetic over the next three-quarters of a century: journalism did turn to science. Why remains a question that must continue to be pursued, especially when we note that one of the key proponents of this turn, Lippmann, had serious second thoughts about the practice of science in general.

Perhaps even more important, now as the turn to science begins to unravel, as the borders between fact and fiction, news and entertainment, news and advertising continue to blur, is the need to re-examine this historic moment for what insights it can provide for creating a new vision of democracy and for the role that a new press might play in that vision. Where Lippmann feared the decline of factuality for the relativity it implied about the world, Dewey welcomed it for exactly that reason.

The relativity of truth called attention to the problem of authority in determining what will be called the truth. Dewey was happy to be done with false gods, whether they were based on religion or scientism.

The test of truth must be in its consequences for the people and judged by the people who experience those consequences. Science, as a way of knowing the world, is not separate from the world. Science is an outgrowth of the interests of the human community that produces it and therefore carries the imprint of those values in the knowledge it delivers. When science forgets, or obscures, its connection to community it becomes only detached reason, and potentially dangerous reason, at that.

Democracy is not just another innovation in government administration. Democracy is the ideal of community realized in practice. It is a constant experiment whose goal is to provide for the greatest development of individual men and women in relationship to the community. For Dewey, we have always lived in the post-factual age, but have denied it. Mistaking scientism as the ushering in of a new age of facts, of objectivity, was simply the latest form of denial. The consequences of this mistake were serious. Democracy was at stake.

To pretend that science was some form of independent knowledge divorced from the interests or concerns of the peopled, established the conditions for the powerful to use science for their own interests. Public opinion could be engineered by playing down the "public" in the formation of that opinion.

Dewey presented a strong challenge to Lippmann and to a scientized understanding of the press, citizenship and democracy.

This challenge was based on Dewey's understanding of the interrelated character of epistemology, communication, and politics. However, where Lippmann's scientistic view became the dominant perspective on the relationship between the press and democracy, Dewey's view was marginalized. But the conflicts between scientism, news, and democracy that Dewey began to make visible have not gone away, but only continue to resurface in different forms. It is perhaps ironic, that the Deweyian idea of communication as both the means for inventing social reality and for constructing community are being wielded by advertisers in the service of fostering the consumption of goods rather than in the service of promoting and deepening democratic life.

SYMBOLS AND POLITICS

Lippmann provides an analysis of the political use of symbols that anticipates some of the more sophisticated arguments about post-factual age politics to be addressed in this monograph. Interestingly, this less scientistic aspect of Lippmann's work has been almost entirely neglected in traditional mass communication theory and political science. The power of symbols, Lippmann argued, rests in the irrational character of human emotions coupled with the ambiguity of symbols themselves. In terms of human emotions, Lippmann wrote, "There is no end of things which can arouse the emotion, and no end of things which can satisfy it."

The consequence is that emotions are transferable, both in terms of what stimulates them and what satisfies them. Lippmann wrote:

If, for example, one man dislikes the League [of Nations], another hates Mr. Wilson, and a third fears labour, you may be able to unite them all if you can find some symbol which is the antithesis of what they all hate. Suppose that symbol is Americanism. The first man may read it as meaning the preservation of American isolation, or as he may call it, independence; the second as the rejection of a politician who clashes with his idea of what an American president should be, the third as a call to resist revolution. The symbol in itself signifies literally no one thing in particular, but it can be associated with almost anything. And because of that it can become the common bond of common feelings, even though those feelings were originally attached to disparate ideas.

An effective symbol can mean many things to many people, generating the illusion of solidarity while at the same time deflecting rational analysis. Modern democracy is therefore less rule by the people than creating the illusion that the people rule. As Lippmann put it, "A leader or an interest that can make itself master of the current symbols is master of the current situation."

UNREALISTIC EXPECTATIONS OF THE PRESS

Given traditional democratic theory's belief in the mysterious, but natural endowment of citizens for self-government, Lippmann wrote, it is not surprising that little thought has been given to "the idea that men have to go forth and study the world in order to govern it." The existence of civil liberties, such as freedom of speech, freedom of the press, and freedom of association, were assumed to guarantee the formation of wise public opinion. But if truth is not something that spontaneously springs to life or if obstacles stand in the way of finding the truth, then this is a dangerous assumption

Lippmann argued that the truth about events and affairs outside of one's direct experience is not self evident and that the "machinery for assembling information is technical and expensive," and yet the political science of the time had not come to "grips with the problem of how to make the invisible world visible to the citizens of a modern state."

The task of informing the public, consequently, has been unthinkingly dropped at the feet of the press. The problem is, according to Lippmann, the press is ill prepared to perform this task. "It is too frail to carry the whole burden of popular sovereignty, to supply spontaneously the truth which democrats hoped was inborn."

Part of the problem is due to the nature of the public, part to the nature of news itself, and part to the organizational structure of the news. All three parts share an economic premise. The public is to blame for its interest primarily in themselves and in their unwillingness to pay the true price of gathering quality information. The consequence of the public's self-interest is that editors serve up news that does little to contribute to the formation of rational, critically reflective public opinion. "The theory," Lippmann wrote, "is that if enough people see their own names in the paper often enough, can read about their weddings, funerals, sociables, foreign travels, lodge meetings, school prizes, their fiftieth birthdays, their sixtieth birthdays, their silver weddings, their outings and clambakes, they will make a reliable circulation."

The flip-side of this self-interest is that the public is unwilling to pay the true cost of news gathering, believing that a "free press" means that "newspapers are virtually given away." The consequence is that the only way readers will pay for the news is when a major part of the cost is hidden in advertising. Put somewhat differently, if readers are unwilling to pay the true cost of the news through the subscription price, the only way for the commercial press to survive is to turn the readers "into circulation which can be sold to manufacturers and merchants." The reader is seen more as a target for advertising than as a citizen in a democracy.

The outcome, that news serves the interests of advertisers and the reading public that buys the advertisers' goods, should be of no surprise. It is the readers' collective fault, Lippmann stated. As a business practice this is all quite understandable. However, it is an uncomfortable situation if one wants to believe that the press makes up for the failings of traditional democratic theory in the creation of a rational common will.

The contradiction between news and advertising is played out in its most concentrated moment in the person of the news editor. "His enterprises," Lippmann wrote, "depend upon indirect taxation levied by his advertisers upon his readers; the patronage of the advertisers depends on the editor's skill in holding together an effective group of customers." Consequently the news editor must mostly provide news that fits within the existing range of expectations and stereotypes of the reader, emphasizing local over national, so as not to lose circulation, the economic base of the organization.

But it is not just the public, Lippmann wrote, but the economics of advertising and circulation make the press ill prepared for the task of informing the public. More important, Lippmann argued, it is the nature of news itself. For Lippmann there is a significant difference between news and the truth. "The function of news is to signalize an event, the function of truth is to bring to light the hidden facts, to set them into relation with each other, and make pictures of reality on which men can act." News then is not a "mirror of social conditions" but simply a report on some aspect of the ongoing stream of social existence that has made itself visible.

Judging which of the infinite events that make up this ongoing stream are newsworthy forces newspapers, as commercial organizations, into making decisions based as much on efficiency of selection in terms of time and effort as on the public importance of the event. Much of what is of public importance may not easily translate into an easily accessible and easily reportable event. Perhaps the most significant indication of the extent of this problem is the existence of the press agent.

Lippmann wrote,"The enormous discretion as to what facts and what impressions shall be reported is steadily convincing every organized group of people that whether it wishes to secure publicity or avoid it, the exercise of discretion cannot be left to the reporter." But to ask the press to address these limitations is to ask it to produce truth, not news. The detailed investigations that would be required"cost time, money, special talent and a lot of space," resources which, Lippmann argued, are not available to the daily press.

While economic limitations impinge in numerous ways on the quality of the press, the most important limitation is not economic but the quality of information that is officially gathered and recorded. The news"is precise in proportion to the precision with which the event is recorded. Unless the event is capable of being named, measured, given shape, made specific, it either fails to take on the character of news, or it is subject to the accidents and prejudices of observation."

Lippmann concluded that the failure of traditional democratic theory to take account of the problem of informing its citizens to allow them to engage in rational self-government is leading to a dangerous state of affairs."In the absence of institutions and education by which the environment is so successfully reported that the realities of public life stand out sharply against self-interested opinion, the common interests very largely elude public opinion entirely, and can be managed only be a specialized class whose personal interests reach beyond the locality. This class is irresponsible, for it acts upon information that is not common property, in situations that the public at large does not conceive, and it can be held to account only on the accomplished fact."

TOWARDS A"REALISTIC" THEORY OF DEMOCRACY

For Lippmann, the result of his analysis is that democracy is in danger because we have overburdened it with false hopes about the capacity of the average citizen to engage in self-rule. Even the hope that somehow the press would or could provide the means to conjure up"a mystical force called Public Opinion" is not workable.

To save democracy requires the development of a"machinery of knowledge" to overcome the"failure of self-governing people to transcend their casual experience and their prejudice." What is needed, Lippmann argued, is the development of a network of intelligence divisions supporting the various agencies of government. These divisions would be staffed by social scientists freed from the stifling confines of academia to take on the practical problems of society.

The position of the social scientist would be radically changed:

Instead of being the man who generalizes from the facts dropped to him by men of action, he becomes the man who prepares the facts for men of action. This is a profound change of strategic position. He no longer stands outside, chewing the cud provided by busy men of affairs, but he takes his place in front of the decision instead of behind it.

Lippmann recognized that he was proposing a potentially new selfinterested faction be added to government and spent considerable time sketching out some of the ways these intelligence divisions would operate but also how checks and balances could be built into a system to keep this new scientific aristocracy"neutral to their prejudice, and capable of overcoming subjectivism."

Nevertheless, Lippmann was developing a strong argument for the redefinition of what would be called"democracy." Power would be substantially withdrawn from the hands of the ill-informed mass of citizens and invested in the hands of a few"men of action," public policy analysts and political leaders.

Lippmann's justification for this shift of power was two-fold. First, traditional democratic theory asked too much of its citizens in becoming allknowing, wise, and rational directors of government. Second, proponents of traditional democratic theory had mistaken the goal of democratic government. The true point of democracy, Lippmann argued, is not simply to allow individuals the pleasure of engaging in self-government. It is as much about his desire for the"good life."

The point of democracy is not the process of government, not active citizenship, but the results of government. The purpose of the organization of intelligence divisions,"then, is not to burden every citizen with expert opinions on all questions, but to push that burden away from him towards the responsible administrator." This, in Lippmann's mind, was realistic democracy.

Lippmann was caught between two epistemological poles: truth as empirical, objective reality and truth as a construction of the mind. As much as his analysis revealed the inconsistencies of both positions, he finally felt he had to choose and he chose science, the science of Bacon, the science that believed a reality could be revealed untainted by human desire or interest.

Lippmann came to a deep understanding of the politics of truth, but not to an understanding of the politics of science as truth. Lippmann's understanding of the symbolic dimension of politics was, in many respects, as sophisticated as much political semiotic work sixty years later. What Lippmann could not accept in the 1920s was that the authority of science might be as open to question as the authority of public opinion.

In August 1921, Lippmann dropped off the manuscript for Public Opinion with his publisher and left, with his wife, for an extended trip to Europe, part vacation and part a first-hand examination of the post-war status of the European nations. When he returned in January 1922, Lippmann assumed his new post as the chief editorial writer for the New York World.

Dewey:"The most effective indictment of democracy as currently conceived ever penned...." When Public Opinion appeared in early 1922, the critics were impressed. The book was viewed as a significant breakthrough in the field of political science, revealing new and significant problems to be addressed and at the same time starkly challenging the possibility of democratic government in a modern society. At the same time the book, in many ways, ushered in modern communication studies as a critical new field.

By 1922 Dewey shared Lippmann's more general pessimism about the possibilities for democratic government following the war as well as his specific concern for the growing manipulation of public opinion. Immediately after the war Dewey held out hope that the conflict had so weakened the existing order that there was an important opportunity to reconstruct a deeper and more meaningful form of democracy.

However, this hope was quickly transformed into cynicism as the post-war reconstruction unfolded. Nationalistic strivings and economic self-interest quickly replaced any vestige of common mission that the war had generated. In addition, the management of public opinion, such a prominent technique in this first modern war, now promised to become a matter of everyday life, not only for government but for commerce.

The war had demonstrated the capacity for a new and dangerous alliance among powerful, elite interests in business, government, and the news. Their motto was, Dewey wrote,"Let us make democracy safe for the world by a careful editing and expurgation of the facts upon which it bases the opinions which in the end decide social action."

However, while Dewey shared Lippmann's concern for the current health of democracy, he did not necessarily share with him either the meaning or purpose of democracy. As early as 1892, Dewey had come to the conclusion that the class divisions brought about by industrial capitalism were contrary to the ethics of democracy." For Dewey democracy was not just a mechanical form of government, it was a recognition of the fundamentally social and interdependent nature of human existence.

"What does democracy mean," Dewey asked,"save that the individual is to have a share in determining the conditions and aims of his own work; and that, upon the whole, through the free and harmonizing of different individuals, the work of the world is better done than when planned, arranged and directed by a few, no matter how wise or how good intent that few?"

In industrial capitalism, Dewey argued, the division of labour, the means by which individuals are assigned the work they will do, is far removed from the control or interest of the worker. The consequence is that"his activity is made a means to benefit others. It can't be complete till he does that for which he is best fitted - and in which he finds the most complete expression of himself."

According to Dewey, the core of democratic politics was the effort to create the conditions for individuals in a society to develop to their fullest potential. This, Dewey believed, was not possible where democratic action was restricted to the political sphere."There is no need to beat about the bush in saying that democracy is not in reality what it is in name until it is industrial, as well as civil and political."

The importance of democracy in the workplace as well as at the ballot box, and the idea of democracy as an ethic as well as a political mechanism were to become central features in Dewey's idea of democracy. Given this expansive notion of participatory democracy and Dewey's commitment to it, it is not surprising that Lippmann's book posed such a challenge for Dewey.

Lippmann's national position and the sophistication of his argument captured Dewey's attention. In addition, Dewey was impressed by the art and force of Lippmann's argument. A few months after the book's publication, Dewey published a review of it in The New Republic. Dewey wrote,"The figures of the scene are so composed and so stand out, the manner of presentation is so objective and projective, that one finishes the book almost without realizing that it is perhaps the most effective indictment of democracy as currently conceived ever penned."

Dewey wrote that"Lippmann's relentless and realistic analysis of the limitations of the pictures in our head about the environment and his account of the methods by which the privileged few supply a supplement and substitute, so skillfully that the mass still thinks that its opinions are valid and spontaneous, is the undeniably successful part of his book.... It shivers most of our illusions, and this particular Humpty Dumpty can never be put together again for anyone who reads these chapters with an open mind."

Dewey found himself in substantial agreement with Lippmann's analysis of the rise of the"manufacture of consent" and the dire consequences it holds for democratic government. However, Dewey was uneasy about the solution Lippmann advanced. Where Lippmann dismisses the newspaper-the press-as inadequate to the task of enlightening and directing public opinion, Dewey argued that the press must continue to serve as a vital link between government and the people. Many of Lippmann's criticisms of the press are valid, but they are criticisms of the press as it now operates. The press, Dewey argued, is what is in need of reform. In the press there must be a union of social science in gathering the facts and art in the presentation of those facts in order to engage the individual as a citizen.

In a democracy, Dewey wrote,"The enlightenment of public opinion still seems to me to have priority over the enlightenment of officials and directors."Sz Dewey recognized Lippmann attempted to sketch out the means to control the new aristocracy of administrators from becoming a dangerous self-interested power block. However, for Dewey, the safeguards Lippmann proposes were not only inadequate but undemocratic. The only true safeguard is the democratic process itself.

Dewey was clearly shaken by Lippmann's argument and although he pieced together a response to Lippmann's elitist solution, Dewey acknowledged that his response at this time was based more on"feeling" than careful argument. Before Dewey could construct that careful argument, Lippmann issued his second major attack on participatory democracy in his book The Phantom Public.

POLITICS ON THE COUCH

The intention is to test and explore the boundaries that exist (we have been told) between therapy and politics, between the inner world and the outer world, between being and doing, and even between what people still call "feminine" approaches to life and "masculine" approaches to life-no matter how problematic those words are.

This paper is divided into a number of sections. It begins by addressing the questions, Why me? Why here? Why now? Then there follows a discussion of how, particularly after the 2004 U. S. presidential election, politics in the West can be understood as changing in the direction of what I call "transformative politics." Third, the question, "Can therapists really make a difference in the world today?" is asked. Fourth is a markedly experiential section entitled "The Inner Politician." I conclude with a few reflections on therapy, politics, and spirituality.

Introduction: Why Me, Why Here, Why Now?

The bases for these remarks, which are grounded in clinical work with individuals, also lie in my involvement with a number of political organizations and recent political developments. I have carried out consultations and conducted workshops in Britain, Europe, the United States, Japan, Brazil, Israel, Australia, New Zealand, and South Africa. These activities are designed to see how useful and effective perspectives derived from psychotherapy may be in forming policy, in creating new ways of thinking about the political process, and in resolving conflict. It is difficult to present therapy thinking so that mainstream politicians-for example, a senior U. S. Democrat senator or a British Labour Party committee-will take it seriously. And the problem is only slightly reduced when the politicians and organizations are alternative or activist.

I have also been involved in the formation of three organizations in Britain that are relevant to the themes of the paper. One is Psychotherapists and Counselors for Social Responsibility, an organization intended to help therapists and counselors use their knowledge and experience to intervene as professionals in social and political matters. The second organization is Antidote, a psychotherapy-based think tank cofounded with Susie Orbach.

It fosters multidisciplinary work, and links are sought with people working in fields other than psychotherapy. Antidote has undertaken research into psychological attitudes towards money and economic issues and is also involved in trying to apply ideas about emotional literacy/intelligence to politics.

The third organization is called the St. James's Alliance. Based at a beautiful Wren church in Piccadilly in central London, it consists of individuals from diverse fields such as politics, economics, ethics, religion, nongovernmental organizations, activist and pressure groups, the media, and psychotherapy.

It attempts to incorporate psychological, ethical, and spiritual concerns into the political agenda and to facilitate dialogue between various single-issue and pressure groups.

In the past, these groups were unsympathetic to other groups' goals-poverty workers did not have time for animal rights activists, for instance, and neither group seemed interested in the problems of the Middle East.

But in a suitably facilitated environment, it has been possible to find whole areas of common ground in relation to politics, and there are so many emotional and spiritual similarities to share. This is an experiment in gathering and using the shards of political energy that are normally split up and dissipated. Politics in many Western countries is broken and in a mess; we urgently need new ideas and approaches. Psychotherapists, along with economists, social scientists, religious people, environmentalists, and others, can contribute to a general transformation of politics.

Today's politicians leave many with a sense of deep despair and disgust. They seem to lack integrity, imagination, and new ideas. Across the globe, and in response to the challenge, a search is on to remodel politics. Psychotherapy's contribution to this search depends on opening a two-way street between inner realities and the world of politics. We need to balance attempts to understand the secret politics of the inner world of emotional, personal, and family experiences with the secret psychology of pressing outer-world matters such as leadership, the economy, environmentalism, nationalism, and war.

Our inner worlds and our private lives reel from the impact of policy decisions and the existing political culture. Why, then, do our policy committees and commissions not have psychotherapists sitting on them as part of a range of experts/This is not a call for a committee of therapists, but just as a committee will often have a statistician present (someone whose role may not be fully appreciated by the other members), there should also be a therapist at the conference table. We expect to find therapists offering views on social issues that involve personal and familial relationships or matters to do with mental health but they may also have ideas to contribute on the" hard" issues-war, violence, poverty, and the economy.

Is it possible to imagine a world in which people are encouraged to sharpen their half-thought-out, intuitive political ideas and commitments so as to take more effective political action? There are probably buried sources of political wisdom in many people, particularly those who do not seem likely to function in such a way. More and more, I have come to see that one does not have to be politically active or knowledgeable and talkative about politics to have something creative to say. Poets and mystics, introverts, those who eschew politics, and those who are ashamed at what they take to be their own ignorance often know something that the more overtly political do not. These anti-political citizens are a great aid in finding out how secret thingschildhood experiences, intimate relationships, fantasies (including sexual fantasies), dreams, and bodily sensations-may be reframed and turned to useful political ends.

Thinking about those who usually do not say much, I find that they make a profound contribution to what I call" political clinics." These are large-group events, often composed of persons who have nothing to do with therapy and psychology at all but come together to explore their emotional and feeling-based reactions to major political themes such as terrorism, the troubles in Northern Ireland, the conflict in the Middle East, racism, and homelessness.

I have discovered that those who say" I am not interested in politics" are often deceiving themselves, caught in a reaction formation. As the political clinic unfolds, it becomes clear that they are indeed extremely interested, knowledgeable, and wise about politics but have always doubted, because they have been taught to doubt, that the emotional reactions they are experiencing are a legitimate part of political process. We are taught, in the Western countries, not to deny that we have emotions about politics, because that would be impossible, but to put those emotions rather low on the scale of what we value in official political debate and political discussion.

Sometimes at the conclusion of these political clinics, we start to talk in terms of citizens as" therapists of the world" who have a large set of usable countertransferences to the political cultures in which they live. This idea constitutes an intellectual challenge to much psychological theorizing about citizens, especially in psychoanalysis, wherein the citizen is regarded as a kind of baby, who has a transference and a collection of fantasies towards the" parental" society in which he or she lives. Turning that around, so that the citizen is seen as a kind of therapist or parent figure for the society can have a radical, uplifting, and empowering effect, overturning the tradition-especially in psychoanalysis-in which the citizen is seen as the baby and society as the parent. This claim, that the citizen is capable of being the therapist (parent) of the world, is one that embodies many possibilities as we struggle to work out what functions citizens might perform in a society in which their voices are distorted by the mass media, and their internal lives unfold in a highly fraught political climate dominated by corporations and cartels.

TRANSFORMATIVE POLITICS

Politics is slowly changing in Western countries, and we are at a very interesting moment in political consciousness. What used to be an elitist insight about how everything is secretly political is now becoming an element in mass awareness. For years now, feminists, academics, intellectuals, and some therapists and analysts have lived happily with the idea that our personal, psychological, and private worlds are full of political tensions, dynamics, and energies. But actually this has been a superior form of knowing, a political gnosticism.

We knew that politics has expanded its definition to include all of the private stuff, but the masses did not. They have continued to be taught (but many now accept it less) that politics means official politics, party politics, congressional or parliamentary politics, power politics, the politics that money can buy, and so on. What helped to accelerate the democratization of the personal-is-political insight were the huge eruptions of feelings about certain events or political trends in recent years, turning those events into what can be called archetypal or at least numinous experiences: I am thinking of disparate phenomena, ranging from grief at the death of Princess Diana, to global anger at the role of the United States in world politics, to intense debates about the role of women in societies across the planet.

The most ruthlessly successful contemporary politicians (such as Tony Blair) have perceived this move into general awareness of the elitist, gnostic, private knowledge about how politics has changed, and they now couch their utterances in the language of the emotions.

Another way in which politics has changed is that it has become more of a transformative process. By this I mean that engagement in political activity and processes of personal growth and development are seen increasingly as the same thing, or at least as the two sides of a coin.

If one interviews persons active in post-Seattle politics, in the environmental movements, in certain sectors of feminism or the men's movement, or in ethnopolitics, one sees that what they are doing is in many respects self-healing in a positive sense that is familiar to psychotherapists. So politics starts to carry an overtly psychological, transformative burden. Sadly, this kind of transformative politics is not only progressive and left leaning, but it can also be spotted in many right-wing and reactionary movements, as the recent election showed.

A third way in which politics has changed is that there is now something that can be called" political energy" to be considered along with political power. Political power is what you would imagine it to be: control over resources such as land, water, oil-or indeed, information and imagery.

Especially today, the issue of who controls information and imagery (*e.g.*, on the Internet and on television) is almost as important as the issue of who controls oil or water. Political power is held by those you would expect to hold it: men, white people, the middle and upper-middle classes, and those who run the big institutions of finance, the military, and the academic and professional worlds, including the world of mental health.

Political energy is different. It is almost the opposite of political power. Political energy involves idealism and an imaginative and visionary focus on certain political problems with a view to making a creative impact on those problems (not necessarily with the goal of solving them). Political energy seeks more political energy, attempting to build to critical mass. It is different from political power because those who have political energy, imagination, commitment, idealism, and real compassion almost by definition lack political power.

Conversely, in contemporary societies, those who have political power tend to lack political energy. This is a funda-mental and radical claim that I am sure will be much disputed. Indeed, the very idea of political energy will upset some intellectual applecarts, because most analysts cannot entertain this notion. In their view, energy does not exist; it is only a mechanistic 19th-century way of looking at things. But there seems to be a possible middle position in which energy, in the sense of psychic energy, is maintained both to exist and not to exist. Jung suggested that, contra Freud's conception of libido, there is a neutral form of psychic energy that can run down various biological, psychological, spiritual, and moral channels. My proposal is that there is also a social channel and that a subset of the social channel will have to do with politics and political energy. As indicated just now, I use the term energy in both a metaphorical and a literal sense.

Jung's idea that there is a specifically moral channel for psychic energy is extremely interesting, resonating with much evolutionary, ethological, genetic, and psychoanalytic thought-Klein's idea of an innate superego, Winnicott's insistence that children have an inborn sense of guilt and hence are not born amoral, Milner's counsel that we stop seeing morality solely as something implanted in children by parents and society. Freud foreshadowed this train of thought with his remarks about the innate disposition of the self-preservation instincts to become more socially oriented.

People with political energy are doing something rather new and different in the Western world today in comparison with what those who have political power are doing. This thought can be liberatory if you are working in a small neighborhood group, in a social and political project with limited resources and support, or with people who have been abused, or if you are trying to build an environmentally informed movement for sustainable development and worldwide economic justice. If you are doing any or all of these things, then you probably do not have much power and it is very easy to judge yourself the way that the conventional political world might judge you-as a waste of time and space when it comes to real politics.

But the very notion of political energy is intended to shift this way of thinking. Very often when I talk about this, people say (as they did for example, at a conference in BeIo Horizonte, Brazil), "Yes, and we wonder what would happen if our country valued political energy as much as it values political power." If political energy is not to be found in the sites of official politics, then where may we find it? Politics has left its home base and gone out into the world to redefine itself and find other and new places to settle. I am not advocating removing political energy from moribund formal institutions; this has been happening in Western societies anyway over many years in one of the most significant sociocultural and collective psychological shifts to take place in the developed countries since the end of World War II.

A striking feature of the past 20 years in such societies has been the spontaneous growth of new social and cultural networks. More and more people are now involved in such networks, increasingly aware that what they are doing may be regarded as political.

The contemporary elasticity in our definition of politics is not something that has been worked out by intellectuals. Nor has there been a concerted effort to achieve such a shift, because the new social movements operate in isolation from each other.

Yet, as we have found in the St. James's Alliance discussed previously, they have something psychological in common. They share an emotional rejection of big politics-its pomposity and self-interest, its mendacity and complacency.They share a Weltanschauung and set of values based on ideas of living intelligible and purposeful lives in spite of the massive social and financial forces that work against intelligibility and purpose.

Such new social changes include environmentalism; the formation of groups working for the rights of ethnic and sexual minorities, animal liberation, complementary medicine; spiritual and religious groups devoted to paganism and neo-paganism; rock and other kinds of music and art; finding God in the new physics; an explosive growth in the participation in sports; organic farming-and psychoanalysis, psychotherapy, and counseling.

Elsewhere, I referred to the social movements as participating in a "resacralization" of politics. Sacral means holy, and the intent was to pick up on the attempt to get a sense of purpose, decency, aspiration, and meaning back into political culture. When I consider attempts by analysts and psychotherapists to do their bit, I have no alternative but to count us as part of this general, worldwide resacralizing movement.

Psychotherapists may want to be different and special, but in our attempts to work the borders between psychotherapy and society, we are part of something bigger, even if the rhetoric sometimes feels too New Agey. Psychotherapists tend to share with other resacralizers a sense of disgust with present politics and politicians. In political clinics, this is often an actual physical disgust involving the gagging reflex, an ancient part of the nervous system that is absolutely necessary for survival in a world full of tangible and metaphorical toxins.

Let me conclude this section by accepting that a transformation of politics is not going to happen in any kind of simple or speedy way and may not happen at all. There is an impossibility to the whole project because the social realm is as inherently uncontrollable as the drives and images of the inner world and the unconscious. Once human desire enters a social system-as it always will-that system cannot function predictably. There are no final solutions to social questions. The social issues that face Western societies are as incorrigible, as unresponsive to treatment, as the psychological issues that individuals face.

Moreover, many will dispute that the cumulative public significances of these movements is positive. It can be argued that the proliferation of new networks and cultural practices is merely a further symptom of social malaise-a selfish retreat into personal, individual preoccupations, reflecting an abandonment of the aspiration to truly political values. It can also be pointed out that reactionary, fundamentalist, religious movements can be seen as attempting, in their own rather different terms, a form of resacralization. But what gets highlighted when religious fundamentalism is brought into the picture is the vastness of the energy pool available for the political reforms that are urgently needed.

Although I am enthusiastic about psychotherapy's role in the refreshing of political culture, I am also somewhat skeptical. So my answer to the question "Can therapists really make a difference?" is both "No" and "Yes." Let's deal with "No" first-with the pessimism. James Hillman and Michael Ventura wrote a book called We've Had a Hundred Years of Psychotherapy-and the World's Getting Worse. It is fairly clear what they were getting at-that psychotherapy makes little or no impact on an unjust world and that persons in therapy are cut off from taking responsibility for ameliorating injustice (cut off from their political energy by therapy, which takes all available psychic energy for its own project of personal exploration).

Yet I think that a much more accurate title for their book would have been We've Had a Hundred Years of Psychotherapy, Trying to Improve the World, But the World Has Stayed Pretty Much the Same, because it is not new for psychotherapists to want to do something in relation to the world. Freud wanted it, Jung wanted it, and the great pioneers of humanistic psychotherapy-such as Maslow, Rogers, and Peris-all wanted it as well. All of these people and their followers invited the world into therapy, but the world didn't show up for its first therapy session.

There are good reasons why the world didn't show up, other than mere resistance. One reason is that therapists so much want and need to be right. (Me, too-this shadow issue of the analyst's maddening rectitude is not one I pretend to have fully dealt with.) Therapists want to reduce everything to the special knowledge that they have. This kind of reductionism gives therapy a bad name when it comes to political and social issues. For example, I remember reading in the London Guardian an article-later the object of intense ridicule-by a Kleinian psychoanalyst about the phallic symbolism of cruise missiles going down ventilator shafts in Baghdad.

My Jungian colleagues are just as bad when they tell us that the military-industrial complex is all the responsibility of the Greek God Hephaestos. The world won't listen to that level of explanation from psychotherapists and is right not to. The priority for psychotherapists is to embark on multidisciplinary work.

But other issues besides therapy reductionism have stopped us from being useful outside a few specific areas such as psychoanalytically influenced social casework or, in some countries, child welfare legislation. Overall, there is a fairly bad record to own up to. Psychotherapists have colluded with oppressive regimes in Nazi Germany, the former Soviet Union, Argentina, and South Africa.

We have been involved in dubious activities such as sending soldiers suffering from shell shock and battle fatigue back to the line of battle in both world wars. There is also the ever-present collusion of many psychotherapists with all manner of normative and oppressive practices, ranging from the psychopathological stigmatization of lesbians and gay men.

And therapists all over the world easily join in right-wing politicians' attacks on father-lacking lone-parent families. According to the right-wing reading, these families-totally responsible for spoiling our wonderful world, only need a father or father figure to come back and sort them out. I love fathers and was one of the first to write about what good-enough fathers actually do, especially with their bodies, to further the sexual, aggressive, and spiritual development of their children. But I utterly loathe the damaging idealization of fathers that so many Western politicians have gone in for, backed by complacent analysts, therapists, and other mental health professionals.

Then there is the problematic matter of psychotherapy's implicit claim that Western androcentric, middle-class values and ways of thinking hold and have value universally and are superior to/should be imposed on the values and ways of thinking of non-Western cultures.

Clearly, these unspoken assumptions reflect the typical caseloads of analysts and therapists, especially in private practice, in many countries. The treatment of women in much psychoanalytic thinking and practice has also been damaging to some. The rise of feminist and gender-sensitive psychotherapy has had an important impact in ameliorating this situation. And what a lot of therapists and analysts say about men is also beginning to receive the same kind of critique that definitions of and generalizations about women used to receive.

Another reason why people are not so likely to listen to therapists who want to make a difference in the world is that therapists are completely crazy in their own professional politics, and the way they organize themselves radiates that craziness. No profession has been quite as subject to splits as the therapy profession; no profession has so frequently used personal demonization and pathological pigeonholing to deal with and get rid of troublesome outsiders and those who question from within. As I continue to look at why we world-oriented therapists do not have a client, I note that-for reasons I do not fully understand even now-the therapy world has tragically split its clinical project off from its sociocritical project. Frankfurt school writers and Lacanian theorists rarely talk of clients, or in an ordinary way about people: mothers, fathers, families, marriages, dreams, symptoms, sexuality, aggression, the inner world of the imagination. And when we read most clinical texts, the external world is hardly mentioned. Much therapy still seems (or claims) to take place in a political vacuum.

There are several delusional aspects of this virginal fantasy about what we do. One delusion is that there are no politics going on the session itself, whereas many clinicians know how the power dynamics and imbalances of the typical therapy setup cannot be wished away by reference to parental transference or the law of the father. These power imbalances often involve the denial of difference of any kind between therapist and client, the bending of the client to the moral will of the therapist, and the ongoing scandal of sexual misconduct.

Another delusion is that it is not possible to find a responsible way to work directly with political, social, and cultural material in the clinical session. There is not sufficient space here for a full discussion of this topic. Succinctly, my position is that it is time to think together about how we can change our practices and our thinking about clinical work in order to incorporate these taboo themes.

To explore empirically what has been happening at the interface of psychotherapy and politics in the actual session, I surveyed 2000 analysts and therapists of many schools worldwide about which political issues their clients mentioned in therapy, how frequently the clients raised such issues, whether such mentions were increasing or decreasing, and how the therapists reacted.

Approximately 700 responded: I also asked the respondents about their own political views and histories. The survey revealed that the therapy profession is far more politically sensitive than one would think, and that politics is a welcome theme in a significant minority of clinical offices.

It underlined the importance of shopping around for and interviewing a potential analyst or therapist. The answers to the questions about which political and social issues are raised also made it clear that clients are raising economic, environmental, and gender-political issues (including issues that do not seem to affect them personally) in their therapy sessions much more than they used to. The respondents clearly wanted to honour and respond to this development, but almost all admitted that they lacked training, helpful texts, and general encouragement to do it on a regular, professional, reputable basis. In fact, many felt that it would be regarded as bad practice even though they wanted very much to engage more expertly with such material when clients bring it to the session.

There is a big difference between a mutual exploration of some huge external event that has dominated everyone's lives (such as the terrorist attacks on September 11, 2001) and struggling to develop ongoing, ordinary ways of working in the session with the client's political selfhood (and that of the therapist) as it has evolved over a lifetime.

Though it can be a fascinating and important moment in any therapy, responding to the impact on the analysis of a moment of high political drama that has affected everyone is not the same as extending what we regard as contemporary good practice to include all aspects of work on the political dimensions of experience.

For example, the Psychoanalytic Dialogues symposium entitled "Reflections on September 11, 2001" (2003, 13/3), though moving, and insightful, did not refer to an ongoing need to develop clinical principles by which to explore the transformative aspects of what I call political discussion within the sealed vessel of an ordinary therapy relationship.

Such work might include (but not be restricted to) the following:

- Exploration of the role played by the joint immersion in the social order on the part of analyst and client in making relationality possible in the first place, whether at a conscious level or at that of unconscious-to-unconscious communication: citizenship facilitating countertransference;
- Considering the functioning of nonpersonal fields that cause distress in individuals who are not personally affected-for example, economic injustice, species depletion, domestic violence (my experience being that the strongest imaginable affects, disturbances in self-image, and psychological conditions-such as depression-involve etiologies at least partly rooted in such nonpersonal fields); and
- Refining technique so as to work out ways of managing states in the analyst that are difficult to manage due to the presence of political viewpoints in the client that feel offensive, upsetting, or disagreeable to the analyst (we all work with people whom we sometimes find unpleasant, and we can build on this capacity so as to encompass our responses to what we find personally unpleasant in the political positions held by the client).

The Inner Politician

Where did your own politics originate? I think this is a question worth asking. What influence did your mother have on the politics you now have? Or your father? And what about differences between your parents in political outlook? Some people have been influenced in their political development by significant others in their lives, such as teachers, clergy, older friends at school. Were you? Your gender is really very significant in the kind of attitude to politics that you have, and your sexual orientation is equally important. Lesbians and gay men live more closely to the political aspects and nuances of life than straight people do. Class and socioeconomic factors are obviously central, too, and so is ethnic, religious, and national background. In Western societies, the feeling of being oppressed by a domestic tyrant, whether male or female, or of seeing other family members as oppressed, can give rise to a sharp sense of injustice and embryonic revolutionary feelings.

Sometimes when I talk to people about what has formed their politics, they start to speak about an event or moment that they remember-their first political memory, the first time they became aware that there is a political system with power at its core, including disparities of wealth and influence. Did you explore these first political memories with your own analyst?

Another way to look at the notion of the inner politician is to imagine a political energy scale on which ten stands for political fanaticism, even martyrdom, and zero stands for absolute passivity, a total lack of interest in politics. Where would you place yourself right now in your life-what level of political energy do you have? Play around with the scale. When you're with people of the same sex, does the energy level go up or down or stay the same?

Is it higher at home or at work? Are there some issues that send it skyrocketing and some that bring it down? Think of the last big interpersonal disagreement or fight with someone you love. Could it be that there was a different level of political energy at work in each of you?

Let's take this thinking right into the traditional heartland of psychotherapy. What was your mother's level of political energy compared with yours, or with your father's? What was your level compared with the typical level of those from the street or neighborhood where you grew up? Continuing to sketch the inner politician, I come to the question of political style. I have noticed in my conflict resolution work that those in conflict are often operating not only with very different levels of political energy, but also with very different political styles. Hence, in my work as a political consultant, I am using the idea of conflicting political styles in many settings.

My inspiration in overall terms was Jung's model of psychological types: extroversion, introversion, thinking, feeling, sensation, intuition. As in life generally, for a variety of reasons (some having to do with personal backgrounds, some with inborn political constitutions), people live out the political aspects of themselves in different ways. Some are violent terrorists; some are pacifists.

Some want empirical backup for their ideas; others prefer to fly by the seat of their pants. Some definitely enjoy cooperative political activity; others will suffer the nightmare of working in a group only because they passionately believe in the ends being pursued. As we begin to work out a psychologically driven transformative politics, let us not make the mistake of insisting that everyone do it in precisely the same way.

If we are to promote political creativity, we need to value and honour diverse political styles and types, and to think of ways of protecting such diversity. (I am indebted to Muriel Dimen [personal communication] for the observation that political style and self-state have something in common as approaches to the diversity of personality.)

As I mentioned, the notion of political style is useful when addressing conflict, whether interpersonal or within organizations or even between nations or parts of nations. Just as introverts and extroverts suffer from mutual incompre-hension, persons who employ a particular political style often have very little understanding of how other persons or groups are actually doing their politics. This is not to say that political content per se is irrelevant, only that there may be more that divides opponents than their different views.

One might list words that evoke images of differing political types as follows, in a spectrum ranging from active styles to passive ones: warrior, terrorist, exhibitionist, leader, activist, parent, follower, child, martyr, victim, trickster, healer, analyst, negotiator, bridge builder, diplomat, philosopher, mystic, ostrich. When working on questions of political style, it is not necessary to encourage anyone to stick to just one style.

In fact, the opposite is true. The context in which the politics in question is taking place needs to be borne in mind. Some people will use one political style in one setting and quite another in a different one.

A negotiator at work may be a terrorist at home. Some may have a superior political style, an inferior political style, and auxiliary styles, to borrow the words of Jimg's typological schema. Thus, a warrior may have neglected her philosopher or a diplomat his activist.

This approach was partially fashioned on the basis of my work with a mixed group of Israeli Arabs and Israelis of Jewish background in Jerusalem in the early 1990s.

It became clear that, aside from the obvious irreconcilable differences in how the Middle East political scene was understood, there were individuals on both sides of the divide who were participating in the group in very similar or identical ways.

I pointed this out and reorganized the spatiality and seating plan of the group along style lines rather than content lines.

There were discernible improvements in comprehension, and even, to a limited extent, in goodwill. The warring factions were presented not with an analysis of what they were saying (that came later), but with a panorama of the ways in which they were saying it-that is to say, with the style of politics they were using.

I have also found the same approach useful in addressing organizational and theoretical disputes in the psychotherapy field and, most recently, in work with senior administrators in Britain's beleaguered National Health Service.

Psychotherapy, Politics, and Spirituality

Attempts are constantly made to improve things in the political world, usually by redistributing wealth or changing legislative and constitutional structures or defusing warlike situations. It is not that nothing is being tried to make things better. Equally vigorous attempts are made to resist and to contest such changes, and most social systems have a gigantic, impersonal capacity to resist change anyway.

But projects of reform are valuable and necessary and generate their own psychological changes. For example, the consequences of fair and effective minimum wage legislation or devolving power to the regions of a country or amending the constitution would have effects that would show up on any national emotional audit.

But a materialist approach deriving exclusively from economics, or one that depends solely on altering the structures of the state, will not refresh those parts of the individual citizen that a psychological perspective can reach.

Our disappointment at liberal democracy's failure to deliver the spiritual goods and our growing realization that there are limits to what can be achieved by economic redistribution or altering constitutional structures strengthen my overall argument: something is missing in contemporary Western politics, something that involves a calamitous denial of the secret life at its core. We can change the clothes and shift the pieces around, but the specter that haunts materialist and constitutional moves in the political world is that they only ruffle the surface. They do not (because-alone-they cannot) bring about the transformations for which the political soul yearns.

The perspectives advocated here may never, ever be applied to our political culture. Everything psychotherapists and analysts have said or done may fail to make one iota of difference in the condition of the world. So I conclude with a few words about failure by Samuel Beckett, who lived and struggled as intensely as anyone with what it might mean to be a good-enough citizen, involving a profound acceptance of the need to go on in the face of not being able to go on: "No matter. Fail again. Fail better."

DEBATE ABOUT THE POLITICS OF NEWS

There is a long held and often repeated assumption within liberal pluralist theories of the press that modern democracy rests on the foundation of the informed citizen who makes decisions based on rational, objective criteria and that the news media are perhaps the most crucial source of this information. The citizen, the media, and democratic government are neatly stitched together in this civic trilogy. And it is this assumption that has been eroding as we appear to have moved into a post-factual age where the border between fact and fiction, news and entertainment, information and advertisements has increasingly blurred.

For a long time now this assumption has been challenged by liberal and critical theorists for underestimating the role of ideology in the production of news. This is, what might be called, the"bias" critique, although on rare occasions the critique goes beyond bias to consider the very epistemology of news objectivity. The"bias" critique, perhaps the most dominant form of news criticism during the last three-quarters of a century, holds out the hope that the errors of accuracy and factuality may still be corrected, saving both the press and the democratic process.

More recently the liberal assumption has been challenged by liberal and critical theorists for misunderstanding that the role of the news as an institution is much more than the provision of information. This is what we might call the"cultural" critique and has taken two forms. Critical theorists have focused on the concept of the public sphere, asking where and under what condition is public opinion formed? And liberal theorists have begun to ask, under the guise of the public journalism movement, what is the role of news in the creation and maintenance of a democratic culture?

These are important challenges and important efforts to address what has been seen as the latest crisis of the press, a crisis of irrelevancy marked by declining readership, declining viewership, declining trust, and a decline even in a taste for the serious.

Much has been written to substantiate the bias as well as the cultural critique of news and citizenship. However, the present monograph will argue that there is a connection between these challenges, as well as the original impetus to the traditional assumption of the informational role of the news, which has only been hinted at, a connection that links what is seen as a problem of bias or a problem of civic participation to what might be called an"epistemological politics"that is, the politics of what we know and how we act as citizens is linked to the politics of how we know.

This monograph will argue that this link can be usefully illustrated and its importance explored by returning to a unique moment in United States media history: a debate between social commentator and journalist Walter Lippmann and philosopher John Dewey.

This debate is not unfamiliar to those concerned with the interconnections of citizenship, media, and democracy. In fact this debate, significantly brought to the attention of communication scholars by James W. Carey in the early 1980s, has in the last few years achieved a remarkable celebrity even in the popular press.

In large part this has been due to the work of Jay Rosen, director of the"Project on Public Life and the Press" at New York University. Rosen saw this dialog between Lippmann and Dewey as illustrative of the contemporary need for the press to see its role in activist terms, both serving to rekindle a vital public life and serve as an active member of that public life. Rosen's work has, in turn, been drawn on and popularized by James Fallows in his recent book Breaking the News. Of particular concern here is the reconstruction of the Lippmann-Dewey exchange as it emerges as the theoretical foundation for the public journalism movement. Carey was acutely interested in what this exchange revealed about the interconnection between epistemology and values, and this interest was carried forward by scholars such as Daniel Czitrom in his intellectual history of modern communication theory, and John Peters in his consideration of the intersection of theories of democracy and theories of communication.

However, in the work of public journalism movement writers like Rosen and Fallows, the significance of the connection between epistemology and values, not to mention power and politics, has faded considerably.

Of crucial importance to Dewey's position in this exchange was his critique of science as an ideology and the connection of this critique to the meaning of democracy. Dewey was not simply calling for a more activist press and public, but was at work unriddling, for the sake of democracy, one of the most pervasive new forms of power in modern society: science as a way of knowing and science as a new value system which claimed to be valuefree.

A key challenge of this monograph, then, is to recover this critical dimension of the Lippmann-Dewey exchange in order to broaden the discussion as to what is the deeper nature of the current crisis of the press and how this crisis should be addressed. At the same time it is hoped that this work can help establish an intellectual bridge between the public journalism movement and the current interest among communication scholars in the more theoretically sophisticated and more critical idea of the public sphere, particularly as represented by the work of Jurgen Habermas.

The guiding question, in this historical revisitation, will be how the turn to an information model of the news did, some might say a"scientization" of the press, affect the role of public opinion in U.S. democracy and contribute to a redefinition of citizenship as well as democracy in America? Lippmann's answer, which in many ways has turned out to be prophetic, was that America's turn to liberalism and particularly to a scientific vision of liberalism would end up undermining all moral authority.

As Lippmann more bluntly put it"Liberalism had burned down the barn to roast the pig." Dewey's answer expressed a greater hope for a democratic future. But this faith was not based on the ideals of liberalism as much as in an understanding of the living character of democracy as a process rather than an end and in an understanding that the creation of knowledge is a social process that must be visible and responsive to the collective will of the people.

THE LIPPMANN-DEWEY DEBATE

In the 1920s an obscure debate took place between Walter Lippmann and John Dewey at an extraordinary moment in U.S. history. Not only was the press experiencing a major credibility crisis in its role as a democratic institution, but significant doubts were being raised about the viability of democracy itself as a form of government.

Lippmann, in his twenties, was already a nationally prominent and influential journalist. Dewey, in his sixties, was considered one of America's pre-eminent philosophers.

The context for the debate was the growing despair about the future of democracy. President Woodrow Wilson's work to secure what he thought were the conditions for a lasting peace after World War I had collapsed in the face of rising nationalism and international commercial interests. Efforts to establish democratic governments in Germany and Italy had been thwarted. The tremors of the Bolshevik revolution were still being felt across Europe and in the United States. The belief in the fundamentally irrational nature of humankind was spreading.

The depth of doubt over the future of democracy manifested itself not only in the halls of academia and on the editorial pages of major newspapers, but also in the nooks and crannies of everyday culture. For instance, an official, widely used 1928 United States Army Training Manual stated that democracy led to"mobocracy," the rule of mobs, and that the democratic attitude towards property was"communistic." Democracy, the manual concluded, led to"demogogism, license, agitation, discontent, anarchy."

Against this backdrop, the debate came to focus on the meaning and role of the news and"the public" in a democratic society. Lippmann, because of his grave doubts over the capacity of the average citizen to engage in rational self-government, advocated a turn to positivistic science, not just for journalism, but for the practice of democracy as a whole. For Lippmann, given the inevitable tendency of individuals to distort what they see, coupled with the basic irrationality of humankind, the only hope for democratic government was to reinvent it. This new, more"realistic" democracy would be tempered and guided by a form of knowledge which, Lippmann believed, rose above subjectivity and politics: science. The Pandora's Box of the relativity of truth would be carefully resealed and a line drawn, if not neatly then at least boldly, between fact and fiction.

For Dewey, the crisis of the individual subjectivity and the crisis of democracy were not to be solved by science alone. Science had its own problems. For Dewey, one of the great ironies of science was that after it had performed such an efficient job of shattering belief in a metaphysical truth, in absolute truths such as God or the spirit of history, it attempted to claim that position for itself.

That is, the positivist notion of science made the ironic claim that its truth existed outside of the influence or control of human action. Yet positivism provided no basis for this claim. For Dewcy scientific knowledge was human-made knowledge. To claim that science was the answer to the crisis of subjectivity and the crisis of democracy was not to solve either of those problems, but to avoid them or worse, hide them. Dewey argued that democracy has suffered from the bureaucratization and impersonalization of industrial life and from the growing power of economic forces to secure their interests in government either directly through compulsion or threat or indirectly in the manipulation of public opinion.

The answer to these problems, Dewey argued, is not to establish an intellectual aristocracy in the name of science -- where the pretense is that they have access to a truth untainted by human interests.

The answer, Dewey argued, is to work to revive the power of the public so that it can speak for itself and demand that its interests, the public's interests be discovered, heard, and followed.

The path for Dewey meant a direct confrontation with the interrelationship of science, the press, and democracy. The heart of this relationship, Dewey said, was communication. But by communication Dewey did not mean the machinery of communication, but the art of communication, the process by which citizens in a society came to understand the nature of their interdependence through a system of shared meaning.

In terms of the press, the path for Dewey was a turn to what might be called public journalism, although the term public journalism as it is being used today contains much less than what Dewey was calling for.

For both Lippmann and Dewey, somehow the problem of epistemology, about how we come to know what we know, was connected both. to communication and citizenship.

AN ODD DEBATE

In many respects the debate between Lippmann and Dewey was unusual. Simply as a debate, it did not take the form we typically associate with debating. There was no face-to-face confrontation. No live coverage. In fact it was carried out over a period of years, mainly in the form of books and essays. And one might even wonder if Lippmann knew he was even part of the debate. Where Dewey, in his essays and book, felt compelled to answer directly Lippmann's arguments, Lippmann never returned the courtesy.

As a rising political superstar, perhaps Lippmann believed he had bigger fish to fry. Dewey certainly was not a small fish. In his sixties as a professor at Columbia University, he was generally regarded as one of the pre-eminent American philosophers of the time. However, his influence on government and politics was no match for Lippmann's. While Dewey had access to the editorial pages of the New York Times to express his opinions about the issues of the day, Lippmann dined with the presidents and occasionally wrote their speeches. Lippmann, it would seem, had more on his mind than Dewey.

Lippmann appeared less interested in achieving consistency in his philosophical and political positions than in influencing the movers and shakers with his vision. For Dewey, a long-time outsider, Lippmann was a mover and shaker, worthy of being addressed and valuable if he could be persuaded.

It was also an odd debate in that the two men had often stood on the same side of many political issues. They both had supported Woodrow Wilson's re-election bid for the presidency and, unlike many progressives of the period, they both stood behind him when he led the country into war.

During the war when efforts to censor any statements critical of the United States were being stepped up, both men actively protested such action. The two men were known for their faith in the scientific method as a useful tool for solving the problems of society as well as industry.

They both supported the women's movement and voting rights for women, but neither seemed to have thought much about the more profound implications of the women's movement for political theory, particularly as it concerned the relationship between domestic and public life.

In fact, a good bit of Lippmann's formative thinking about society was influenced by Dewey. When Lippmann, at the age of twenty-three, made his appearance on the national political scene with the 1913 publication of his first book A Preface to Politics, the thinking of Dewey, or at least Lippmann's interpretation of Dewey, was a major part of the solution advanced by the book for the various ills of society.

In this book, Lippmann managed to weave together some of Dewey's thoughts on the role of science in social change, as well as William James celebration of what he called "experience," Nietzsche's affirmation of the will, H.G. Well's utopianism, and Freud's notion of the unconscious.

The book also represented the opening salvo by Lippmann on the middle-class reform efforts of the progressive movement, favoring instead the "radical" idea of scientific management. Lippmann's second book, Drift and Mastery, published in 1914, was also indebted to Dewey's ideas concerning the scientific management of society, ideas which, as we will see, may not have been interpreted quite as Dewey intended.

The two men began a personal working relationship in 1914 when Lippmann became the first editor of The New Republic, a national monthly magazine "of politics and arts."

Dewey was enlisted as one of the many prestigious contributors to the magazine, a magazine that served as a vehicle for Lippmann to continue his ascent into national political prominence and provided Dewey with his first truly national forum to move outside of philosophy to serve as commentator on national politics. Lippmann's esteem for Dewey was also visibly revealed in other ways. In a 1916 review of Dewey's book Democracy and Education, published in The New Republic, Lippmann wrote that the result of the book "is not information or propaganda but a book which is the mature wisdom of the finest and most important intellect devoted to the future of American civilization." During the war Lippmann was appointed to coordinate a team of specialists to advise President Wilson on the shape of the peace plan to be implemented at the war's end. Lippmann invited Dewey to head a special branch of the Enquiry to be based in Moscow. The branch never materialized, but the invitation indicated Lippmann's continued high esteem for Dewey.

Following the war, faced with disruption and uncertainty at home and abroad, the contrasts between their ideas became more visible as they turned their attention to what must be done to rescue democratic government. Lippmann's blend of liberalism and elitism became more pronounced and Dewey's commitment to participatory democracy deepened.

EXONERATING POPULAR CULTURE/SHAKING THE BLAME

As the implication of a popular-culture product in the murder case became old news, new theories of blame started to circulate. During this time, a few weeks after the murder, two key suspects shared the blame for Amedure's murder with the "Jenny Jones Show"-Jonathan Schmitz himself and what was called the "homosexual panic defence." Paul E. Gainor, reporting for The Detroit News, March 26, 1995, was one of many who explored this theory.

Richard S. Sinacola, a Royal Oak therapist for 12 years...says the case of Scott Amedure and John Schmitz...may have involved homosexual panic as a trigger point.... Sinacola theorizes that Schmitz "couldn't handle the fact that it involved homosexuality." For him, it touched on some deep-seated homophobia.... What he was killing was not so much the victim, but his own sense of homosexuality in the victim.

The "homosexual panic defence" theory quickly took centre stage in news articles after stories about Jenny Jones' irresponsible behaviour began to subside. The homosexual panic defence made headlines a few weeks after the murder and reappeared as a secondary object of blame when the media began covering Schmitz's first trial. From The Seattle Times, reporter not listed, on October 6, 1996:

Focusing on the "Jenny Jones Show" shifts blame away from the defendant to homophobia... Society's problem is not that these TV shows are on. Society's problem is that we've created a world where a guy feels he can go out and kill a guy because he is gay.

As the "hate, not humiliation" theory became the new focus of news stories, a small contingent began to blame Schmitz again for the murder. Robert Strauss of The Los Angeles Times said that Schmitz would have to be pretty gullible to have no idea what he was in for on the "Jenny Jones Show." Strauss argued that even if the show's producers encouraged Amedure to be "flamboyant" towards Schmitz, Schmitz still purchased the gun, sought out Amodure, and killed him.

UNIQUE ELEMENTS

While Scott Amedure's death is undoubtedly a tragedy, his death did not reach the magnitude, in terms of press coverage or public outrage, of the Columbine High School shootings or Princess Diana's death.

The "Jenny Jones" talk-show case also differed from the other two cases in that it involved two trials and a negligence suit brought against the show.

In the late fall of 1995, hearings on the "Jenny Jones" murder case began, and throughout late 1995 and 1996, the "Jenny Jones" talk-show murder began making news again. While more than six months had passed between the murder and the first round of hearings, Jenny Jones, the show, and its producers still remained the objects of blame for Amedure's murder.

As the trial neared, Schmitz's new defence attorney again tried to focus on the talk show's tactics. While on the stand, Jenny Jones herself maintained that Schmitz knew his secret admirer could be a man or a woman.

Ron French, for The Detroit News on February 21, 1996, wrote several stories about the trial stages of the case.

...defence attorney James Burdick will try to deflect responsibility for the slaying from his client to the "Jenny Jones Show" and its ambush interview tactics. Schmitz claims he was misled by producers who persuaded him to fly to Chicago to appear on a show about secret admirers.

On November 12, 1996, Jonathan Schmitz was convicted of second-degree murder, yet jurors for the trial said the show deserved at least some of the blame. Ron French of The Detroit News, November 13, 1996, covered the case's outcome from the jury's point of view.

"We saw the show as a catalyst for this," said juror Joyce O'Brien. "They destroyed one person's life and his family, and another young man is dead and his family ruined. It is a terrible injustice all because of the show."

As the trial came to a close, reporters from the "elite" media again began bashing the "Jenny Jones Show," the show's producers, and daytime TV for the "corruption of society " The Boston Globe, AP story, Dec. 8, 1995). An Associated Press story, written by Frazier Moore, discussed the details of the verdict in a November 29, 1996, column.

Obviously Jonathan Schmitz wasn't prepared for what he got by Jones or any of the Jenny Jones staff. Quite the opposite. Evidence indicates that for the sake of lively talk TV, Schmitz was set up to believe he would be meeting the girl of his dreams. Instead, he met Jenny Jones.

After the much-publicized trial and verdict, the two years following the trial, 1997 and 1998, were fairly quiet. News of the murder and trial popped up sporadically, mostly in the form of editorials. Schmitz was convicted in 1996, but in 1998, his conviction was overturned on a technicality in an appeals court. In May of 1999, a jury awarded the Amedure family $25 million in a negligence suit against the "Jenny Jones Show." From a Los Angeles Times story (byline merely indicating it was from wire reports) on May 15, 1999: A jury finds the "Jenny Jones Show" liable for the 1995 shooting death of Scott Amedure, a gay man who admitted during a never-aired show that he had a crush on Jonathan Schmitz. The jury awarded $25 million in damages to Amedure's family, saying the show tricked Schmitz and humiliated him into committing the murder.

In September 1999, Jonathan Schmitz was convicted for the second time in the death of Scott Amedure. Circuit Judge Wendy Potts handed Schmitz a 25 to 50-year sentence-the same sentence he received in his first trial.

The $25 million civil-suit award for the Amedure family represents a new turn in state and federal courts holding entertainment media liable for a tragedy. Culpability in the "Jenny Jones" talk-show murder case was easier to prove than the culpability of the violent video games, music, and films linked to the Columbine High School shooting and of the paparazzi linked to the death of Princess Diana. The title of the segment, "Secret Admirers," the "ambush-style" tactics, and the notion that a talk-show guest was allegedly "goaded" to "act flamboyantly" have all been cited as evidence that the show and its producers incited the murder.

CONTEXT OF POPULAR-CULTURE BLAME

At the same time the entertainment industry was being held accountable for Scott Amedure's death, news of other tragedies, including the Columbine High School shootings, hit the airwaves and newsstands, and some producers of popular culture were again the target of blame. From the time of the murder to the time of Jonathan Schmitz's first trial, the "Jenny Jones Show," the producers of the show, daytime talk shows in general, homophobia, and Schmitz had all been blamed for the death of Amedure.

The news stories acknowledged Schmitz was responsible for pulling the trigger; however, many reporters seemed intent on finding an additional source of blame. Through the selection of sources used in news stories to the focus of the news stories themselves, the "elite" media seemed to assign blame to the "less-than-legitimate" talk shows. Within a month after the murder, many of the "elite" media jumped on the bandwagon of accusing the popular media of polluting America. From The Washington Post, on October 31, 1995:

Still, there's no question many talk shows exploit and often humiliate people for entertainment-especially the ambush-style Programmes like the infamous Jenny Jones episode that was accused of sparking a murder.

Some of the news stories even tried to draw distinctions between audiences of the "trashy" daytime talk shows and the audiences for other news-oriented Programmes. Sharon Waxman in The Washington Post described viewers of the daytime talk shows as "gullible...often unemployed...leeches" who had nothing better to do than to live vicariously through the lives of other "trailer park trash."

This cycle of blame became all the more evident as Jonathan Schmitz headed into his first trial and then his second trial. "Elite" newspapers such as The Washington Post, The Los Angeles Times, The Dallas Morning News, The Detroit News, and The Chicago Tribune appeared to draw a clear distinction between themselves and the popular media. Furthermore, these news outlets criticized the talk shows for uncovering secrets, exposing wrongdoings, and "harping on the perversion in society." Yet many of these publications were doing the same thing by giving the story so much coverage. The difference is that the talk shows were reaching one audience, and the "elite" media used the same "trash" to reach another audience.

During the four-and-a-half-year-long evolution of the story, several theories of blame circulated. While the blame was shared, the daytime talk shows took the biggest hit for allegedly causing a larger social problem, "cultural pollution." Jonathan Schmitz's lawyer, James Burdick, said when Jenny Jones asked her television audience, "Is your life better than television?," culpability rested in her hands and in the hands of the show's producers. Burdick's contention is that in Jones' quest to focus on the drama of interpersonal conflict in a public forum, she theoretically put the gun in Schmitz's hands.

CONNECTIONS WITH THEORY

Pauly's discussion of the "elite" media's criticism of Rupert Murdoch parallels the "elite" media's criticism of the talk shows in the "Jenny Jones" case. Rupert Murdoch was accused by many in the "elite" press of devaluing journalistic ideals, and in a similar sense, journalists covering the "Jenny Jones" case accused the talk shows of not maintaining a high standard of practice. This can be seen quite clearly as many newspaper reporters covering the story implicitly or explicitly distinguished themselves as "serious" journalists.

Media mogul Rupert Murdoch was criticized for his style of promotional journalism, and the news organizations covering the "Jenny Jones" story capitalized on the promotional qualities of the pop-culture products they were criticizing by giving the story so much news coverage. The news media would have a difficult time rationalizing the prominent play the story received, especially the length of time the story was in the news, because over the course of time, new details were not uncovered. More simply, the story was essentially old news with a high level of sensationalism and a presumed high level of public interest. It seems fairly clear that as news editors made decisions regarding the newsworthiness of the story, promotional journalism was a driving factor in continued coverage.

The examples from the "Jenny Jones" case parallel Bird's discussion of the way "serious" journalists speak out about "low taste." The "elite" journalists and the sources they chose made overt references to the media producers they felt were responsible for Amedure's death. Adjectives such as "trashy" and "tabloid" clearly placed the talk shows in a very different category from the "elite" journalists; thus, by distinguishing the talk shows as a media product very different from what the journalists were producing, the journalists were able to keep the blame away from themselves.

The "elite" media's classification of the talk shows as "smut" entertainment is what Jensen would classify as an assumption of the masses as the "lowest common denominator." As the "elite" newspapers critiqued their popular media counterparts by using words such as "trash," "smut," or "tabloid," they elevated their own status by drawing a clear distinction between themselves and those ostensibly not like them. One application of Jensen's theoretical framework to this study is an understanding of how the popular media were blamed for each of the tragedies. In the "Jenny Jones" case, the "elite" journalists accused the talk shows of pandering to the "sick" predilections of viewers-in a sense, doing anything for ratings.

The talk shows were blamed for giving audiences what they wanted rather than news and information they needed. In many news stories, the "elite" journalists directly condemned the talk shows, the talk show producers, the talk show guests and the talk show viewers of lowering the cultural standard of art in America. This analysis can also be tied to McDonald's discussion of journalists speaking out against "low taste." In the "Jenny Jones" case, some newspaper quotes actually addressed this issue explicitly, arguing that part of the blame lies squarely at the feet of the public whose taste for sensationalism is merely answered by television talk shows.

Shoemaker and re-ese's discussion of the five levels of influence on media content is central to explaining much of the coverage of the "Jenny Jones" case. At the individual level, reporters and columnists frequently took the show to task in the form of editorials, thereby providing an outlet for their own unfavorable views of the show and others like it.

The newspaper journalists covering the "Jenny Jones" case often seemed to have taken a "holier-than-thou" tone in their stories of Scott Amedure's death. It is possible the professional background of these reporters and columnists enabled them to view the talk-show host and producers as professionally careless in their attempts to achieve higher ratings via exploitative means.

At the routines and/or the individual level of influence, newspaper reporters often presented a relatively one-sided story via the sources they used in their stories. Some stories, while seemingly objective, contained a position simply by the use of some sources and not others. It seems as if the "elite" newspapers relied on Thompson, the prosecutor, heavily because he provided a voice for the point of view that was presumed to sell more newspapers.

Thompson readily blamed the "Jenny Jones Show, " Jenny Jones herself, and the talk-show producers for the murder. Numerous news stories quoted family members and friends of Schmitz in addition to psychologists and analysts hired by the defence team. Furthermore, "elite" journalists were able to work many expert and official sources into their stories by relying on murder experts and psychologists who provided a rationale for Schmitz's actions and in some cases even took the blame away from Schmitz and placed more blame on the talk show.

Following Amedure's murder, several members of Congress also spoke publicly about the negative and violent content of television talk shows, and some even advocated removing the shows from television altogether. The inclusion of these sources in the news stories was certainly justifiable, yet few stories provided the depth and analysis that would represent alternative views.

Initially, the "Jenny Jones" case did not receive the prominent news coverage of the other cases reviewed here. The murder was not considered newsworthy until the entertainment media were accused of helping to commit the crime. The story seemed to illustrate the routines of "status conferral" and of pack journalism.

As the story and its subjects became more prominent, it began to appear in more and more newspapers. Some newspapers devoted one story and several sidebars to the case for weeks and even months.

Other newspapers ran stories for several days in a row, even though new information had not been uncovered or released. While this behaviour may be standard practice in many newsrooms, it also illustrates the way news editors are often "forced" to allow more space for a story simply because the competition or national newspapers are running the story.

From an ideological or hegemonic standpoint, blaming the "Jenny Jones Show" and its producers meant the "cause" for the tragedy was easily pinpointed. American society could point its finger at the media, and then, in a figurative sense, rest comfortably with the thought that the villain was identified. As de Mooij suggests, American culture strives for a source of blame, an identifiable cause, and views tragic events as a consequence of blame-worthy factors.

Blaming the media, in this case, helps maintain order because members of society do not necessarily have question the social forces that pit members of a dominant group (heterosexuals) against those from a non-dominant group (homosexuals) with potentially fatal consequences once the media have been isolated as the villain.

The underlying theme of the press coverage is that ordinary citizens do not have to fear for their safety unless they appear on a talk show themselves, rather than suggesting homophobia and hate are all too common in society. Initially, this well-publicized case may have temporarily heightened fear and feelings of uncertainty in members of society. With the elevated fear, they searched for a culprit, and once the talk shows were identified as the "cause," the fear subsided, and members of society, as well as those in the "elite" media, were able to feel more secure about their status quo social world. It seemed much easier to blame the products of popular culture when the finger-pointers could step back and draw a clear distinction between themselves and those they were blaming for the tragedy.

By making daytime television seem sleazy, trashy, and outlandish, the "elite" media improved their own image by comparison. However, the oversight seems to be that these same "elite" media were using similar stunts to draw in larger audiences themselves.

On April 20,1999, just before lunchtime, 18-year-old Eric Harris and 17-year-old Dylan Klebold, armed with guns and homemade bombs, opened fire on their classmates at Columbine High School in Littleton, Colorado. The siege lasted over four hours and ended with 15 dead, including the two gunmen, and several others wounded.

It was the bloodiest school shooting in the history of the United States and was carried out with well-orchestrated and disturbingly cold and calculated precision-as well as visible glee on the part of the gunmen.

The series of events and its aftermath left many to grapple with the difficult question of what had gone so terribly wrong that two young men would wreak such awful havoc on their peers. This case study attempts to illustrate how the print news media covered this tragedy, with an emphasis on how journalists dealt with the task of addressing the issue of why the shooting occurred.

In the course of investigating and discussing possible entities at fault, the news media quickly came to focus on popular-culture and entertainment-media products as causal contributors to the massacre at Columbine High.

Extensive quotes drawn from major newspapers around the world (searched via LEXIS-NEXIS) illustrate and also place into context the tendency of the news media to point the finger of blame at popular culture following this tragic event. The very first accounts in the news media of the school shooting in Littleton, Colorado, followed traditional journalistic ideals of reporting on who, what, where, when, and how. The first day of coverage was a veritable news media frenzy, with blow-by-blow accounts broadcast live across the United States on the major radio and broadcast television networks and extensive coverage of gory details on cable news networks. News that day featured terrified testimonials from students.

Expressions of immense relief were broadcast as parents were united with their children. But above all, the view of a bloodied student escaping from a second-story window was perhaps the most memorable image, because of both its profundity and the number of times it was shown.

Quotes from print news media on April 20, 1999, document the tragic and frightening sequence of events and reflect the journalistic tradition of conveying the particulars (who, what, when, where, and how) of the event. The first newspaper articles on the topic came out before all the facts were known and thus included attempts to find out what exactly was happening inside the school, reporting the harrowing estimations of how many were killed, how many wounded. From The Denver Rocky Mountain News, reporters Mike Anton, Manny Gonzalez, Kevin Vaughan, Charley Able, and Lou Kilzer, on April 20, 1999:

At least 21 people were injured today when two or three gunmen dressed in black overcoats and masks opened fire inside Columbine High School in Littleton. Witnesses said the gunmen, reportedly students, appeared to fire randomly and set off explosives, possibly pipe bombs, laughing as they went. From The Denver Rocky Mountain News, reporter Mike Anton, on April 20, 1999: Authorities said some victims were still inside the school as of 2:15 p.m.

About 30 students were reported hiding in the choir room.... Seconds after the shooting began, hundreds of students and teachers poured out of the school while others sought refuge inside, hiding under desks and locking themselves in bathrooms.... Said another student "We were all under the table and the girl across the table from me was shot in the head right there."

A finger pointing of sorts occurred on this day, but served to merely answer the most pressing question at hand: who was responsible for this tragedy? Early blame was narrowly focused on those quickly identified as the gunmen, Eric Harris and Dylan Klebold. News stories traced the steps of the siege, its consequences, and its perpetrators.

The next day, however, on April 21, 1999, the basic facts had largely already been gathered and disseminated. News coverage would now be dominated by placing blame and assigning responsibility to various people, institutions, and entities. Exceptions to the blame-laying patterns that prevailed in the aftermath of the shooting were stories about vigils and grieving processes, connections made in communities around the country with those involved, and decisions to cancel sporting and other events in light of the tragedy. Most other stories appearing for more than a month later attempted not to repeat the who, what, where, when, and how issues, but rather tackled the far more complex issue of why.

Instances of popular culture being blamed came quickly, on the day of the tragedy to help fill the broad expanse of time that cable news networks devoted to coverage, and in the days immediately following in print. The tradition of many news sources picking up the same angle or the same threads of the story was also readily apparent. Wire reports appeared in newspapers across the nation, and the same shocking footage became less and less troubling as American television news viewers were exposed to it again and again. Once popular-culture products were introduced as culprits in early coverage, journalists across the world made a similar connection.

Those who pointed the finger of blame at media and popular-culture products in newspaper coverage largely fell into three categories: students at Columbine and other area schools, experts-typically professors, counselors, attorneys, and police officers-and reporters and newspaper editorial staff writers themselves.

Many popular-culture products were implicated as causal contributors to Harris and Klebold's violence. Movies (especially The Matrix), television, video games, the Internet, and recorded music were all scrutinized as antisocial influences on the gunmen. In fact, though there is plenty of precedent for a single film or book, for instance, inspiring real-life antisocial behaviour, the Columbine shooting stands out as the one historical incident in which so many different popular-culture products were seen as responsible in so many different ways.

From The Atlanta Journal Constitution, reporter Mike Williams, on April 22, 1999: According to their friends, Harris, 18, and Klebold, 17, were part of a loose-knit group called the 'Trenchcoat Mafia' and often dressed in black, favoring leather and the long coats that have been featured in many violence-filled Hollywood movies. The boys played violent computer games for hours, friends said.... Harris set up an Internet home page that spouted Nazi ideology and condoned violence. The shootings came on the 110th anniversary of Hitler's birthday.

From The Daily Telegraph (London), reporter John Hiscock, on April 22, 1999: The two laughing teenagers who shot and bombed their way though the halls of Columbine High School were members of a Gothic-style group known as the Trenchcoat Mafia. Students at Littleton, Colorado, yesterday described Dylan Klebold, 17, and Eric Harris, 18, as "satanic individuals" who talked about Nazis and were fans of the "shock rock" star Marilyn Manson.

From The New York Daily News, reporter Helen Kennedy, on April 21, 1999:

A Web page attributed to one of the members contained crude sketches of demons along with juvenile nihilism like "Anything I don't like sucks." There were song lyrics, from a German underground band called KMFDM an acronym for Kein Mehrfeit Fur Die Mitleid (No pity for the majority) including "What I don't like I waste," "I am your apocalypse," and "Chaos panic/no resistance/ detonations in the distance."

From The Daily Telegraph (London), reporter John Hiscock, on April 22, 1999: The Trenchcoat Mafia was born about three years ago when about a dozen students at Columbine started wearing black and listening to German techno music. They often wore German slogans and swastikas on their clothes. Both were obsessed with the Internet-widely used by neo-Nazi groups-and computer games. Their favourites were Doom and Quake-violent fantasies where the aim is to kill everything you meet.

From The Denver Post, reporters Susan Greene and Bill Briggs, on April 21, 1999: "It appears you have a bunch of kids who've been into black metal music-Marilyn Manson-who basically have apocalyptic fantasies and (who operate under) a heavy code of neo-Nazism," said (Dr. Carl) Raschke (author of Painted Black, which explores violent youth culture).

From The Denver Rocky Mountain News, reporter Robert Denerstein, on April 22, 1999: In the enormously popular new movie The Matrix, Keanu re-eves wears a black duster and battles the forces of evil with two-fisted bursts of gunfire. He stages an attack on the conspiracy that has turned his life into a living hell. The movie already is being mentioned as a possible source of influence on the Trench Coat Mafia, two of whose members entered Columbine High School Tuesday carrying weapons and wearing long black coats. It's not the first time movies have been connected with real-life violence...

The above quotes demonstrate the wide variation in types of popular-culture products blamed, as well as the unique combinations of those entities that were viewed as responsible. They also demonstrate other aspects of youth culture, including hairstyles, body art, and means of dress, that were indirectly implicated in the news coverage of the Columbine shootings. The entire nation was introduced to "gothic" culture in a manner that was at times valiant in its pursuit of value-neutral reportage. At other times "gothic" culture was implicated as a menacing desensitization to and even morbid fascination with death and dying that purportedly helped explain why Harris and Klebold acted with such utter disregard for human life.

The short amount of time it took to blame popular media and popular culture was partially explained by the relationship of the events that occurred in Littleton that day to other school shootings with young perpetrators in other areas of the country. It was an eerily familiar formula, and attempts at explanation linked Columbine to these other school shootings as sources and reporters struggled to make sense of the lot. In fact, one newspaper account used the media and popular culture to link the tragedy at Columbine to another recent high-profile student shooting.

From The Ottawa Citizen, reporters Bob Harvey and Christopher Guly, on April 22, 1999: Just last week, parents of three girls killed in 1997 in Paducah, Kentucky, sued the makers of another film, The Basketball Diaries, starring Leonardo DiCaprio. The Paducah killer, Michael Carneal, said his decision to open fire on a school prayer group was influenced by that film.

Certainly the media and popular-culture products were not the only entities blamed for the Columbine tragedy, though they were among the most frequent targets. Other sources of blame included poor parenting, unsafe schools, uninformed school and police officials, teen cliques, feelings of ostracism, and, perhaps the most frequent additional target of criticism-the prevalence and accessibility of guns.

Some of those who assigned blame in the Columbine shootings chose to focus on only one of these culprits, while others argued that these factors acted in concert to explain the tragedy that had occurred. Some took the position that other societal factors outweighed the role of popular culture in contributing to the tragedy. Others seemed to feel that those entities should share the responsibility. From The Los Angeles Times, reporter Josh Getlin, on April 22, 1999:

The shooting also brings up an old question. How much responsibility does the culture bear for images of violence and retribution, which fill movies, TV, video games, the Internet, recorded music and even the most elementary cartoons today? "We've seen a steady escalation of violence as entertainment, and it reaches people in disturbing ways," (Joyce) Appleby (American history professor) said. "Billions of people watch these pictures around the globe, but somewhere a handful of boys weren't horrified, they were fascinated."

From The Ottawa Citizen, reporters Bob Harvey and Christopher Guly, on April 22, 1999: Those especially vulnerable to violent media messages are individuals-like the two gunmen in the Denver suburb Tuesday-who are "separated away from the mainstream," said Mr. (Andrew) Osier (media professor at the University of Western Ontario), who researches media and violence at the university's Faculty of Information and Media Studies.

A few reporters and experts alike voiced concern that media and popular-culture products were serving as scapegoats in the wake of Columbine, possibly masking other, ostensibly more important causal factors. Articles defending these entities, however, were in the minority and tended to occur in response to the preceding typos of popular-culture accusations. From The Chicago Sun Times, reporter Richard Roeper, on April 22, 1999: It's impossible-and unfair-to point to a band or a movie or a TV show and say "That was the cause," and then to turn to a slaughter and say, "This is the effect." If that's the way it worked, how can it be that hundreds of thousands of fans the world over have been exposed to the spine-thumping music of KMFDM without turning violent?

From The Los Angeles Times, reporter Josh Getlin, on April 22, 1999: "The media influences people, but you don't march into a school armed with guns and grenades and kill 13 people overnight. It doesn't come from nowhere," he (Todd Boyd, an author and professor at the USC School of Cinema and Television) added.

From The Denver Rocky Mountain News editorial, on April 21, 1999: What, many Americans wonder, is going on? We don't profess to know, yet surely part of the answer is a relatively simple phenomenon: unbalanced, resentful kids imitating the highly publicized actions of other unbalanced kids. Most other explanations-the influence of violent entertainment, for example, or too-easy access to guns-suffer from the weakness of having long predated the recent trend of gun-toting students invading their schools with guns.

Do news accounts merely blame the content of popular entertainment media without assessing the media companies and the production and distribution processes that create that content? The answer in this case appears to be yes. Noticeably absent in coverage of the Columbine school shootings was a larger, more macroscopic context for popular-culture blame. Newspaper articles that mentioned either the corporations involved in the production of the content that many found objectionable or the commercial structure of American media that de-emphasizes social responsibility in the creation of content were noticeably rare.

Indeed, though many an allegation was made against popular-culture products for their role in this shooting, most blamers did not accuse the producers of these products but rather just the products themselves.

This seems to suggest media and popular-culture content were "naturalized," perceived as a given in this case. Most accounts did not tend to acknowledge that there were people making decisions that dictate what types of content we see in entertainment media and popular culture.

Though very rare, we will share the few exceptions in which producers of the objectionable content were blamed. From The Boston Globe, reporter John Ellis, on April 22, 1999: The television networks, the major movie studios, record companies, video game software producers, print and other media are spending hundreds of millions of dollars every year to adapt children to this diet of violence and carnage. Once addicted, they'll want more of it, which can and will be provided at a slightly higher price.

From The London Independent, reporter David Aaronovitch, on April 22, 1999: Film-makers who allow violence to seem cool and attractive should examine their consciences.

And we should criticise them more. Organisations like CNN, who offered "uninterrupted live coverage" of events at Columbine High School, should consider whether that isn't exactly what the avenging dweebs want.

Some news accounts were acutely aware of the blaming tendency and viewed it as a defence mechanism for coping with the tragedy, also noting that at the most fundamental level, there truly was no sufficient explanation for a tragedy of such magnitude.

These atypical news articles drew the most macroscopic picture possible, speculating on broad problems at issue in society or simply conceding that an accurate and fair assessment of blame was impossible. From The Arizona Republic editorial, on April 21, 1999:

Whatever that elusive answer may be, it is no longer enough to simply wag our fingers at the usual suspects. This time, we can't allow ourselves to simply scowl at the National Rifle Association. Or at disintegrating families and bleak, cynical television that trivializes life. We can't simply rage at bloody video games.

From The Boston Globe, reporter John Ellis, on April 22, 1999: We have surrounded ourselves with violence. It is everywhere we turn. It is in our music. It is on our televisions. It is in our movies. It is on our video games. It is prominently featured in print media and on popular Web sites. If it bleeds it leads and it leads because it sells. Tuesday's massacre at Columbine High School in Littleton, Colo., was not an aberration. It was and is a fact of modern American life.

From The Denver Rocky Mountain News editorial, on April 21, 1999: But as we said, we don't know what the explanation is and don't care to speculate right now. The moment is too solemn, the bloodletting too extensive for the mind to even grasp. For the time being, our thoughts remain focused solely on those who lives now will never be the same.

The role of popular culture in the Columbine school shooting is a rather complex phenomenon. In addition to the basic and pervasive tendency to blame popular-culture products (films, television, video games, recorded music), there were three additional sources of media-related blame in newspaper coverage. First, many questioned the role of the local news media-universally picked up by the national news media-during the tragedy, in that their actions may have inadvertently jeopardized the safety of the students in the school.

Others blamed the news media for being unnecessarily sensationalistic, insensitive to the trauma experienced by those involved, and inordinately intrusive into the lives of members of the community. (It is important to note that still others applauded the local news media for accurate and compassionate reporting, though those accounts are not reported here as they do not involve blame.) These quotes also demonstrate the way in which some news organizations differentiated themselves from others in order to elude blame by association. From The Atlanta Journal Constitution, reporters Don Aucoin and Drew Jubera, on April 21, 1999: In the heat of the moment, missteps occurred. At one point, the information was broadcast that one youth was trapped inside the schools' "choir room," a potentially risky step if the gunmen were watching TV inside the school.

From The Chicago Sun Times, reporter Phil Rosenthal, on April 21, 1999: From ground zero of the melee at Columbine High School in Littleton, Colo., a student hiding under a table with his cell phone called to alert others of his predicament. His call went not to his parents or police, as some did. It went to Denver's KUSA-TV, which broadcast his report live in Denver (and nationally via CNN, MSNBC and CNBC), oblivious to the fact the school had TVs in every classroom and that the inside information might be aiding the gun-toting assailants behind the siege.

From The Boston Herald, reporter Monica Collins, on April 22, 1999: On television yesterday, it was a mop-up operation after Tuesday's horrendous live coverage of the massacre at Columbine High School in Littleton, Colo. Bigfoot network reporters arrived, interviewing shell-shocked student survivors. Sobbing parents who awaited their children's corpses at a nearby elementary school were not spared from the intrusive lenses. Viewers still shudder at the memory of those macabre, unfiltered visions captured at the height of the evil event...

Second, many critics of the news media also speculated on the possibility of copycat instances following the very extensive coverage the news media gave the event. Critics mentioned the unwitting tendency of the news media to elevate the perpetrators to cult celebrity status, which may, in turn, encourage similar behaviours from young people elsewhere.

One might expect newspaper reporters to omit such instances in which news media were implicated, albeit indirectly, out of self-interest. However, sources consulted for the stories often thrust this angle into the news discourse about the event. Furthermore, newspapers were able to protect their own interests by emphasizing local strategies to avoid hypercoverage that may lead to copycat phenomena.

From The Atlanta Journal Constitution, reporter Phil Kloer, on April 21, 1999: As the sheriff spoke to reporters, news helicopters circled overhead. He was immersed in a sea of reporters, their microphones all lined up in concentric circles, pointing inward. "We've had a lot of media attention of these kinds of situations," the sheriff said, "and you don't know how much that gives other people the idea to do it."

From The Boston Herald, reporter Monica Collins, on April 22, 1999: Detective Sgt. Margot Hill, the Boston police media relations director who helped hammer out the pact (setting standards for the airing of live tragedies) with Boston broadcasters, says "There's no value in airing live. If you air live, you're ghouls and you'll probably create a copycat within a week. We've become a nation of voyeurs."

From The Columbus Dispatch, reporter not listed, on April 22, 1999: "Media attention has given a star quality to such incidents," (Richard) Hazier (a professor in Counselor Education at Ohio University) said. "Kids now have the thought in their minds that it is possible to bring guns into school and get revenge that way," he said..."That's why copycat issues are such a concern today."

Third, another subtopic of media-related blame involved Harris and Klebold reportedly learning how to make pipe bombs on the Internet. From The New York Daily News, reporter Kevin McCoy, on April 22, 1999: A Colorado prosecutor confirmed the cybersearch yesterday as new details emerged about violent imagery and pipe bomb assembly instructions on a Web site linked to gunman Eric Harris. "The Internet is very involved in this case," Jefferson County District Attorney David Thomas said when asked whether Harris and Dylan Klebold used computer expertise to plot the rampage.

From The London Independent, reporter David Aaronovitch, on April 22, 1999: Ah yes, but Eric and Dylan also had home-made pipe bombs. Where did those come from? Almost certainly from the pages of the Internet, where Randy from Idaho, or the Urban Terrorist's homepage, will give any teenager all the information he needs to know to blow up his enemies...Perhaps they were rendered immune to the reality of what they were planning to do as a consequence of long, crepuscular hours spent at the keyboard, blasting punks and decapitating jerks to earn record scores. After a while, real flesh may become confused with pixellated gore and guts in the adolescent mind.

The quotes from the newspaper coverage of the Columbine tragedy demonstrate many of the theoretical foundations outlined earlier in this chapter. Just as Pauly and Eason discuss in essays about Rupert Murdoch and the news story "Jimmy's World," respectively, analysis of the press coverage of the Columbine school shootings reveals rather ingrained, idealized notions about the nature of journalism. Journalists reporting on Columbine seem to deem themselves above the fray, even when discussing the apparent mistakes made by fellow journalists in covering the story, such as being too intrusive or insensitive or having coverage that is so extensive it could inspire a copycat shooting. In fact, some of the stories-either through the comments of sources or the words of journalists themselves-suggest disdain on the part of "serious" journalists for their more sensationalistic or entertainment-oriented counterparts.

Rarely was a distinction between "serious" journalism and more "frivolous" and presumably "harmful" entertainment media content made explicitly by a reporter in the story. Rather, the distinction was made implicitly in the tone of the stories, in the words and phrases chosen, and in the angles pursued in the telling of the story. The distinction that we argue is made here is similar to the one discussed by Bird in her analysis of tabloid newspapers and their relationship to "serious" journalism. In the case of Columbine, the distinction may, in fact, be easier for newspaper reporters to argue because the medium is often different, with newspapers or print journalism seen as "serious," informative, and helpful, and video games, recorded music, television, and movies seen as more "frivolous" and "harmful."

The same types of assumptions that Jensen argues underlie major strains of media criticism are apparent here. There is a sense of protectionism that borders on elitism on the part of those who criticized popular media in major newspaper coverage of the Columbine shootings, with the notion that the newspapers provide what is good for the public, and entertainment media provide what is bad. The newspaper's role is one of savior. By pointing out the evils of the popular media that Dylan Klebold and Eric Harris enjoyed, newspaper coverage can help save other impressionable youth or raise a warning flag for their parents.

The newspaper coverage of the Columbine school shootings can also be examined in terms of Shoemaker and re-ese's levels of influence on media content. On the individual level, for instance, the tone of the coverage suggests that the journalists may have shared the sadness and outrage of the American public and were thus inclined to point the finger of blame as a way of coping with and trying to make sense of the tragedy. In fact, the immediate deaths of Klebold and Harris served to remove them as a target for continuing feelings of grief and anger. Assigning responsibility to an ongoing social institution such as the popular media provides both reporters and their readers with an enduring target at which they can vent their anger.

The individual reporters and their editors may also have chosen this angle because it corresponds with their own personal values or opinions regarding popular culture and media influence. The quotes that imply disapproval or the ones that adopt a moralistic tone would support this as one factor shaping coverage. Also on the individual level, reporters and editors at the newspapers whose coverage was examined may have felt a "holier than thou" attitude towards entertainment-oriented popular media. This influence bridges the theoretical structure of Shoemaker and re-ese.

On the media routines level, the routines regarding the selection and use of sources as well as the traditional emphasis on localism were apparent in coverage. For example, schoolmates and area residents were often called upon for first-hand accounts of possible popular-culture blame, and experts such as police officers or college professors were often utilized for verification. The coverage also evolved from reporting "who, what, where, when, and how" to also including "why," the latter leading to the popular-culture blame explored here. Finally, the routine of providing simplified, uncomplicated explanations for events was followed in some of the coverage of the Columbine shootings that advanced one particular or more compelling explanation for the tragedy (often popular culture) rather than discussing multiple and complex factors.

In either the organizational or the extramedia level as defined by Shoemaker and re-ese, ownership issues and the chain of command may have influenced coverage of the Columbine shootings. With such a broad range of media and popular-culture products implicated, a conflict of interest was possible because of growing cross-media ownership. A newspaper owned by the same company that owns a record label whose recording artists or types of music were criticized for their role in the shootings may have been disinclined to emphasize the possible effect ofthat music on the shooters because of pressure from the top.

On the other hand, a newspaper relatively free of those direct connections with the popular media being implicated (or with holdings in competing media that would benefit from a possible boycott of the particular popular media criticized) may be more likely to point the finger of blame.

In the case of Columbine, it is possible that manufacturers and distributors of popular-culture products that advertise in newspapers would be displeased with coverage that implicates those video games, the Internet, television, or movies in such a high-profile tragedy. For instance, the newspapers from which we have quoted may carry lucrative advertising inserts for retail outlets offering or even specializing in media-driven products (TV sets, DVD players, video game consoles). Perhaps popular-culture culpability would havo been even more extensive or scathing if it were not for this influence that may have trickled down from the owners and managers in the newspaper's organizational structure.

Also on the extramedia level, the sources used to cover the Columbine tragedy helped shape the content. The students of Columbine High School were quick to report the violent and nihilistic media and popular culture content that attracted Klebold and Harris, as is apparent in the quotes from coverage above. This early angle may well have helped define the story from that point on. Similarly, the efforts of other media organizations to establish the popular-media culpability angle, including the hometown Denver newspapers who had the earliest and most extensive coverage, may have set the tone that other media organizations followed.

Finally, influences found at the ideological level may have shaped coverage of the Columbine shootings, as well. For instance, in many of the quotes from newspaper coverage outlined above, occasional resistance to assign blame to producers of content is evident, as writers relied instead on accusations against media content itself as divorced from those who created it.

This may have been, consciously or not, a defensive strategy on the part of the newspapers to deflect criticism from their possible role in creating "a culture of violence" by helping to obscure the connection between the decisions and approaches of creators of content from content itself. Also evident in the language used to implicate popular media are the lines of distinction implicitly drawn in coverage of the Columbine tragedy between the news media who covered the event and the entertainment media who were blamed.

The emphasis was often on the blood, gore, and generally antisocial content of particular music lyrics, video games, and movies, and the apparently disturbing notion that this is what is used to entertain young people in our society. Thus, responsibility was placed firmly at the feet of media who are merely entertaining the masses rather than the news media who are providing a public service by informing them. In the case of Columbine, there exists an underlying assumption that something is dreadfully wrong with the people who tune in to violent media fare and that the news media are trying to save them by pointing this out.

Also at the ideological level, blaming the media for the Columbine tragedy could help maintain comforting notions of social order and reassure the public of social stability. The discomfort that comes with leaving such a tragedy unexplained is evident in the very few editorials that expressed that they were mystified by the tragedy and admitted this created a disquieting sense of chaos.

It is also evident in the majority of newspaper stories that did, indeed, offer the popular-culture culpability argument as an explanation. As de Mooij suggests, Americans are comforted by a sense of rationality and order, of things occurring for a reason.

Advancing the popular-culture culpability attempts to bring rationality to the otherwise senseless nature of the tragedy, compounded because of the young age of the assailants and victims, the seemingly safe setting, and the apparent glee with which Klebold and Harris perpetrated their crimes.

This study uses three high-profile cases to investigate conceptions regarding the moral consequences of popular media in contemporary soci-ety. In analyzing the discourse generated in news coverage of the three events, the theme of popular media's moral culpability was quite apparent.

Whether it was for the car crash that claimed the life of Princess Diana, for the shooting that followed an apparently incendiary taping of the "Jenny Jones Show," or for the multiple-weapon assault enacted on Columbine High School, newspaper coverage included the assignment of blame to popular media and popular-culture products for these tragedies.

Analysis of the news discourse surrounding these events points to a number of themes regarding cultural and social practices. First, we can examine views and perceptions of "the media" as having potentially different readings and carrying quite disparate critical connotations depending on one's perspective. Some conceptualize "the media" as a relatively homogeneous and powerful force in the contemporary social structure with only slight, if any, important differences based on news versus entertainment content.

This view holds that each media outlet exists for the purpose of profit and seeks that profit by appealing to audiences of specific sizes or characteristics. Differences between news and entertainment are seen as minimal and shrinking, in a time in which "infotainment" abounds and the "news hole" in newspapers and on television is diminished by the amount of space or time allotted to weather, sports, and "light" features.

Yet, the discourse examined in newspaper coverage of these three events shows a very different view of "the media." Rather than assuming similarities between news and entertainment and rather than newspapers sharing a sense of responsibility for a "culture of violence" or sensationalism such as is criticized in these cases, "the media" is seen as a heterogeneous collection of very different types of organizations with very different functions.

Implicit distinctions are drawn between those "serious" journalists whose function is to inform the public of important information related to their health and well being and those producers of popular media who allegedly instead jeopardize public health by irresponsible practices and the transmis sion of potentially harmful content. The notion of irresponsible practices can be seen in the condemning tone in newspaper coverage that discusses the paparazzi in the case of Princess Diana's death and talk show producers and creators in the case of the "Jenny Jones Show" murder.

The notion of harmful content is also an explicit element of the news discourse surrounding sensationalism, sex, and violence in talk shows as related to the "Jenny Jones" murder and antisocial and violent themes in popular media as related to the Columbine shootings.

Thus, there are some parallels to the theoretical argument made by Jensen. Jensen would argue that the view of the media described first above, as a homogeneous force, is an example of modern media criticism that may better be viewed as a criticism of modernity. Yet, she would presumably also object to the defensive strategies embarked upon by the newspapers whose coverage we examined because of their underlying assumptions regarding popular preferences and morality. These lines of distinction between "serious" and "popular" media comprise the second major theme revealed in this analysis.

As mentioned in the case studies, the distinction between "us" and "them" was not always made explicitly in the news coverage of the events. However, in the pursuit of the popular-culture culpability angle, in the disapproving tone of sources turned to or in reporters' own words, and in the lack of connection established between the newspaper itself and the other forms of media criticized, the distinction appears as an underlying assumption.

The assumption of a stark distinction between the "elite" press and other media forms is tenuous at best. As Bird andPauly suggest, those who position themselves as "serious" journalists and those who are viewed as "tabloid" journalists (and even those who create and disseminate entertainment media content) have more similarities than differences in terms of practices and goals. Yet, even when the connection between the accuser (the newspaper) and the accused seems most obvious, as in the discussion of excessive news coverage paving the way for a copycat following the Columbine tragedy, no elements of the discourse suggest similarity or recognize potential involvement on the part of the accuser.

Rather, the newspapers reported from a presumed position above the fray, akin to an omniscient and impartial observer, who then adopts an interpretive role to further the public good by helping to cure social ills. This not only reveals a privileged position for "elite" journalists but also suggests an artificial, unrealistic isolation of the newspaper from surrounding society.

At the centre of the issue of what makes a media professional "serious" or not is an assumption about the nature of the audience. The analysis of news discourse provided here shows further evidence of a protectionist, somewhat elitist view of audiences as being drawn, like moths to a flame, to content that is bad for them. Whether one blames the producers of such content or the audience members themselves for this assumed preference, the premise is the same: audience members must be encouraged to see the error of their ways in their enjoyment of or tolerance for violent, sexual, sensationalistic, and intrusive media content.

Some of the quotes we have cited from newspaper coverage of these three events appear to adopt the position that deaths such as these are the price we pay for the moral decline evident in the popularity of certain types of media content.

Others reveal a tone of warning for local communities to prevent similar tragedies from occurring or recurring. Still others call directly for greater governmental regulation, stricter parental control, and more responsibility on the part of the media industry. All such angles suggest a need for those wiser and more moral-led, in this case, by the "serious" journalists - to help save audience members from themselves.

Underlying the blame of popular media and culture in the media discourse examined in our study is the "serious" journalists' notion of audience members preferring what is "easier to digest" or more appealing (popular media and culture) rather than what is good for them. What is good for them, in the case of our study, is presumably more "elite" media and culture, including the reading of newspapers such as those that are blaming their more populist counterparts.

By focusing on the aspect of each story that involves the purportedly appealing qualities of the popular media criticized, "elite" newspapers can capitalize on those qualities (*e.g.*, violence in the case of Columbine, sex in the case of "Jenny Jones") at the same time that they implicitly draw a distinction that separates them as more "tasteful."

Shoemaker and re-ese's theory of influences on media content also provides insights about situated, particular practices of news professionals, constraints and traditions in news gathering, and the interplay of producers, content, and public. Of the five spheres of influence identified by Shoemaker and re-ese, we would argue that media routines were among the most likely to have a direct and measurable impact on how these three events were covered in the news.

Routines including news values, ideas of what makes a "good" story, and traditional practices and constraints of news reportage are also presumably the influences that would most likely be listed by journalists themselves if asked what factors affect how events are covered, because of their practicality and concrete nature.

The other, more microscopic spheres of influence are slightly less compelling in this context. For example, though many journalists would welcome a work environment in which their own preferences, opinions, and values could dictate coverage, few achieve this degree of autonomy and write articles that run unchanged by higher-ups in the organizational structure.

We believe the more macroscopic factors of extramedia influences and ideology also play a crucial role, but one which is less apparent and more insidious. It is this element of the Shoemaker and re-ese theory that can be linked to the theoretical contributions of Jensen, Bird, Pauly, and Eason. Though these forces are not always obvious, we argue that the factors comprising them are among the most potent in shaping news content in general, and coverage of these events specifically. The influence of ideology encompasses cultural elements such as the cause-and-effect paradigm that de Mooij suggests is expected in American culture. This cultural norm is readily apparent in news-media discourse surrounding each of these three events, evident in the attempts to answer "why" the tragedies occurred in a simple and straightforward manner.

The ideological level also encompasses the issues of journalists (and others) holding rather unflattering perceptions of audience members and espousing a somewhat idealized role of the "serious" journalist as watchdog in contemporary society. In this scenario, there is a protectionism that borders on elitism. A key element interwoven throughout these theoretical foundations is hegemony.

A revered and respected role reserved for "serious" journalists assures their position in society. Economics also play a crucial part. Newspapers tell stories in a certain way to sell copies in order to sell space to advertisers. Popular-culture culpability, by its very populist nature, is a virtual guarantee of public interest. Yet, the public may be surprised to find the news discourse generated is one of shame, guilt, and danger associated with popular media.

We would like to caution our readers, however, about assumptions that underlie this research endeavor. Our aim here was not to blame the "serious" news media for, in turn, blaming more populist news and entertainment media because we feel that blame is not deserved. On the contrary (and perhaps contrary to the position Jensen would adopt), we do believe there are irresponsible practices and potentially harmful content in tabloid news and entertainment media that may have contributed-though certainly not as the sole culprit-to these three tragedies, and to other events as well.

Our purpose here was to examine how this blame took shape, to illuminate forces and factors that led to the pursuit of this blaming as a common angle, and to elucidate the implicit strategies to keep "serious" journalists above blame. It is this distinction that is made between accuser and culprit in the news coverage we examined, when the distance between the two is arguably quite small, that we suggest is the most interesting finding from our study.

7

Theories of Crime

INTRODUCTION

The three views have clearly placed very different constructions around the phenomenon of crime. The view taken by the individual criminologist, together with his or her own background in sociology, psychology, and so on, will influence the way in which research evidence is gathered, data interpreted, and theories constructed. The following section briefly examines how the three views have been translated into theories of crime.

CLASSICAL AND POSITIVIST THEORIES

The consensus view of crime is linked to two schools of thought within criminology. The *classical* theorists hold central the concept of free will in explaining why a person commits a crime. When the opportunity for crime arises, the individual has a free choice between criminal and non-criminal behaviour. If the payoffs for the criminal act are greater than the retribution it will bring, so the probability of a crime increases. At its most basic this suggests that severe retribution will deter people from any criminal act. Indeed, this simple philosophy was one which guided the process of justice through to the mid-1700s and even into the early 1800s, when acts such as stealing or vagrancy were punishable by severe physical punishment such as flogging or even death.

The eighteenth-century Italian economist Cesare Beccaria was in accord with the general view of the time that humans are rational beings, able to choose and control their behaviour. Beccaria was also concerned that the punishment should fit the crime and so argued, with eventual success, that extreme measures are unnecessary and, indeed, may be counter-productive. There is more than a grain of truth in the saying that 'it is as well to be hung for a sheep as a lamb'. Around the turn of the eighteenth century, the British philosopher Jeremy Bentham similarly argued that a balance between profit and pain guided the free choice of a criminal act. Bentham formulated a number of rules by which to regulate the administration of punishment; with the justification for punishment always presented in terms of its preventing a greater evil than it creates.

Classical theory, as presented by Beccaria and Bentham, was the dominant force in Europe and America in the late eighteenth and nineteenth centuries, guiding both judicial philosophers and criminal justice system of the time. With the advent of positivist theories the classical school waned in popularity and influence throughout the twentieth centry. However, the 1970s and 1980s have seen a renewed interest in classical criminology. The *neoclassical* or *conservative* criminologists have emerged as a strong voice in contemporary theorizing. Fuelled by a general failure of positivist theories to discover the causes of crime and to develop effective strategies for controlling crime, some of the basic ideas associated with classical theories are beginning to return. The call for greater deterrence in the form of longer prison sentences, the return of the death penalty, and the notion of 'just deserts' for lawbreakers, has been heard increasingly over the past decade.

The *positivist* theorists, while sympathizing with the consensus view of crime, differ from classical theorists with respect to the role of free will in determining behaviour, including criminal behaviour. Positivist theories grew from the arguments, advanced from the mid-nineteenth century onwards, that influences outside the realm of free will are the most important in determining behaviour. As theories have advanced and fallen so these influences have ranged from biological factors such as genetic transmission, to psychological constructs such as personality, learning, and moral development. While from a more sociological perspective, there are *social structure* theories which emphasize concepts such as 'anomie', and 'strain' which result from class structure and poverty; and *social process* theories which focus on the effects of, for example, education, peer relationships, and the family. Positivist theories are generally seen as more liberal in orientation, with their suggestions that some form of helpful intervention—be it welfare at a social level or treatment at an individual level—is the optimum strategy for reducing crime.

Radical Criminology

While conflict views of crime encompass a range of opinions, it was those theorists who emphasized the Marxist position who advanced the framework for a new model within criminology. The new criminology promised by I.Taylor *et al*. quickly became more popularly known as radical criminology. It is incorrect to say that radical criminology represents a unified theory; rather since 1973 it has put forward a series of associated coherent statements which combine to form a body of knowledge and opinion. While radical criminology has its roots in the writings of Marx and Engels, it was theorists such as Willem Bonger who began to formulate a full Marxist critique of crime. In contrast to classical theories it is proposed that no act in itself is naturally immoral or criminal;

definitions of crime are socially determined, reflecting current social values. This emphasis on social determination also runs counter to those positivist theories which incorporate genetic or other biologically based explanations of crime.

Within a radical framework, criminal law is designed to suit the purposes of the dominant ruling class, those within society who hold wealth and power. In a capitalist system, the unequal distribution of wealth means that those without finance have to resort to crime to enjoy the luxuries and advantages seen to be enjoyed by others. Crime therefore is in some instances a function of poverty.

The rich also commit crimes for the purpose of gaining further wealth and power. However, as the rich control the means of regulating crime, their legal sysem will discriminate against the poor. So while the poor, the proletariat, may commit the same number of crimes as the wealthy, the bourgeoisie, they are arrested and punished with much greater frequency. A number of modern writers have clarified, elaborated, and extended the position defined by Bonger and articulated by I.Taylor *et al.*

In terms of a solution for crime, radical criminology suggests that changes must occur at economic, political, and social levels. Specifically if progress from the present capitalist system to monopoly capitalism can be made, then redistribution of wealth can take place. It is argued that crime will then no longer be necessary; any crimes which do occur will be the result of individual psychopathology. T.Platt presents a blueprint for the formulation of alternatives to the present system of 'law and 'order' which follow a radical criminological approach. Radical criminology has been subjected to fierce criticism, with some carefully constructed commentaries and others with more than a touch of naivety.

Labelling Theory

The interactionist view of crime gave rise to a theory of criminology which relies on a mixture of social and semantic processes to explain deviance. In common with conflict theories, labelling theory suggests that the law is applied to the benefit of those who hold social and economic power. Thus disadvantaged groups within society, such as the lower socioeconomic classes and minority groups, are more likely to be prosecuted and to receive harsher penalties. An individual becomes a criminal when the people who hold power—judges, parents, police, teachers, etc. —decide to confer the label 'criminal'. As Becker notes: 'Deviant behaviour is behaviour that people so label'.

Here there is a clear contrast with a moral view: behaviour is not seen as 'right' or 'wrong', rather 'deviant behaviour' is a judgement by certain sections of society towardss certain classes of behaviour. This argument does not, of course, apply only to criminal behaviour: the same reasoning has been used to explain the creation of groups variously labelled 'alcoholic', 'mentally ill', 'sexually deviant', and so on. While writers such as Gove have offered explanations within a labelling theory framework to account for the involvement of people in criminal acts, the main force of labelling theory has been to examine the consequences of labelling. Two consequences are emphasized—the creation of stigma and modification of self-image. The term *stigma* refers to the public attitude of condemnation of the deviant and the associated exclusion of the labelled individual from some parts of society.

The label 'criminal' is associated with undesirable traits and so, in the public eye, the criminal is a person to be avoided and treated with suspicion. Thus the criminal will find that he or she is barred from certain types of employment; the young offender may find that their school or their family is unwilling to offer a welcome; those with criminal records may attract an undue amount of attention from the police. The force of these social pressures can lead to the second major consequence of the label: the individual comes to believe society's judgement and so modifies his or her self-image to match the label. The prophecy becomes self-fulfiling: the individual becomes the person described by the label. As the label becomes a role for the labelled individual, so the role is reinforced so that the person's life changes to suit the role. More crimes are committed, the peer group changes to others playing the same role, the person's identity becomes that of a 'criminal' with all its associated values, attitudes, and beliefs. Lemart calls this process *deviance amplification*.

The irony of any attempt at intervention, either by punishment or treatment, is that it serves only to reinforce the individual's self-perception of him- or herself as a criminal. Like all other theories of crime, labelling theory has its critics. There are a range of objections from a failure to specify why some individuals set off on a path of crime, to a failure to acknowledge that some crimes such as murder and rape are universally judged as 'wrong'.

As Siegal points out, several criminologists who were at one time strong advocates of labelling theory have in the 1970s and 1980s shifted ground to favour more radical theories, principally the conflict theories. In summary, it can be seen that the three influential theories explain crime in very different ways. It is true that there is a degree of overlap between certain aspects of some theories, which has been examined by experimental methods but in the main the theories remain independent of each other. While these theories offer explanations for crime, they do not inform us as to the numbers of crimes committed.

Knowledge of the numbers of crimes committed is important both theoretically and practically: if crime is a low frequency behaviour then criminals may differ in some important way from those who do not perform such acts; if on the other hand it is a high frequency behaviour this may mean quite the reverse. The practical reasons are concerned with the allocation of finance to those establishments concerned with controlling crime: if there is a great deal of crime, and it is society's wish to control it, then the forces of law and order will demand a proportion of the public purse—the higher the frequency of crime, the greater the demand on the purse.

MORAL DEVELOPMENT AND CRIME

The process of socialization is linked with moral development in the theories of both Piaget and Kohlberg. There are various accounts of Piaget's theories on moral development and Aronfreed compares the views of Piaget and Kohlberg. However, Kohlberg has used his theory to develop an explanation for offending and therefore this particular theory is of interest here. Kohlberg, like Piaget, argues that moral reasoning develops in a sequential manner as the individual attains maturity. Kohlberg describes three levels of moral development, with two stages at each level.

At the lower stages moral reasoning is concrete in orientation, becoming more abstract at the higher stages and involving concepts such as 'justice', 'rights', and 'principles'. Offending, Kohlberg argues, is associated with a delay in the development of moral reasoning so that given the opportunity for offending the individual does not have the internal mechanisms to control and resist the temptation.

A number of recent reviews have both elaborated this basic premise and discussed the empirical evidence. The main body of experimental evidence compares the moral judgements of delinquents and non-delinquents. The results are mixed with some studies finding that young offenders use less mature reasoning than non-offenders; others failing to show any distinction between the two groups.

There are two procedural explanations for these varied results: the first is the failure to control for behavioural and personality correlates of moral development; the second is the possibility of variations just as to the type of offence within the offender population. Indeed, Thornton and Reid reported that convicted criminals who had offended for no financial gain showed more mature moral judgement than those who offended for money.

Thus, as Jurkovic notes: 'Not only do they vary from one another in stage of moral judgement, but they also fluctuate in their own reasoning level on different moral problems'. As both Ross and Fabiano and Arbuthnot and Gordon point out, the concept of moral development is not a simple one and a number of important distinctions require clarification within the overall framework. While research has focused on the *content* of the offender's moral code, that is the offender's beliefs and attitudes, this contextual aspect can be contrasted with the *process* of moral reasoning. It is an assumption that process is related to content: while delayed development may be the cause of an antisocial moral code, it is also possible that as Ross and Fabiano suggest: 'One can argue eloquently and convincingly about social/moral issues yet have a personal set of values which are entirely self-serving, hedonistic or anti-social'.

Further, the assumption of a relationship between moral reasoning, moral values, and behaviour must also be queried: several well-known experiments have shown that people will behave in ways which they believe or know to be wrong. In summary, there are a number of doubts about the general applicability of moral development theory to crime. A direct causal link between moral functioning and criminal behavour remains to be established.

Further, tests of moral development which assess answers to hypothetical moral and social issues have also been criticized as having little relevance to the type of thinking an offender engages in when deciding whether to commit a crime. Indeed, studies of thinking prior to offending show that the criminal is not concerned with moral issues, but rather with the likelihood of being successful. Cognitive, social, and moral development are the subjects of much recent research and it may be that these advances will be applied to delinquent populations in the future to respond to some of the doubts expressed.

Eysenck's Theory of Crime

Eysenck's theory, which is also a control theory, incorporates biological, social, and individual factors. The basis of the theory is that through genetic endowment some individuals are born with cortical and autonomic nervous systems which affect their ability to learn from, or more properly to *condition* to, environmental stimuli. An individual's behaviour, influenced by both biological and social factors, defines that person's *personality*. H.J.Eysenck defined two dimensions of personality, *extroversion* (E) and *neuroticism* (N); later work described a third dimension, *psychoticism* (P). Each of these dimensions is conceived as a continuum with most people falling in the middle range and, it follows, with comparatively few people at the extremes of each scale. Extraversion runs from high to low; similarly neuroticism runs from high to low; as also does psychoticism. The extravert is considered as cortically *under*aroused and therefore is continually seeking stimulation to maintain cortical arousal at an optimal level: thus the extravert is impulsive and seeks excitement.

The introvert is cortically *over*aroused and therefore tries to avoid stimulation to keep arousal levels down to a comfortable, optimal level: introverts are therefore characterized by a quiet, reserved demeanour. In terms of conditioning, that is learning by Pavlovian conditioning or association rather than operant conditioning the theory maintains that extraverts condition less efficiently than introverts. Neuroticism, sometimes called emotionality, is argued to be related to the functioning of the autonomic nervous system. Individuals at the high extreme of this continuum are characterized by a very labile ANS, which causes strong reactions to any unpleasant or painful stimuli:

High N individuals display moody, anxious behaviour. Low N individuals have a very stable ANS and so display calm, eventempered behaviour even when under stress.

As with E, N is also linked with conditionability: High N leads to poor conditioning because of the vitiating effects of anxiety; Low N leads to efficient conditioning. As assessed by standard psychometric tests, each individual scores on both E and N; therefore their position on these two dimensions of personality can be plotted as shown in Figure. As conditionability is related to levels of E and N it is further suggested that stable introverts will condition best; stable extraverts and neurotic introverts will be at some mid-point; while neurotic extraverts will condition least well.

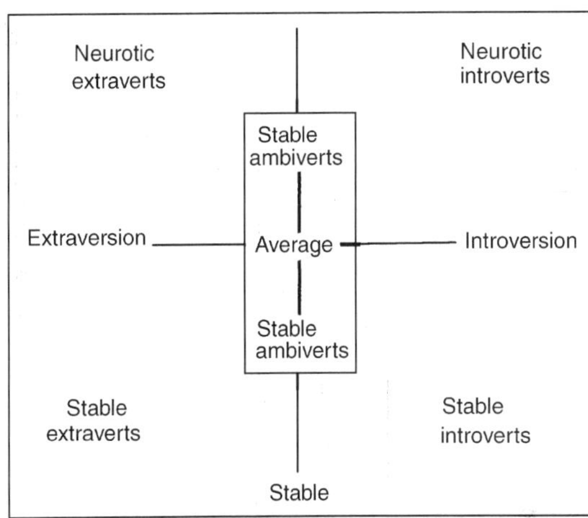

Fig. Eysenck's Personality Dimensions of Extraversion and Neuroticism

The third personality dimension, psychoticism is not so well formulated as E and N: while maintaining a genetic basis for P, its biological basis has not been described in detail. Indeed, various descriptions of P have been offered: initially intended to distinguish the personality underlying psychosis, as opposed to neurosis, the suggestion was later made that P might better denote psychopathy than psychoticism. The P scale assesses attributes such as a preference for solitude, a lack of feeling for others, sensation-seeking, toughmindedness, and aggression. Although recently revised, there is still some doubt about what exactly the P scale is measuring.

The relationship between personality and crime has been described and refined by H.J.Eysenck, and recent summaries are available. The principal assumption is that children learn to control antisocial behaviour through the development of a 'conscience': this conscience, Eysenck maintains, is a set of conditioned emotional responses to environmental events associated with the antisocial behaviour. For example the child who misbehaves incurs parental wrath; the fear and pain this brings is associated with the antisocial act, and through this conditioning process the child becomes socialized. The speed and efficiency of social conditioning will mainly depend upon the individual's personality in terms of E and N. As the High E-High N combination leads to poor conditionablity then such individuals will be least likely to learn social control and therefore, it is predicted, will be over-represented in offender populations. Conversely Low E-Low N would lead to effective socialization, so that these individuals would be predicted to be under-represented in offender groups.

The remaining two combinations, High E-Low N and Low EHigh N, fall at some intermediate level and so would be expected in both offender and non-offender groups. The third personality dimension, P, is also argued to be strongly related to offending, particularly with crimes which involve hostility towards other people. H.J.Eysenck suggests that 'In general terms, we would expect persons with strong antisocial inclinations to have high P, high E, and high N scores'. It is important to note the use of the term *antisocial*: as H.J.Eysenck is at pains to point out, not all crimes are antisocial in the general sense of that term. There are politically motivated crimes, impulsive crimes, crimes committed by the intellectually disadvantaged, and so on. In other words, some allowance has to be made for the heterogeneity of the offender population. Eysenck's theory of crime has generated a great deal of empirical research and there are several reviews of the findings up to 1980.

The broad position is that there is unanimous support for the contention that offenders will score highly on P, and the majority of studies show that offender samples score highly on N. The evidence is mixed for E: some studies reported high E scores as predicted in offender samples, others found no difference between offender and non-offender samples, and a small number of studies reported *lower* scores in offender groups. The general pattern for P, E, and N is similar with both young and adult offender groups. In seeking to account for the discrepant findings for E, S.B.G.Eysenck and H.J.Eysenck suggested that E might be split into two subscales, Sociability and Impulsiveness, with only the latter related to offending. A study by S.B.G.Eysenck and McGurk confirmed that an offender sample scored higher than a non-offender sample on Impulsiveness, with no difference between the two samples on a measure of Sociability.

There are two important points to note with regard to these early investigations: the majority of studies have examined the personality traits singly rather than in combination; and few studies have attempted to control for the type of crime. It will be recalled that Eysenck's theory is specifically concerned with the combined effects of different personality traits and with antisocial crimes. A small number of studies have attended to these specific aspects of the theory. Two studies by Allsopp and Feldman suggested that P, E, and N in combination provided support for Eysenck's theory.

The most compelling evidence is presented in a more recent study by McGurk and McDougall. McGurk and McDougall report the results of a cluster analysis of the P, E, and N scores of 100 delinquents and 100 non-delinquent college pupils. The analysis showed four personality clusters in each group: both groups contained Low E-High N and High E-Low N clusters, but the clusters predicted to be related to criminal behaviour—High E-High N and High P-High EHigh N—were, indeed, found only in the delinquent sample. The Low E-Low N group, which the theory would predict to be highly socialized, was found only in the non-delinquent group.

McEwan attempted a similar analysis with a delinquent population and also found four personality clusters. With a more rigorous definition for 'high' and 'low', McEwan's analysis gave rather different clusters to McGurk and McDougall. While the High E-High N combination figures prominently, the other groups show varying degrees of dissimilarity with those reported in the previous study. Another study by McEwan and Knowles also produced four clusters, once again with similarities and differences to the other studies. With regard to type of offence, Hindelang and Weis found mixed support for the predicted relationship between personality type and nature of offence.

Their findings indicated that the High E-High N cluster was significantly associated with general deviancy but not with major theft and aggression. S.B.G.Eysenck *et al.* compared the P, E, and N scores of groups of offenders: 'conmen' showed lower P scores than the other groups, while property and violent offender groups had lower N scores. The groups did not differ on the E scale. McEwan and Knowles failed to show any significant variation in the types of offences committed by the personality clusters in their study. In terms of numbers of offences, McEwan compared the criminal records of the subgroups defined in the first part of his study.

The subgroup with the high P score proved to have significantly more previous convictions than the other subgroups. The weight of empirical evidence lends support to Eysenck's thesis that there is a relationship between personality and crime. Indeed, a self-report study of a range of predictors of delinquency showed that P was by far the strongest predictor. Exposition of the theory Feldman concludes that the 'Eysenckian personality dimensions are likely to make a useful contribution to the explanation of criminal behaviour'. While this may prove to be the case, a number of reservations, as Eysenck acknowledges, need to be made. The theory does not explain all crime and, with its concentration on extremes of the scale, is not applicable to all offenders.

Further, one of the theoretical bases of the theory, the link between classical conditioning and socialization, remains to be established satisfactorily. On a broader front the Eysenckian personality traits are not the only personality traits to have been described; studies have pointed to other personality dimensions which may be associated with criminal behaviour. Still further, the theory demands acceptance of a trait theory of personality which is only one of a number of ways of conceptualizing 'personality' and one which has come under fierce attack. In summary, Eysenck's theory is important, emphasizing the interaction between biological, environmental, and psychological factors. Integration of the theory into mainstream criminology, bearing in mind the various shortcomings, would be one way of bringing individual factors into more sociologically oriented views of crime.

COGNITION AND CRIME

The term 'cognition' is an imprecise one, used in a variety of ways by different authors: in general terms it refers to concepts such as memory, imagery, intelligence, and reasoning; although perhaps its most widely used meaning is as a synonym for thinking. In explanations of offending, cognition is implicit in the theories of a number of writers who suggest that various styles of thinking, such as 'impulsive' or 'concrete', are characteristic of criminal populations. The link between cognition and crime is perhaps at its most explicit in the controversial writings of Samuel Yochelson and Stanton Samenow.

In the first volume of *The Criminal Personality,* Yochelson and Samenow describe their conclusions drawn from interviews with male offenders referred to their hospital for 'determination of competency'. From these interviews, they claim to have discovered the 'criminal thinking patterns' which characterize all criminals. While cautious social scientists might exercise some restraint in accepting the conclusions of investigators who assert that 'The criminal has revealed the working of his mind to us' and 'We fractionate the criminal's mind and then synthesize it', it cannot be denied that Yochelson and Samenow present some fascinating and idiosyncratic views.

They describe a number of styles and errors of thinking—Ross and Fabiano have counted fifty-two—which define the criminal mind. These thinking patterns include concrete thinking, fragmentation, failure to empathize with others, a lack of any perspective of time, irresponsible decision-making, and perceiving themselves as victims. While there is much of interest in this work, there are a number of criticisms and shortcomings, some methodological, others theoretical. The sample used by Yochelson and Samenow is an unusual one in that it consisted of 240 persistent offenders, many of whom had been judged 'Not Guilty by Reason of Insanity'.

It is questionable just how far it is possible to generalize from this sample to the remainder of the offender population. Their conclusion that all criminals share the same thinking pattern, must therefore be treated with caution. Further, as they failed to include a non-offender control group, it is not established that the thinking patterns they describe are peculiar to criminal populations. The interview method of data-gathering, while a rich source of material, does require a check for reliability and validity which is not given.

Similarly, there is no indication of any attempt at standardization across interviews. At a theoretical level two principal issues arise: the first is with the concept of 'mind' and the associated assumption that thinking caused behaviour.

There are a number of theoretical variations on both mind and the primacy of cognition over behaviour, none of which is fully explored. The second issue lies in their assertion that, by processes which are not well explained, criminals are like a different breed of person. Indeed, comments of this latter type have led to charges of 'neo-Lombrosian' being levelled against this work. In summarizing the cognitive approach of Yochelson and Samenow, Ross and Fabiano express regret at the shortcomings of this work, which has led to a great deal of controversy rather than establishing a valuable contribution to clinical criminology. However, the approach of Yochelson and Samenow is not that of other cognitive models of criminal behaviour. More recent studies have looked for more explicit cognitive variations between offenders and non-offenders. Although the distinction may not be exact, Ross and Fabiano distinguish between *im*personal cognition and *inter*personal cognition.

The former is that aspect of cognition which 'deals with the physical world'; the latter is concerned with 'understanding people and their actions', sometimes called social cognition. While impersonal cognition may be a factor in the development of criminal behaviour—for example the research which points to intellectual imbalances in offender samples— Ross and Fabiano argue that interpersonal cognition may well be more important in understanding crime. In reviewing studies of social cognition with criminal populations, Ross and Fabiano described a variety of types or styles of cognition which characterize offenders. A failure in *self-control,* leading to *impulsivity,* figures repeatedly in explanations of crime. Ross and Fabiano suggest that impulsivity may be seen 'as a failure to insert between impulse and action a stage of reflection, a cognitive analysis of the situation'. This failure, they further suggest, may be due to one of a number of factors: a failure to learn to stop and think; a failure to learn 'effective thinking'; a failure to generate alternative responses; or a reflection of hopelessness. The empirical evidence is mixed. Some studies suggest that offenders are more impulsive than non-offenders others that offenders are unable to delay reward. However, other studies have not found such differences.

The difference between studies may be due to differing definitions and measures of impulsivity, and the heterogeneity of the offender population. The concept of *locus of control* refers to the degree to which individuals perceive their behaviour to be under their own *internal* control, as opposed to being controlled by *external* agents such as luck or authority figures. A number of studies have shown that offenders tend to external control, that is they explain their behaviour as being controlled by influences beyond their personal control.

However, other studies have failed to show any difference in locus of control between offender and non-offender samples; while Lefcourt and Ladwig found offenders to be more *internally* controlled than nonoffenders. The varied findings are probably due to two unfounded assumptions: that locus of control is a unitary concept, and that offenders form a homogeneous population.

With regard to the former point, a number of studies have shown that there are several dimensions to locus of control, such as belief in control over one's immediate environment as opposed to belief in control over political events. In terms of the latter point, locus of control within an offender population may be a function of race; type of offence, for example, violent offenders tend to external control or time spent in prison. If locus of control does have some relationship with offending, it will require rather more sophisticated research than is presently available to discover its exact role. As social perception develops so the ability to 'see things from the other person's point of view' matures and influences our own behaviour.

A long-standing finding with offenders is that they see situations only from their own perspective, not appreciating the view of the other person. This is reflected in low scores on measures of empathy and role-taking ability: although variations have been reported just as to length of criminal career and type of offence. If social perception is the ability to discriminate social cues and understand their significance, then the next step requires using these perceptions to decide upon suitable social behaviour. This requires a range of cognitive skills such as the ability to generate a range of solutions to a social problem, considering the various consequences of the different solutions, and planning the steps to achieve the different outcomes.

These cognitive skills have become more widely known as 'cognitive problem-solving' over the past few years. Several studies have found that offenders show poorer social problem solving than nonoffenders. Although some doubt has been expressed about the validity of one of the measures used in some of these studies, and also about the functional relationship of these cognitive skills with offending. In total the evidence does indicate some differences in social cognition between offenders and non-offenders. However, two points require clarification: the relationship between impersonal and interpersonal cognitive abilities, particularly with regard to offender populations; secondly, and perhaps more importantly, the process by which the cognition results in offending.

It seems likely that the answer to this latter point will come from studies, not yet attempted, of social *decisionmaking* in offenders. While social decision-making in offenders has not been researched, decision-making regarding the commission of crime has received a growing amount of attention.

This line of enquiry portrays the offender as a rational decision-maker, a 'reasoning criminal'. The beginnings of this cognitive view of crime are, somewhat ironically, to be found in studies which focused on environmental rather than individual factors in explaining the crime. Simply, this view suggests that for a crime to be committed, the opportunity must be afforded for the offence to occur; the criminal is one who decides to take advantage of this opportunity. L.E.Cohen and Felson elaborated on this view of 'crime as opportunity', suggesting that for example the increase in burglaries over the past decade can be explained in terms of increased opportunity as more family members go out to work, so leaving houses empty for longer periods.

Studies have similarly investigated the effects of opportunity on car theft violence robbery and theft and vandalism. The cognitive component involves the decision-making process when the opportunity to offend arises. A crime is seen therefore as the result of the offender's consideration of the risks and costs of offending; indeed previous studies have addressed the relationship between risk perception and likelihood of offending. Cornish and Clarke summarize this view of crime:

- Its starting point was the assumption that offenders seek to benefit themselves by their criminal behaviour; that this involves the making of decisions and choices, however rudimentary on occasion these processes might be; and that these processes exhibit a measure of rationality, albeit constrained by limits of time and ability and the availability of relevant information.

Cornish and Clarke also make the distinction between criminal *involvement* and criminal *events*. The former is the process by which individuals choose to become involved in crime, while the latter refers to the short-term, immediate decisions in a given set of circumstances. Thus the approach is an interactional one, in which the offender reacts in a reasoned manner to environmental opportunities. While this represents a move away from 'dispositional' theories which focus exclusively on the offender, it does not dismiss the importance of personal variables, but rather attempts to place such variables in a wider context. As an example Cornish and Clarke work through the process of an individual's initial involvement in the crime of burglary, followed by the event decision for a specific burglary, and finally the process underlying the individual committing more and more such offences.

The initial involvement includes factors such as type of upbringing and other social variables; the event decision considers the influence of factors such as the presence of a dog or a burglar alarm on the decision to enter a particular house; while the increase in frequency is related to a growing sense of 'professionalism' in committing the crime, and accompanying changes in self-evaluation, life-style, and peer group. As well as burglary the rational choice model has been applied to shoplifting, robbery and drug use.

The rational choice model can also be applied to the decision to give up crime. In total, the traditional learning theories have concentrated upon the acquisition of criminal behaviour through reinforcement and modelling. The cognitive theories have followed this trend, but have recently considered the alternative of explaining why offending does *not* occur even when the opportunity arises. This notion of not offending is central to another group of theories which see crime as a failure to learn control behaviour.

POLICE RECORDING OF CRIME

If an offence is reported to the police is it guaranteed to appear in the official statistics? An American study cited by Hood and Sparks suggests not: only about two-thirds of serious crimes which victims claimed to have reported to the police were actually recorded in police files. A British survey similarly found that there were discrepancies between reported crime and police-recorded crime: the percentage shortfall— crimes reported but not recorded—ranged from 75 per cent for robbery to 27 per cent for bicycle theft. However, three offence categories—sexual offences, thefts of motor vehicles, and theft in a dwelling—showed no shortfall between reporting and police recording.

While human error may play a part in misrecording or 'losing' crimes, and the exact figures involved may be open to question, it is also true that the police have considerable discretion over the recording of reported crime. Bottomley and Pease present a full discussion of police work and criminal statistics; however, for present purposes the emphasis will be on the process of recording. As Hough and Mayhew note, the police may, with justification, feel that a reported 'crime' is a mistake, or there is a lack of evidence to support the report. In other instances an informal caution may be given in which case the offence will not appear in the official figures.

In a similar vein, the criminal incident may be satisfactorily resolved by the appearance of a police officer: family disputes and arguments in public houses are examples of this type of situation in which the crime is reported but goes unrecorded. Alternatively it could be that after reporting a crime the injured party asks for the crime to be dropped and so the incident is written off as 'no crime' —again failing to appear in the criminal statistics. In a survey of three London areas, Sparks *et al.* found that 'no crime' cases accounted for between 18 per cent and 28 per cent of all initially recorded crimes. The time lapse between the committing of the crime and its reporting to the police is also important; those judged as being too 'stale' to merit investigation may fail to be recorded. Thus for these and perhaps other reasons the discrepancy between the number of crimes actually committed and the number recorded by the police suggests that the official statistics are not telling the full story—at least for some types of crime.

While crimes can be 'lost' and so distort official figures, variations in police activity can also cause fluctuations in the crime statistics. A crackdown on some criminal group, say drug offenders, can cause a 'bulge' in the figures.

Of course this does not mean that there has been a dramatic increase in that type of crime—despite what some newspaper headlines might say—rather that, to use an experimental metaphor, improved sampling has given a better estimate of the true population. In other words, the official figure moves closer to reality.

Similarly a change in public attitude or improving the means of communication—it is more convenient to telephone the police at 2 am than to walk to the station—may shift both the quality and quantity of crimes reported to the police. So while, say, the real amount of violent crime in society is decreasing, higher levels of reporting can cause an *increase* to appear in the official figures. The first British Crime Survey showed that victims were selective in the crimes they reported to the police: there was, for example, a high rate of reporting for theft of a motor vehicle but a low rate for theft in a dwelling. M. Hough and Mayhew also examined the reasons offered by victims for not reporting a crime. The main reasons were the view that the crime was too trivial, or that the police could do nothing, or that it was appropriate to deal with the matter personally. In total these explanations show why victims may decide not to report a crime, although other factors can also be considered.

The victim, or perhaps witness, may not realise an act is criminal: physical violence, for example, may be perceived as bullying rather than assault. In cases of fraud or theft from an employer the victim might be unaware of the crime. Alternatively the individual may be a 'willing victim': for example, some homosexual behaviour, drug dealing, and prostitution all involve willing victims. Finally there are 'victimless crimes': if a telephone box is vandalized, or a false income tax return submitted, who is the victim to report the crime? In summary, crimes are committed, some serious, which fail to appear in the criminal statistics. The amount of this 'unknown' crime is traditionally referred to as the *Dark Figure*. In attempting to shed light on the magnitude of the Dark Figure researchers have turned away from official bodies towards the other two parties involved in crime—the offenders and the victims.

OFFENDER SURVEYS

In the 1960s a number of offender surveys were carried out for which reviews are available. The most commonly employed methodology was to select a sample either on the basis of age or geographical location, then to ask the members of the sample whether they had committed any crimes, either detected or undetected. This information was gathered either by questionnaire or interview, conducted with the target person themselves or with someone who knew them well. A British study of theft conducted by Belson illustrates a typical survey. A sample of 1,445 boys, aged from 13 to 16 years, was randomly selected from a large sample of London households. Interviews with the boys revealed that approximately 70 per cent of the sample had stolen from a shop, and about

17 per cent had stolen from private premises. Thus the majority of boys had committed an offence for which, had they been caught, they would have been liable to prosecution. The general picture which emerges from the self-report studies is that the official figures underestimate the true extent of crime, especially amongst the young. Indeed, Hood and Sparks suggest that the official figures represent on average only one-quarter of those who actually commit offences; in other words, they estimate that the Dark Figure is actually about four times greater than the official figure. The initial impact of the self-report studies was to give pause for thought about whether crime, especially in the young, can legitimately be considered a deviant activity.

If so many people are committing offences perhaps that is the norm rather than remaining within the limits of the law. Critics of self-report studies pointed to several shortcomings, the principal one being confidence in the veracity of the data. Does the respondent always tell the truth? Are some crimes withheld, others invented or exaggerated? Further research showed that a number of interviewer and interviewee characteristics—age, sex, socioeconomic status, and race—could influence the quality of information. Additionally there may be sampling problems: if a survey is carried out at a school, for example, it will lose those absent or playing truant—who may be engaged in committing the more serious crimes. Advocates of self-report studies pointed to the advantages of the methodology in that it not only gives a picture of crime involving victims, but also includes 'victimless' crimes such as drug abuse and vandalism. Such doubts led a number of investigators to refine the self-report methodology to include reliability checks on the data.

The most frequently used verification technique is to compare selfreport with police records. Studies using this check have found high degrees of agreement between the two measures of offending. Other verification methods include using peer informants to ensure reports match; testing respondents twice to determine if their answers remain constant; and including lie questions in the schedule as a general check on honesty. Hindelang *et al.*, following a comprehensive review of self-report methodology, conclude that the match is a good one between self-report data and official recording. However, despite the assurances of researchers such as Hindelang *et al.*, the trend in recent times has moved away from offender surveys to victim surveys. One reason for this is that not only can victim surveys reveal information about crime, but also they can be used to gather data on other issues such as public attitudes towards crime and public fear of crime.

VICTIM SURVEYS

The first contemporary victim surveys were carried out in the USA in the late 1960s, followed by the first American national survey in 1972. Similar surveys were carried out in other parts of the world including Australia and the Scandinavian countries. Smaller-scale victim surveys have been conducted in specific parts of a country, for example in England surveys have been conducted in the Midlands, in Islington in London and on Merseyside or in areas of the same city, such as the survey in different parts of London. Victim research has a range of available methodologies but *household surveys* offer perhaps the most important means of data collection. This methodology is typified by the first British Crime Survey. This survey selected 16,000 households from the Electoral Register, with the aim of interviewing one person aged 16 years or older from each household.

The survey achieved an 80 per cent success rate in striving to achieve that particular sample. In the context of an interview respondents answered questions about any crimes in which they had been the victim, gave details of the crime and answered questions on their attitudes towards crime. Surveys such as the British Crime Survey have thrown up a vast amount of data, but across studies a consistent pattern of findings emerges. The most notable is the extent of crime, as Sparks notes: 'Criminal victimization is an extremely rare event...crimes of violence are extremely uncommon'. The first British Crime Survey was in agreement with Sparks's observations.

Trivial crimes such as theft from a motor vehicle are the most common, while serious offences such as assault and robbery have a very low frequency of occurrence. Indeed, M.Hough and Mayhew estimate that the 'statistically average' person over the age of 16 years can expect to be burgled once every 40 years, and to be robbed once every 500 years. Crime is not, however, a random event and crime surveys illustrate this point. The majority of respondents, Sparks estimates about 90 per cent, report no experience of crime. On the other hand, some people report being involved in a series of incidents, having been the victims of two, three, four, or even more crimes. This leads to the important distinction between the *incidence* of victimization and the *prevalence* of victimization. The incidence is the average crime rate over the whole population; the prevalence is that percentage of the population who actually experience crime. Thus surveys reveal that burglaries are most prevalent in inner city areas; cars parked on the street at night are more likely to be stolen; and that it is not the elderly but young males, who typically have assaulted others themselves, who are the most likely victims of assault. If surveys are repeated over regular periods trends in crime rates may be described.

Sparks discusses some figures from the American National Crime Survey over the period 1973–79: rates for burglary and robbery dropped over that period, while rates for household and personal larceny fluctuated over that time. In Britain such trends cannot be calculated as only two national crime surveys have been completed. The second of these showed rises in almost all categories of offence. It can also be seen that the rises detected by the survey closely parallel changes in the amount of crime recorded by the police.

Table. Percentage change in British Crime Survey Estimates and Offences Recorded by the Police in the same Period

Offences	Survey Estimates	Recorded offences (% Change)
Vandalism	+ 9	+ 15
Theft from a motor vehicle	+ 7	+ 12
Burglary in a dwelling	+ 21	+ 24
Theft of motor vehicle	0	– 2
Bicycle theft	+ 34	+ 13
Theft in a dwelling	+ 2	+ 13
Theft from a person/robbery	+ 9	– 1
Total	+ 10	+ 12

Victim surveys provide a good picture of the type and amount of crime but they are not without drawbacks. The figures they produce will always underestimate the amount of crime: they focus on offences against the person and against property, omitting the whole area of 'white-collar crime' such as fraud and embezzlement. The problems of respondent accuracy, as with offender surveys, also apply to victim surveys. Other factors such as the type of interview, interviewer characteristics and the use of multiple interviews can all influence the quality of information gained by the survey. Similarly Sparks *et al.* found that the amount of crime reported was related to the respondent's level of educational achievement. Nevertheless, the figures produced by crime surveys are an important source of information about crime: as such they therefore have great potential for shaping theories of crime and influencing political and social policies towards managing and controlling crime. In summary, surveys of both offenders and victims confirm that the Dark Figure exists, and that it is substantially greater than official figures. However, given the methodological limitations of surveys, it is prudent to exercise caution in attempting to ascribe exact numerical values to the Dark Figure.

MENTAL ILLNESS AND CRIME

In truth, the term 'mental illness' causes more problems than it solves: Ashworth and Gostin note that mental illness is not defined in the Mental Health Act and therefore 'much will depend upon medical opinion'. In practice the term is used for a wide range of diagnostic categories including psychoses, affective disorders, anxiety states, hysteria, and so on. Inspection of admissions to Special Hospitals shows that by far the greatest number of mentally ill serious offenders are diagnosed as schizophrenic, with depression the next most frequent diagnosis. Does any special relationship exist between these two particular disorders and crime?

SCHIZOPHRENIA

The most important indicators of schizophrenia, which would *not* all be found in one person, include disturbances of thought, perception, affect, and motor behaviour. Thought disorder refers to a disturbance of the process of making associations between thoughts. Perceptual disturbances are evinced by hallucinations, which may be visual or tactile but are most commonly auditory, typically as voices commenting or giving instructions. Affect can be flat and expressionless or alternatively it can be inappropriate such as anger without provocation, or laughter at misfortune. Finally, motor disturbances can take the form of bizarre facial grimaces, repeated gesturing, or excited agitation of the body; alternatively unusual postures can be adopted and held, in a state of immobility, for long periods.

As noted, not all these behaviours would be found in the same person, although some pattern does emerge: disorganized or hebephrenic schizophrenia is characterized by hallucinations, delusions, and inappropriate affect; catatonic schizophrenia by motor disturbances; and paranoid schizophrenia by delusions of persecu-tion, incorporating 'ideas of reference' in which personal significance is continually perceived in the actions of other people. Given this range, it may well be expedient to think of schizophrenia as a group of disorders rather than a single disorder which always manifests itself in the same fashion.

While of uncertain aetiology, contemporary theories favour a complex interaction between genetic, neurochemical, and social factors as an explanation for schizophrenia. It is generally accepted that the incidence of schizophrenia is close to 1 per cent in the general population: this sets a baseline against which to compare the rates of schizophrenia in offender populations. Spry reviews the evidence on the incidence of schizophrenia and crime and notes a division in research findings: with studies of nondisordered offender groups the incidence of schizophrenia is around the 1 per cent mark with selected samples of offenders referred for psychiatric treatment, typically having committed serious offences, the incidence is much higher.

For example, Green reports that 74 per cent of a sample of fifty-eight men admitted to a Special Hospital having committed matricide were schizophrenic. Does this suggest that schizophrenia is related to serious offences? As Spry notes, many people associate schizophrenia with crime, particularly violent crime. Indeed, there are indications that a relationship may exist between paranoid ideas and violence, and that the victims of violent attacks are often those who figured in the schizophrenic's delusions.

Crimes of this type catch the public imagination: Prins notes the case of Ian Ball, in which delusional thought processes were manifest in a plot to kidnap a member of the royal family: Prins discusses the crimes of Peter Sutcliffe, the 'Yorkshire Ripper', in which there was some controversy as to the role of his paranoid schizophrenia in the murders he committed. It should be stressed, however, that the publicity generated by these cases is in inverse proportion to their frequency; the deluded and paranoid people who commit such crimes are rare. While these extreme cases are infrequent, the finding remains that schizophrenics are slightly more likely to commit violent offences than other disordered groups or the general population.

While schizophrenia may be directly related to violence, with delusional and paranoid beliefs of apparent importance, a simple relationship between the disorder and the crime is unlikely to exist. P.J.Taylor suggests that: 'It is not unusual to find that the violent act of a schizophrenic cannot be directly explained by the current psychopathology. This does not, however, negate the relevance of the illness...social and illness variables must be considered together'. The point Taylor makes is an important one: as well as considering a causal relationship between schizophrenia and violence, attention should also be paid to the similarities in social, environmental, and organic antecedents common to both violence and schizophrenia. More recent findings by the same researcher reinforce this point. From a survey of 121 psychotic offenders, Taylor concluded that '20 per cent of the actively psychotic were directly driven to offend by their psychotic symptoms, and a further 26 per cent probably so'. When social factors such as homelessness were considered along with the nature of the crime, so that 'the direct and indirect consequences of psychosis are considered together, then over 80 per cent of the offences of the psychotic were probably attributable to their illness'.

Depression

Clinically two types of depression are distinguished: *major depression* and *bipolar disorder*. Major depression is characterized by profoundly sad mood, overwhelming feelings of selfblame, guilt, and worthlessness, appetite disturbances, fatigue and long periods of sleep, lethargy, and recurrent thoughts of death and suicide. Bipolar disorder is typified by bouts of mania as well as periods of depression: during the manic phase the individual shows elated or irritable mood, high levels of furious physical activity, goes long periods without sleep, and displays a general air of self-importance and inflated self-esteem.

Of the two, major depression is by far the most common, with estimates suggesting that 8 per cent to 11 per cent of men and 18 per cent to 23 per cent of women will be clinically depressed at least once in their life; bipolar disorder is less frequent, appearing in about 1 per cent of the population. Theories of depression incorporate a wide range of biological, cognitive, behavioural, and social factors. As with schizophrenia—or, indeed, any mental illness—there are difficulties in establishing the relationship between depression and crime.

A range of possibilities exists: the crime may have been committed because the offender was depressed; the offender may become depressed after the crime, either because of guilt or imprisonment; the offender may have been depressed when committing the crime, but the depression was not instrumental in causing the crime. In terms of a direct causal link, one of the more familiar and tragic associations between depression and crime occurs when an individual becomes convinced that life is hopeless and before committing suicide kills his or her children and other members of the family. West studied seventy-eight cases of murder followed by suicide and estimated that twenty-eight of the offenders were depressed at the time of the offence. Lawson suggests that a general pattern in certain murders by depressives lies in the 'social circumstances and pathological features of the domestic killing'.

The social circumstances involve a negative life event such as an upset in a long-term relationship, while the act itself shows no sign of planning or even malice. As well as murder, depression has been associated with other crimes including shoplifting and violence. With regard to violence, Häfner and Böker found that the violence was principally directed at relatives, suggesting similarities with the 'extended suicides'. As Howells notes, depressed in-patients are not a violent population, suggesting that the relationship between depression and crime is closely tied to social, particularly interpersonal, factors. Although most studies do not indicate which type of depression is present, it is reasonable to assume that major depression is involved.

However, McCulloch and Prins do describe a case involving a manic episode, a car salesman, and violence towards property. While Blumberg suggested that, after schizophrenia, manic depressive episodes were the disorder most commonly found in arsonists; Gunderson similarly suggested that firesetting during a manic state may be more common than is generally acknowledged. The broad picture which emerges for mental illness and crime does not really take us much further than the general evidence for 'mental disorder' and crime. Mental illness, particularly schizophrenia and depression, are found in criminal populations but the exact nature of the relationship between the two remains unclear. P.J.Taylor's work is however beginning to show how psychosis and crime may be seen as complex psychosocial phenomena, rather than in a simple relationship in which one factor has a linear causal effect on the other.

ANALYSIS OF THE VIOLENT SITUATION

The situational approach to understanding violence is firmly established in the psychological literature as one which seeks to analyse the environmental factors associated with violent acts. The focus is on research which has analysed the contexts in which the crimes of serious assault, robbery and murder occur.

SERIOUS ASSAULT

Serious assault may be defined as an attack which inflicts severe wounding and physical assault on the victim. M. Henderson reported an exhaustive analysis of violent incidents following lengthy interviews with forty-four prison inmates serving sentences for wounding, attempted murder, grievous bodily harm, and actual bodily harm. The transcripts of the interviews were coded across a range of categories such as victim age and sex, place of incident, and time of day. A cluster analysis of the 246 violent incidents described by the interviewees revealed eight distinct types of incident. The immediate impact of these findings is the variety of settings, the different types of violence, and range of victims involved in the violent act.

The majority of offenders reported being involved in more than one of the types of incident, with 'bullying' the most common and 'crimerelated with the offender alone' least common. Within this analysis four broad categories are apparent: violence in conjunction with another crime; family violence; 'public violence'; and institutional violence. The others deserve mention. Family violence has rapidly become one of the social problems of the 1980s and a number of reviews are available. Henderson's analysis shows that family violence, particularly towards women, takes place at night without the presence of other people.

There is usually a history of violence between offender and victim, with the incident following an argument in which the victim has retaliated verbally but not physically. Child abuse has attracted a great deal of public and specialist interest. The physical abuse of the child typically takes the form of maltreatment such as burning or beatings with hand, feet, or weapons; alternatively the abuse may take the form of extreme neglect leading to starvation, illness, and so on. In either case the effects are severe and can be fatal. The dynamics of family violence between husband and wife were described in a study by Dobash and Dobash of over 100 battered wives. From both personal interviews and official records Dobash and Dobash constructed a pattern of violence, most often taking place in the family home, which began with a verbal confrontation, often construed by the man as a challenge to his authority.

As the pattern unfolds the woman typically attempts to avert the forthcoming violence using strategies such as attempting to withdraw from the situation, or trying to reason or debate with the man. As the attack begins, involving slapping, punching, butting, hitting with sticks and other weapons, the woman continues to try to negotiate a way out of the violence. The woman hits back physically in only a very few instances, then out of anger or frustration; the general effect of this was to increase the level of violence. During the majority of assaults there were bystanders present, most often children. The bystanders mainly tried to support the woman, either by begging the man to stop or by running for help.

After the attack, which resulted in a range of physical injury inflicted on the woman, the men were reported as acting as if nothing had happened, with few expressing remorse or regret. The injured women sought contact with friends, social and medical agencies, or voluntary bodies for both solace and help. Dobash and Dobash suggest that the quality of the response to this search for contact is vital: an outright condemnation of the violence is entirely more supportive than an implicit blaming of the woman by looking for ways in which she might have caused the violence to take place. M.Henderson's analysis showed that 'public violence' is of two types—either involving gangs or taking place in pubs or clubs. Henderson describes two types of gang violence.

In the first a group attacks a victim at night, usually after drinking hours; the victim is not known to the attackers but is also liable to have been drinking; weapons are used, as well as kicking, which can result in death. The second type of gang violence Henderson describes as 'bullying', in which younger victims are slapped and pushed, resulting in serious injury. Violence associated with pubs tends to be between individuals, with the offender's associates as onlookers rather than fellow attackers. The offender and victim have both been drinking and violence follows an argument instigated by the victim. In the fight both offender and victim sustain injuries. Finally Henderson describes two types of institutional violence: violence towards either fellow inmates or towards authority figures.

In Henderson's study the violence was towards other prisoners and police and prison staff, although violence can occur in other institutions. W. Davies discusses prison violence in detail, including hostagetaking; and Drinkwater reviews violence in psychiatric hospitals. *Robbery* Robbery is the theft, or attempted theft, of property or money directly from another person; the theft is accompanied by the use of physical force or the threat of physical harm. In some cases the robber is armed, although most armed robbers use their weapons to intimidate rather than to inflict injury. This is not to say that, given the circumstances, the weapons would not be used. McClintock and Gibson carried out a study of robbery in London and described five situations in which the offence occurred. The first takes place in a bank or jewellers, involving the offender and the staff of the shop or bank.

In the second, the offence takes place on the street, including crimes such as 'mugging' and handbag-snatching. The third, robbery on private premises, is unusual in that it involves breaking into a house to commit the offence. When the robbery takes place indoors it is more commonly between two people who know each other: thus in the fourth and fifth types of robbery, the offence takes place either between people who have only a short acquaintance, say at a party, or between people who have known each other for longer periods. McClintock and Gibson found overall that stranger-to-stranger robberies are much more common, accounting for over three-quarters of all robberies. M.Henderson described two situations in which violence occurred during the course of stealing. In one the violence was directed towards a stranger, often older than the group of offenders, within the victim's home during daylight hours. Weapons are used causing serious injury and the offenders report a lack of emotion in committing the offence. In the second type the offender is alone at night in the victim's house.

The violence, typically involving women or elderly people, takes the form of kicking and can be fatal. The offender reports being drunk at the time of the offence, feeling anxious, losing control, and afterwards saying that the victim did not deserve their injuries. These two types of robberies can be described in terms of the distinction referred to previously between 'instrumental' and 'hostile' aggression. In the first instance the violence is simply instrumental in achieving the goal of obtaining money. The second instance bears the hallmarks of a 'burglary gone wrong': upon discovery the offender panics, loses control, perhaps because of the effects of drink, and hits out at the householder; the simple burglary escalates to robbery or even murder.

Murder

Murder is the *intentional* taking of the life of another person. The emphasis on intent is crucial: if a life is taken without premeditated intent to kill then the act is termed manslaughter. It is, of course, often a matter for the courts to decide whether an act was premeditated and therefore one of murder not manslaughter. Murder is not a common crime: in England and Wales, for example, the 1985 Criminal Statistics show that there were 173 convictions for murder, with a further 35 convictions for attempted murder.

Similarly, Siegal notes that in 1984 the murder rate in the USA was 7.9 offences per 100,000 inhabitants. Official figures do not necessarily reflect the real levels of a particular crime. This is true of murder: some murders go undetected, in other cases the murderer commits suicide after killing; nevertheless it is probably the case that, in relation to the total number of crimes committed, murder is an uncommon act. Wolfgang presents an analysis of the situations in which 588 murders took place in Philadelphia between 1948 and 1952. In a substantial number of cases the killing followed a relatively trivial event such as an argument, threat, or insult; in the majority of cases the offender and victim knew each other; the offender and victim were almost always of the same race. The majority of murderers were male, usually less than 35 years of age; most victims were also male; and stabbing was the most common means of causing death. The offender, victim, or both had usually been drinking, and offenders typically had previous arrest records, usually for violent crime.

The murders most frequently occurred in a domestic setting during the summer months, most often between the hours of 8 pm Saturday and 2 am Sunday. The incidents which were the most violent in character occurred between husband and wife. Most subsequent surveys broadly agree with Wolfgang's findings, although there are several exceptions. An English study found that the majority of victims are female; a study in Chicago found that offender and victim were related in fewer instances, and that firearms were more frequently used. Goldstein presents an analysis of the motives for murder from the 1983 American figures and suggests that about 20 per cent of murders were related to another crime such as robbery, while 44 per cent were associated with arguments. In total, the general picture is of a crime which commonly takes place between people who are at least acquainted and have argued, perhaps following drinking.

While the surveys paint an overall picture, a study by Luckenbill vividly illuminates the fine detail. Luckenbill analysed the interactions between offender and victim in the time immediately before the act of murder. From this analysis he described six stages in 'transactions resulting in murder'. In stage one the opening move comes from the victim in the form of a verbal comment, or refusal to comply with a request or some physical act such as flirta-tion. In some instances an insult was clearly intended, in others the offender interpreted the victim's behaviour as offensive. In stage two the offender seeks confirmation of the insult, either by verbally checking with the victim, or with anyone else who might be present; the victim's continuation of the behaviour can also act as confirmation of the insult. In some instances the 'confirmation' is inferred: for example a child's continued screaming confirms refusal to comply with the instruction to be quiet. At stage three the offender opts not to retreat but to stand his or her ground and retaliate. In most cases the retaliation at this stage is verbal, although in a minority of instances it is physical and the murder results. At stage four the victim replies to the retaliation; as Luckenbill notes, 'The victim's move appeared as an agreement that violence was suitable to the transaction'. The victim's move is a continuation of the offensive behaviour, a verbal counter-challenge, or physical attack.

This move was often supported by onlookers or others present. With stage five battle commences, usually with a weapon to hand: the act is generally brief, Luckenbill reports that in over half the murders the offender 'dropped the victim in a single shot, stab, or rally of blows'. In the sixth and final stage the murderer acts in one of three ways: he or she voluntarily waits for the police; is held by others present; or flees the scene. Luckenbill portrays a crime which is not simply perpetrated by one person: 'Rather, murder is the outcome of a dynamic interchange between an offender, victim, and, in many cases, bystanders'. This view of the victim as playing a role, perhaps even a causative role, in determining their fate has been a source of some controversy.

Dobash and Dobash, for example, concluded their study of battered wives discussed previously with the note that their research failed to support any interpretation which shifted the blame for the attack from the aggressor to the victim. While not discounting the possibility that Luckenbill's analysis may have some relevance in understanding violence between males, Dobash and Dobash argue that gender and its associated roles and meanings must be considered when male violence is directed at female victims. However, at a general theoretical level, Dobash and Dobash are unhappy with the notion of victim-precipitated violence: 'We would argue that many violent episodes should be understood as often constructed intentionally by the aggressor'. While an analysis of social exchanges may be efficacious in explaining some murders, particularly domestic murders, there are other types of murder which seem to demand a different level of explanation. *Mass murderers* kill a number of people simultaneously: two American mass murderers, Charles Whitman and James Huberty, killed fourteen and twenty-one people respectively in sustained violent acts, and during the time of writing this book there was in Britain the massacre at Hungerford. The *serial killer* is a mass murderer who kills over a period of time rather than in one outburst.

The victims of the serial killer are typically tortured or sexually assaulted before being murdered. In some instances the serial killer may terrorize a city, such as the 'Yorkshire Ripper' in Leeds, or Kenneth Bianchi in Los Angeles: in other instances the serial killer travels the country, taking life as they move from location to location. Levin and Fox have estimated that about thirty-five mass murderers, including serial killers, are active in America at present. Before moving on to look at the research findings from studies of the violent individual, it should be noted that there are violent crimes. Assault and murder, for example, can occur through means other than direct physical violence, such as firesetting, although in some instances this may be violence towards property rather than people and poisoning or leaving bombs in public places.

ANALYSIS OF THE VIOLENT OFFENDER

Taxonomies

This approach seeks to classify types of violent offender just as to one or more variables. Conklin for example suggested that there are four 'specialist' types of robber. The *professional robber* views robbery as a highly effective means of earning a living: robberies, perhaps three or four a year, are carefully planned by organized teams with the victim generally a commercial institution. The *opportunist robber* steals only small amounts as and when a vulnerable target, such as a young or old person, presents itself; the act is not planned in advance. The *addict robber* and the *alcoholic robber* steal to obtain money to purchase more drugs or drink: these robberies are not likely to be planned or organized, and are generally aimed at 'easy' victims. While this general approach can be helpful in illustrating that different people commit violent crimes for different reasons and under different conditions, it does not say a great deal about the *person* involved. A body of work which has attempted to investigate the psychology of the violent offender is concerned with the link between personality and violence.

Personality

The model which prompted the main line of research in personality and violence was proposed by Megargee. The basis of the model is that violence occurs when the instigation to violence, mediated by anger, exceeds the individual's level of control of aggressive feelings or impulses. The *undercontrolled* person has very low inhibitors and therefore frequently acts in a violent manner when provocation is perceived. The *overcontrolled* person has extremely strong inhibitors and violence will occur only if the provocation is intense or has been endured for a very long period of time. Megargee predicted that an overcontrolled personality would be found in those who have committed acts of extreme violence, but would not be found among those with histories of frequent minor assaults.

Blackburn compared the personality profiles of a group of 'extreme' violent offenders, convicted of murder, manslaughter, or attempted murder, with a group of 'moderate' violent offenders who had committed acts of assault. In keeping with the prediction, the extreme group were significantly more introverted, conform-ing, overcontrolled, and less hostile than the moderate group; although Crawford failed to replicate this finding. Quinsey *et al.* and M.Henderson reported that the overcontrolled violent offender showed deficiencies in assertive behaviour. Henderson also found that violent offenders who scored low on a psychometric measure of control reported significantly more difficulty in controlling their temper and avoiding fights. While the weight of this research lends support to a distinction based on an overcontrolled-undercontrolled dichotomy, the most significant advances have come from an approach which searches for types, or clusters, of offenders based on their scores on personality measures.

Blackburn carried out a cluster analysis on the MMPI scores of fifty-six male murderers detained in a secure psychiatric hospital. The Minnesota Multiphasic Personality Inventory is a collection of psychometric measures, including scales such as 'psychoticism', 'dominance', 'hostility', and so on. Initially devised over forty-five years ago, the MMPI is a widely used device in psychological research. Blackburn's analysis of MMPI scores showed four clusters of violent offenders: two of these clusters were classed as overcontrolled, and two as undercontrolled.

The *psychopathic* group is characterized by poor impulse control, high extraversion, outward-directed hostility, low anxiety, and few psychiatric symptoms. The *paranoid-aggressive* group also displays high impulsivity and aggression, but also high levels of psychiatric disorder, particularly psychotic symptoms. These two groups are sometimes referred to as *primary psychopaths* and *secondary psychopaths*. The overcontrolled classification contains a *controlledrepressor* group which exhibits a high degree of impulse control and of defensiveness, and low levels of hostility, anxiety, and psychiatric symptoms. The second overcontrolled group is labelled *depressedinhibited* and is characterized by low levels of impulsivity and extraversion, inward-directed hostility, and high levels of depression.

Blackburn replicated this finding, as did McGurk with a sample of 'normal' murderers from a prison, rather than hospital, population. M.Henderson found essentially the same four types in a sample of violent offenders from the prison population. McGurk's study also pointed to the existence of a fifth group; while Blackburn found the same four groups, a fifth similar to McGurk's additional group, and a new sixth group. However, McGurk and Blackburn are agreed that these 'extra' groups are variants of the four principal groups rather than distinct types: one is a less aggressive and withdrawn secondary psychopath; the other a more introverted variant of the controlled-repressor group with high levels of mental illness.

The evidence therefore supports the fourfold classification of violent offenders. However, before beginning to explain *violent* crime, the prevalence of the four groups in other types of offenders has to be considered. In two studies with non-violent prisoners, Holland and Holt and Widom found four personality clusters: in both studies three of the clusters corresponded to the original clusters with the exception that the depressed-inhibited group was not found. McGurk and McGurk similarly found three clusters with non-violent prisoners, once again the groups corresponded to the original groups with no depressed-inhibited group appearing in the analysis.

M.Henderson also found four clusters in an MMPI analysis of non-violent offenders, and this time the clusters matched the original analysis; that is a depressed-inhibited group was found in a non-violent population. M.Henderson then compared the non-violent depressed-inhibited group with the same group from the violent population in her earlier study: 'Although the defining characteristics of the two are similar, the violent offender of this group, tends to be more disturbed, introverted, anxious and hostile than his non-violent counterpart'. It appears, on balance, that the four personality clusters are to be found in the offender population generally, rather appearing exclusively in the violent offender population. The depressed-inhibited profile seems the most characteristic of violent offender populations and may therefore give some clues towards explaining at least some violent acts.

The theoretical position is a matter of debate. Bartol suggests that the low inhibition of the undercontrolled offender corresponds with Eysenck's proposition that anti-social behaviour is the result of a failure to condition impulse control. While in interpersonal terms, M.Henderson found that violent inhibited offenders reported difficulty in making friends and functioning as part of a social group. This strikes at the heart of the debate: violence can be seen as resulting from the effects of a stable personality trait; or it can be understood in social learning terms, with the emphasis on a person-situation interaction. Blackburn offers a succinct summary of the position to date.

In the case of the primary and secondary psychopaths, the probability of a violent outcome seems likely to be increased as a result of their typically coercive or hostile approaches to interpersonal problem-solving. For controlled and inhibited individuals, on the other hand, violence may represent a last resort when attempts to resolve a situation through compliance or avoidance break down. In these terms, this broad classification may provide a first stab at understanding a violent act in the individual case. Blackburn 1986:268)

While empirical research has supported and refined Megargee's original proposition of undercontrolled and overcontrolled offenders, it seems unlikely that this approach will provide an explanation for violent crime in itself. This is not surprising in that theories of aggression and violence which have relied heavily on individual factors—the instinct and drive theories—have been less than satisfactory. What is required is a marriage of the situational and individual approaches: the social detail of studies like those of Luckenbill, and Dobash and Dobash, together with the intricate psychometric profiles of Blackburn or Henderson alongside the cognitive aspect as described by Novaco.

The question which remains to be answered is why some people, in some situations, commit violent acts. The 'people' part of the equation may contain elements from personality theory, or perhaps other factors such as intelligence or preference for personal space, styles of attribution or imitative behaviour.

The 'situation' may contain the deliberate actions of another person, comments from onlookers, or prolonged stress such as a child who will not stop screaming. Distillation of the vital explosive elements awaits further investigation.

8

Interviewing Skills Required for Reporting

IMPORTANCE OF THE INTERVIEW

There are various ways of gathering information and knowledge of the media. One can do so from books, magazines and journals, or incidents, and by meeting people who hold important positions. Meeting or interviewing them is one of the most significant and important ways of gathering information, facts and knowledge. The interview is a very useful input for all media-print and electronic. It depends on how one would like to use an interview. It may be used as a programme to make the audience/reader get information/ facts from the source directly. The interview can form the basis of an article, a feature or a commentary. Or, segments of an interview can be used to substantiate an argument or a point in an article or a radio/television feature.

The Importance of Preparing Oneself to Conduct an Interview: One may like to presume that you have written something in your life; a letter, an application, an article or a poem. One can also assume that you might not have been satisfied with the first draft. Therefore, you may have re-written it changing sentences, paragraphs, words, etc. It is also possible that after changing the draft twice, thrice or more times, you were satisfied with your written material. Let us call this the preparatory stage. To do an interview is also something like doing an original work in which you create something. Thus, to do a meaningful interview—both for yourself and for the person whom you plan to talk to—it is necessary that you do your homework right. It is only then, that an interview conducted after proper preparation, would make a certain impact. It is said that to speak for five minutes over the radio, a person must prepare Himself/herself at least for five hours. Therefore, preparation is very important.

On the Record and Off the Record Interviews: Interviews can be on the record or off the record. On the record interviews are those whose contents can be attributed to the person interviewed. In this case, unless there is a prior agreement to use the whole of the interview verbatim, portions of the interview, that have some use for the reporter can be utilized and the rest discarded or canned for future use. Off the record interviews are those in which the information is given, but the source is not to be identified by the interviewer. In such cases, the source identifier is "a source in the, Defence Ministry" or "a General Commanding a division etc. In such cases it is normal to crosscheck the facts from another source, since the man giving the information is not willing to stand up and be counted. There can be interviews which are partly on the record and partly off the record. That is, some information given can be attributed to the person who gives it and some can be attributed to "a source" or "a Defence Ministry Official" or "a General", etc.

HOW TO PREPARE FOR AN INTERVIEW

The most important part of the interview is to know your subject as completely as possible. It could be a VIP, an important member of the bureaucracy, the art world or the corporate sector or just an ordinary citizen. Accordingly, you should prepare yourself by reading about the person. It is imperative for you to not only fully research the information you want from your subject, but also the person behind it. You should also have all the essential background information on the interviewee, *e.g.,* His/her family, hobbies, interests. This will help you to build an instant rapport with the interviewee. It will enable you to get on with the job most comfortably. A reluctant interviewee only acts as an obstacle and foils the very purpose of the interviewer.

Research: It is most important to research your subject matter. It could be a subject in which you neither have any interest nor adequate knowledge. But once you are fully armed with the basic and important information acquired through books, newspapers, journals or magazine articles, you will be much more comfortable and should be successful in your venture. For example, if you are required to interview a criminal lawyer, a policeman or an accused, you should have enough knowledge of criminal law —cognizable and non-cognizable offences, various Acts/ Sections which govern the offences, and other legal provisions. This will help you extract the required information. You must know your subject matter as well as the person whom you intend to talk to about the subject matter.

Editing Interviews for Use: All journalists must remember two fundamental factors: First, all interviews is subject to editing. So there is no harm in culling more information than you can use. The information that you need to buttress an argument or to refute another or to make a point, can be used at the appropriate place. The rest can be stored for use in future. Second, no statement made in the interview is allowed to be used out of context. If, for instance, a Government authority vehemently denies that any human rights violations were made during a particular clash in Kashmir, one cannot quote him to create the impression that no human rights violations are made by security forces during any clashes. If the authority interviewed does not generalize it, the reporter or sub-editor is debarred from generalizing it.

Strategy: It is important to establish contact with the interviewee much in advance of the interview. How do you do this? It could be a direct contact-physical or through telephone. More often than not, where important interviewees are concerned, there is a channel you will have to go through. It could be the private secretary or the members of the family-referred to as the "protector of the interviewee." So, the first thing to do is to establish a rapport with the protector. To get to your subject matter or the person, you must be able to play to the gallery to defeat all the obstacles imposed by the "protectors".

What You Want from the Interview: If the first thing is to establish contact and to build up a rapport, the most important part of the preparation is to decide what you want to get out of the interview. May be you want substantiation of a fact you have discussed; Or the refutation of something; Or maybe you want the interviewer's views on some proposition you or someone else is making. Here, an experienced journalist recalls for our benefit one such exciting interview that he had conducted some years ago. In 1962 an International Invitation Table Tennis Tournament was held in Lucknow. Taking part were Victor Parua of England, Ferem Sido of Hungary who was among the first five in world Table Tennis.

The cream of Indian Table Tennis was also there. The foreigners were lodged in Carlton Hotel the best in Lucknow those days, and the Indians in Capoor Hotel, the city's second best those days. Both were declared out of bounds for reporters because while the players played in the evening and until late at nights, they used to rest undisturbed during the day. I was the Sports Editor of M. Calapati Rau's National Herald. The Sports Reporter did the spot reporting of the matches. I devised a way of getting past security to get to the players. A codeword prearranged with Meena Parande, who had been India's No. 1 player among women for seven years, was used by me to get to Meena's room in Capoor's at 1 1.30 a.m. one morning. As I knocked at and entered Meena's spacious room, in walked T. Thiruvengadam, K. Nagaraj and Pappu Haldankar, the three top male players of the country. I was clear in my mind that the objective was to find out about Meena's future plans. Though some of the questions might relate to Meena's past, background, experiences, etc., they were to be used only as ballast. The focus had to be in the future, since her past was already much written about and well known. As I plied her with questions, she seemed unclear about her future plans. This puts me on the alert.

The plans of such high-ranking players are usually charted at least six months in advance. If this was not so, there must be something else in the offing. What was it? Meena was 25 or 26. She had been on top in India for seven years. By now it must not be very exciting to get one win over the other, to put it mildly. If one puts it bluntly, it should be quite boring. I decided to probe from another side. Was she contemplating marriage? Considering that 25 or 26 is supposed to be a pretty ripe age for the marriage of an Indian girl. Neena gave me a look as if say, "How did you know?" Then she replied diplomatically, "Not before retiring from competitive table tennis." Was she planning retirement? Meena spoke the whole truth. What else? She had been on top of Indian Women's table tennis for seven years and had no more worlds to conquer. In international table tennis she was not in the top 50 among women, and 26 was not the age to go up. She could only go down. The wise thing was to retire now when she was at the peak. "Now?" I asked incredulous as I realized I was on the trail of a scoop. "Well", she said after a pause, "now or after the next Nationals", which were coming up in two months. I asked some more probing questions. The male players echoed Meena's argument. All of them were going to retire. They had remained on top in India for years and had no hope of making good in the world arena.

They were 27 to 29 arid had to look forward to raising a family and carving a career for themselves. It was high time they retired. I had got the confirmation that I wanted. Coming back, I reported that India was losing the cream of its table tennis and quoted copiously from the interview. It was an all-India cream. The lessons to be drawn from this example are two. First, it is vital for an interviewer to decide what he wants out of the interview. It is not a fishing expedition in which your net whatever you get. It is a hunt where you go after a target and get it. Second, one has to keep his senses on full alert and the antenna unfurled to catch nuggets of news which have a knack of falling from the lips of the interviewee at the most unexpected moments.

Preparing Yourself: It is important and essential, to make a deep study of the, individual you plan to interview. Let us say that the person is particularly fond of dogs. When you go to interview her/him, it will be fatal to talk about how you abhor dogs or how they are dangerous. As interviewer, you cannot afford to convey your general wariness about the canine species—not verbally, not even through body language. The information you seek to extract from the person may have nothing whatsoever to do with dogs. Yet, the person may react by remaining uncommunicative through the rest of the interview if you start off on the wrong note. Paying attention to such minute, apparently insignificant matters really help in conducting the interview smoothly. You must build a personal rapport to begin with, so you may start the interview comfortably.

Physical Preparation: In the electronic media, there are two ways of interviewing: with the Prime Minister or the President, the setting would be as designed by the Public Relation Officer or the Principal Information Officer. If it is a television interview, then you need the following:

(a) Cameraman;
(b) Sound records;

(c) Lighting technician; and
(d) The sound technician.

The other way could be that the interview is to be held in a studio. In that case, you should adequately arrange the setting in the studio. For the radio studio interview, you would need a very good recording machine. You use a lip microphone which prevents extraneous sound from getting injected into the microphone.

If the interview is only a part of what you are actually going to air, then it should be transcribed. Mark the important segments, and tailor the interview to the actual slot requirements with a suitable link to give necessary continuity. To do this, you would require an editor to do a proper cut and paste work of the tape. In radio and TV interviews, it is important for the interviewer and the interviewee to discuss what they respectively want out of it. Frequently a mini interview is held until a few seconds before the recording devices are switched on.

HOW TO GET AN INTERVIEW

Getting an interview can often be difficult because the interviewer is generally viewed with suspicion! To overcome this handicap, the interviewer has to be imaginative. The interviewer Labours between two competing factors. One, the public has the right to know and you are the tool employed to gather the information. Two, from the legal point of view nobody can be forced into talking and hence, the job can be tiresome and at times, very frustrating. If you have seriously completed Activity-1 and done Cheek Your Progress-1 then you may proceed further. Remember that an interviewer or a reporter would in most cases, like to get information, facts and opinions from the interviewee. Therefore, it is very important that one's own participation in the interview is secondary. One must let the interviewee do most of the talking. To make this happen smoothly, a number of skills and techniques have to be deployed to get your feet inside before the door is slammed and you have your feet stuck up half way. We list some skills here.

- There is the direct approach: to telephone and tell the interviewee what you want.
- The end round: A secretary in a business or government office will generally try and give you the "brush-off", although the interviewee may be totally unaware of the secretary's action. You must recognize the go-between and try and make that person your friend. Remember, it is just a habit for the private secretary to say that the boss has no time. The attempt of the interviewer/reporter should be to try and make the secretary/protector 'one's friend.
- When faced with repeated failure; find out the person's hide-out and with an overdose of apology, just barge in.

- Sit-in: It pays to just sit and wait till the subject of the interview shows up in spite of secretaries and protectors saying that "the boss has no time to see you". Take your lunch or dinner packet along with you to emphasize your determination.
- The appeal: As soon as you get a glimpse of the reluctant interviewee, make your appeal as quickly and strongly as possible, *e.g.*, "We have some information that you are to be shifted from your department/ officer or something which will capture the attention of the object of your interview.
- Be courteous and polite: Tell the interviewee that there are two sides to every story, and we want to know yours. Thus, you arouse the interviewee's curiosity and attention. In many cases, it pays to tell the interviewee of the other side.

Teaching someone how to conduct an interview is like telling him/ her to conduct a conversation. Some are direct and aggressive-which can help. But shyness is no serious handicap: people tend to tell the shy interviewer their "secrets".

DOS AND DON'TS FOR AN INTERVIEW

- *Be operational in time for the interview*: This is very important. It shows the importance of the interviewee and that he has not been taken for granted. "To be operative" is a journalistic term described in the book Advanced Journalism. In a nutshell, you must be ready right on time to start the interview. Arriving on time may be good in most cases, for one has to do things like setting up the camera, or recording devices before the interview. One should arrive 10-15 minutes before time in order to be operational on time.
- Outline your reasons for being there, unless you are working on something very sensitive. If you do not specify your reasons, it may create problems.
- *Stan the interview with a broad question*: This helps you to size up the person and also collect your thoughts. It also helps to receive information you may not have anticipated and to chart out your course of action-a correct direction that the interview should take.
- *Do not interrupt until the interviewee has relaxed*: Avoid making the interviewee uncomfortable at the outset. It would be of little value. An interviewee kept at complete ease can be most helpful.
- *Let him speak at length on his favourite topic/achievement/escapade/feat*: You will get nuggets of information. The irrelevant facts can always be edited out. Be inquisitive, even enthusiastic about his achievements. He will loosen up 6 d be willing to come to the subject you want to discuss at length.

- Grunt and chuckle occasionally.
- Stick to your subject.
- Avoid commenting except to egg him on to talk more: Let the interviewee do most of the talking. This makes that person feel good and wise.
- Do not end the interview till you have the basics-how does he spell his name, official title, age, etc. Never ever assume that you know these things. Preferably get these details in advance from his staff and then get it confirmed by him.
- Be understanding: Do not be insensitive. Even a convict will remember that you were nice to him. Taking notes is a part of the interview. Also, make the interviewee feel important-often it is the interviewee who takes down notes. Relax and double check the contents. Keep the interviewee at ease.

SETTING UP AN INTERVIEW

Most interviews begin with a phone call. This phone call may be to set up an interview time, or to obtain background information to help you to devise the questions. Ideally, you would want to conduct the actual interview face-to-face, and preferably one-to-one as well, though on-the-spot media conferences (called "doorstops") are an increasingly common method of interviewing.

Sometimes you will have to conduct your interview over the phone, or via e-mail, either because the person you want to interview is too busy for a face-to-face meeting or because the workload of the newsroom requires reporters to complete stories as fast as possible.

Of course, sometimes all you will want is a short comment, so a phone interview will be the quickest and most efficient means of getting it. But for longer interviews, phone and e-mail lack a vital ingredient—the non-verbal communication (or body language) which is part of a face-to-face exchange.

The telephone at least will provide you with some clues from the person's tone of voice, or if they laugh or sound abrupt, but e-mail will not provide any of these. The latter is ideal for contacting people from all over the world, but can be even easier to ignore than the phone if the source does not want to talk to you.

What do you want from the interview?

When you set out to conduct an interview, it's important that you know *what* it is that you want to achieve. The first step should be to get a firm idea of the story and the angle, and how the interview will contribute to this. You should be able to summarise your story in about 30 words (or write a possible intro) and, if you can't, you need to spend some time getting this straight before going any further.

Author of a leading book on interviewing, Shirley Biagi, believes you should also establish the interview *why* or the goal or purpose of the interview. She asks: "Will you: Gather facts? Look for quotes? Collect anecdotes? Characterize a situation? Confirm what you know? Show that you were there?"

Once you have determined *what* you want to achieve, and *why* you need to conduct the interview, now is a good time to look at the *who* of the story. Who are the key figures involved? Who can you contact? In other words, who should be interviewed. Make a list of the sources you want to interview for the story.

Shirley Biagi also notes that time should be spent ensuring you have the best source for your story.

People become part of the news for one or more of several reasons:

- Their jobs are important
- They accomplish something important
- They know something or someone important
- They have watched something important happen
- Something important has happened to them
- They represent an important national or international trend

Sometimes the nature of the news will present the obvious choice for the interview. As we've seen already, news can come from events that are managed or that occur spontaneously, from the watching briefs or from reporters" rounds. To a certain extent, these will dictate who you speak to and how you interview them. For instance, with a managed event such as a media conference, the person conducting the conference will be your main source. Today, doorstop interviews are probably the most common method of interviewing politicians, CEOs and other busy people.

Doorstops usually involve representatives of the different media—print, radio and television—all of them with different interests and deadlines. Political reporter for *The Age,* Richard Baker, says asking a question in this environment can be "quite Newsmakers often find it more convenient to give "all-in" interviews rather than talk to reporters individually.

Intimidating" for young reporters. But reporters have to get used to working in front of their peers. Richard says confidence comes with practice and he recommends journalists new to the job should tag along with more experienced reporters to see how these doorstops operate, and how other journalists handle them.

INTERVIEWING STYLE

The style of interviewing each journalist uses reflects not just their training but also their cultural background and personality. That means some reporters may adopt a combative style to get the answers they want, while others may find it difficult to be sufficiently pushy to get more than superficial responses.

The Editorial Training Consultant for Victoria's Leader Newspaper group, Jane Cafarella, has written of the need for young journalists, especially women, to overcome a tendency to be "nice", saying it's not the best characteristic for a journalist. She says too often these young journalists want the interviewee to like them and that makes them gullible. Jane tells her cadets that their job is "to represent the reader and to ask what the reader needs to know". She says reporters conducting interviews should always imagine the reader looking over their shoulder asking "Why?"

Editor of *The Fraser Coast Chronicle,* Nancy Bates, says a reporter needs to think about the expression on their face and the tone of their voice during an interview. Reporters shouldn't give the impression that they're on one side or another of a debate. Nancy tells her journalists, "If you are asking questions, be detached"; though she concedes that "it's easier to be detached on some issues than on the ones more inclined to arouse sympathy".

REMEMBER

A reporter must accurately represent the views of the interviewee. But that doesn't mean you need to agree with them. A reporter is there to represent the public's interests, not the interviewee's.

Reporters wanting to improve their interviewing style will probably benefit from watching top interviewers in action. But it is not recommended that you copy someone else's style. Richard Baker believes a journalist's interviewing style is instinctive, but techniques can be learned.

It's only by being around a bit and getting experience that you can get the guts to say to someone "Hey hang on you're not answering my question. " You learn that and it comes with being around people and having a bit of experience and confidence.

DIFFERENT MEDIA, DIFFERENT STYLES

Always collect more information than you need, it's easy to cut out material later, but extremely difficult to pad out a story if you have not got enough information. However, this tip is only useful if you have the luxury of time. Generally, broadcast journalists have to gather just enough for what they need (sometimes only a seven-second grab) and then run to get it back to the newsroom to edit their story.

This is just one way in which different media make different demands on the way reporters conduct interviews. They also often want different *types* of responses. Print reporters often want a lot of detail as well as comment to help to expand their reports.

By contrast, radio reporters usually want raw information—"When is something going to take place?" "How many people will this affect?" That's because radio news reports are brief and to the point. Television news is good at conveying the emotion of a situation, but not good at presenting large amounts of detail. Television reporters will often ask "emotional" questions, the "How did that make you feel" style of question.

The types of interviews reporters conduct, and the skills required, also vary according to the type of publication a reporter is working for. Jane Cafarella says many of the people who are interviewed by reporters working in metro media outlets are accustomed to being interviewed and they know what's expected of them when answering questions. By contrast, she says, journalists working for suburban or regional papers have to be prepared to coax information out of ordinary people who are not used to dealing with journalists.

A lot of the time the people we interview aren't newsmakers. They're not used to being interviewed. So it's not so much a question of trying to get information from people who are holding back because they've got big company or hot political secrets. It's people who either won't shut up or won't say anything. So there's a skill in drawing those people out.

THE FIVE Ws AND H

There are six questions which should be answered in every story—who, what, when, where, why and how—commonly known as the five Ws and H. Even the smallest news brief, of two or three paragraphs or sentences, should answer the first four of these questions at the very least.

The two main question types are:

- Closed (requiring only a "yes" or "nO' answer).
- Open (inviting more explanation and detail).

It is very easy to turn a closed question into an open one, simply by adding one of the five Ws and H. For instance, if you were to ask a netball player, "Do you think you'll win the game?" you would probably elicit just a "Yes". However if you ask, "*What* will influence the outcome of the game?" you should get so much more simply by adding *what* to the question.

Jana Wendt says early in her career she made the mistake of trying to make things too complicated. She believes the best advice for those starting out in interviewing is to keep it as simple as possible because there's "nothing like a simple question—the classic who, what, when, where, why and how questions".

They're a sure-fire way of getting a flow of conversation. They give you time to think about what you are being told, and any weakness in an argument, and how you might be able to draw a person out. Simple is always best.

However, occasionally you will require someone to answer a closed question to confirm important information. For instance, if you were to ask the prime minister if taxes were going to increase next year, you need a firm "yes" or "no' answer before asking for any details. Another useful question is described by Sedorkin and McGregor as the "bigger, brighter, better" question.

These are the sort of questions the public would want to ask if they were conducting the interview themselves. For instance, an interview with a police detective about a drug raid invites the "bigger, brighter, better" question. The curious journalist should be wondering: What makes this raid different, special, unusual or worthy of coverage?; What gives it that newsworthy angle?

Example: Q: Is this the biggest drug raid in this area/state/country? A "yes" answer to this question could easily result in a front page story.

Richard Baker advises against excessive formality. He says, "If you're interviewing someone for a newspaper, magazine or E-zine, you don't want to make them feel as though they're being quizzed on *Four Corners* or *60 Minutes.* You want your interviewee to feel comfortable."

That means if you have the time to conduct the interview face-to-face (rather than by phone or e-mail), you should try to schedule the interview in a place where the interviewee is most likely to feel relaxed. That might be their office, or a coffee shop and so on. A reporter needs to be adaptable. They also need to be patient. Richard says he would never start an interview with his toughest question.

You've got to get the interviewee at ease and gain a bit of trust. So, if it's a contentious issue, start with a few general questions—let them get their side of the story out and then work into the harder questions and then pull back. You don't want to batter them around the head because very rarely will it get you anywhere. You just want to try and seduce them into speaking honestly and without feeling that they've been driven into providing a certain answer.

Jane Rocca, who often interviews people in the entertainment industries, believes it's important not to shy away from uncomfortable questions. She says an interviewer can afford to be "a bit daring", as long as it's done with respect.

If you want to confirm a rumour or something you read about that person (for instance in the tabloids), approach the topic gently. Don't patronise the artist but simply ask what they think of a specific article. Be daring to get their opinion on something completely off the wall. If it is a music interview, don't be afraid to venture into family chit chat, religion, spirituality, drugs etc. You often get the best material by just being yourself and digging more than just beneath the surface.

In their book *Talk Straight, Listen Carefully: The art of interviewing,* Paterno and Stein say it's important to avoid "overloading" questions. One way of overloading is to pose a double-barreled question, which contains two or more questions in one. The problem with overloading a question is that it gives a "source with something to hide" the opportunity to "keep it hidden".

For example, when reporters were trying to find out if then US president Bill Clinton had had a long-standing affair with a woman named Gennifer Flowers, a well-known television reporter misused his opportunity by asking an overloaded question.

Reporter: "Was Gennifer Flowers your lover for 12 years?" Clinton: "That allegation is false." What allegation is false? That she was his lover? Or that she was his lover for 12 years? Maybe she was his lover for 11 years or seven years, in which case Clinton answered truthfully. By asking imprecise questions, reporters allow sources to wriggle out of responding to issues that are difficult for them.

Different reporters have different opinions about whether a reporter should have all their questions written down, though most journalists agree that when someone is just starting in journalism, they should at least write down their first few questions and perhaps any complex questions they might otherwise forget. Others suggest it is more useful to have a list of key areas to be covered in the interview, rather than specifically worded questions. The concern with written questions is that journalists can, and do, stick slavishly to their lists, rather than listening and taking their cues from what the interviewee is saying.

Presenter of Radio National's *Breakfast* programme, and former presenter of the SBS television current affairs programme *Insight,* Vivian Schenker says she finds it very useful to have a list of questions, for two main reasons:

One, if your mind goes blank, but morc importantly because I refresh my mind as I'm going with the sorts of areas I want to cover. I remind myself that "yes, that's still really important and I want to get back to that, but those four in the middle are much less important" and "how do I get from here to here?". I'm thinking while I'm listening and while they're talking.

Ask any experienced interviewer the secret of a good interview and they'll usually say it's *listening* to the interviewee. Vivian Schenker at ABC Radio National. So I think it's not a bad idea to have done the preparation and the work and have an idea of what you want out of the interview, as long as you're prepared to throw it away, and as long as you listen really, really hard— not just with one ear. Vivian says the best tip she can give people doing interviews is *listen.* She says, "I'm still staggered by how many people there are who think they don't have to concentrate really hard during the interview—that if they'd done their homework, then that was the work done. To me, homework can sometimes be thrown right out the door."

Vivian also believes that the really crucial part is the actual interview, not the preparation. She says, "Preparation makes you feel more confident going in, and I would always have the first questions written down, and I would always actually have a script and 10 questions. You just have to be prepared not to ask them, and not be sorry about it."

Former *60 Minutes* reporter and ABC foreign correspondent, Jeff McMullen, agrees that the most important skill to use during interviews is listening. He says one of the finest broadcast journalists he watched was Bill Moyers.

What he really did best was listen. He never had the rapier-thrust of Mike Wallace [a veteran reporter with the US *60 Minutes*] and he's not like the great British conversationalists, but he was such a strong mind. What he really did was sit with a brilliant person and listen.

Jeff says he took that lesson on board and from then on started to structure interviews differently. He says he's never worked with a clipboard or notebook in front of him. "I would, whether I was recording a *Four Corners* interview or a *60 Minutes* interview, study the subject, plan a very elaborate interview, commit it to memory, and then throw it away."

Jeff says he did what Moyers had shown him; that you have a conversation with people, and they will tell you which ways to go in the interview. "Your own mind, your improvisational skills, will take it where you need to go. But really that's more about listening than having the "smarty-pants" questions."

These days many people who deal with the media regularly, such as business people, politicians, sports people and so on, have been given media training to help them make the best of media appearances. These people know how reporters work and how to side-step reporters" questions to get their message across. In cases such as this, it's important not to let a person in a position of authority bluff you. Reporters need to develop the confidence and authority to stand their ground and, if necessary, tell the interviewee that they are not answering the question and ask it again.

Certainly some interviewees are intimidating, either by design or simply because of their job or position. Broadcast journalist Sally Spalding says whenever she has to interview someone like that, she falls back on a piece of advice she was given early on in her career:

One tip that someone gave me was that, if I was ever intimidated when I was going out to do an interview, just to imagine the person I was going to interview with no clothes on! I've used that a lot. But it didn't help me once when I had to interview Gough Whitlam because he was still so intimidating—naked or clothed.

Jana Wendt believes the important thing to remember when you are feeling overawed is that you *are* the media and the conduit for the interviewee's words. "They know that, " Jana says. "So you may look stupid and inexperienced and overawed, but ultimately you will be delivering this person's words and attitudes and style to the general public. So if they're smart they will realise, in a sense,*your* power, even if you're a very young journalist."

Jana says the best way to deal with someone who is overwhelming is to stay focused on what *you* want to achieve in your interview with this person.

Presumably you will have done your research. Presumably you will know what the key issues are, you know what this person's vulnerabilities and strengths may be, where the cracks are in any particular argument—hopefully you know that. So you craft your questions around those key important issues.

OBSERVATION

Observation is also very important with both "hard" and "soft" news interviews. Keep your questions short and let the interviewee speak as much as possible. In broadcast interviews, people want to hear the interviewee—not you. With print, you want quotes with *their* words, thoughts and opinions—not yours.

Interviewing requires more than just accurately taking down a person's responses to your questions. It means noticing their surroundings and general demeanour, because that might be an important part of the story.

Threadbare furniture and empty cupboards may tell you more about the plight of a family where the parents are out of work than anything the family says. Similarly, anger or frustration in the voices of consumers fighting a large corporation tells you something fundamental about their position.

Checking

Before you leave any interview you should check that:

- You have correctly taken down the interviewee's name and title.
- You have covered the five Ws and H and any other crucial questions.
- You have all the interviewee's contact details.

Journalist and media adviser, Andrea Carson, says she was given two really good pieces of advice when she first started interviewing.

One was to check that she had correctly taken down all the important information such as name and title. The other was that, before finishing an interview, she should always ask if there was anything else the interviewee would like to add that hadn't been covered. Invariably, she says, this produced some very important information and some really strong quotes on an area she had not thought to ask about.

It's important to check and clarify information as you go along, not just at the end of the interview. News director at 3AW, Rob Curtain, says checking throughout the interview ensures that you have understood what the interviewee is saying. One way of doing this is to paraphrase the inter-viewee's responses—for example, "so you're saying ..."—and use them as questions. One thing that's important for younger reporters—particularly doing stories you may not know much about—is that you need to keep putting back to the person you're interviewing your understanding of what they are saying.

It's almost as though you are writing the story in your head and putting it back to them because then, if it sounds completely different to them from the way it should, you know you're on the wrong track.

Remember

If an interviewee says something defamatory or in contempt of court, the outlet that publishes or broadcasts the comment is just as accountable as the person who made the comment and more likely to be sued or charged. As a reporter, you are responsible for what you write or broadcast, regardless of whose words you are quoting.

It's also important to remember that the mere fact that someone (no matter how highly placed they are) says something, doesn't make it true. All claims and comments need to be evaluated and checked. How much say should an interviewee have in the final product?

There's one question reporters are regularly asked by the people they interview: "Can I see the story before it's published/broadcast?" Interviewees have every right to be concerned about the way their comments will be used. They've probably heard of, or know of, incidents where interviewees felt they were misquoted or otherwise damaged by a media report. But does that mean you should give someone the right to veto your work? In most cases the answer is "no'.

For one thing, deadlines make it almost impossible to realistically promise to check back with every interviewee before publication.

But that means the onus is on the reporter to quote accurately, with sensitivity where required, and in context. In denying an interviewee the right to revise what they have said and check the way you've used it, you are asking them to trust your professional standards.

Quoting someone accurately won't guarantee that they approve of the finished story. That's because reporters must canvass opinion widely and weigh up competing interests in their stories.

Many reporters, even those with good shorthand, use recording devices during interviews. If you have a choice about the device you buy or use, choose a digital system, either solid state or MiniDisc.

These systems allow you to mark every significant point in the recording and later find each marker instantly. This overcomes the main criticism of cassette recorders, which is that it takes too long to spool though the tape when you're writing the story.

In addition, these digital devices are highly portable and, as long as they're equipped with a good quality microphone, will record audio at broadcast or webcast quality, if high quality audio is needed.

Ensure that the machine has a microphone input as well as a line input and line output. Unless the machine has a "mic in" socket, you will not be able to connect an external microphone. If you are buying a tape machine, you should spend the extra money to get one equipped with a counter.

Many reporters record interviews conducted over the phone for backup notes. There are a couple of devices that make this simple and easy.

One is a suction cup or "inductive phone line pick up", which can be attached to the phone's earpiece. The other is a small microphone that fits within an earpiece worn by the person recording the conversation. Note that for legal and ethical reasons you should *always* tell someone when you want to record them over the phone. Print reporters who also want to use their interviews for broadcast or webcast have to learn one of the basics of interviewing for broadcast, which is to stay silent during the interview unless they are asking a question. Print reporters often encourage their interviewees by using common phrases—"really?", "uh huh", "go on" ... and so on. But these little interruptions sound silly when the audio is edited for use on air or online as a soundbite. So, if you need to edit your interview for use as audio soundbites, keep quiet when the interviewee is talking. Using a suction cup or an earpiece microphone, both shown above, makes it easy to record phone interviews, but interviewees should always be told they are being recorded.

INTERVIEWING SKILLS

Advance preparation for the interview by-way of well-thought out question and a thorough consideration of approach is very helpful. One need not fear that the final outcome will sound stilted with no natural spontaneity. Usually the reverse is true.

One will be able to pose the most appropriate questions when one is well-versed with the subject. But how should one conduct oneself when conducting an interview? At the outset, arrive on time for the interview. This will help keep the interviewee in good humour.

Taking Notes: Taking notes is an essential part of interviewing: the two cannot be separated. Some take down everything, even irrelevant and redundant remarks. Take down only what is important (and save time). However, that may not always be possible. People sometimes stop talking when you start writing. You do not always know what is relevant until you have written it all down and reviewed it. You must train your mind to have a flawless recall. A wrong quote can be most embarrassing professionally. It costs you your credibility. Nowadays, there is the help of a recorder. Take permission of the interviewee before using it.

- Write as fast as you can; knowing shorthand can be a great help
- Keep hands and mind together, listen to key phrases; note the book references/citations. Verbatim quotes are especially valuable on touchy subject matters. A tape recorder helps you to review the interview in toto. It is a must for a question and answer story. There are also disadvantages.

Always carry a notebook. Never run out of tape or be faced with dead batteries. Remember to take down notes as well.

Off at Record: Remember, you are honour-bound to respect and keep it secret in the best interest of journalism.

- Whenever you get a glimpse of the reluctant prospective interviewee passing within a running distance, make your appeal as quietly and dramatically as possible. "Oh... Mr. / Mrs. So-and-so, we have information regarding........ which could prove sensational, Would you care to comment?"

- But be courteous: "We know there are two sides to every story. We want to hear yours".
- Sometimes nothing works better like an appeal to a person's sympathy. To interview a survivor of a tragedy, you might explain how uncomfortable you feel asking questions, and, how sorry you feel for him. But say, "Could you please tell us what Chitra (the victim) was like? Do you have a picture?"

Good planning makes the interview successful and leaves happy memories for both the interviewer and the interviewee.

Conducting an Interview: Know your subject, in this case, the interviewee, so that you can size him/ her up, with some reliability, in a matter of seconds. Is the person being honest? What is he trying to hide? Read the person's eyes, and mannerisms since these offer a reliable clue on how an interview is to be handled. Draw up a list of ten questions. But remember, an interview rarely goes as planned. The interviewer, therefore, requires a lot of instinct. The persons who know when and how to ask questions based on one's sheer instinct would be able to save an interview anytime.

HOW TO ESTABLISH RAPPORT WITH THE INTERVIEWEE

- In many small and big ways, try to make your interviewee feel nice, cheerful and important.
- Outline your reasons for being there. Bring the interviewee upto-date on what you are looking for.
- Start with a board question. This helps you to size the person and collect your thoughts. It also gives you an opportunity to receive information which you may not have anticipated.
- Stick to the subject. Do not ramble or chit-chat. Neither is it advisable to beat around the bush. So go ahead and simply ask your questions straightaway.
- Doodling or writing down a lot of useless matter in your notebook can be, helpful. Those who have important information to transmit, like to feel they are being recorded. Even so, try not to con your interviewee in this manner for too long! You might be asked to show what you have taken, down. For all that, jotting down points helps you to prepare the transcription of the interview-session for publication.
- Listen Listen Listen: Not only does this make the interviewee feel good and wise, but it also helps you to control the interview. An interviewer might start speaking with good intentions and slowly digress. You can bring him back to point. "You were saying something about the time you were in college, prison, etc. When was that?" And you are back on the track.

- Be understanding: Nobody likes insensibility. The interviewee is often quite nervous while discussing his/ her wrong doings, sin or tragedy. Help him/ her to relax. If your mind goes blank, just say, "Excuse me. I forgot where we were and what I need to ask".

THE INTERVIEW AS AN EXTENSION OF THE CONVERSATION

The interviewer must not only be conversant with the subject matter of the interview but must also be a good conversationalist. All the important features of interpersonal communication come into play in an interview. In a face to face meeting, the stress is on both the language used in speech and the non-verbal body language. But, in a telephonic interview, the stress would be on the tone and inflection given to the words. In this type of interview, it can be rather difficult to assess the intended meaning for the other person's actual expression is hidden from sight.

We shall now discuss the salient points to be kept in mind when conducting an interview in person. On occasion, an interview may not be planned or rehearsed before it actually takes place. But then there are a few thumb rules that are fundamental to any interview. Preparing oneself to interview a personality, a celebrity or even the person-on-the-street is actually an on-going long-term process. This is because one must be a well-rounded interviewer, skilled in the art of handling a variety of topics and areas as also a range of idiosyncrasies that are inherent in people in general. One must be prepared b t for any turn of events and still be able to take it all in of its stride, that is to say, with equanimity. One cannot acquire these skills overnight but must nurture them over a period of time. A great deal of deep study of persons and happenings is called for. The would-be interviewer must yearn to learn.

Your Part as the Interviewer: Send and receive messages accurately. Choose words that your receiver will understand. Avoid technical words and terms. Words should be very simple.

How to Generate Ideas for Your Interview: Some interviews are simply old wine in new bottles. Others seek to convey an innovation or idea that the interviewee has recently come up with. Yet other interviews have been made out of the interviewer's idea(s): giving a new twist to an event, throwing new light on a discovery that had been accepted at face value, and such like. One must develop a keen sense of identifying material for use in an interview. One must also have the knack to read more into matters than is at first apparent: something like reading between the lines. That way, a much-interviewed person may reveal a fresh side of the matter being discussed and perhaps also of his/ her own personality hitherto hidden from public view.

Having a finely-tuned news-sense helps to generate ideas for Interviews. It enables one to capture a glimpse of the extra-ordinary in the most 'ordinary' things and persons. It depends on the situation whether one comes upon a fresh insight during the interview by asking hard-hitting questions or by putting queries in a gentle manner. These are tactics that ought to be learnt by assessing and recognizing the opportune time and place when it comes your way. Alternately, you could create the right atmosphere to make your interviewee reveal material which would form the basis for a good interview. In effect, the interviewer gives shape and direction to the interview; always allowing enough leeway for the unexpected utterance.

One could then build carefully on what is sometimes said in such an offhand manner. The interviewer must, therefore, remain alert and latch on to every word that is said during the conversation. One can become adept at this technique only with practice.

EXPOSITORY WRITING

Many students experience difficulties mastering the writing process. Data from the National Assessment of Educational Progress shows three out of every four 4th-, 8th-, and 12th-grade students exhibited only partial mastery of necessary writing skills and knowledge at their respective grade levels, and only 1 in 100 students demonstrated "advanced" writing skills. Negotiating and coordinating basic skills, knowledge, strategies, and conventions of written language can be difficult even for skilled writers, because writing demands that students plan, generate content, organize their composition, translate content into written language, and revise and improve their initial draft. Additionally, many children are not equipped with appropriate strategies to overcome obstacles presented by written expression.

One group of children who may be at particular risk for difficulties with written expression is children with attention deficit hyperactivity disorder (ADHD). ADHD is one of the most commonly diagnosed psychiatric disorders of childhood. Prevalence is typically reported as between 3 per cent and 7 per cent, and it is estimated to affect more than 2 million school-age children. Students with ADHD are generally at risk for academic underachievement and are likely to experience difficulties with all aspects of the writing process. Problems with prerequisite skills, including transcription and spelling, are well documented. Difficulties in using language to express thoughts or produce coherent narrative are also well documented.

Another potential area of difficulty is in planning and organizing compositions. Using a deliberate, planful, and organized approach to attack a task is a complex mental ability considered to be a component of executive function (EF). Problems with EF are symptomatic of ADHD. EF impairments also have been shown to negatively influence academic functioning of students with ADHD. Because writing requires planning, organization, and attention to the composing process, it is likely to be a difficult task for students with ADHD.

Written expression skills among students with ADHD have not been well studied. We located only two studies that reported data on the level of composition skills among children with ADHD. Mayes, Calhoun, and Crowell (2000) reported data on a sample of 86 students, 8 to 16 years old, who had been referred to a university-affiliated department of psychiatry. Students were divided into two groups: ADHD with learning disabilities (LD) and ADHD without LD. Students in the ADHD with LD group had a 26-point standard score discrepancy between IQ and written expression achievement.

Students in the ADHD without LD group demonstrated a 7-point standard score discrepancy between IQ and written expression achievement, which suggested some degree of impairment. Similarly, Resta and Eliot reported data on 21students with ADHD. Students, ages 8 to 13, were clinic referred. The compositions of the children with ADHD were significantly below controls in terms of word complexity, written language, productivity, and general writing ability.

One intervention that could be used to improve the composition skills of children with ADHD is the strategy instruction approach using the Self-Regulated Strategy Development (SRSD) model. There are several reasons why the SRSD model is promising. First, SRSD has demonstrated effectiveness with children with LD. There is considerable overlap between LD and ADHD populations, which suggests SRSD may be effective for children with ADHD. Second, current theories of ADHD stress that ADHD is the result of a deficit in self-regulation. Problems with establishing goals, holding goals in memory, persisting in efforts towards goal completion, and shaping and directing behaviours in order to achieve goals are seen as central to ADHD.

The SRSD model directly addresses these problems--goal setting is discussed, the importance of goals is stressed, and progress towards goals is expressly monitored. In addition, SRSD explicitly develops self-regulation strategies (*e.g.*, self-monitoring) that have demonstrated efficacy with children with ADHD in improving ability to maintain focus and effort. Third, working memory deficits are common in children with ADHD. SRSD instruction reduces demands on working memory by presenting instruction in small steps, teaching strategies to achieve automaticity, and providing systematic scaffolded practice. Additionally, prompts, cues, and organizers are provided initially to support efforts. This decreases the burden on working memory and allows students to focus on the task at hand--performing the strategy.

A small but growing body of research supports the use of SRSD for students with ADHD. De La Paz (2001) examined the effects of SRSD on planning and writing expository essays (opinion essays). One participant was a middle school student with ADHD. Results indicated instruction had a positive effect on the student's approach to writing and overall writing performance. Improvements were maintained over a 4-week period. Lienemann, Graham, Leader-Janssen, and Reid (2006) examined the impact of SRSD strategy instruction on the narrative compositions of struggling second-grade writers. The study included one student with ADHD. After instruction, the student with ADHD composed stories that were longer, more complete, and qualitatively better.

In this study, we investigated the effects of strategy instruction on opinion-essay writing. Fourth- and fifth-grade participants with ADHD were taught a general, three-step planning strategy and a strategy for writing opinion essays. The planning strategy, POW, required students to (a) Plan their essays by choosing a topic or idea to write about, (b) Organize their notes and ideas into a comprehensive writing plan, and (c) Write their essays using their writing plan and add to it as they wrote their composition. This general planning strategy provided the framework for the genre-specific strategy--TREE: Topic sentence, Reason, Explanation, and Ending.

TREE is an opinion writing strategy including a series of prompts about the basic elements of a persuasive essay. Both the POW and TREE strategies have demonstrated efficacy with general education and special education populations. Additionally, students were taught how to facilitate writing performance through self-talk, goal-setting, and self-monitoring.

The present study had two aims. First we replicated the use of SRSD for written expression with students with ADHD. At present, SRSD instruction has been reported with only five students with ADHD. Second, we expanded the writing genres used with students with ADHD. Two of the three previous SRSD studies focused on narrative writing.

The only study focusing on expository text had only one middle school student. There is a clear need for exploring the efficacy of strategies that can improve students' skills at expository writing. In particular, students with disabilities commonly experience difficulties with expository text. Expository text structure is more complex than that of narratives and does not follow the familiar conventions of narrative text. For students with ADHD to attain mastery of written language, it is necessary to validate effective strategies for expository text genres. We hypothesized that as a result of instruction, (a) students would write longer essays, (b) essays would contain more essay elements, and (c) the overall holistic quality of essays would improve.

EXPERIMENTAL DESIGN

A multiple baseline across participants with multiple probes during baseline was used to address the study hypotheses. This design required the researcher to introduce the independent variable in a systematic, sequential fashion with one student at a time. A functional relationship between the independent variable and participants' progress was established if the target behaviour improved only after the completion of SRSD instruction and if the noninstructed participants' (*i.e.*, those still in baseline) performance stayed at or near preintervention levels across baseline.

SETTING

The study was conducted during the fall and early spring semesters in a predominantly middle-class, rural elementary school in the Midwest. The demographics of the school were as follows: 96 per cent Caucasian, 1 per cent African American, 2 per cent Hispanic, and 1 per cent Asian. A total of 8 per cent of the students received free or reduced lunch.

PARTICIPANTS

Participants included students in fourth and fifth grades.

Criteria for participation in the study included:

- The student was teacher nominated as a poor writer;
- The student's parents verified that the student had been diagnosed by either a pediatrician or clinical psychologist as having ADHD;
- The student had at least average intelligence (*i.e.*, > 80) on the Wechsler Abbreviated Scale of Intelligence;
- The student received a standard score in the below to low average range (*i.e.*, 79-91) on the written expression subtest of the Wechsler Individual Achievement Test II;
- The student had a stable medication status if medication for ADHD was being taken (*i.e.*, participant's medication type or dosage was not to be changed during the course of the study).

All screening was done by the school psychologist for this study. A total of four students, two fourth graders (one boy and one girl) and two fifth graders (one boy and one girl) met the criteria for inclusion in this study. Teachers' ADHD Rating Scale-IV ratings were in the normal range for two students; however, teachers' ratings were based on students performance while medicated, and medication can normalize teachers' ratings of behaviour in many children with ADHD. All participants were Caucasian.

The first student to receive instruction was a fourth-grade boy, Stanley. He was in the referral process for special education services at the time of the study and was subsequently identified as Other Health Impaired. Macy, a fourth-grade girl, was the second student to receive instruction. She was also in the referral process for special education services at the time of the study and was subsequently identified as Other Health Impaired. The third student to receive instruction in the strategy was, Sidney, a fifth-grade girl.

During the time of the study she was receiving special education services for behavioral disorders. The final student to receive instruction was a fifth-grade boy, Trevor. He had been diagnosed as having a specific learning disability in the area of written expression and was receiving special education services for reading and writing. Stanley, Sidney, and Trevor had previous experience with SRSD instruction. They had all been taught a narrative writing strategy the previous school year.

SCREENING MEASURES

The WASI is designed as a reliable, brief measure of intelligence. It is an individually administered measure and is appropriate for children and adults ranging in age from 6 to 89 years.

Both internal consistency and test-retest reliability are at or above.88 indicating acceptable reliability, and construct validity based on correlations with other IQ scales is also acceptable.

The WIAT-II is an individually administered achievement test. The Written Expression subtest incorporates items assessing word fluency, sentence construction, writing fluency, and written responses to visual or verbal cues. Additionally, it incorporates descriptive and narrative writing tasks. Internal consistency for this subtest is above.70. Criterion validity estimates range from.47 to.71.

The ADHD Rating Scale-IV is designed to identify ADHD symptoms as reported by a parent or educator. This measure is intended for children 5 to 18 years old. There are two versions of the measure--the ADHD Rating Scale-IV: Home Version and School Version. The scale items reflect the DSM-IV (American Psychiatric Association, 2000) ADHD criteria. A 4-point Likert rating scale of 0 (never or rarely) to 3 (very often) is used to describe the frequency of different ADHD symptoms. Nine of 18 questions seek to investigate symptoms suggestive of "inattention" and the other 9 measure "hyperactivity-impulsivity.

" Three raw scores are derived from each version, including inattention, hyperactivity-impulsivity, and total. Raw scores are converted into percentiles based on the child's gender and age. Internal consistency estimates range from.88 to.95. Concurrent validity estimates with other ADHD rating scales range from.77 to.94.

PROCEDURES

Treatment was individually administered by the first author who has conducted two previous studies using the SRSD model.

BASELINE PROBES

Students were given a prompting opinion question (*e.g.*, Should children be punished when they do something wrong?). Students were told to plan their essay, include all elements of a good opinion essay, and write as much as they could.

Students did not receive assistance from the instructor, nor did they receive any cues. Baseline probes were taken until stability was achieved. A minimum of three continuous baseline probes were taken prior to a participant beginning the treatment phase.

INSTRUCTION

The first participant received instruction in the opinion-essay writing strategy until criterion level was achieved (*i.e.*, independently writing an opinion essay with all the parts of TREE). Once criterion level was achieved, the student moved into the independent performance phase. Instruction did not begin for the next child until the first student's performance reached a criterion level of eight essay elements. These same procedures were used with the third and fourth students in treatment.

INDEPENDENT PERFORMANCE

Immediately following the treatment phase, each student wrote three opinion essays. During the independent performance phase the students did not receive assistance from the instructor. After the essay was completed students were given a graph to monitor the use of the strategy (*i.e.*, number of essay elements included) and length of their essay.

MAINTENANCE

Maintenance probes were conducted 2 and 4 weeks after the end of the independent performance phase. These writing probes were completed under the same conditions as in the independent performance phase.

TESTING MATERIALS: ESSAY WRITING PROMPTS

Prompts in all conditions included labels with prompting questions adhered to a blank sheet of writing paper. These questions had been used previously by Graham and Harris. The order in which the essay prompts were presented was randomized.

They were then administered in the same order to all participants. When presented with an essay writing prompt, students were asked to read the question and write an essay. They were told to plan their essay, include all the elements of a good essay, and write as much as they could. Students were allowed as much time as they desired to write their essays.

DEPENDENT MEASURES

Each opinion essay was scored for number of essay elements, number of words, and overall quality. We computed percentage of nonoverlapping data for the number of essay elements and number of words.

Number of Essay Elements. Number of essay elements was scored by tabulating whether students included the following eight essay elements in their papers: topic sentence, three reasons, an explanation for each reason, and a concluding statement. Students could include extra elements (*e.g.*, additional reasons or explanation) so there was no ceiling for this measure. Students were awarded a point for each element that was included. Two independent raters read and scored the number of essay elements. Interrater agreement (agreements divided by agreements + disagreements) was.98.

NUMBER OF WORDS

Each essay was entered into a word processing programme. Spelling and punctuation were corrected. The number of words written was computed by using the word processing program's word count function. Because this measure was machine scored, no reliability was computed.

QUALITY RATINGS

Quality of essays was evaluated using a 7-point holistic scale, with a score of 1 representing the lowest quality and a score of 7 the highest quality. Two graduate students, both with a background in special education, scored the essays for overall quality. Raters received a brief training period. Raters were given anchor papers representative of low-, medium-, and high-quality essays. They were then provided with practice essays and allowed to practice rating stories.

Raters were asked to read the essay attentively to get an overall impression of writing quality and then, using the anchor papers as a reference, score the essays. Raters practiced until 80 per cent reliability was achieved. This was achieved in approximately I hr of practice. Procedures for obtaining anchor essays were similar to those used in previous studies.

Anchor essays were obtained by administering an opinion essay prompt to two classrooms in the school where the research was being conducted (*i.e.*, 1 fourth-grade classroom and 1 fifth-grade classroom). These classrooms did not have any participating students. Two former elementary school teachers then selected the anchor essays for both the fourth- and fifth-grade essays. Selection was based on ideation, organization, aptness of word choice, grammar, and sentence structure.

After reliability was achieved, raters were given actual participants' essays. All essays were assigned code numbers to ensure that there was no reference to phase (*i.e.*, baseline, independent performance or maintenance); or participant. Raters were given essays in a random order. All scoring was donc independently. Separate anchor essays were used for the fourth-and fifth-grade students to allow age appropriate ratings. The two raters independently scored each essay for overall quality. Before essays were scored, they were transcribed and entered into a word processor. Because problems with spelling and punctuation can affect quality ratings, all spelling and punctuation errors were corrected prior to scoring. Interobserver agreement for the essays was.96.

GENERAL INSTRUCTIONAL PROCEDURES

SRSD was used to teach an opinion essay planning and writing strategy. With this approach, students are explicitly and systematically taught a task-specific strategy for accomplishing an academic task or problem (*i.e.*, opinion essay writing). Self-regulation is enabled by teaching students how to set goals, self-monitor their performance, and to use self-instructions, and/or self-reinforcement to manage their use of the strategy, the task, and their behaviours. Background knowledge is established by teaching any information (or skills) students need to know to use the strategy. Motivation is boosted through a variety of procedures, including emphasizing the role of effort in learning, making the positive effects of instruction concrete and visible (through self-monitoring and graphing), and promoting an "I can do it" attitude.

The emphasis during SRSD instruction is on students' independent use of the strategy and accompanying self-regulation procedures. This includes learning when, where, and how to apply these procedures. Instruction is scaffolded so that responsibility for using the strategy and self-regulation procedures gradually shifts from the instructor to the students. The level and type of feedback and instructional support are individualized so that they are responsive to children's needs. Students are treated as active collaborators in the learning process. All instruction is criterion- rather than time-based. Students move through each instructional stage at their own pace and do not proceed to later stages of instruction until they have met criteria for doing so.

All instruction took place in a hallway outside the classroom. Detailed lesson plans were used during each stage of instruction. Instruction was designed for participants to receive individualized instruction 20 to 30 min, 4 days a week for 2 to 3 weeks. Students continued with instruction until criterion was achieved. Criterion was defined as independently writing an opinion essay with all eight elements. Macy and Sidney achieved criterion in five sessions, Stanley and Trevor required eight sessions. Instruction for Stanley and Macy took place during their special time (*i.e.*, music, computers, and character education). Instruction for Sidney and Trevor took place during their study hall.

INSTRUCTIONAL PROCEDURES FOR TEACHING THE PLANNING AND WRITING STRATEGY

The planning and opinion essay writing strategies used in this study were developed by Graham and Harris. The TREE strategy was used to guide students' composition of opinion essays. The TREE strategy is comprised of four self-directional prompts used to guide the fundamental form of an opinion essay. To most effectively use the TREE strategy, students were taught to use TREE within a general three-step writing strategy, POW, for planning and writing. The POW strategy was used to frame the writing process; TREE was used to organize the written prose.

First, students were asked to Pick an idea (the first step of POW). Picking an idea helped the students narrow their focus, and begin to formulate their thoughts. Then, students were prompted to Organize their notes (the second step of POW) using TREE. Students organized their thoughts and ideas in the fashion of a typical opinion essay, starting with a Topic sentence (the first step in TREE). Students were taught that a topic sentence "tells what you believe clearly and concisely."

The topic sentence makes clear what the author's opinion is. Students were then asked to provide three or more Reasons to support their opinion (the second step in Tree). These reasons were then to be supported with Examples (the third step in Tree). Students were prompted to ask themselves "Why do I believe this?" and "Will my readers believe this?" This not only helped the students elaborate and support their opinions, it also prompted them to consider the audience's thoughts on their rationale.

The final step in the Tree strategy is the Ending. Students were taught to write a concluding statement. A statement that will "wrap it up right!" The final or ending statement lets the reader know that the essay is complete. This statement finishes off the essay and usually reiterates the opinion. The final step in POW is to Write and say more. Students were prompted to check over their compositions for completeness. If any areas were found that needed further development, students worked on them until the composition was complete and fully expressed their opinion.

In the first stage of instruction, Develop Background Knowledge, the students were introduced to the POW and TREE strategies. The instructor explained that these strategies will assist the student in planning and remembering the essential elements of an opinion essay. POW was introduced first, and the importance of each step in the planning process was discussed. After the instructor introduced the three steps in the planning process, the student was asked to explain the three steps and the importance of each step. Next, the instructor and student discussed what makes a good opinion essay.

Here the instructor emphasized that an opinion essay tells the reader what you believe, gives the reader at least three reasons why you believe it, and has an ending sentence. A good opinion essay also makes sense and has several parts. Then, the instructor introduced the Tree strategy as a "trick" to help the student remember the important parts in an opinion essay.

After reviewing the parts of the strategy, the instructor read an opinion essay to the student and had the student listen for the parts of TREE (*e.g.*, what I believe, at least three reasons why, three examples, and an ending sentence). Students were given a graphic organizer with a picture of a TREE to assist them in remembering the parts of TREE. Then, the student was given a copy of the opinion essay and asked to raise his or her hand when he or she heard what the writer believed, each reason why, the examples, and an ending sentence. Each time he or she found an essay element, the instructor wrote it down on a graphic organizer. Next, the student was orally quizzed over the parts of POW + Tree.

Then, the instructor read another opinion essay and had the student practice finding the elements again. Next, the idea of transfer was discussed, and the instructor emphasized that she wanted the student to "transfer" what he or she learned about POW and Tree from this instruction to other classes and other writing tasks. Finally, the goals for the next session were discussed; the student was asked to report any time he or she transferred either strategy to an appropriate situation.

In the second stage of instruction, Discuss It, the student was instructed to continue to focus on the importance and uses of the two strategies. At the beginning of the session, the student was tested to determine if he or she remembered what the POW and Tree strategies stood for. The student was required to memorize the steps of the strategy. Then, he or she practiced finding essay elements in two more opinion essays. Next, the student analyzed one of his or her own opinion essays, written during baseline, to determine if all the essay elements were included. During the analysis and discussion of the student's opinion essay, the instructor explained that essays can be improved and that improving an essay makes it more fun to write and more fun to read.

After determining how many parts the student included in his or her essay, the instructor discussed the importance of goal-setting. The goal in writing a good opinion essay is to tell the reader what you believe, give at least three reasons and examples why, and have an ending sentence. Also, good opinion essays are fun to write, fun for others to read, and they make sense. The students then were taught to self-monitor the number of essay elements they included in their opinion essays by counting and recording them on a bar graph in the shape of a group of rocket ships.

In the third stage of instruction, Model It, the instructor explicitly modeled the process using the POW and Tree strategies by focusing on self-instructions and self-talks. First, the student was reminded of the goal of writing an opinion essay. Then, the instructor, in collaboration with the student, generated an opinion essay including all the essay elements. The instructor modeled working through the planning and writing process.

As ideas were generated, the instructor recorded the responses on the planning sheet. While using the strategy, the instructor used a variety of self-statements to assist with the problem definition (*e.g.*, "What is my goal?"); planning (*e.g.*, "What is my next step?"); self-evaluation (*e.g.*, "Does that make sense?"); self-reinforcement (*e.g.*, I like that part!"); and coping (*e.g.*, I'm almost done!"). After taking notes, the instructor discussed the importance of self-talk.

After the essay was written, the instructor and the student identified all elements in Tree by marking each element with a highlighter, counting the number of elements, and graphing the results. They also counted up and graphed the number of words written. The next stage, Support It, is a collaborative writing experience. The instructor and the student write opinion essays together using POW + TREE and a graphic organizer. This stage was student-controlled; the instructor only provided support when necessary. As the student became more proficient with the strategy, instructor support faded. Based on the notes generated, the student wrote the opinion essay. After the essay was written, the student identified each part of TREE by highlighting each part. Then the student determined if he or she had met his or her goal and graphed the results (*i.e.*, the number of essay elements and the number of words) on his or her rocket sheet.

The final stage, Independent Performance, was reached when students could successfully write an opinion essay independently without assistance from the instructor. The student mastered this stage when he or she could independently write an essay including all the parts of TREE.

FIDELITY OF TREATMENT

To ensure consistency in implementation of the SRSD treatment, the following procedures were employed. First, the instructor practiced how to apply instructional procedures until she could implement them without error.

This was verified by an observer who checked each step in turn as it was practiced. Second, the instructor had a checklist with step-by-step instructions for each lesson. Third, 25 per cent of all lessons were observed by an individual who was familiar with the implementation of the strategy. The observer had the same step-by-step checklist as the instructor and checked off items as they were performed by the instructor. The point-by-point method was used to calculate interobserver agreement. Fidelity was 99 per cent.

All students exhibited stable baselines, and none of the students included all eight elements in their essays. Mean number of essay elements in baseline, respectively, for Stanley, Macy, Sidney, and Trevor were 2.0, 1.5, 2.8, and 2.3. During the instruction phase, performance increased immediately and stabilized. For the independent performance phase all essays contained all eight elements.

During independent performance, mean increases over baseline for Stanley, Macy, Sidney and Trevor, respectively, were 533 per cent, 578 per cent, 357 per cent, and 343 per cent. Two students produced essays with more than eight elements. For all students, effects maintained across 2- and 4-week follow-ups. PND for all students for all phases was 100 per cent. Mean baseline number of words for Stanley, Macy, Sidney and Trevor, respectively, were 18, 27, 34, and 19. During the instruction phase, all students exhibited an immediate and pronounced change in level. The improvement maintained during the independent performance phase.

Mean number of words in independent performance for Stanley, Macy, Sidney and Trevor, respectively, were 115, 114, 107, and 73. Mean increases for Stanley, Macy, Sidney, and Trevor respectively were 639 per cent, 422 per cent, 315 per cent, and 384 per cent. For Stanley, number of words decreased somewhat across 2- and 4-week follow-ups, but still remained well above baseline levels. For Macy and Trevor, effects maintained across 2- and 4-week follow-ups and were only slightly below independent performance levels. For Sidney, effects were maintained across 2- and 4-week follow-ups and were actually above all other phases. PND for all students for all phases was 100 per cent.

HOLISTIC QUALITY

All students' quality ratings improved markedly after instruction. Mean percentage increases for Stanley, Macy, Sidney, and Trevor, respectively, were 417 per cent, 357 per cent, 285 per cent, and 350 per cent. All students were above the median (*i.e.*, 3.5) on the rating scale suggesting their performance had been normalized. All students' quality ratings remained well above baseline over 2- and 4-week follow-ups. Macy, Sidney, and Trevor's quality ratings decreased somewhat on the 2- and 4-week follow-ups, but remained well above baseline levels and remained above the median on the rating scale, suggesting their performance remained normalized. Stanley's quality rating increased slightly on 2- and 4-week follow-ups.

EFFECTS ON DEPENDENT MEASURES

Prior to instruction, students' essays were short, largely incomplete, and qualitatively poor even though three of the four students had previously received strategy instruction for narrative compositions. The three students who had received strategy instruction previously, in an unrelated composition genre (*i.e.*, stories), performed only slightly better on average than the student who had not (Macy). Although Macy included an average of 1.5 essay elements, Stanley, Sidney, and Trevor included 2, 2.8, and 2.3 essay elements respectively. Previous research has found that strategy instruction can generalize across genres with common elements (*e.g.*, stories to personal narratives).

The lack of generalization we found might be due to the lack of common elements across stories and essays. Following instruction, all students wrote longer, more complete, and higher quality essays. PND for number of essay elements and number of words was 100 per cent for all students, suggesting that the intervention was highly effective. One of the most dramatic improvements was in the quality of.essays. Quality scores for writing increased by 285 per cent to 417 per cent, and quality ratings were in the normal range. Previous studies using SRSD (Reid and Lienemann) had similar results for quality ratings. It is important to note that quality ratings were at or above the normal range. The fact that a brief intervention was able to normalize performance stresses the importance of such systematic instruction for students with ADHD.

SRSD AND STUDENTS WITH ADHD

An important aspect of the current study was that SRSD combines self-regulation (*i.e.*, self-instructions, self-reinforcement, goal setting, and self-monitoring) and academic strategies. Self- regulation strategies are intended to be an integral part of the SRSD model. This is a desirable feature, because self-regulation strategies have demonstrated effectiveness with children with ADHD, and current conceptualizations of ADHD suggest that ADHD is the result of a deficit in self-regulation.

One problem children commonly experience is failure to monitor task performance. Lack of awareness of performance is thought to be one reason for academic difficulties among students with ADHD. In this study, self-monitoring was used to provide feedback on performance. Students self-monitored the number of essay parts and the number of words in their essays. Self-monitoring also served as a cue to remind students of the overall goal of writing good essays (*i.e.*, including all the parts). Based on observation, it also appeared that the self-monitoring component had a significant effect on persistence.

The self-monitoring component was introduced during instruction. When the graphs for the number of words were introduced there was an immediate and pronounced effect on the length of students' essays. The same effects were noted in previous studies with children with ADHD and with LD. We would note that although students in this study self-monitored academic performance, other studies that used self-monitoring of attention have also demonstrated effectiveness with children with ADHD.

Another concern for children with ADHD is problems with goal-related behaviour. Children with ADHD have problems in establishing goals, holding goals in memory, persisting in efforts towards goals, and shaping and redirecting behaviours in order to achieve goals. The SRSD model is designed to systematically address these deficits. Students are taught explicitly how to establish goals, monitor their progress towards their goals, and recognize when goals were achieved. Self-monitoring also appeared to help with goal-setting. After the introduction of the graphs, students began spontaneously setting goals for the number of words for their next essay.

We found it interesting that although the number of words did not increase during the instruction, independent performance, and maintenance phases, students' goals for the number of words increased with each essay.

SRSD AND RESPONSE TO INTERVENTION

Although the primary focus of the study was the use of SRSD with students with ADHD, there are broader ramifications. With the recent legislative push to change the process of identification of students with LD from a discrepancy-based model to response to intervention (RTI), it is increasingly more important to identify effective, research-based interventions for struggling students. The premise behind the RTI model is that students should receive effective instruction with progress monitoring before being considered for special education. There has been considerable research done on RTI in the area of reading, but little if any in the area of written expression.

There is now good evidence to suggest that SRSD can be a highly effective instructional technique for young children who struggle with written expression; additionally, progress monitoring can easily be (and typically already is) incorporated into SRSD instruction. Thus, SRSD instruction combined with self-regulation techniques should be investigated as a research-based RTI method for written expression.

LIMITATIONS

There are several limitations to the current study. First, maintenance probes were taken only 2 and 4 weeks after independent performance. With such a short maintenance period, it is impossible to determine whether or not long-term effects were maintained. Long-term maintenance is a serious concern for students with ADHD. Second, all instruction was on a one-to-one basis. Future studies will need to establish whether or not this type of instruction is as effective in small-group or whole-classroom settings with students with ADHD. Third, the instructional regimen only focused on planning and writing a composition. Other important aspects of the writing process were left out (*e.g.*, editing, revising, and publishing).

There is good reason to suspect that revision tasks would present problems for students with ADHD, as they require attention to detail and redoing a task. Fourth, all the students participating in this study were receiving medication for ADHD. This is important because there is evidence to suggest that EF deficits are sensitive to medication; thus, students who do not receive medication may not respond in the same manner. This is an issue because up to 25 per cent of children are not responsive to medication and for others medication is discontinued after 1 or 2 years. Future research should investigate the effectiveness of SRSD instruction with students with ADHD who are not on medication. Fifth, this study demonstrated the effectiveness of SRSD instruction in only one area of expository composition.

Future studies should include other expository composition types (*i.e.*, compare/contrast, explanations, and problem/solution). Finally, although the results of this study are consistent with the earlier findings of Reid and Lienemann (2006) and suggest that content strategies combined with self-regulation techniques are well suited for students with ADHD, we cannot say whether improvements resulted from the content strategy, the self-regulation strategies, or both. Because the students used the self-monitoring procedures in independent performance and maintenance phases, we cannot separate the effect of the strategy from the self-monitoring procedure. Future research utilizing components analysis will be necessary to clarify this issue.

IMPLICATIONS

These findings add to a small but growing body of literature showing that strategy instruction using the SRSD model can significantly improve the written expression skills of students with ADHD. These findings replicate and extend previous studies investigating the use of SRSD with students with ADHD. Previous studies by Lienemann et al. and Reid and Lienemann focused on story writing. Stories are essential to early academic success, but as students progress through elementary, middle, and high school, expository text becomes increasingly more important.

The results of this study suggest that SRSD instruction can be highly effective in improving the essay composition skills of students with ADHD. Even relatively brief interventions, such as the one studied here, can have a marked effect on these children's writing performance--essentially normalizing performance. The fact that two students had comorbid conditions in addition to ADHD is important. Children with ADHD commonly have other conditions that impact academic performance (*e.g.*, learning disabilities, behaviour disorders). Thus, the fact that SRSD is effective with students with comorbid conditions is encouraging. An important aspect of the study is that all techniques used were "off the shelf." SRSD-based strategy instruction, goal-setting, and self-monitoring are well validated, widely used, practical, and, most important, readily accepted by classroom teachers.

Furthermore, lesson plans were modified only slightly to include self-monitoring and detailed lesson plans for TREE and other strategies are now commercially available. Thus, translating this research into the classroom should be relatively straightforward. Given the concerns over composition skills of students in general, and students with ADHD in particular, effective interventions such as the ones used in this study should be a high priority.

The assignment is especially appropriate for a class such as mine, which is an upper-division reporting techniques class for business majors and some engineering and international business majors. However, the assignment can also be adapted to any class that requires knowledge of negotiation and/or proposal development.

The assignment has two major components: proposal skill development and negotiation skill development. The proposal development requires students to complete an individual proposal assignment; the negotiation skill development requires students to integrate the skill into a team. The first component of the assignment consists of two 75-minute sessions on proposal development and two more 75-minute sessions for oral presentations of the proposals. The second component consists of two 75-minute sessions on negotiation, one 75-minute session to develop teams, and one session on team negotiation for proposal selection.

This assignment can be modified to fit a shorter academic term, or modified when you cannot devote so much time to one assignment. For example, sessions 1-2, proposal discussions, can combine into one session. Sessions 3-4, negotiation discussion, can combine to one session, presentations can be limited to three minutes instead of five minutes, and sessions 7-8 can combine to one session. Also, using your judgement, some of the content can be eliminated or covered by students on their own.

PROPOSAL SKILL DEVELOPMENT

In developing proposal skills, I use a number of supplemental resources, which are listed at the end of this chapter. Required readings for students are in Technical Communication by Lay (2000), which is the course textbook. In the proposal skills development, we discuss definition, purpose, description, and components. After the comprehensive discussion of proposal development, I give the following assignment:

Write a proposal to solve a specific problem or opportunity related to your major. Select a topic of sufficient complexity to warrant research. However, do not tackle a topic beyond the scope of the time allowed for the assignment. Conduct a preliminary investigation on the topic, obtaining at least eight sources, and develop an annotated bibliography for the proposal. Submit the proposal in an attractive format. I do not specify a length for the proposals. My experience is that when a length is specified for assignments, students focus on quantity rather then quality. I tell students that their "assignments should be as long as it needs to be to achieve their purpose." After all, in the "business world," one does not always have artificial boundaries to produce a report of a certain length. However, I do point out to students that they should make sure they have addressed all the components of each assignment in a clear and complete manner.

Topic selection is a difficult task for some students, but I encourage them to use critical thinking skills to select a topic about which they want to gain more knowledge or a topic on which they want to become an expert. Initially students are intimidated by having the freedom to choose their topic, but after I explain the benefits of selecting their own topic and share with them some of the topics used in the past, they are more comfortable with meeting the critical thinking challenge and enjoy the opportunity to explore a topic of interest to them.

Here are some example topics:

- Implementing an internship requirement for business majors
- Developing fund-raising Programmes for business student organizations
- Implementing a network system for x company

- Reducing the wait time at the San Ysidro border crossing
- Implementing a Unix system for x company
- Developing an investment seminar for college students
- Developing an html training programme
- Developing an import/export trade business between the US and Japan
- Developing marketing strategies to promote a start-up catering business
- Developing a "dress for business success" workshop

NEGOTIATION SKILLS DEVELOPMENT

In developing negotiation skills, I use the lecture-discussion approach to define negotiation, to explain purpose and importance, to discuss myths, to discuss elements, to explain strategies, and to explain negotiation errors to avoid. The following sections highlight the content of these discussions.

NEGOTIATION MYTHS

Therefore, before beginning the negotiation skill development, I use the principles from Thompson to discuss the myths of negotiation. The unsubstantiated theories about what it takes to be an effective negotiator are addressed with discussions of negotiation myths.

ELEMENTS OF NEGOTIATION

Negotiation takes many forms; therefore, students must know and understand the elements of negotiation.

The following are the elements for discussion:

- Parties--are people who negotiate; the parties are the focal negotiator; the opponent is termed the target negotiator; and the key parties are termed the principals.
- Issues--are the resources to be allocated or the considerations to be resolved in the negotiation. The more issues, the better because they provide opportunities for tradeoffs among the issues and the parties.
- Alternatives--are the choices available to the negotiator for each issue to be resolved. Negotiators must identify and create choices, and the more choices to resolve the issues, the better.
- Positions arid interests--are the stated wants a negotiator has for an issue. Interests are the underlying needs that a negotiator has and wants from the negotiation. Negotiators' needs may be met by a variety of positions. A key to successful negotiation is to move away from positional bargaining into a discussion of underlying interests and needs.
- Negotiation process--are the events and interactions that occur between parties before arriving at the outcome. The process includes all of the verbal and nonverbal interaction among parties, the

execution of bargaining strategies, and the external or situational events affecting the interaction between negotiators. The negotiation process also includes the degree and level of concessions that each party makes, the use of threats and promises, and the medium of communication between negotiators.

- Negotiation outcome--is the endpoint of the bargaining. The analysis of negotiated outcomes does not stop with the attainment of mutual agreement. Emotional reactions to negotiation must also be negotiated because some parties will feel satisfied, others may feel cheated, and some may feel guilty. These feelings can dramatically affect the likelihood of settlement and the relationships and reputations of the parties.

NEGOTIATION STRATEGIES

In the past, the negotiation process could be characterized by lots of warlike imagery and words such as trickery, intimidation, and manipulation that resulted in "winners" and "losers." However, there is now less emphasis on the war-zone approach that demands an "I win, you lose" mentality. Negotiators should search for common ground because long-term relationships are at stake. They are more likely to achieve success if the negotiation helps all parties.

Therefore, I instruct students to focus on developing a supportive communication climate using the following strategies:

- *Plan and prepare for the negotiation*: Establish your goals and the strategies you will use to negotiate your position.
- *Find a way to reach all members' goals*: Orient members to the problem and how developing a solution will benefit them. Focus on what needs to be done in practical terms and lead the discussion within the wider context of the team's goals. Clarity is essential; therefore, continue discussion of the problem or issue until all members understand.
- *View the team members as partners*: To have a win-win style, view team members as equals in the contributions they can make in executing the proposal plan. Treat each team member fairly without favoritism, and recognize that each will have valid concerns.
- *Help the members*: Communicate empathy in the problem orientation. Show genuine concern for all team members.
- *Develop and examine alternatives*. Make provisions for the team members to be a part of the solution by asking for other methods of solving the problem. Be open, and realise that your solutions may not fit current circumstances.
- *Accept other ways of doing things*. Allow for spontaneity, and be flexible in the problem solving or development process. Avoid having a preconceived notion that you have the best solution for the problem by working with the process as it unfolds.

- Realise the necessity to be receptive and non-threatening. An open communication style of verbalizing and active, receptive listening can make the difference between a constructive or destructive climate.
- *Agree to evaluate agreed upon solution*(s). When a solution is treated as tentative, consensus is easier to gain.

AVOIDING NEGOTIATING ERRORS

Errors in negotiation can occur; therefore, students need to know what some of the errors are so they can avoid them. We use this checklist for discussion of what the errors are and their significance in the negotiation process. I encourage students to use this checklist as an editing feature in their negotiation tasks.

PROPOSAL ORAL PRESENTATIONS

Each student must give a five-minute informative oral presentation on his or her proposal topic. In this way, potential team members gain knowledge of proposal topics that they may be interested in implementing for a team project.

Following the oral presentations, students submit their written proposal for grading. I want the teams to make their decision on which proposal to implement based on their analysis, not mine. I make clear to them that the proposal with the highest grade is not necessarily the best proposal for the team project. Note: Do not hand back the graded proposals until after teams have made their proposal topic selection. In the past when I have handed back the graded proposals before the decision of the teams, the teams selected the proposal with the highest grade and ignored all they learned about negotiation for proposal selection. Students make a copy of their proposal for themselves so that they have something to work with when they negotiate for proposal topic selection.

The oral presentations are the only exposure the class has to potential topics because they do not receive copies of their classmates' proposals.

Therefore, students must make sure their presentations are concrete, complete, and clear. This process forces students to do a good job on their presentations. Students have the choice of using visuals in their presentations, but they must make sure the presentation is informative and not persuasive. I tell students to view their presentations as briefings on their proposals, and the persuasion will come within your team.

TEAM DEVELOPMENT

The growth in teams has done much to highlight teamwork as a vital communication aspect of organizational life. Therefore, 21st century academic institutions are challenged by increasing demands from corporations for graduates who are able to function as knowledge workers in teamwork-oriented organizations. In a work world of restricted resources, complex problems, renewed focus on quality, and increased competition, the need to work together for common goals has become evident and imperative. This assignment is designed to help prepare students for a teamwork-oriented work environment.

Wilson indicates that group size is directly related to the evolution of a team. The sense of cohesiveness is at risk when a group is too small or too large. He recommends that groups not be larger than 10 or 11 members, but five to seven members would be a good workable size.

With these concepts in mind, I have students develop teams of five. Depending on the class size, I may adjust that number up or have some teams of five or seven so that the odds of everyone being selected are greater.

Students self-select five team members by looking for those who are interested in and/or have expertise in particular aspects of their proposal topics. However, interest in a particular topic does not imply agreement on the direction or approach of the topic. Members may be selected for their disagreement, which can lead to healthy discussions.

Therefore, according to Wilson, selection of group members should include the following questions:

- Who should participate in the group because of special qualifications or expertise?
- Who should participate in the group because of sensitivity of the potential subject matter?
- Are there any duplications of participants that may inhibit the group?

If the teams are formed before the oral presentations, students seem to limit their team selection to students they know or have worked with in the past. Therefore, students will receive the most value from this exercise if teams are selected after the oral presentations.

Some teams may have members that have similar or related proposal topics and they may be able to negotiate the blend of the topics. Teams with all team members from the same major occur sometimes, but it is not a problem because each student's major includes the same core courses, while each member brings a different perspective to the team discussions.

Therefore, by having students' team member selection based on the selection criteria presented above, students do not need to concern themselves about the makeup of the team by gender, race, ESL, or other criteria that are not related to getting the project done. Students must keep in mind that in the business world, they are not to discriminate and must make their team member selections performance- and task-based.

When students are not selected to participate in a team, I have a backup plan. I accompany that student to a team that does not have enough members or a team that has some members with a related topic. Such a circumstance is always uncomfortable and difficult no matter what method is used, but my strategy is to point out the benefits that person can contribute to a team.

TEAM NEGOTIATION OF PROPOSAL SELECTION

After the teams have been formed and they have completed the initial phase of getting acquainted and establishing team relationships, they are ready to discuss the proposal selection for team implementation. Only one proposal can be selected for implementation; therefore, using the negotiation skills they learned, students must convince team members that their proposal is the best one for the team to implement. From this segment of the assignment, students experience the competitive nature of proposals and the importance of a clear, persuasive product.

Each team member uses negotiation, interpersonal, and written skills to convince the team to select their proposal for implementation. Armed with their newly acquired knowledge of negotiation skills, students negotiate how their proposal can benefit each team member and the team project. Of course, if team members have similar or related topics, the negotiation process is easier because they can blend the topics for the team project.

To help get students started with the process, each student must prepare a written plan for their negotiation and submit a copy to me. Their strategy plan must be written in an organized and attractive format. In their written negotiation plan, they must include their topic, the application of the negotiation elements, the application of the negotiation strategies, and specific negotiation errors they will avoid. By making students accountable for the use of their negotiation skills, they are forced to give thought to the negotiation planning process.

IMPLEMENTATION OF THE TEAM PROJECT

After a proposal is selected, the team starts the process of implementing the proposed plan. The team has approximately five weeks to develop all aspects of the proposed plan and to submit a written report on the final product. They must execute the tasks in the proposal plan to meet all of the objectives and to achieve the purpose of the proposal.

During the execution of the proposal tasks, teams are allowed, where necessary, to make changes from the original proposal. In addition, team members must thoroughly familiarize themselves with the proposal, and in most cases, the teams must conduct additional research. After the implementation of the proposal, the team writes a report documenting their execution of the project's implementation and submits the final product to me for grading.

ASSIGNMENT BENEFITS

The most important benefits students get from this assignment are the opportunity to develop a proposal, to practice negotiation skills, and to develop their critical thinking skills. In addition, many students have been able to share their problem-solving skills by implementing their proposal at their workplace.

Many students work full- or part-time and have the opportunity to apply their knowledge and skills in their workplace. In my upper division classes, I find that more students are non-traditional working students, balancing work and school. These students are dedicated, motivated, and focused in this class.

Some five years ago, my university embraced its identity as an urban institution and revised its mission statement to emphasize connections among the university and various constituents in the surrounding metro community. The technical writing programme found itself in a strong position to contribute to the implementation of the urban mission simply by virtue of the pragmatic nature of the discipline. The metro region is a popular and growing area for major technical industries such as semiconductor manufacturers and chemical and environmental engineering groups. A liaison with these firms would be a natural fit: the writing programme could provide technical writers to meet their communication needs while the firms themselves could enhance the education of writing students by offering internships and other opportunities.

In light of the university's urban mission, I became interested in involving such firms in curricular development. Put simply, I want local organizations who might hire our students to recognize a degree from the writing programme as a credential qualifying our graduates to do the job. To move towards this goal, I formed an advisory board made up of key managers and executives in the metro region. I first approached them by modifying an accepted classroom assessment technique - the annotated portfolio - for use in a contest. The idea was to get the targeted companies interested in assessment of student writing and then to solicit their representatives' interest in continuing to serve on an advisory board.

Representatives from Arthur Andersen, Cascade Earth Sciences, CH2M Hill, First Interstate Bank, The Harris Group, Intel, Sequent, and Tektronix participated in the initial contest, awarding cash prizes donated from the companies. More important, each representative committed to an ongoing relationship. Subsequently, representatives from Timberline Software and US West have joined the advisory board.

I draw on the board to advise me regarding curricular developments, including course content and offerings. They keep programme faculty informed of important needs in the local community of technical and professional writers, and faculty in turn can share this input directly with students. The board also represents a potential pool of adjunct teachers and guest speakers. This winter, for instance, the senior technical editor from C[H.sub.2]M Hill taught our technical report writing course and received outstanding reviews from students who recognized this voice of authority as a working expert in the field. Other board members have designed and proposed new courses for the curriculum. Additionally, board members regularly visit classrooms as guest lecturers to share their experience and advice with students. These visits translate into sincere mentoring relationships in some cases. And, in line with the university's efforts to catalyze education in the community rather than containing it within classroom walls, the board facilitates internships, capstone experiences, and community-based learning courses that get students learning by doing.

But the annotated portfolio remains central to the relationship: each year the board comes together to determine first, second, and third place portfolio winners, awarding cash prizes in recognition of communication excellence. The portfolios provide a touchstone for important and ongoing dialogue about what works and what doesn't in technical and business writing.

This chapter offers guidelines for those who might wish to establish a similar advisory board to improve student learning outcomes in their Programmes. It advocates student portfolios as an effective assessment technique and shows how devising an annual portfolio contest can encourage students to develop and retain their portfolios in order to prepare for their careers.

Additionally, portfolios that students enter into the contest can be used to identify and exemplify standards and criteria for performance success, and programme administrators can use this information to inform decision making. Involving experts outside the university in determining these standards is the key feature of this process and, at an urban university such as mine at least, speaks to the larger institutional objective of building strong community partnerships.

PORTFOLIO ASSESSMENT

While a full discussion of issues related to student portfolio work in writing courses lies beyond the scope of the present paper, a review of the recent literature seems in order.

In general, writing instructors value student portfolios because portfolio creation emphasizes revision and gives the student writer primary control over the creative process.

Portfolios represent the student's best work over time rather than simply giving a snapshot of a single performance and thus provide a more complete picture of writing competence.

Most important, portfolios provide a means for self-evaluation rather than simply giving the instructor a set of symptoms to evaluate; that is, portfolios generally require students to comment on the work showcased and to explain the rhetorical strategies that informed their production - especially revisions. In some cases, portfolios can contain various drafts of a single document to show the revisionary work.

Engaging students in this metadiscourse raises their awareness of the writing process. In turn, encouraging a greater scrutiny of the writing process leads to self-reflexive learning and validates portfolios as authentic assessment instruments.As adaptations of the annotated portfolio described by Angelo and Cross, the student portfolios proposed here engage the learning process in the ways indicated above but do not contain revisionary drafts of single documents. Note the emphasis on the introductory letter, which asks students to explain the rhetorical strategies and the communication context for each of the elements contained within the portfolio. This letter acts as an abstract for the whole and gives advisory board judges the background they need to evaluate the writing performance.

One purpose of the contest is to make students realise that a well-prepared portfolio can contribute to the job search process. While most discussions of how to create and administer student portfolio assignments remain grounded in composition theory, the potential benefit the portfolio offers as an employment-gaining strategy receives almost exclusive attention in business communication pedagogy.

In my programme, the portfolio contest is open to any enrolled student and is linked to the required introduction to technical writing course, which uses traditional portfolio assessment as part of the classroom learning experience. The idea is to get students to produce a portfolio early in their programme that they can modify and develop into an effective job-application tool as they gain experience over time.

The contest itself is open to students at any level, but generally those who enter are about to graduate from the programme, and their portfolios represent a wide array of technical and professional writing documents compiled from community-based as well as classroom activities. The portfolio thus is an important feature of the programme, but students retain the choice of whether they wish to expand the assignment in the introductory course into a more formal document for later use, whether in the contest or in the job market.

Nevertheless, the portfolio contest does facilitate decision making and build consensus among programme instructors regarding expectations and performance since a faculty panel reviews all contest entrants in order to narrow the pool to five finalists that advisory board members judge. The existing literature effectively documents the benefits of involving nonacademic partners in an advisory capacity. Obvious benefits include an advisory board's potential for raising dollars, the enhanced ability to recruit students for the professions that the advisory board represents, and overall programme and institutional improvements that come about as a result of advisory board recommendations and intervention.

In the case of communication disciplines including public relations, marketing, and technical and business writing Programmes, advisory boards specifically facilitate internship and career enhancing contacts for students and increase the Programmes' credibility and visibility in addition to improving curricular planning. For technical writing Programmes, especially, advisory board participation effectively bridges the gap between classroom and workplace and benefits board members as well as students and faculty. Serving on such a board represents an effective networking opportunity for professionals who otherwise might not be able to contribute to local educational objectives. Most analyses generally follow the "how-to" approach adopted here and distinguish from among advisory boards that serve on institutional, programme, and ad hoc bases.

In short, advisory boards are recommended vehicles for improving student learning by ensuring that programme goals are consistent with desired outcomes in the community.

9

Contempt of Court and Media

INTRODUCTION

The right to a fair trial, uninfluenced by extraneous pressures is recognized as a basic tenet of justice. The Constitution of India and the Contempt of Courts Act, 1971 contain provisions aimed at safeguarding the right to fair trial. Restrictions are imposed on the discussion or publication of matters relating to the merits of a case pending before a Court.

The problems raised by trial by media involve a tug of war between two conflicting principles free press and free trial. The freedom of the press stems from the right of the public in a democracy to be involved on the issues of the day, which affect them. People cannot adequately influence the decisions that affect their lives unless they can be adequately informed on the facts and arguments relevant to the decisions. Much of such fact-finding and argumentation necessarily has to be conducted vicariously, the public press being a principal instrument. This is also the justification for investigative and campaign journalism.

At the same time, the right to fair trial, uninfluenced by extraneous pressures is recognized as a basic tenet of justice. The Constitution of India and the Contempt of Courts Act, 1971 contain provisions aimed at safeguarding the right to fair trial.

Restrictions are imposed on the discussion or publication of matters relating to the merits of a case pending before a Court. A journalist may thus be liable for contempt of court if he publishes anything which might prejudice a fair trial or anything which impairs the impartiality of a court to decide a cause on its merits, whether the proceedings before the Court be a criminal or civil proceeding.

In relation to freedom of speech and expression, there are three types of contempt of court:

(a) One kind of contempt is scandalizing the court itself;
(b) There may likewise be a contempt of court in abusing parties who are concerned in causes in the court;

(c) There may also be contempt in prejudicing mankind against persons before the cause is heard.

However, the above classifications are by no means exhaustive. Very broadly speaking, the conduct may refer to anything that tends to bring the administration of justice into disrepute or to obstruct or interfere with the due course of justice.

PRE-TRIAL PUBLICITY

Sensationalized journalism has also had an impact on the judiciary. For example, in upholding the imposition of the death penalty on Mohammed Afzal for the December 2001 attack on the Indian Parliament, Justice P. Venkatarama Reddi stated, (t)he incident, which resulted in heavy casualties, had shaken the entire nation and the collective conscience of the society will only be satisfied if capital punishment is awarded to the offender.

A media trial began almost immediately after Afzals arrest. Only one week after the attack, on 20 December 2001, the police called a press conference during the course of which Afzal incriminated himself in front of the national media. The media played an excessive and negative role in shaping the public conscience before Afzal was even tried. Similarly, S.A.R. Geelani, one of Afzals co-defendants in the Parliament attack case, was initially sentenced to death for his alleged involvement despite an overwhelming lack of evidence. Large sections of the Indian media portrayed him as a dangerous and trained terrorist. On appeal, the Delhi High Court overturned Geelanis conviction and described the prosecutions case as at best, absurd and tragic.

PROTECTION OF THE RIGHTS OF THE ACCUSED

Taking exception to the media interviewing witnesses and commenting on cases during trial, the Law Commission has recommended changes in the Contempt of Courts Act, 1971 to protect the rights of the accused and ensure the proper conduct of trial in its latest report titled *Trial by Media*, headed by Justice M Jagannadha Rao. It has also emphasised the need to sensitise journalists through proper training in certain aspects of the law. What is going on in the media may indeed be highly objectionable. Merely because it is tolerated by the courts, it may not cease to be contempt, the Commission noted in the report. The Commission said: In our country the lack of knowledge of law of contempt currently shows that there is extensive coverage of interviews with witnesses.

The panel said that this is highly objectionable even under the current law of contempt if such interviews are conducted after the chargesheet is filed. We are of the view that there is considerable interference with the due administration of criminal justice and this will have to remedied by Parliament, the report said. In its report submitted to the Government, the Commission said, Today there is a feeling that in view of the extensive use of the television and cable services, the whole pattern of publication of news has changed and several such publications are likely to have a prejudicial impact on the suspects, accused, witnesses and even judges and in general on the administration of justice. The report said, according to our law, a suspect/accused is entitled to a fair procedure and is presumed to be innocent till proved guilty in a court of law. None can be allowed to prejudge or prejudice his case by the time it goes to trial. It said that publications, which interfered or tend to interfere with the administration of justice would amount to criminal contempt under the Contempt of Courts Act, 1971 and if in order to preclude such interference, the provisions of that Act impose reasonable restrictions on freedom of speech, such restrictions would be valid.

The report noted that at present, under Section 3 (2) of the Contempt of Courts Act, 1971 such publications would be contempt only if a chargesheet had been filed in a criminal case. The Commission has suggested that the starting point of a criminal case should be from the time of arrest of an accused and not from the time of filing of the charge sheet. In the perception of the Commission such an amendment would prevent the media from prejudging or prejudicing the case.

The United States and Australia both have stringent provisions regulating media trials, and the solutions that are envisaged to the damage caused to the right to a fair trial of the accused range from sequestering of the judge/jury for the duration of the trial, to transferring trials to more neutral jurisdictions, to declaring mistrials and acquitting accused persons, and in extreme cases, even barring further criminal complaints against an accused whose character has been so tarnished by media scrutiny that it would be impossible for him to be given a fair trial. In India, the Press Council of India does have regulations concerning reporting of *sub judice* matters, but a violation of these norms will only call for sanction against the media organization and will not necessarily ensure justice to the accused. At present, in India, the impossibility of a fair trial for an accused can possibly be a ground for transfer of cases to another jurisdiction. The Supreme Court has come down on trials by media, especially in dowry cases, where public sympathy is clearly with the victim and her family, and out pours of public outrage against the errant husband and his family easily find place in local publications.

In *M P Lohia v. State of West Bengal*, Justice Santosh Hegde of the Supreme Court felt compelled to note the disturbing factor. The case concerned the death of one Chandni in February, 2002 and the complaint in this regard was registered, the investigation was in progress and the application for grant of anticipatory bail had been disposed of by the High Court of Calcutta when an article has appeared in a magazine called Saga titled Doomed by Dowry written by one Kakoli Poddar based on her interview of the family of the deceased. Justice Hegde remarked that all material narrated therein are those that may be used in the forthcoming trial, and was convinced that they would certainly interfere with the administration of justice.

THE NEED FOR OPENNESS

There is a concern that the above regulations may result in the restricted reporting of important cases. In the interests of ensuring fair trials, the media in UK for instance have restricted the reporting of terrorist trials for long periods. Conviction following a fair trial is a major weapon to combat terrorism. The case with family courts is also similar. There is a feeling that the workings of, and the decisions made in family courts are too secretive. The argument runs that without increased openness there can be no confidence in the workings of the family court, and therefore no confidence in the process or the outcomes. To a consultation in the UK on the issue, the Newspaper Society wrote that:

We fully support the proposal that the media should be allowed to attend ALL family courts as of right and the principle of a general presumption of openness must be the established if public confidence and accountability is to be achieved. The role of the media as representative of the public particularly in relation to attendance at court proceedings is well established and understood. Media groups argue that the solution lies in letting journalists in as of right to act as a proxy for the public. To restrict them would be to deny the public and mean that miscarriages of justice could go unrecognised and unreported.

The contempt law is as old as Common Law itself. The Court, however, will act only where justice is jeopardized by a gross and/or unfounded attack on the Judges, where the attack is calculated to obstruct or destroy the judicial process. The judiciary cannot be immune from criticism. Judges and courts are alike open to criticism, and if reasonable argument or expostulation is offered against any judicial act as contrary to law or the public good, no Court could or would treat that as contempt of court. It is only the scurrilous abuse on a Judge in his character as a Judge, which would be actionable under the Contempt of Courts Act.

The freedom of the press and the independence of the judiciary are two of the most important indices of democracy in a country. It is essential to preserve both. Pliable press and subservient judiciary are the first step in the process of extinguishment of democratic lights.

STRUCTURE OF THE MEDIA

A healthy media environment should be plural and diverse, able to carry the wider range of views, information and opinion that exists in any society. For example it may be that the media environment is fragmented, or politically partisan. The history of dictatorship, repression or conflict may mean there is little tradition of independent professional journalism. Each set of circumstances will require a different approach. In most societies there is some kind of state broadcaster, however discredited. Alongside the stimulation of a healthy and vibrant private media it is important not to neglect the state broadcaster. New and restored democracies should begin the process of transforming it into a genuine public service broadcaster. The requirements of the print media and the broadcast media are quite different in this respect. Within the general confines of the law, the print media can be left alone to develop in so far as the market permits.

But to achieve the right plural mix of broadcast media – the balance between public service broadcasting and straightforward commercial interests- requires state intervention. The first, basic task is for any administration to ensure that people can access the means of communication – including the reception of broadcasts, provision of electricity supplies, access to telephones and Internet. There is a need to ensure the infrastructure exists to develop a broadcast industry.

INDEPENDENT REGULATOR

Another early task should be the creation of an independent regulator to allocate wavelengths and undertake the necessary licensing procedures. This body should be established by law and be independent of any government interference, either directly by appointing its membership, or indirectly by controlling its funding. Its members should be chosen through an open and public process and it should be accountable to the wider public through the legislative arm of the state. (For a more detailed elaboration of these principle see *Access to the Airwaves* published by Article 19). The regulatory authority should rapidly produce a frequency plan showing how the airwaves will be shared between the public and private broadcasters and community broadcasters. In addition – where relevant-it should specify the regional and local allocations and how the status of minorities will be guaranteed.

PUBLIC SERVICE BROADCASTING

It is sometimes assumed that the policy objective in a new or restored democracy is simply to allow the maximum private ownership of the media, on the grounds that this will produce the widest and most diverse range of voices. Some caution should be exercised however. In a bitterly divided society, the profusion of media, with no overall "national voice" capable of helping foster an imagined community can exacerbate rather than heal divisions. In these circumstances a high priority should be given to establishing a national public service broadcaster whose composition and programming can reflect the diverse strands of the society in question. Experience shows that the production of programmes, which arc informative, educative or demonstrate distinct cultural or linguistic strands, which are crucial to the development of national identity – are most easily achieved by the creation of an effective public service broadcaster. This is not an easy task however. A public service broadcaster requires a clearly articulated vision, some kind of national consensus on its objectives, complete freedom from political interference and a conscious attempt to engage viewers and listeners. The goals of public service broadcasting should be defined in law.

These will include the provision of comprehensive and balanced news coverage, the promotion of local programme production – including through the use of quotas – guaranteed universal access and a commitment to serve all regions, cultures and linguistic groups. The first stage is to establish the PSB overseen by a fully independent governing body whose autonomy and independence is guaranteed by law–as with the regulatory authority.

Specific guarantees should be given on editorial independence and on funding arrangements. The governing body should be accountable to a multi-party body of some kind – the legislative assembly if one exists-and its primary role will be to appoint the managers to run the PSB and to ensure subsequently that the public service mandate is being fulfilled. The governing body should not interfere in the day to day running of the broadcaster; appointments processes should be open and transparent and staff be protected from unfair dismissal. Another option is to establish a framework where all media have a public service function. In this case, public service obligations will be placed upon all broadcasters, probably through the regulatory authority that issues licenses. This approach needs to be considered very carefully. It may well be appropriate in a very divided society where all the media has been affected by conflicts in the transition to democracy, or in circumstances where state revenues are so scarce that there is no realistic possibility of providing any state funding for a single PSB (as is the case where fiscal revenues are very low).

Whichever approach is adopted, independent civil society has a role to play as a watchdog, ensuring that the public service remit is fulfilled. Consideration should therefore be given to the creation of media forums which involve civil society and which can consider the performance of the public broadcaster and the policies of the governing body. There needs to be a consistent commitment to consultation with the public, through civil society organisations and through the political parties and other forums. In new or restored democracies establishing the legitimacy of a single national voice is vital. There needs to be – for example – news bulletins and programmes which everyone in the society can watch, regardless of their position on issues of the day, confident that they are receiving balanced and authoritative coverage.

PRIVATE BROADCASTING

A crucial role for the governing authority and the regulator is providing the ground rules that enable fair competition between the public broadcaster and the private broadcasters. The government's main responsibility is to ensure a level playing field economically. In particular there should no attempt to use the tax system to favour one broadcaster over another.

The allocation of government advertising must be strictly monitored to ensure fair access by all media. License fees should not be set so high as to favour the wealthiest and most powerful corporations – the ideal is to create relatively low entry costs. In general, while it is impossible to be prescriptive in the abstract, any economic measures that affect the media should be fair, transparent and non-discriminatory. The regulator has an important role to play in overseeing more complex issues that involve the fostering of a dual broadcasting system (public and private). It is unrealistic to think that modern PSBs can be created solely on the basis of public funds – they will nearly all require a degree of advertising. There is a role for a competition regulator in this field as well as the broad cast regulator – the mix of powers being dependent upon the general capacity of the state to support such institutions.

ECONOMIC SUPPORT

In many societies the market for the media is very weak. In these circumstances the media, particularly newspapers are funded by powerful groups – parties, factions, businesses – to act as mouthpieces for their own interests. A good public service broadcaster is one possible antidote to this. Creating a climate where a genuine media market can develop is another. International support can be crucial in providing support with start up costs, professional expertise, even equipment and materials. What new and restored democracies should be wary of however is allowing the international community's funding to act as a substitute for the development of a domestic market.

One possible model is to establish a Media Development Fund, administered by respected local media professionals from across all communities, which can provide low cost loans to help new media get established. Models for this exist in different parts of the world. Loans are preferable to grants as they encourage serious business plans and moves towardss genuine economic independence. While financial support should not be made conditional upon a particular editorial approach, which would compromise the independence of the media, it is reasonable to impose some conditions that will help produce professional balanced journalism. For example, financial support could be made conditional upon non-discriminatory employment practices, or on an insistence that jobs are not the exclusive preserve of one ethnic group. Another approach would be to establish a not-for-profit holding company that has a major stake in leading media companies, which guarantees editorial independence and uses its profits to promote the objectives of free expression through grants and activities.

CULTURE AND JOURNALISM

Laws are the foundations of a democratic society and economic structures and reality determine the broad shape of the media. Neither however is any guarantee of independent, balanced, professional journalism. They can provide the conditions for independent professional journalism to flourish but no more than that. New and restored democracies should consider how to help build a culture of professional journalism. There are a number of international organisations of journalists and employers that support this activity and the programmes may be of value.

In some areas media centres have been established to provide a professional base for journalists to work, receive training and support. It seems sensible for new and restored democracies to encourage media organisations to cooperate in establishing such a centre – in the past competing proposals or even competing centres have complicated the media environment.

Journalism training should be given a high priority. Past experience suggests that such training concentrates on the following areas:-

- Building a general awareness of democracy and human rights
- Encouraging independent analysis and thought
- The techniques of investigative journalism.

Most professionals are influenced by their peers – in fact peer pressure is the most likely means of improving skills and ethics. For this reason the establishment of an independent journalist association should be given a high priority, linked to a respected international association like the International Federation of Journalists. Such an association can provide a direct advocacy on behalf of the profession, particularly on pay and conditions issues and on questions such as unfair dismissal cases between local staff and employers, in which it would be unwise for the international community to intervene. In parallel to this, steps should be taken to foster – through civil society initiatives – the development of employers associations, linked in turn to the World Association of Newspapers or the Association of Independent Broadcasters.

The most important role for these associations is in creating a climate of self-regulation. Self regulation is always better than imposed regulation because it is likely to be more effective (people are always more committed to freely chosen values than to those forced upon them) and, of course, it respects the independence of the media. Such associations provide useful means of disseminating good practice, and can help create peer pressure to respect editorial independence, human rights norms and democratic values.

CIVIL SOCIETY

Trade unions and employers associations are one manifestation of civil society but there are many others which play an important role in helping foster the conditions for media development. One weakness that may have to be overcome in a new or restored democracy is the absence of a stable civil society and of a culture in which the values of freedom of expression are assumed. While regulation can play and important role in creating the climate for this culture, it cannot guarantee it. A whole range of civil society groups will have an interest and a stake in the media coverage of their society. They can monitor the media regularly and can play an important role during elections checking for evidence of bias. They can also play a significant role in helping shape media policy providing an interface between the practitioners, public officials, the international community and the general public.

Providing the structural stability for the media in new and restored democracies requires the right blend of a mix of approaches. It will almost certainly need a legal and policy strand, some kind of economic support, careful thought given to establishing the right mix of media structures. It will require fostering an active climate of professional journalism and civil society intervention. In these circumstances there will be a need for on-going research, monitoring and evaluation of the approach adopted.

Local organisations and media professionals can work with international organisations and experts but primacy should be given to local control and direction of policies. New and restored democracies should be aware that the media environment of a country is not just shaped by domestic forces. Local communities will have access to international media outside of the country's context – the World Service, Voice of America and a range of European alternatives will provide coverage that does not derive from local experiences. The internet and VoIP protocols permit a new kind of citizen journalism that transcends traditional media boundaries. The priority for a new or restored democracy is to create a domestic media that can help support democracy and human rights in the country concerned. This in turn will require sustained and serious commitment by the country and by any international donors that are involved in reconstruction. It will also require the ability to learn from past mistakes– a process that is assisted enormously if new and restored democracies can share information and expertise.

MEDIA AND THE COURTS

No area of media law has attracted more attention by the courts in both countries than the one involving media coverage of the courts. This area directly involves the conflict of constitutional guarantees: first, freedom of the press with its companion need to gather information and cover government, including the courts and, second, the defendant's constitutional right to a fair trial. In the United States, the conflict is between the First and Sixth Amendments. In Canada, it is the conflict between freedom of the press and other media of communication in Section 2(b) and the right to a fair and public hearing in Section 11(d) of the Charter of Rights and Freedoms.

In Canada, prior to the enactment of the Charter in 1982, the rights of individuals and the media to attend and report on court proceedings were much more limited than was the case south of the border.

Since then, however, the courts in Canada have issued important decisions that have expanded these rights considerably, but still not to the extent that the courts have in the United States. For example, trial court judges in Canada still have considerable authority to restrain the publication of certain information arising from hearings (publication of evidence tendered in a preliminary hearing is usually banned until after a full trial can be held before an unbiased jury), and journalists have no general right of access to court documents unless specifically provided by statute or court rule.

During the first year of the new Charter, the Ontario Court of Appeal ruled that an absolute ban on the press and public from attending court proceedings was a violation of Section 2(b). While recognizing that the guarantee of freedom of the press is not absolute, the Court acknowledged that "There can be no doubt that the openness of the courts to the public is one of the hallmarks of a democratic society. Public accessibility to the courts was and is a felt necessity; it is a restraint on arbitrary action by those who govern and by the powerful."

It concluded, however, that while absolute bans excluding the press and public from court proceedings did not constitute a reasonable limit, such closures requiring judicial discretion would be allowed under Section 1 of the Charter. The Supreme Court of Canada offered further instruction in the application of Section 1 in matters relating to the courts in one ruling that struck down an Alberta law prohibiting publication of materials from court proceedings, ruling that such limits were not justified under Section 1.

In another decision, the Supreme Court ruled that an injunction restraining picketing and other activities calculated to interfere with the operations of the court was justified under Section 1, even though the lower court record included an affidavit from a member of the Law Society of British Columbia explaining that the "picket line was orderly and peaceful" and that "Persons appearing to have business inside the Courthouse entered and left the building at will and at no time appeared to be impeded in any way by the picketers."

Further, in Canadian Newspapers Co. v Canada (A.G.), the Supreme Court held that a mandatory ban on publishing the identity of a sexual assault victim was allowed under Section 1, since it was required to achieve Parliament's objective of facilitating complaints by victims of sexual assaults. In a recent decision, the Canadian Supreme Court set aside a ban on CBC from broadcasting a fictional account of sexual and physical abuse of children during a trial in Ontario with similar facts and circumstances.

While ruling that such a ban did not meet the "reasonable limits" test of s. 1, the majority justices offered an interesting observation about differences between the Canadian and American constitutional approaches to issues like this: "Publication bans, however, should not always be seen as a clash between freedom of expression for the media and the right to a fair trial for the accused. The clash model is more suited to the American constitutional context and should be rejected in Canada." This review of developments in three areas of media law in Canada shows that, while the courts on both sides of the border have expressed a strong commitment to the principle of a free press, Canadian courts have been less likely to provide strict protections for the media to publish without government restraint or interference.

This is most obvious in matters related to coverage of the courts, where judicial restraints on the news media have been more allowable in Canada, although the Court has moved in recent years to balance the importance of press freedom and the constitutional right to a fair trial. Also, Canadian courts have permitted government bans on the publication of truthful information, lawfully obtained, while American courts have held that such bans constitute an unconstitutional prior restraint.

And while media in the United States are allowed greater latitude to criticize public officials, Canadian courts have been reluctant to adopt the American approach to public libel and false light privacy. In other areas, however, involving newsgathering, the duty to testify, and access to information, the courts in both countries have attempted to balance the individual rights of the news media against the broader community interests of society.

DIFFERENCES IN JOURNALISTIC PRACTICE

In order to make some generalized comparisons of journalists and journalistic practice in the United States, in English-speaking Canada, and in French-speaking Canada, it is necessary to indulge in some oversimplifications about groups which, in themselves, tend to be rather complex and diverse. Lysiane Gagnon, in her discussion of "Journalism and Ideologies in Quebec," offers a useful starting point in her review of the classic work by Siebert, Peterson, and Schramm on The Four Theories of the Press, which provides a framework for generalizing about differences between these three groups of journalists and for beginning to identify the French, English, and American influences on the practice of journalism in North America.While the so-called "social responsibility" theory of the press grew out of the 1947 report of the Hutchins Commission on Freedom of the Press in the United States, American journalists have tended not to accept its basic premise, which calls for government intervention when and if the media fail to act responsibly.

For the most part, they continue to subscribe to the more libertarian view and its imperative that the press be free from government control and influence. However, the most recent national survey of journalists in the United States reveals a shift in the perceived functions of journalism favouring some of the original recommendations of the Hutchins Commission. As Weaver and Wilhoit explain, "most journalists in 1992 appeared to have a `belief system' that reflected the Commission's goal of investigating `the truth about the facts' and providing `a context which gives them meaning.'"

Concerning the appropriate role for government, journalists in English Canada, who share British traditions allowing for more government secrecy and control of information and the reporting of information, are more tolerant than their American counterparts of government intervention and control. And by further comparison, journalists on French-language media in Quebec subscribe even more to the tenets of the social-responsibility theory and are willing to accept an even greater role for government involvement in media matters to assure the public's right to information.

According to Fulford, English-Canadian journalists have inherited most of their techniques from Britain and the United States, except for the extensive foreign correspondence of British journalism and the investigative reporting in the United States. Further, and perhaps more important, is his observation that English-Canadian newspapers tend to mix elements of British and American heritage and share the ideal which involves truth, completeness, and justice.

Explaining that English-Canadian journalists seek "to report the truth," Fulford quotes publisher Stuart Keate who wrote that "Any publisher, editor or reporter worth his salt recognizes that he has only one basic duty to perform: to dig for the truth; to write it in language people can understand; and to resist all impediments to its publication."

While changes in English-Canadian journalism during this century have paralleled similar changes in the United States, journalism in Quebec has been more influenced by French models that include government distribution agencies, newspapers with more readily identifiable political leanings, and greater acceptance of government intervention in media affairs. The latter is linked to the basic tenet of the social-responsibility theory of the press which, according to Gagnon, has become more accepted by journalists in the province of Quebec than anywhere else in North America. One of the recent presidents of Quebec's federation of professional journalists, Real Barnabe, supported this observation by writing: "Now that they have acquired the conditions under which they may practice their profession with dignity, never have they Quebec journalists been so preoccupied by their responsibilities."

Gagnon further explains that the notion of freedom of the press, which was widely accepted by Quebec journalists in the 1940s and 1950s, has given way to a more complex concept of the public's "right to know," and that this has enjoyed considerable success in Quebec, certainly more than it has in English Canada and, with even more reason, the United States. Part of the explanation for this has to do with the French traditions and perspectives which place a greater value on collectivism over individualism.

As Siebert, Peterson, and Schramm explain in their classic work, the social responsibility theory is "in closer harmony with a collectivist theory of society than with the individualistic theory from which the libertarian system sprang."

Other ways in which the French tradition has contributed to differences between French and English journalism and journalists in Canada include: the emphasis on analysis over simple reporting of facts; the tendency to treat matters conceptually rather than in terms of people and events; the need to rationalize; and a greater personalization of articles and editorials. This is not to say that Quebec journalists are less committed to the facts and to being factual. A recent study by Pritchard and Sauvageau, for example, found that Quebec journalists are more likely than other Canadian journalists to think that it is important to accurately report comments from news sources. Similarly, an earlier study by Langlois and Sauvageau, which also documented this commitment to the facts, found there to be considerable variation among newspaper journalists in Quebec.

Concerning the greater personalization of articles and editorials, mentioned above, Siegel found in his study of the coverage of the FLQ crisis in 1970 that the French-language papers tended to project an image of self-importance in a variety of ways including "frequent reference to media and journalists; personalized coverage which, at times, included the raising of rhetorical questions which they then proceeded to answer; and editorials written in the first person." Another conclusion he reached point to still another important difference between journalism in English and French Canada. Following a comparison of coverage of several major issues or events, as well as a comparison of French and English broadcasting, Siegel found a homogeneity of outlook in the French press system.

"Of particular interest is the leadership role in French-Canadian society in which French-language journalists see them-selves. The articulation of a clearly defined value system is evident in French-language journalism, a practice that goes back a long time."

He found no such uniformity of outlook on the part of the English press, which he termed "fragmented." His conclusion is reinforced by David Thomas, an English-speaking journalist from Quebec: "Unity of thought was, and remains, infinitely more obvious in Quebec's French-language media—a phenomenon implicitly recognized by politicians and journalists who repeatedly point to the harsher treatment accorded the government by the English media."

Dominque Clift, a Montreal author and free-lance journalist who worked for major Canadian newspapers in both French and English Canada, characterized this uniformity of French-language journalists in a different way: the way in which they viewed themselves and their role in Quebec society. In his article, "Solidarity on a Pedestal: French Journalism in Quebec," he charged that "French journalists see for themselves a much more exalted role in society than do their English-speaking counterparts," adding that: "It is in the actual practice of journalism that French and English writers differ in the most pronounced manner. It has to do with the way in which journalists look upon themselves, their profession, their public, as well as on their employers."

But Florian Sauvageau, in his more systematic study of journalists on French-language dailies in Quebec, could find no such homogeneity in Quebec's journalistic circles. Instead, he found changes in Quebec media to parallel those in the modern corporate media of North America. Those include: the tendency to view newspapers as, first and foremost, businesses and journalists as "news workers"; journalists talking not so much in terms of "news" but of the "product"; and business and marketing functions gradually replacing the news function. Journalists are far from all being those radicals trying to control the news, as depicted a few years ago with some help from the pronouncements of the most militant of them. There are some, of course, who still turn for inspiration to the theses of the news as a driving force, and journalism as a tool for development, seeing themselves as agents of change and keeping up with the rhetoric of the 1960s and 1970s.

However, a good number are content simply to report the remarks of the dignitaries they meet, or to get the news out as quickly as possible. The result, he said, is that the work of journalists is becoming more and more routine and fairly unfulfilling, and that this is partly due to the rigid application of certain clauses in collective agreements between journalists and management. In summary, this brief review of research and commentary on journalists and journalism in the United States, English Canada, and Quebec provides some insight into how the practice of journalism in these different settings has been influenced in a variety of ways by English, French, and American traditions. Our concern, however, is in how these different traditions or perspectives may have resulted in journalistic practices that vary in their tendencies to promote individualism or to serve the community or broader societal interests.

ANECDOTAL EVIDENCE

Despite the growing body of literature from systematic studies of journalists in Canada and the United States, most of the "evidence" about how journalists and journalistic practices differ between the two countries tends to be anecdotal rather than the result of formal research. There are some exceptions, of course. For example, we already reported how the most recent national survey of journalists in the United States shows a shift towards some of the values articulated by the Hutchins Commission, which advanced the "social-responsibility" theory of the press.

Also, French-language journalists in Canada tend to be more willing than their English-Canadian and especially their American counterparts to perceive the press as a public service that can be regulated by the government. As evidence, Langois and Sauvageau found that nearly two-thirds of the French-speaking journalists in their study agreed that the state should intervene in the field of information. Even before the Kent Commission issued its report and recommendations in 1981, Sauvageau argued that the government might intervene to assure the citizen's right to information, similar to the way it has done in education and health care. More often, though, evidence is used to explain how the traditions and perspectives of journalists in Canada and the United States vary considerably in terms of tolerance for intervention by government and the courts in ways that limit the media and the practice of journalism.

This chapter began with a good example of this variety by comparing reactions to the decision in the United States to publish the Unibomber's manifesto with reaction to CBC cooperation with the RCMP in meeting broadcast demands of a group of renegades in British Columbia. Another example is reaction to certain recommendations of the Kent Commission on Newspapers. Following the simultaneous sale of newspapers in Winnipeg and Ottawa by two major Canadian newspaper groups, the federal government established the Kent Commission in 1980 and authorized it to study the new newspaper industry and make recommendations to the government. One of the more controversial recommendations called for the establishment of a Press Rights Panel within the Canadian Human Rights Commission.

Response came mainly from representatives and publishers of newspapers owned by large newspaper groups in Canada. The reaction was tempered and mild compared to what one would expect in the United States if similar recommendations were to come out of a government committee that spent more than $3 million to investigate the daily newspaper industry. Reactions in the United States to any threat of government intervention or control in media affairs tend to be immediate and predictable. Media owners and spokespersons for associations of journalists, particularly in the print media, are quick to call "infringement" and issue charges of improper violations of cherished First Amendment guarantees of freedom of the press.

Still another example has to do with media coverage of criminal trials. During the months of exhaustive coverage and commentary related to the O.J. Simpson trial in the United States, a trial court judge in Ontario issued a restraining order on the media in the Paul Bernardo murder trial that included, as well, a ban on publication of most information from his wife's trial several months earlier. Canadian journalists complained but complied with the court order, while American journalists in neighbouring border cities did not, continuing what one U.S. newspaper editor had earlier referred to as a "border battle with Canadian law."

These examples help illustrate the differences between Canada and the United States in terms of their legal systems, judicial traditions, and accepted journalistic practice and show a stronger commitment in Canada to the values of community over the individual rights of journalists and the news media.

Discussion

Important differences in the traditions of law and in the practice of journalism in Canada and the United States result in different approaches to how the rights of the news media are appropriately balanced against the needs of the community and the broader interests of society. To begin with, while the two legal systems share a similar tradition in English Common Law, their judicial and political approaches are different in important ways. As Lipset and Pool explain, while both nations seek to protect the rights of the individual while promoting and protecting the general welfare of the community, they do "strike different balances, with Canada tipping towards the interests of the community, and the United States towards the individual."

This review of the development of media law in the two countries shows that the courts on both sides of the border have expressed a strong commitment to the principle of a free press. However, Canadian courts have been less likely than those in the United States to provide strict protections for the media to publish without government restraint or interference. This is most obvious in matters related to coverage of the courts, where judicial restraints are more allowable in Canada.

Also, Canadian courts have permitted government bans on the publication of truthful information, lawfully obtained, while American courts have held that such bans on the press or punishment for publishing such information is unconstitutional. Also, media in the United States are allowed greater latitude to criticize public officials than are media in Canada, where the courts have been reluctant to adopt the American approach to civil libel. In other areas, however, involving newsgathering, the duty to testify, and access to information, the courts in both countries have attempted to balance the rights of the news media against the broader interests of society.

Apart from differences in the law are differences in the practice of journalism in Canada and the United States. Journalists in Canada are more inclined towards a "social responsibility" view of the role of the media in society. While this particular perspective was proposed by the prestigious Hutchins Commission on Freedom of the Press in the United States, American journalists have tended not accept its basic premise, which calls for government intervention when and if the media fail to act responsibly. For the most part, they continue to subscribe to the more libertarian view and its imperative that the media be free from government influence and control.

Canadian journalists, however, whether sharing British traditions that allow for more government secrecy and control of information or French traditions that are more accepting of government intervention in media affairs, tend to be more tolerant of government intervention in ways that directly affect the media while serving the broader needs and interests of society. The most recent national survey of American journalists suggests that there may be some shift towards some of the goals of the Hutchins Commission, which originally proposed the social responsibility model.

Some Future Considerations

There is, and has been, considerable discussion about the Constitution in Canada since the Charter of Rights and Freedoms was adopted in 1982. However, little if any of the controversy centers around concerns over government control of the media or court limitations of Charter guarantees of press freedom. This is not to say that journalists and media owners in Canada do not have concerns about these issues or that they would not prefer greater freedom and less government control. It is just that these are not major concerns, at least not compared to the larger constitutional issues being discussed.

This is not the case in the United States, where journalists and media owners have long been eager and vocal critics of any attempts by government or the courts to limit press freedoms and violate their First Amendment guarantees. However, the growing criticism and concerns about court interpretations of the speech-press clause in the United States are coming from non-media sources who are concerned about too much freedom at the expense of other interests, particularly the rights and interests of disadvantaged groups like women and minorities. In particular, concerns being raised by feminists, critical scholars and, especially, critical legal theorists are that the court's continuing emphasis on protecting press freedoms serves only to advance the status quo and favours the special interests of corporate-owned media conglomerates.

These are variations of the same kinds of criticism and concerns expressed by Jerome Barron, who argued nearly thirty years ago that "Our constitutional theory is in the grip of a romantic conception of free expression, a belief that the `marketplace of ideas' is freely accessible. But if ever there were a self operating marketplace of ideas, it has long ceased to exist." He went on to argue for a legal right of access to the media to provide citizens with the kind of marketplace originally intended by the Founding Fathers. Barron, an American, raises these same concerns over recent developments in media law in Canada, and a growing number of critical theorists and legal scholars in Canada are expressing concerns of their own about constitutional developments related to court interpretations of the Canadian Charter of Rights and Freedoms. Michael Mandel, for example, frames his criticisms in terms of what he calls "The legalization of politics in Canada," and argues that the representative institutions like Parliament, the legislatures, and municipal councils "are now being pushed from centre stage and told what they can and cannot do by judges elected by and accountable to nobody."

David Schneiderman, in his edited volume on Freedom of Expression and the Charter, explains that critics are not optimistic about the consequences of the constitutionalization of freedom of expression in Canada and are concerned that the Charter favours the value system of liberal individualism over the collectivist aims of the modern welfare state. In the United States, concerns are also being raised in journalistic circles about the status of American journalism, about public criticism of the press, and about the appropriate roles and responsibilities of the media in a free democratic society.

One of the best recent books on this subject is by Anderson, Dardenne, and Killenberg, who argue for a more ecumenical, constructive, participative, and democratically responsive role for journalism's institutional future. Other recent authors like Davis Merritt, Jay Rosen, and James Fallows have called for a revision in journalistic practices in order to promote community through civic or public journalism. This approach has challenged the way responsible media report on and relate to the communities they serve.

As Dennis and Merrill put it, "The new communitarians are waging a rhetorical war against Enlightenment liberalism—against individualism and libertarianism." More specifically, Christians argues that journalists should discard the liberal politics of rights, which "rests on unsupportable foundations," and that such rights should be "given up for a politics of the common good." In response, critics of this approach argue that it "confuses journalism with community organization, a social work concept" and are concerned that if journalists became activists and took positions on community issues, they would lose "any claim to impartiality and would sacrifice credibility." In summary, what emerges from a review of issues like these is the fact that some of the basic foundations of law and journalistic practice are being challenged in very significant ways by credible practitioners and scholars in Canada and the United States alike.

This is all part of the important ongoing discussions about how to appropriately balance the freedoms of the press and other media of communication against the larger interests of society, and about how to frame the practice of journalism in the best way possible to serve the democratic process. The quality of these discussions on both sides of the border can be enhanced by examining the experiences in both countries and, indeed, in other societies, to see how these issues are being played out against the backdrop of different traditions, practices, values, and beliefs.

MEDIA THEORY AND ETHICS

In evaluating what media ethics has accomplished and assessing its academic status at present, theory is the most obvious place to begin. Ethics is a world of ideas. The mission of colleges and universities is critical thinking, creating new knowledge, building scientific models that are transferable and testable. Higher education is our home for teaching ethics, and the centerpiece of our vocation is ideas. Obviously, abundant things happen in media ethics, but we need to focus on its intellectual substance to ensure that it is equipped for the globalized 21st century. A crucial issue is whether our theorizing is adequate. What foundations undergird our enterprise? We find our pathway now and in the future conceptually. If we understand ethics as a world of ideas, our primary task is credible theory.

In the first half of the 1980s, the material was largely atheoretical, with media ethics typically defined as descriptive in character. Taking a complex professional arena seriously seemed to demand war stories rather than abstractions. The prominent text by John Hulteng, The Messenger's Motives: Ethical Problems of the Mass Media, first published in 1976 with a second edition in 1985, used ethics codes and accepted professional practice as the standards for how the media ought to operate. Hulteng's 1981 book was descriptive also, Playing It Straight: A Practical Discussion of the Ethical Principles of ASNE. Gene Goodwin's Groping for Ethics in Journalism examined a variety of issues such as conflict of interest and privacy in terms of interviews with quality professionals and codes of ethics. Tom Goldstein in The News at Any Cost: How Journalists Compromise Their Ethics to Shape the News focused on the techniques used by the press when dealing with plagiarism, money, accuracy, and so forth. The framework in Philip Meyer's Ethical Journalism was the First Amendment and written and unwritten codes of ethics.

While journalism values rather than ethical theory dominated the field as this period opened, John Merrill's work has been the exception and theoretically inclined from the beginning. The first anthology in media ethics, Ethics and the Press, edited by Merrill and Ralph Barney in 1975 includes a section on theoretical issues. His Philosophy and Journalism with Jack Odell in 1983 treats the substantive issues philosophically. And over the two-plus decades under review, the orientation of the field has changed in like fashion. On occasion, book-length studies in media ethics at present develop a philosophical framework. From journalistic morality or descriptive ethics or values in the early 1980s, normative ethics has become mandatory at present.

The major textbooks currently in use introduce students to philosophical ethics-classic and contemporary. Some examples are Philip Patterson and Lee Wilkins, Media Ethics: cases and Issues; Thomas Bivins, Mixed Media: Moral Distinctions in Advertising, Public Relations and Journalism; Louis Day, Ethics in Media Communications: cases and Commentaries; Richard Johannesen et al.'s Ethics in Human Communication; and Clifford Christians, Mark Fackler, Kathy McKee, Peggy Kreshel and Robert Woods, Media Ethics: cases and Moral Reasoning. The 2006 book Contemporary Media Ethics, by Mitchell Land and Bill Hornaday, is centered entirely around the debate in ethical theory between utilitarianism and communitarian philosophy, as Jay Black's Mixed News: The Public/Civic/Communitarian Journalism Debate was earlier in different form. Stephen Ward's The Invention of Journalism Ethics is rich in intellectual history.

Christopher Meyers's anthology on journalism ethics, currently in development, and The Handbook of Mass Media Ethics edited by Lee Wilkins and Clifford Christians for Erlbaum both take ethical theory seriously. Jay Black has always welcomed theoretical ethics for the Journal of Mass Media Ethics, of which Chris Meyers's "Appreciating W. D. Ross: On Duties and Consequences" and Stephen Ward's "Philosophical Foundations for Global Journalism Ethics" are illustrative. In fact, a recent special issue of the Journal of Mass Media Ethics deals with ethical theory throughout.

The bi-annual "National Communication Ethics Conference"-originally at Gull Lake, Michigan, and now at Duquesne University-has featured theory over its 16 years, through scholars-in-residence, papers, and plenary sessions. "Colloquium 2000 in Applied Media Ethics," the brainchild of Jay Black and Ralph Barney to enrich the field through a series of annual workshops on critical issues, has produced some groundbreaking work in ethical theory. Ed Lambeth's week-long seminars on Teaching Journalism Ethics consistently had a theoretical component. The colloquium hosted at the University of Oregon by Tom Bivins focused on the ethics of care as a theory in addition to its application to media practice. Several book-length treatments from university presses illustrate theories of communication ethics and present possible options for bringing the Summits' history to philosophical maturity. The four that follow develop normative models for communication as an enterprise in general or the press as a social institution in particular.

Ronald Arnett established the field of communication as a whole around Martin Buber and his legacy. In terms of the focus on media ethics in this Summit review, Edmund Lambeth's Committed Journalism: An Ethic for the Profession is the first of this genre. He advocates an ethical system of five principles: truthtelling, humanness, justice, freedom, and stewardship-derived from a combination of ethical theory, ideal institutional guidelines, and the "toughest minds and truest spirits in the field". Within this framework of prima facie obligations, journalists "become stewards of free expression".

John Merrill proposes a deontelic ethics that integrates theories of duty with those grounded in consequences. A synthesis of principles and consequences results from a dialectical process true to the dynamic world of journalism. In the existential moment, classical and neo-liberal antinomies, altruism and egoism, positive and negative freedom are reconciled. The foundation for Merrill's "organic unification of opposites" is the dialectical tradition from Heraclitus.

Good News: Social Ethics and the Press identifies individual autonomy as the axis of Enlightenment ethics and advocates a communitarian philosophy instead. The community is understood to be ontologically and axiologically prior to persons. Organizations in this model operate with the standard of mutuality rather than power pragmatism. Reporting facilitates public life and represents the moral landscape within which the human community is formed. Land and Hornaday (2006) apply communitarian theory to news, advertising, and public relations by contrasting its appeal to community values with an emphasis on individual liberty and consequences. The forthcoming Ethics for Public Communication by Fackler, Christians, and Ferré puts the communitarian model into textbook form, centered around those critical episodes in the world media that signal a democratic "tipping-point." The political communitarianism represented by Good News has been integrated with feminist ethics to establish it outside neo-conservative politics. Dialogic communitarianism is the most advanced version of the theory, ensuring its multiculturalism and gender inclusiveness.

The long-term future of the field depends on the common language of theory, not as an abstract authority, but to assist us in thinking more systematically about the major league issues. While academia is generally committed to theoretical media ethics as necessary for the complicated agenda at present, there are several issues in theory that need ongoing debate and resolution. Some are perennial issues requiring continual clarification, and others can be resolved.

THE CANONICITY PROBLEM

We ought to solve the canonicity issue rather than be immobilized by it. As the media ethics literature matures philosophically, its appeal to classical ethicists and contemporary intellectuals is soured by the savage attacks at present on Eurocentric paternalism within the liberal arts as a whole. Hostile students weary of learning about "the dead white guys" can be ignored if their exasperation is no more articulate than that. However, in astute and systematic terms the philosophically inclined in ethics are currently mounting an attack on canonical authority that is inescapable. Enlightenment notions of the good are now recognized as the morality of the dominant gender and ruling class. The canon of media ethics has been largely monocultural, and for all the achievements within it, the field must become multicultural, gender inclusive, and transnational instead.

The expanding and deepening work in feminist ethics is of particular importance in confronting the challenge of canonicity. Nel Noddings sets feminist ethics at odds with rule-based systems, that is, with the traditional Western trajectory grounded in prescriptions and norms external to society and professional practice. Formalist media ethics presumes autonomous moral agents who apply rules consistently and self-consciously to every choice. In Noddings's terms, an ethics of moral reasoning that "arranges principles hierarchically and derives conclusions logically" is "peripheral to or even alien to, many problems of moral action....Moral decisions are, after all, made in real situations; they are qualitatively different from the solution of geometry problems". The feminist ethics of Seyla Benhabib and the neo-Aristotelian social ethics of Martha Nussbaum are fundamentally restructuring ethical theory. Daryl Koehn supports the emphasis in feminist ethics on a relational order rather than individual selves adhering to formal codes. However, she opposes the feminist tradition of care and nurturance, and argues for a dialogic ethics that stitches feminist ethics into dialogic communication theory. Linda Steiner's work demonstrates, during the period under review, how feminist ethics establishes a politically and morally ambitious agenda for media institutions and practice. On a broader level than feminist ethics, another approach is to reconceptualize the canonicity problem. Some issues do not disappear from our agenda. This is true about virtue, duty, and consequences. They are fundamental components of the moral life. We may reject the European formulation but the issues remain. Our prevailing theories need not be considered canonical-defined in this case as a body of self-evident truths without contradiction.

The Greek Kanon means measuring stick, taxation table, or a blueprint. Canons do grant privilege to certain texts on the grounds that without boundaries there is only chaos, dissipated energies, "a babble of...complaints rather than a settled critique." Diversity arises out of unity; without a buffer zone, struggle is impossible. The canon "depends on who is teaching it how;...living in the same place does not mean living with the same history". We should go beyond the original without forgetting it. Socrates makes that point in the Crito-recognizing that the fact he criticizes, what he criticizes, and how he criticizes is made possible by the very city he is criticizing. Theorists are not abstract authorities, but enable us to think on our own.

In Aristotle, moral virtue is a middle state determined by practical wisdom. Of the four cardinal virtues, temperance is the capstone and gateway to the other three. In Confucius's golden mean, moral virtue is the appropriate location between two extremes. Islamic ethics is a version of virtue ethics. The majority of Islamicists consider it a virtue ethics system. In the 12th century, for example, wisdom, justice, and courage were considered the primary virtues, though here influenced by the Greeks through alGhazali, Islam's greatest philosopher. The feminist ethics of Edith Wyschogrod's Saints and Postmodernism is a version of virtue ethics too, in that moral principles are only conceivable in the context of good persons. In the tradition of Emmanuel Lévinas, but in terms distinctively her own, the saintly life is one in "which compassion for the Other, irrespective of the cost to the saint, is the primary trait". Reciprocal care and understanding, rooted in emotion and experience, and not in formal consensus, are the basis on which moral discourse is possible.

In addition, for solving the canonicity problem, we need to reconstruct the character of theorizing. Theories ought not be treated in static, scholastic terms. The Greek tradition of rational universals and the Enlightenment commitment to Cartesian non-contingency privilege the conceptual logos. Philosophical proclivity towards reason presumes an objective, ahistorical foundation of knowledge. However, theory should be redefined as meaningful portraits and not statistically precise formulations derived from artificially fixed conditions. Theorizing in these terms is not an examination of external events, but the power of the imagination to give us an inside perspective on reality. Thomas Kuhn calls this revolutionary sciencethe constructing of paradigms-rather than the normal science of verifying that propositions are externally and internally valid.

Theories are not ex nihilo. They are not conceptually immaculate, arising out of nothing. Theories are not abstract theorems, but oppositional claims about the world. We identify niches and inconsistencies and conundrums over against existing conventions and theorize how to start over intellectually. Moral Engagement in Public Life: Theorists for Contemporary Ethics meets the test of valid theory. Two classical thinkers are included, Aristotle and Confucius, and 10 contemporary thinkers crossculturally and internationally who are epistemologically legitimate but not gendered male, one-dimensional, and Western thinking is rooted in core beliefs rather than epistemic certainty, and in this way they give us ethical discourse for grounding professional practice.

RELATIVISM

Working on media ethics in 21st century terms, the most fundamental challenge is Friedrich Nietzsche's. In his totalizing attack on ethical rationalism, Nietzsche insisted that life can be justified only as aesthetic phenomena. In a world where God has died and everything lacks meaning, morality is appearance, even delusion. Since there is no transcendent answer to the why of human existence, we face the demise of moral interpretation altogether. In the era beyond good and evil, ethics has been replaced by aesthetics. Only aesthetic values matter. One can speak of beauty without implying that anything ought to be beautiful or that anyone ought to create something beautiful. For Nietzsche, morality has reached the end of the line. In its contemporary version, defending a suprasensory good is not beneficent, but imperialism over the moral judgement of diverse communities. Popular culture gets caught up in the technological imperative, producing the visually interesting, creating Programmes at times of artistic wholeness, but driven by the conditions of aesthetic space rather than ethics.

Communications is one crucial laboratory for addressing this predicament. It is not a discipline per se with a discrete subject matter; communications is pervasive and integrative rather than specialized. And communications makes possible all cultural forms, all community life and socio-political institutions without being absorbed into any of them. Therefore, in today's wideranging assault on the foundations of knowledge, the communication infrastructure has no place to hide. Nietzsche was a philologist and today's conundrums typically come to a head at the nexus of language theory and theories of culture.

Communication studies often bear the brunt of the attack-along with literature, philosophy, history, and theology.Beyond epistemological relativism in the Nietzschean tradition, cultural relativity is unquestioned and celebrated-that is, the right and valid are only known in local space and native languages. A context that is intelligible, a proposition that is true, an argument that is legitimate, and judgements of right and wrong are accepted by such a culture's internal criteria. And therefore these concepts, propositions, arguments, and judgements are considered to have no validity elsewhere.

One could argue that relativism ultimately founders on Mannheim's paradox: "Relativists claim that truth is culture bound. But they cannot proclaim relativism without rising above it, and they cannot rise above it without giving it up." At least to me, Mannheim's argument appears unassailable. Deni Elliott casts it in empirical terms, demonstrating that without shared values, the practice of everyday journalism is impossible. Although reporters and editors are pluraliste, they are not relativists.

However, in addition to attacking relativism on the practical level, our constructive task is formulating a normative position that does not rest on first foundations and Newton's static universe. Appealing to unconditional a prions or a fixed human nature or philosophical prescriptions carry little resonance at present. But we can successfully embed norms within culture and history. In this intellectual strategy, transcendental criteria are shifted from a metaphysical, vertical, punctiliar plane to the horizon of community, world, and being, but compelling norms they remain nonetheless. As an indicator of our distinctiveness, the human species generates symbolic patterns along the boundaries between moral norms and actual behaviour, the deepest self and our collective roles, the intentional and the inevitable. Thomas Nagel's View from Nowhere documents those epiphanal moments coming with dynamic force from outside us, though not grounded a priori.

Refusing to fashion a normative framework on every level weakens our ethical agenda. How can we appeal to human dignity, to social change, to social responsibility in our media institutions without accepting a network of non-negotiable norms such as justice, compassion, and stewardship? Without norms that are more than contingent, we cannot finally condemn oppression except on the arbitrary grounds of personal preference. Without a defensible conception of the good, the by-product is moral agnosticism. In an ironic twist on conventional skepticism, normative claims are not a medieval remnant but the catalyst for innovation. Certainly no provocation will be as formidable over the long term as relativism. A viable media ethics of the future has a considerable stake in the outcome and an opportunity to contribute substantially.

UTILITARIANISM

Developing a credible normative ethics in media studies faces another major obstacle. Given the dual character of professional ethics, the morality of the practitioners' world interacts with the philosophical framework of academics. On one side of the equation, the conventions and guidelines of media practice are basically utilitarian. In print and broadcast journalism, public relations, advertising, and entertainment, the modus operandi is self-consciously or superficially determined by consequences. In news and editorial departments, advertising agencies, and media companies, the overarching appeal is to benefit the greatest public good with the least possible harm. In academic ethics, John Stuart Mill's treatise on political freedom in 1859, On Liberty, and his Utilitarianism in 1861 work in and through each other, as does the natural affinity today in democratic life towards determining the morally right alternative by the greatest balance of good over evil. Mill, in the legacy of Jeremy Bentham, contended that happiness was the sole end of human action and the test by which all conduct ought to be judged. With later utilitarians expanding the notion of pleasure, assessing Tightness or wrongness in terms of the total amount of value is a definitive guideline for aiding our ethical choices.

A utility calculus fits hand-in-glove with the press's zeal for the public's right to know, as well as with the commitment in public relations and advertising to provide clients with the maximum benefits at the least cost. For the entertainment industry, utility resonates with capitalism's supply-and demand principle and an institution's risk-benefit calculations. Moreover, the utility principle does not presume commands from heaven or a universe of natural laws and brings together disparate segments of a diverse society. The press's actions in Watergate, for instance, were considered appropriate by most people; the public saw the pain inflicted on a few as proper because the overall consequences for the many were beneficent.

Although the utilitarian perspective is powerful, utilitarianism presents serious difficulties for theory formation in ethics at this Summit juncture. It depends on making accurate measurements of the consequences, when in everyday affairs, the results of our choices are often blurred, at least in the long term. In addition, utilitarians view society as a collection of individuals, all with their own desires and goals. Thus, institutions as structures are not analysed in a sophisticated manner, and an atomistic, procedural view of democracy is presumed. Moreover, the principle of the greatest public benefit applies only to societies in which certain nonutilitarian standards of decency prevail. And on a deeper level, there is mounting criticism of utilitarianism's commitment to an exceptionless norm as determining all ethical judgements. As a matter of fact, consequentialism in its various forms is intellectually appealing in the same way scientific theories are-a single principle constitutes all moral judgements. However, the exactness of this one-factor model represents a "semblance of validity by leaving out whatever cannot be calculated.

In some media situations, consequences are a reliable guide. But practitioners usually find themselves confronting more than one moral claim at the same time, and asking only what produces the most good is too limiting. In the full range of human relationships, we ordinarily recognize that fulfilling promises, preventing injury, providing equal distribution, and relieving distress are moral imperatives. But utilitarianism renders irrelevant other moral demands that conflict with its consequentialism. In some of the most crucial issues we face at present, utility is not an adequate guide-for understanding distributive justice, diversity in popular culture, violence in television and cinema, truth telling, conflict of interest, and so forth. We face the anomaly that the ethical system most entrenched in the media industry is not ideally suited for resolving its most persistent headaches.

A sophisticated model of utilitarianism emphasizing long-term consequences will eliminate many of the media's day-to-day quandaries and provide an important alternative to the quasi-utility that is typically invoked at present. However, based on a century of experience with utilitarian rationalism, it is arguable that an ethics of duty is a more compelling means of moral decision-making for the media professions.

Duty recognizes that responsible actions are necessary to keep the human community humane. For Emmanuel Levinas, for instance, our duties to others are more fundamental to human identity than are individual rights. Oxford's W. David Ross developed the most influential critique of utilitarianism within philosophical circles and established prima facie duties as a compelling alternative, in which reparations, fidelity, justice, noninjury, gratitude, and self-improvement are given centrality. Therefore, in terms of the overall task of constructing a theoretically credible media ethics, the most promising direction is a deontological one. We face the challenge of moving particular problems (sexism, violence, hate speech, just distribution, for example) from their generally utilitarian orientation to duty ethics instead.

SOCIAL PHILOSOPHY

The emphasis since 1980 has been on professional morality, on the character of the news, on the values and structure of news organizations. While journalism has received primary attention, advertising as a media profession has been studied to some extent, and public relations too. The Hastings studies insisted on a narrow target. In credible versions of applied ethics, the professional worlds of medicine, business, law, engineering, and journalism would be taught from the inside out. Instead of generalizations and artifice, the classroom and research needed to represent the voice of the insider. Team teaching was considered the best method to ensure that both academia and the profession were represented effectively. If teaching and research were done by one person, he or she trained in one area should have at least legitimate competence and experience in the other. This serious attention to the profession as a bona fide entity is what made professional ethics a distinct enterprise.

Though called professional ethics, Hastings more accurately promoted professional morality.4 The agenda was to be set by the field, its struggles and problems as understood from the inside out and the bottom up. The Hastings monograph for journalism identified the content of ethics courses exactly in these terms: problems of daily newsgathering, reporters and sources, invasion of privacy, economic temptations, national security and government secrecy, photojournalism, free press/fair trial, and so forth. There has been substantial growth in free-standing media ethics courses since the first survey in 1978, though they have consistently maintained an ongoing orientation to the subject matter of the field.

The most dominant pedagogical technique, case studies, focuses on concrete problems. As the Hastings Report concluded, cases should be used "to draw out broader ethical principles," but recognized that "the sheer drama" of cases will tend "to overcome the more serious need for sobre analysis". Following generally the same trajectory, Sandra Borden provides a careful review of the pros and cons of case studies within the context of journalism education.

Jay Black, Robert Steele, and Ralph Barney bring the professional ethics strategy to its maturest level by developing a curriculum and teaching strategy for the classroom and professionals centered on the Society of Professional Journalists (SPJ) code of ethics. Dale Jacquette's entry in Prentice Hall's "Basic Ethics in Action Series," his Journalistic Ethics: Moral Responsibility in the Media, is a recent illustration of this tradition, based on 30 case studies from contemporary journalistic practice. Howard Good eschews "tired" and "watered-down philosophers" in favour of a series of eclectic lessons from and debates in the media such as hate speech, hip-hop music, and the Clinton-Lewinsky scandal. Bala Musa and Cindy Price broaden the analysis to include institutional issues such as ownership, public policy, advertising, and public relations. James Ettema and Theodore Glasser provide a sophisticated analysis of the values and moral ambiguities of investigative journalism built around open-ended conversations with newspaper and television reporters who are "designated by other journalists as among the best reporters doing the best reporting". Controversies in Media Ethics make a distinctive contribution to the literature by debating the issues and thereby stimulating thought engagement with them rather than superficiality. In what has become the authoritative empirical source, David Weaver and colleagues document the character and values of American journalism in credible social scientific terms.

GENERAL MORALITY

The rationale for this practitioner-centered genre is obvious. The complexity of the field and its changing dynamics require not only socio-cultural and political economic analyses but ongoing research in professional morality.

However, our challenge at this stage is to ground media ethics education in the general morality, not first of all in professional ethics.

While the apparatus of professional ethics may be necessary logisticalIy, our theoretical work ought to arise from and be accountable to the general morality. Rather than developing rules for experts, our preoccupation should be the moral dimension of everyday life. How the moral order works itself out in community formation must be the focus, not first of all what practitioners consider virtuous. The venerable issues of social ethics should determine the agenda-justice, truth telling, human dignity, for example, with the debates over journalistic practice understood in that larger context. The ultimate standard for media professionals is not role-specific ethical principles but the general morality.

Alan Goldman's critique is a mini-classic and inescapable. He argues in his Moral Foundations of Professional Ethics that the general morality is the ultimate framework for understanding professional norms. In his view, "the most fundamental question for professional ethics is whether those in professional roles require special norms and principles to guide their well-intentioned conduct". For practitioners in medicine, law, business, journalism, government, and so forth, we typically assume that their roles require principles or specially weighted norms. In fact, the standard approach is to define ethical codes as sharply as possible according to the peculiar demands each field entails-aggressive defence in law, for instance, the physician's responsibility to clients, journalists' obligation to sources, and the commitment of business executives to stockholders. Obviously, "special institutional obligations exist when their recognition has better moral consequences than would refusing to recognize them". Yet Goldman concluded: "The central problem in professional ethics as actually practiced is not that professionals often fail to live up to their unique official codes and professional principles; nor that they lack the will to enforce them. It is rather that they often assume without question that they ought to live up to them". The ultimate standard for professionals is not role-specific principles, but the general morality.

The mass media are institutions of power whose decisions and policies can be self-serving, and practitioners defensive when criticized. Competition and careerism often cloud the application of professional codes or ethical guidelines. For example, journalists may have an understanding with their sources that all information will be treated confidentially, but then change their mind when they come under pressure and conclude that the public has a right to know this privileged material after all. Whereas we agree in the general morality that we ought to keep our promises. In this case, canons of professional practice allow self-defined exceptions for the journalist as expert. A preoccupation with privilege and authority cuts journalism loose from the very public it is meant to serve. Rather than refining professional codes of ethics, the challenge for journalists is the moral life as a whole-no harm to innocents, truth telling, reparations for wrong actions, beneficence, gratitude, and honoring contracts. With this focus, reporters operate in the same arena as citizens themselves. After a detailed assessment of codes of ethics around the globe, Christians and Nordenstreng conclude that the compelling need today is a citizens' ethics rather than profession-based ethics per se.

Giving priority to the general morality and making professional ethics penultimate is the task, but it is not obvious how to do this effectively. Our challenge heretofore is working in concert on this re-orientation of our teaching and scholarship. The journal Philosophy and Public Affairs is suggestive in form and content. Colloquium 2003 opened up some avenues through political philosophy. Lee Wilkins and Renita Coleman have given us our deepest understanding to date of the ethical reasoning of journalists. They illustrate the approach the field needs at present by situating their analysis in moral development theory, which itself is linked to philosophical ethics. The explication by Louis Hodges and colleagues of accountability in journalism is situated broadly within the nature of the professions and social theory-through the latter distinguishing accountability and responsibility, for example.

DEMOCRACY AS CONTEXT

The Press opens the right pathway here. Democracy provides the framework for The Press's understanding of the structure and function of the news media. The press is considered "an institution of American democracy.... At the centre of this book is [the] question: What should a democracy expect of the press". Journalism is considered the means; "the end is democracy". The fourth section in the book deals with the journalistic enterprise, its practice, and performance, but section one frames the issues in the larger context of representative, constitutional democracy-its vitality and ongoing redefinitions. While the standard press-government relation is examined in section three-the first amendment, regulation, and public policy-The Press sees democracy philosophically and politically as the overriding concern. James Curran represents the flow of the argument with his chapter title, "What Democracy Requires of the Media". John Keane in coming to grips with global politics focuses on civil society rather than state institutions as he struggles with the question of whether "democracy [has] a chance of taking root in the emerging global order".

The intellectual strategy represented in The Press is analogous to the reorientation we need in media ethics. When we organize our teaching and research around the general morality rather than in terms of professional ethics per se, we participate in the debates over political philosophy and their implications for public communication. Ed Lambeth has demonstrated life-long leadership here on journalism and democracy since his early years as a

Washington correspondent and then founding director of the Washington Reporting Programme for a decade. His Committed Journalism puts ethics in the context of civic life. He published a research essay on "The News Media and Democracy" in the Media Studies Journal and argued in the Journal of Mass Media Ethics that moral reasoning is an essential competence for democratic journalism. The Missouri School of Journalism adopted a capstone course in journalism and democracy for its news majors and Lambeth designed it.

Democratic entities are not merely political and economic arrangements but moral structures. As a matter of fact, democracy is inconceivable without ordering relations. A limited set of fundamental moral commitments such as tolerance are necessary for collective survival. Sissela Bok labels them minimalist values, and they provide a basis for political dialogue and negotiation but do not call for agreement as to their source or character. Without a broad acceptance of such common values, a viable democratic order is impossible. Without a framework broadly owned and understood, the resolution of practical issues is inconceivable.

In political philosophy we call it the common good, and the health of democratic life depends on its vitality. Aristotle's "common interest" is the basis for distinguishing constitutional governments in the people's interest from illegitimate ones on the ruler's behalf. Thomas Aquinas insists on the common good as the ultimate end of law and government. Rousseau understood the common good as the object of the general will and the end of the state, in contrast to "particular wills." Although philosophers have differed on the precise content of the common good and how to promote it, there is a core meaning that the welfare of all citizens should be served impartially, rather than the welfare of factions or special interests. Mass Media and the Moral Imagination argues for enlarging the moral sensibility as the arena in which the common good can be developed, and offers theological and philosophical reflections on how this expansion might be possible.

Democracy will not be successful unless the common good comes into its own conceptually. Citizenship, civic discourse, community activism, and grass-roots participation are only moralistic pleading unless they are grounded in a defensible notion of the common good. The common good is the axis around which communities and politics become a democratic organism. It is a normative principle, a fundamental concept of social morality, not just the majority results of voting or an opinion poll. Since our public life in democracy is not merely functional, but knit together by social values, the media are challenged to participate in a community's process of moral elucidation. If societies are moral orders, the various technologies of public communication ought to stimulate the moral imagination. From this perspective, the news media are obligated to appeal to democratic citizens about human values. News ought to further a community's ongoing values clarification by helping people penetrate through the political and economic surface to the moral dynamics underneath. Rather than merely provide readers and audiences with information, the press's aim is morally literate citizens.

In the tsunami disaster, December 2004, the news included the overwhelming acts of kindness around the world, and our moral imagination was invigorated. Historical documentaries on television relive human morality during the horrifies of the Holocaust and WWII-the benefactors hiding Anne Frank in the Netherlands, and the resistance of Dietrich Bonhoeffer. Out of the turmoil in the Middle East are the inspiring stories of Jews and Muslims working on water projects in Palestine, and teaching their children each other's religion. The great film Hotel Rwanda highlights the virtue of Paul Rusesabagina sheltering 1200 refugees, rather than raw bloodshed and human evil only. The moral dimension of the social order takes on life and inspiration.

Editorials have raised our consciousness of anti-Semitism and heightened our moral awareness of racism and gender discrimination. In the debates over war and worldwide trade in military arms, the moral issues in terms of just-war theory and pacifism have emerged at various times in news and commentary. Affirmative action, environmental protection, health, global warming, gun control, immigration policy, and welfare reform raise moral conflicts that journalists can help the public negotiate. Over time and across the media, one observes a redemptive glow on occasion in which the news and popular culture have facilitated moral discernment by their affirmation of democracy as a people's movement and their insight into humankind as a distinctive species. Along these lines we redeem the media as an agent of democratic formation. Building on its unique capacities as a genre, we are empowered towards moral literacy by reporters appealing to our conscience. Democratic life rests on moral principles. Communication ethics is the foundation of genuine democracy. In meeting this challenge, the media are accountable to the widely shared moral frameworks that orient the society in which they operate and give it meaning.

Index